AN ECONOMIC DETOUR

M. S. STUART

Vice President and Director of Governmental Relations, Universal Life Insurance
Company; Historian, National Negro Insurance Association.

AN ECONOMIC DETOUR

A History of Insurance in the Lives
of American Negroes

By

M. S. STUART

Vice-President and Director of Governmental
Relations, Universal Life Insurance Company,
Memphis, Tennessee; Historian, National Negro
Insurance Association.

McGrath Publishing Company
College Park, Maryland

Reprint McGrath Publishing Company 1969
Library of Congress Catalog Card Number: 75-84100

Manufactured in the United States of America
by Arno Press, Inc., New York

AN ECONOMIC DETOUR

*A History of Insurance in the Lives of
American Negroes*

To:

THE CRADLES OF ORGANIZED ECONOMIC RELIEF
—THE EARLY CHURCHES OF THE NEGRO RACE

PREFACE

The status of the Negro race in America, since the Emancipation in 1865, has been uncertain and queer. The race has been the subject of many theories and a kind of "guinea pig" for sociologists, politicians and statesmen.

But, strangely, none of these, in their various printed and oral expressions, has emphasized the necessity of preparation and assistance for the Negro's commercial advancement.

Enormous amounts in philanthropy have been expended, numerous volumes have been written and tremendous efforts made to improve other phases of Negro life, but little has been said or done to encourage the development of business enterprises and the cultivation of commercial talents.

Educational institutions for Negroes, both those supported by state governments and by private endowments, have placed least emphasis upon preparation for business. Only in recent years have the colleges and universities for Negroes established commercial departments properly equipped for training in this field.

The limited success which colored people have achieved in commerce has been the result either of native ability or of some lucky combination of circumstances; and the enterprises thus organized and operated receive far less attention even in Negro newspapers and magazine articles, and from Negro authors, than less material though more spectacular accomplishments.

No attempt will here be made to assign the causes for this strange neglect. Suffice it to say that in some way the Negro must be considered in the economic pattern of the nation. His presence on the scene puts him in the picture. Whether he finally contributes to the strength of the fabric or proves merely a weak spot in the structure is not only the Negro's problem, but the problem of every American truly interested in the national welfare.

Is the colored race in the United States being fitted into this picture in a way best for all concerned? To what extent is the economic system of the nation being affected or likely to be affected by a haphazard, innovational policy for approximately nine per cent of the whole population? To arouse a sufficient interest in the answer to these questions so that investigations may be undertaken and corrections of maladjustments attempted is one of the objectives of this discussion.

Since "the operation of life insurance is the biggest business conducted by Negroes in the United States,"[1] it is believed that the history of the development of this business and an analysis of the peculiar conditions under which it has to be pursued will expose in a clearer way than any other the awkward commercial role that Negroes must play in trying to operate businesses of all kinds.

To make a record of the Negro's progress in the field of life insurance and its effects on the general economic life of the group; to point out some of the unusual difficulties to be encountered in the effort to promote a specialized, separate system of business; to provoke a spirit of inquiry as to whether or not such a system can be made adequately successful to serve the principal needs of the race; to call attention to the unfairness of a policy that denies to a minority group the opportunity to be employed in the work created by the money its members spend; to leave to posterity a record of the extra struggle required under such a system of restriction; to preserve a record of the remarkable determination of Negro leaders to succeed in business despite these handicaps; to point out some of the business mistakes and failures of Negro business in the true light of all the surrounding circumstances: these are the objectives for which this volume has been written.

It is obviously impossible, in this limited space, to acknowledge by name the hundreds of individuals and institutions to whom I am deeply indebted for cooperation in presenting these pages to the public. The list includes: the Universal Life Insurance Company, which, gratuitously, made available many of the necessary facilities for the work; the National Negro Insurance Association, whose repeated endorsements and patience have been encouraging and sustaining; and the officers of those member companies who have so promptly and efficiently cooperated by supplying the necessary data concerning their companies.

Messrs. J. H. Coates of Mississippi, Murriel Gonzaque of New Orleans, Louisiana, and H. W. Russell, of Atlanta, Georgia, and

[1] The Memphis Commercial Appeal, Jan. 1, 1940.

others of the field forces, too numerous to mention, furnished me highly appreciated assistance.

Among the prominent officials of fraternal organizations whose contributions have been of inestimable value, Messrs. L. H. Lightner, Supreme Commander of the American Woodmen, and William Kelso, Louisiana Grand Master of the Odd Fellows, are foremost.

The following organizations, institutions and individuals were particularly helpful in supplying statistics and reference material for use in the preparation of this work: the North Carolina Mutual Life Insurance Company; the Johns Hopkins University; the University of Virginia; the Index Publishing Company of New York; Mr. James E. Dunne, Editor of Dunne's International Insurance Reports; Mr. Cyrus Campfield, Statistician of the National Negro Insurance Association; Mr. W. J. Trent, author of *The Development of Negro Life Insurance Enterprises;* Mr. M. J. Davis, former District Grand Secretary, Odd Fellows of Georgia, and Dr. H. C. and Mrs. Grace Hamilton of Memphis, Tenn.

I express my gratitude to Mrs. Ethyl Cox Howard of Indianola, Mississippi, without whose assistance I should not have been able to complete the highly interesting story of the lives of her parents.

I also acknowledge my appreciation for the constant interest, assistance and suggestions of my daughter, Mrs. Evarie Stuart Thompson.

It is with the hope that there may be aroused a keener appreciation of the peculiar and difficult economic situation of the American Negro that this work is offered to the public.

M. S. Stuart

Memphis, Tenn.
April 5, 1940.

CONTENTS

CONTENTS— (*continued*)

CONTENTS — (*continued*)

CONTENTS — (continued)

List of Illustrations

(Illustrations are located in relation to the text)

INTRODUCTION

JUST what is a *race business?* Should there, especially in the United States, composite of so many races, be a Jewish, an Italian or a Negro business, or any kind of a separate "race" business, in the sense that it should be exclusively owned by and should cater to only the members of any particular group? Why should there have to be such a thing? Does even prejudice have to have such a device to accomplish its purposes? Must not the very nature of such a policy be in conflict with the fundamental logic of commerce, of trade, which thrives the more by expansion and suffers under constriction? Surely this is so, for the pages of history teem with descriptions of the constant struggles of the human race to open and keep open the avenues of commercial intercourse among the different racial groups of the earth.

Now, surely this desire for intergroup, interracial and international commercial intercourse must spring from obviously natural requirements and advantages or civilized mankind would not continue to strive so earnestly to gratify it. Undoubtedly this course of commerce is the best route to human wealth and progress; for civilized man's major efforts have always been concerned in establishing and improving it.

In the efforts to remove the visible, physical hindrances to free commercial intercourse among the men of the earth, and to conquer the expense and difficulties of intervening space, the citizens of the United States of America have joined with others and have played major parts, through their energy and inventive and constructive genius in transportational facilities.

Our Invisible Barrier

Does it not then seem strange that here in America there is a policy which keeps in a state of repair a high, invisible wall of commercial obstruction, more prohibitive of the greatest degree of commercial profit between the two most important racial groups in America than would be a wall of stone, a range of mountains, or the expanse of oceans? This invisible barrier stands in the way of the development of the great market which the needs of Negroes constitute—a market, the proper development and exploitation of

xvii

which, would prove mutually profitable to members of both races if attempted along lines of interracial cooperation. Yet there is an abundance of evidence to show that leaders in economic thought, both in and out of the Negro race in America, approve—or at least tolerate—this barrier, this doctrine of a separate economy for the Negro; and grant the assumption that the Negro can accomplish that which under similar circumstances no other group has accomplished, viz., a successful, separate"race" business by the side of, and in competition with, the general business of the nation. Dr. Booker T. Washington, perhaps the wisest Negro leader produced in the seventy-five years of the Negro's freedom, gave emphatic proof of his belief in at least the necessity of trying to develop such a racial business, by the establishment of the National Negro Business League: perhaps because that great educator realized the formidable difficulties involved in persuading white America to accept a broader commercial policy for the Negro.

And there can be no doubt that the Federal Government itself assumes that the novel undertaking of a distinct commerce for the Negro is not only possible but practical. The Department of Commerce recognizes the existence of a separate "Negro business," and gives to the effort to prosecute it its active support by setting up a ·separate Bureau of Negro Business Affairs which from time to time releases bulletins and statistical data on various subjects related to such Negro businesses as now exist. From the following letter from that department it will be seen that no such statistics are compiled and released for any other groups except the general group termed "native white Americans":

DEPARTMENT OF COMMERCE
Bureau of the Census
WASHINGTON
August 7, 1939.

Mr. M. S. Stuart, Vice President,
UNIVERSAL LIFE INSURANCE COMPANY,
234 Hernando Street,
Memphis, Tennessee.

Dear Mr. Stuart

We have your letter of August 3, requesting information as to whether special releases have been issued relating to retail stores,

xviii

service establishments, hotels, etc., for any other group of native Americans with the exception of whites and Negroes.

These are the only two groups for which we issue statistics of that character.

Yours very truly,

T. F. Murphy,
Chief Statistician
Publications, General Information
and Records.

GHT :RR

Moreover, this department even mentions in another release certain conditions which it emphasizes as peculiar only to the business of Negro life insurance.

Economic Detour

Since, then, this seems to be a nationally recognized policy, it is obviously necessary to analyze certain strangely peculiar difficulties that not only must be faced and conquered, but which, because of their novel nature, have caused and are still causing some colored philosophers and economists to be skeptical of the wisdom and efficacy of such a policy. Any attempt to dissipate this skepticism would seem to require also that the reasons should be frankly stated why the Negro alone, of all of other groups, must embark upon this queer commercial ship, as well as that a plan be outlined that gives reasonable promise of the success of the scheme on a scale sufficiently broad to serve the needs of at least the majority of the Negro population.

First, the undertaking is an innovation, a departure from the accepted practices of civilization. Of all the cruel mockeries to which, in racial experimentations, the American Negro has been subjected, the "opportunity" to operate a separate business, to employ his commercial talents and make his way in businesses and professions confined to that small fraction of the population of his own people which he may attract and hold in competition with the mass production and marketing, the giant financial combinations, the cumulative wisdom and financial strength of centuries, is perhaps the most ironical and obviously difficult.

Of course, no grounds can be found to justify racial narrow-

ness in any phase of human relations; but in business—commerce—
the very essence of which is the exchange of services and commodities on equitable and mutually agreeable terms, and of providing the greatest convenience in the interchange thereof, the un-
tenable, unprofitable viciousness of racial prejudice bares the
nakedness of its evil purpose more flagrantly than in other fields.
In this scheme, the Negro, admittedly the weakest of all American
groups, economically naked just three-quarters of a century ago, is
expected to establish a separate economy, within the general
economy, without the protection of any distinct political autonomy.

Is such an economy, caged behind the bars of racial prejudice,
right? Can it succeed ultimately if it is not right? Is it necessary
to try to mark out an economic Negro island surrounded by the
intangible, baffling billows of prejudice right here in the heart of
our great America? Altruism aside, is not such a thing unprofitable to all concerned?

The Negro is under no illusions about this matter. He knows
that fundamentally such a policy is *not* best. Even those of his
leaders engaged, because they have to, in the prosecution of such
a commerce understand the unusual difficulties involved in the
adventure. They understand the odds against them in the trade
war they must conduct armed with only fantastic, racial sentiment,
against the hard, tangible, material instincts of thrift and human
selfishness.

They understand the inadequacies of a hot-house economy and
pot-plant businesses to serve material necessities. They know that
until any economy is toughened by getting its roots firmly into the
ground, out in the sunlight of the general commerce of the nation,
it must suffer bruising, mutilation, and, perhaps, final destruction
in the fierce competition with which it must cope. They know that
any economy that must always be "wet-nursed" by racial sentiment
and coddled in the lap of race pride must forever remain puny and
dependent. They know that the natural human desires to profit, to
advance, to take advantage of the best bargains are major appeals
too strong to be overcome by considerations of race loyalty. On the
other hand they know that to survive above a status of peasantry
any group must have an important part both in the production *and
the marketing* of the products of the land on which it lives. Its
members must be serious, unrestricted participants in both of these
processes. They must be left free to develop, by exercise under

equal conditions, such commercial instincts and talents as they may possess, and thereby learn to survive in the general contest of life. They must find an entree and have a part in directing the trends of the markets for their products. They must be allowed to sell as well as to buy.

Inadequate Now

It is obvious that the services now furnished and the results obtained by this "separate policy" meet only the most negligible requirements of the colored race.

The undeveloped status of the Negro's commerce emphasizes this fact: Out of 5,000,000 Negroes gainfully employed in 1930, none were engaged in operating wholesale stores or factories except a few dealing in toilet and hygienic goods. In Negro retail stores of all kinds 28,243 proprietors employed only 12,561 persons with an annual pay roll of $8,523,306. At the same time 213,000 Orientals in this country had 6,432 store proprietors that gave employment to 8,916; and yet the annual pay roll of these 8,916 Oriental employees was $9,253,000 as against the annual pay roll of $8,523,306 for the 12,561 Negro employees engaged in commerce.[1] If the Negro's retail commerce could be developed in the same proportion to population as "native whites'," instead of 25,000 stores employing 12,000 with an annual pay roll slightly in excess of $8,000,000 there would be more than 162,000 retail stores employing more than 381,000 persons with an annual pay roll of something like $422,000,000. While hope for any such realization is too sanguine to be entertained, yet the figures above may be of comparative value in showing how little Negro business has been expanded and how few it employs and serves. They leave no doubt of the woeful lack of development of the so-called Negro Business Economy!

In the light of these conditions, it seems plain that if Negro talent in leadership and energy must in the future be encouraged to concern itself with developing a separate and distinct Negro commerce—if the undertaking, obviously beset with queer and complicated difficulties, is not impractical and fantastic—then there should not only be an announced approval and general support of the policy, but a concrete program, perhaps with special govern-

[1] Dept. of Commerce, *Negroes in U. S.*

mental support, for developing this field on a wider, more useful and self-sustaining scale.

Surely it is known that there is no private Negro capital sufficient to finance the proper expansion. Private white philanthropy has given constant evidence through these years that it is not interested in this phase of the Negro's progress. It appears then that the proper development is possible only through either governmental sponsoring, or through some other program of a more comprehensive nature than now obtains.

Why This Queer Policy?

Why, it may well here be asked, is a separate commerce necessary for the Negro—why can he not participate in the general commercial systems, just like other Americans? That he should, there is no doubt. That he cannot, is equally without question; and the reasons are too well known to require elaboration.

In what way is the Negro's participation in the general commerce of the nation restricted to an extent to make necessary an entire separate and distinct system of racial business? The privilege of being patrons in support of any enterprise ought to carry with it the opportunity to be employed in the work such a business creates in proportion to demand and merit. Discrimination on the grounds of race should not be a factor. If artificial barriers are allowed to intervene to restrict or obstruct the natural talents and opportunities of the members of any group, clearly the dollars spent by such a group for the necessities of life fall short of their broadest function to those who earn and spend them. Their dollars are bereft of their power to employ. They are robbed, in so far as the restricted group is concerned, of one of their most valuable factors—that of creating employment available to that group, a function which every spent dollar helps to perform for somebody.

The Negro has long felt the retarding effects of these commercial restrictions and realizes that he cannot exist always just a buyer—a consumer—certainly not above the level of a peon. He realizes his keen need of all of the employment created by the dollars he spends for the necessities of life; and he knows that he is deprived of most of it through racial discrimination. But, as yet, he has not been able to overcome to any appreciable degree that brazen type of American prejudice which in effect says: *We will sell to you: we want your money. But we will not employ you*

*to sell to others; we will not even employ you to sell to your own
kind. More than that, you and your kind, when you come to buy
from the hands of others, may, at any time, expect discourtesies
and insults. Moreover, we will send agents of other races into your
homes seeking business and there, across your threshold, around
your own fireside, in the presence of loved ones, you may expect
the same kind of humiliation.* Seeking a way, therefore, to have a
chance at the beneficial reaction of his spent dollars in the form of
employment created; seeking a way to avoid buying insults and
assure himself courtesy when he buys the necessities of life; seeking
respect, the American Negro has been *driven* into an awkward,
selfish corner, attempting to operate *racial* businesses—to rear a
stepchild economy.

This is not his preference. Yet it seems to be his only re-
course. It is an ECONOMIC DETOUR which no other racial
group in this country is required to travel. Any type of foreigner,
Oriental or "what not," can usually attract to his business a surviving degree of the patronage of the native American. No matter
that he may be fresh from foreign shores with no contribution to
the national welfare to his credit; no matter that he sends every
dollar of his American-earned profit back to his foreign home or
uses it to help finance organizations dedicated to the destruction of
the government that furnishes him his new golden opportunity;
yet he can find a welcome place on the economic broadway of
America. But the Negro, despite centuries of unrequited toil to
help build and maintain that highway, must turn to a detour that
leads he knows not where. Following this doubtful economic trail,
he knows that he will have to find most of his customers within
his own race in any enterprise he attempts. Yet, within this limited
scope, if only he had an even chance at this approximate nine per
cent of the population, a not too discouraging field might lay before him.

The Negro business man, embarking upon this uncharted
course, must encounter not only *giant financial combinations, cumulative business wisdom, cumulative wealth, mass production and
marketing, the power of advertising,* and *marketing tricks and
schemes,* but finds at least two other big enemies further limiting his
customers and obstructing his way.

Geographical limitations and *population distribution* deny to
most types of Negro business about 60 per cent of the prospective

patronage of the whole Negro population. In thousands of towns, cities, and communities, where the Negro population bears an important ratio to the whole, there is yet not enough race concentration for the successful operation of race enterprises. This fact must be kept in mind in contemplating the degree of development of a distinct racial commerce. It is fallacious to measure the possibilities of such a commerce by the whole population of the race. Clearly, a great proportion of the Negroes scattered throughout the North, East, and West is not available to Negro business. All of the North and East, save not more than a dozen of the larger cities, and the entire West, except three or four places in California, must be eliminated from consideration as areas of possible development of Negro business of nearly all kinds, except on a very limited scale.

The commercial vista of colored people, then, becomes reduced largely to the South; and here there are hundreds of places where the population is too scattered or mixed in for the success of many types of Negro enterprises.

A careful examination of the statistics on distribution of population discloses that the approximate total number of Negroes geographically susceptible to convenient cultivation of Negro business enterprises does not exceed 4,800,000.

Of course, all of this population inaccessable to Negro business supports the general business of the nation. In the light of this, the unusual business difficulties faced by this group, mixed in with the general population, living in the same general areas, becomes clear.

Kinds of Business

Of course, there can be no such thing as a "Negro owned and operated" utility; yet the entire Negro population must contribute to the support of the utilities in every community. This not only denies to Negroes the employment benefits flowing from utility operations, but all collateral benefits resulting from various utility connections and influences. There are many other types of enterprise, the very natures of which make their operation as racial businesses impractical.

The prospective Negro business man must not only select with careful scrutiny the place in which he ventures into the field of commerce; but he must, by the aid of a more complicated analysis, determine the *kind* of business in which he may hope for success. There are comparatively few types of business in which the Negro business man has even a reasonable chance to succeed. He must choose those lines of commerce and personal service that white competitors have either not elected to invade and nearly monopolize, or the very natures of which tend to make less effective the forces of white competition and peculiar racial restrictions.

Among the lines of business and personal service in which colored operators and proprietors may be most free from extraracial obstacles may be mentioned: barber shops and beauty parlors, food service establishments, journalism, hotels,[2] undertaking and life insurance businesses. Only a discussion of the two last named has any pertinent relation to this work; and the undertaking business, though having a direct connection with life insurance, needs here only such treatment as will explain the peculiar relation between the two.

[2] While the hotel business is included in those lines that Negroes could successfully operate without encountering extraordinary racial difficulties yet progress in this business has not been at all commensurate with the apparent needs of the race. The explanation perhaps lies in the very limited extent to which other Negro commercial enterprises throughout the country have been developed. There are few Negro commercial travelers.

Chapter I

RELATED ORGANIZATIONS

THE UNDERTAKING BUSINESS

PRIOR to 1895, there were few, if any, established colored undertaking concerns in existence. In most of the cities with heavy colored population, white undertakers buried the bodies of colored people. The additional expense required to maintain equal, separate accommodations made the colored phases of the business less profitable to white companies; therefore, the advent of Negro undertakers into this field was not entirely unwelcome by most of the white operators. Many colored men soon entered the business with creditably equipped establishments, and during the past thirty-five years have secured almost a monopoly of it, especially in the larger towns and cities in the South and in some places in the North. It has proved to be one of the most profitable of all the lines of business in which Negroes have engaged.

The wide margins of profits supposed to have been realized, emphasized by the display of prosperity by colored undertakers, have invited attacks by critical Negro economists as being excessive and unwarranted; and have perhaps inspired the re-entry into this field, during the past seven or eight years, of white competition of a new and far more difficult type, which seems to hold a possible threat to the future success of colored undertakers as well as to present a new problem to Negro life insurance companies catering to industrial business.

These organizations have appeared in the form of "Burial" life insurance companies or associations. The inspiration for this type of organization seems to have sprung from the knowledge that a large part of the mortality benefits paid by industrial life insurance companies goes to private undertakers to defray the funeral expenses of the insured. Burial life insurance companies, therefore, avail themselves of the greater advantages resulting from the operation of both the insurance and the undertaking businesses. Some of such companies still further widen their margins of profit by manufacturing the supplies their parlors sell. Organi-

1

zations of this type constitute a new form of organized social service; and while the relief most of them render extends only to the disposition of the dead, they probably will enjoy a heavy patronage as long as human sentiment places great emphasis on expensive provisions for interment.

The Union Protective Assurance Company

The Union Protective Assurance Company of Memphis, Tennessee, is one of the prominent Negro burial life insurance companies. It was organized September 13, 1933 and commenced business in January 1934. Its officers are: H. D. Whalum, president, T. H. Hayes, Jr., vice president; Louis H. Twigg, secretary; and Edward R. Kirk, treasurer. Closely allied with it are the following three important undertaking companies of Memphis: T. H. Hayes & Sons; S. W. Qualls & Company, and N. M. Owens & Sons.

THE BUSINESS OF LIFE INSURANCE

On the surface, there appears to be little in the nature of the business of life insurance more peculiarly advantageous to Negro ownership and operation than any other kind of business, or that in any special sense tends to shield colored companies from the effects of the racial handicaps to which other lines are fully subjected. Deeper thought, however, reveals that:

1. The established rates in the business of life insurace are arrived at by calculations based upon the records of the mortality experience of large numbers of human beings during many years. Because of this, Negro companies, and other small companies, are protected against rates arbitrarily fixed to favor commercial units able to deal in great quantity purchases.

2. The "stock in trade"—business in force on the lives of living, thinking people—cannot be easily cornered or monopolized and traded in mass quantities by powerful combines, boards of trade, or other commercial units, as can cotton, corn, wheat, and other commodities. Thus it is that in life insurance the Negro has a fair chance at the commodity in which he must deal.

3. White companies in other lines of merchandise, through friends and relatives, have more intimate and ready contact with the wholesale markets than the Negro merchant engaged in similar lines. By this being able to buy more advantageously and offer at low prices cheap, flashy brands, they are able to lure Negro patronage away from Negro enterprises.

In most of the cities of large Negro populations there are so-called "Negro streets," such as Auburn in Atlanta, Georgia; Beale in Memphis, Tennessee; Central in Los Angeles, California; Eighteenth in Birmingham, Alabama; Farrish in Jackson, Mississippi; Lenox and Seventh in New York City; Lombard in Philadelphia, Pennsylvania; Hall in Dallas, Texas; Market in St. Louis, Missouri; State in Chicago, Illinois; Rampart in New Orleans, Louisiana; Sixteenth in Kansas City, Missouri; Walnut in Louisville, Kentucky; West Ninth in Little Rock, Arkansas; and others. On all these streets there are numbers of mercantile establishments owned and operated chiefly by people of Hebrew or foreign extraction catering largely to Negro trade. The number, the volume of patronage, and the capitalization of business establishments of this type exceed by far Negro business units in the same cities. Negro merchants engaged in the same lines can offer only feeble competition to them. In the life insurance business Negro companies are not subjected to this type of opposition.

4. In the mutual aid, benevolent, burial, and fraternal benefit associations, Negroes learned the superior effectiveness of organized effort. Wtihout realizing it, they learned the first principles of life insurance in their early, crude combination of interests for mutual protection against common misfortune. It was a lesson in rudimentary business and organization which they received in no other line in the early days of their freedom. So, from these blundering forerunners, out of which most of the important Negro companies have developed, Negroes gained exceptional advantages in preparation for the more exacting business details required to operate legal reserve companies.

Church Relief Societies, 1787-1890

In reviewing the origin and progress of those combinational social devices among Negroes which were supposed to provide protection against the losses caused by sickness, disability and death, this study will consider them in three general classes: *Church Relief Societies, Fraternal Benefit Societies,* and *Life Insurance Companies or Associations.*

Following the close of the Revolutionary War there were years of poverty and distress for nearly all the people of the newly created republic. Then, as in every subsequent period of economic distress, the group fartherest down—Negroes in this country—felt

3

the pinch of poverty most keenly. There was much distress among the free Negroes of the North.

It was in the emergency created by these conditions that Negro leadership arose to meet the situation by sponsoring the organization of societies for bearing the losses caused by sickness or other disability, and for burying the dead.

The first of these organizations for relief, bearing any resemblance to the business of life insurance, had their inception in the church. Neither the time of operation nor the type of the church relief societies can be closely confined to any particular period or to any exact definition. Effort here will be made to place them as nearly as possible within the time of their effective operation and to designate them according to their general objectives and plans of operation. The motives that inspired them were born of the warm atmosphere of sympathy which the Negro's conception of religion created. The sponsors of these organizations, with some exceptions, were either ministers of the gospel or active members of the church; and there are many indications that the motives of these sponsors were entirely altruistic and that they had no intention to form relief units that could or would later be developed into regulated life insurance companies of the financial magnitude and cold, corporate nature which now characterize some of them.

As early as 1787, Negro churches in northern cities found themselves called upon to make some provision for the relief of the large number of escaped slaves and free Negroes who came North, destitute and often ill.

The first of these units of relief of which there is any authentic record was the Free African Society founded in Philadelphia, Pennsylvania, April 12, 1787.[3] This society came into existence as a result of the aggressive leadership of members of the St. George Methodist Church. Its organizers were Absalom Jones and Richard Allen. While the society had its inception in that church, it appears that its organization and the success of its operation awoke in Richard Allen a realization of his ability as an organizer and leader and had, therefore, great influence in inspiring him to found the Bethel A. M. E. Church, the mother church of the great African Methodist Episcopal denomination.

The crudeness of the financial scheme of the Free African Society may be seen from the monthly dues required from members

[3] Trent, W. J., *The Development of Negro Life Insurance Companies*, p.2.

4

(one silver shilling, the equivalent of about 16c) and the weekly benefits (three shillings, nine pence, the equivalent of about 57c) promised[4] after one year's membership to those members who should require relief, all payable in Pennsylvania paper money. The assessment was the same for all ages. There does not appear to have been any age limit. There was no requirement of physical fitness on entrance. The greater emphasis seems to have been placed on morality. Sober and clean living was a qualification, and members found guilty of immoral conduct were frequently expelled from the Society.

Of course, the Free African Society soon ran into financial difficulties. In less than nine months after its organization it was compelled to increase its assessments. This, however, must have been in anticipation of claims and obligations expected after the expiration of the first year of operation, before which time no benefits could be claimed.

Not only did the Free African Society serve as a medium for the economic advancement and moral improvement of its members; its meetings were often converted into forums for the expression of opinions of the Negroes of Philadelphia on many subjects affecting their welfare.[5]

That there were other societies similar to the Free African in Newport, Rhode Island, and Boston, Massachusetts,[6] is shown by the existence of correspondence as early as 1789, between it and a society in Boston on the subject of general race migration to Africa, and other questions of race policy.

There were also societies in other northern cities as the dates of organization of the following, established more or less by approximation, show:

One in New York	1810
The Clarkson	1812
The Wilberforce Benevolent	1820
The Union Society of Brooklyn	1820
The Woolman Society of Brooklyn	1820

And, according to Trent, in 1838 in northern cities there were about 100 others in various places with a membership at that time

[4] Ibid. p.3.
[5] Trent, op. cit., p.4.
[6] Ibid., p.4.

approximating 7,500, paying a monthly assessment per member of about 25c. It does not appear what benefits they attempted to pay, but, taken as a whole, it seems that up to this time they were enjoying profitable management. Dr. Dubois, in his *Philadelphia Negro,* shows that in the aggregate they had a surplus of $10,023.

Sick Claim Speculation

It is interesting to note the appearance of what may have been sick claim speculation among these benevolent societies as early as 1849. The Society of Friends[7] of Philadelphia, in 1849, found that 4,904 persons, nearly half the adult Negro population of that city, were members of mutual beneficial societies. The report of the Friends further said: "Many of these persons belong to two or more societies at once with a view to increasing the amount received when sick."

Out of 106 of these societies investigated by the Friends of Philadelphia 76 had a total annual income of $16,812.23 in 1849 and had in funds "permanently invested" $17,771.83.

In several other cities of the North and bordering states there were several societies of similar type organized between the years 1820 and 1855, particularly in Washington, D. C., and Baltimore, the latter having as many as 40 in 1850, according to Brackett in his "Colored People in Maryland Since the War."

Canada, perhaps, more than any other section, was looked to as "the promised land of freedom" by escaped slaves prior to Emancipation. To it the underground railroad ran and terminated. Stranded there from time to time were hundreds of Negroes without sufficient savings ahead to provide medicine and physician's care in sickness or to meet the expenses of burial of their deceased numbers. The organization of societies to meet this situation was necessary. The first of these was formed at Malden in September 1854[8] with 600 members. It took the name "True Band." In two years there were 14 units of this organization in West Canada, all operating under the name True Band. It is almost a certain conclusion that they were all joined in some sort of union, confederacy, or supreme governing tribunal. If so, it is the first instance of which there is record of a number of such Negro organizations in different towns uniting for mutual benefit.

[7] Trent, op. cit., p.5.
[8] Ibid., pp.5, 6.

6

RELATED ORGANIZATIONS

There are indications that mutual benefit of an insurance nature was not the major objective of The Brown Fellowship Society, organized by certain quadroons and mulattoes in Charleston, South Carolina, in 1790[9] although "mutual aid of one another in distress" was included in the purposes for which the society was set up. The major emphasis seems to have been placed upon class distinction and social caste as distinguished from organization for material social benefits. Foolish though the color qualification of these misguided zealots, yet some racial good resulted from even their organization. It inspired the darker hued free colored people of Charleston to organize two other similar associations, and then all three continued in existence for nearly 40 years, competing with each other in the work of relief of the unfortunate. Moreover, there are some indications to support the belief that they all three assisted escaped slaves on their way north.

In the South

It is well known that nowhere in the South were slaves allowed to congregate except in the presence of a white person. They were allowed to have church services and to attend funerals. All meetings for other purposes were forbidden. Despite all this, however, as far back as 1833[10] there were many mutual aid associations among the slaves of the South.

After the War

The coming of freedom, far from alleviating the conditions that prompted the creation of combinational units for distributing the weight of community misfortunes among Negroes before the war, rather intensified them immediately following the emancipation of the slaves. The Freedmen's Bureau, the only semblance of governmental attempt to deal with the situation, was entirely inadequate to cope with the conditions. Hence, it was the Negro Church which again arose to meet a situation that was even worse than that among the destitute free Negroes of the North prior to the war, and, economically, far worse than that among the slaves—a situation which gave to the foolish critics of the Negro's freedom their excuse for saying that the freedmen were not capable of surviving as free men in North American civilization. Naturally there was

[9] Ibid., p.7.
[10] Ib., p.8.

7

great privation, suffering, and disease throughout most of 1865 in a group so large, suddenly thrown upon its own resources. Most freedmen were skeptical of signing any kind of contract for farm work with those who owned land in the South, lest they forfeit the precious freedom granted them under the Emancipation.

For more than a quarter of a century church relief societies grew in popularity and in membership in the South, most of them serving well the purposes for which they were organized. A meeting of representatives of various societies was held in Baltimore in 1884.[11] An aggregate membership of some 2,100 was reported from about 40 societies.

The report further showed the following:[12]

Total number members buried (probably since organization)	1,400
Total amount paid for funeral expenses	$45,000
Total amount paid for sick benefits	$125,000
Total amount paid for widows' relief	$27,000
Total amount paid for house rent	$10,700
Total amount paid for incidental expenses	$11,300

NOTE: About 1840 the Maryland Assembly had passed a measure making it unlawful for colored people to assemble in any kind of a meeting. Two years later, in 1842, on the petition of a number of "highly respectable citizens" that it had "operated with much hardship on many honest and industrious blacks," the law was modified for the city of Baltimore to permit the Negroes of that city to organize mutual aid or benevolent associations. Brackett, J. R., *The Negro in Maryland*, pp.203-4:

That adequate assessments had been collected and good business practiced in some of them is attested by the fact that some $40,000 in unexpended balances—dividends, to be accurate—had been paid back to the members.

The concerns thus far considered, whether known as church relief societies, mutual aid or benevolent associations,[13] had their inspiration in conditions of pressing distress and were organized to

[11] Ibid., p.12.

[12] Ibid., p.12.

[13] The following entirely different type of organization will attest to the high appreciation of the Negroes' insurable value even as a slave: "In 1846, thirty and more citizens of Kent County were incorporated into a 'Mutual Protection Society,' for the insurance of slave property. Every person who insured a slave became a member, and the object was to protect the members from loss of slaves who might run away beyond the limits of Maryland. In 1860, was formed the Southern Slaveholders' Insurance Company of Maryland. Any slaveholder of the United States could have his property insured, and either the runaways were returned or their value paid." Brackett, op. cit., p.91.

meet stern necessities which probably no other agency would have served. To this work, and to it alone, the efforts of their members seem to have been faithfully devoted. There appears nowhere in the history of their operations any trace of gaiety, display of pomp, vain pageantry, or the lighter veins of social indulgences.

Union Central Relief Association of Birmingham, Alabama

The Union Central Relief Association was organized December 1894[14] in Birmingham, Alabama, as the Afro-American Benevolent Association. The Reverend T. W. Walker, resenting the discrimination against and discourtesies to Negro policyholders in the Southern Mutual Aid, a white organization offering health and accident insurance to colored people, promoted the Union Central as concrete protest against the mal-practices of agents of the Southern Mutual.

Almost immediately, however, the white officials of the latter association raised objections to the use of a policy of similar wording to theirs. In 1896 the colored organization changed the style of its policies and the name to Union Central Indemnity Association. In 1901[1] the Alabama legislature was persuaded to grant the sponsors a charter giving exclusive rights to the name "Union Central Relief Association."

This association enjoyed prosperous and useful operation in the state of Alabama for more than a quarter of a century, finally being absorbed by the Atlanta Life Insurance Company without loss to its policyholders. From the beginning of its operation, it installed efficient clerical systems and reliable business principles, as a result of which several leaders in early insurance of this type were developed, some of whom led in the formation of other insurance units, viz.: Anniston Aid Society, of Anniston Alabama; The Peoples Mutual Aid and Great Southern Home Industrial Association, both of Alabama; the Union Mutual Association and Georgia Mutual, of Georgia. All of these finally disappeared through reinsurance.

[14] Trent, op. cit.
[4] Ibid.

Chapter II

FRATERNAL BENEFIT SOCIETIES

THE motives that inspired the organization among Negroes, soon after the close of the Civil War, of those combinations known variously as fraternal orders, secret societies, lodges, or fraternal benefit associations were neither altruistic like the early church relief societies nor frankly and honestly financial for purposes of profit, like the later well-regulated life insurance companies. While benevolent in legal theory and, perhaps, actually so, as conducted by some groups, among Negroes they were steered away from the paths of true charity to serve ends highly commercialized and mercenary in nature and practices.

In the first place, they did not arise to meet and administer to conditions of suffering and distress. They were created not in response to any stern demands of human necessity; but their organization and development were designed to gratify ambitions less economic and helpful in so far as the interests of the masses of Negroes were concerned. While in later years the opportunities for gratifying other motives appeared, in the first years of their promotion there were three principal appeals that drew large numbers of colored men and women into these societies. They were:

1. The love for the spectacular, the gaudy, flashy colors, the illusions of the tinseled grandeur in the showy and pompous ceremonies.

2. The natural human craving to take part in affairs governmental and political.

3. A desire for the advantages of the deep secrets of the lodges.

In explanation of the first: white politicians from the North had already whetted the freedmen's appetite for brilliant regalia in the companies of Negro State Militia with smart, new uniforms, which they had organized in an effort to hold state political jobs in the South. The fraternal organizations imitated the parade features of the militia.

With these rather intangible considerations as inducements, the fraternal orders increased rapidly in membership, in variety, and in the number of units in the first two decades after the war. With increased numbers, the feasibility of other attractions—meetings for social pleasure, outings, and railroad excursions—appeared; and then some of the leaders began to see the opportunity for the creation of lucrative offices and great personal gain in the establishment of a system of state and national units to which the local lodges would be subordinate.

Fifty Years of Fraternalism

The best interests of the masses of Negroes, however, were not forgotten nor subordinated to personal gain in all organizations of the type here discussed. Some sincerely served their members in many useful ways, as will be explained; and yet it would have been far more beneficial to the race as a whole if the organizational genius and energy of the early post-war leaders, which resulted in the creation of so many fraternal associations, had been exercised in the formation and development of some type of industrial enterprise. This would have been better than embarking upon and spending themselves for more than a half century in the prosecution of institutions that contributed nothing indispensable to the economic life of the race.

They produced nothing, sold nothing necessary, employed comparatively few, offered no media for investments of profits; and there is no record of any other racial group having relied upon them as important sources of livelihood; but the incompetence of organizations such as these, to serve the imperative economic needs of a group in such stress of circumstances as were the four or five million Negroes right after the Civil War, is here pointed out not to condemn fraternal orders, but to lament the error of according them major importance at such a crucial time.

Appraisal

While this is to be regretted, yet these societies were not without important racial values:

1. The work in them taught the value and technique of organization.

2. They taught necessary lessons in discipline, cooperation and loyalty to constituted authority. They taught team work.

3. In a sense they were kindergartens in civil government and in the methods and practices of conventions.

4. Race talent in salesmanship was developed in the canvassing campaigns for members.

5. Through them colored leaders came in contact with larger sums of money than, perhaps, would have been otherwise possible, thus causing them to begin to think in greater financial terms, and to organize banks and other financial institutions in connection with some of the organizations.

6. For a time they furnished a profitable field of practice for the budding legal talent of the race, both as attorneys for claimants against the organizations and as defenders of them.

7. While the insurance departments of nearly all of the fraternal societies became insolvent before the vast majority of the beneficiaries realized any of the promised benefits from the premiums paid, yet as a result of the millions of dollars that they collected, thousands of young Negroes were helped in getting educations, hundreds of homes were paid for and mortgages satisfied in the territory of their operations.

8. They laid the foundations for the more reliable and scientifically operated Old Line Legal Reserve Life Insurance Companies that followed them.

Fifty years, from 1865 to 1915, cover the period of most rapid growth, largest volume of business, and highest popularity of Negro fraternal orders. True, several are still in operation, and The American Woodmen, exceptional in its business efficiency, is now highly prosperous; but most of those started within the first quarter of a century following the close of the Civil War had almost reached their zenith in the decade from 1900 to 1910. By 1915 the majority of them, having financial troubles and some internal political strife, were commencing to wane in popularity. With only two or three exceptions, confidence in the secret orders to provide reliable insurance was almost wholly lost by 1925.

The Plan and Frame Work

The plan and frame work of all of the secret orders conformed to a general pattern. The laws governing the qualification and operation of fraternal societies are similar in many states. The theoretical concept running through these laws contemplates an

13

ideal form of representative government; but, as already mentioned, among Negroes it frequently did not work out that way.

In time, almost as a rule, the affairs of all departments of the various fraternal societies came to be dominated by the supreme or grand officers almost as definitely as though they had been owned outright by stock control. For a while in Mississippi there was an understanding among the several grand officers in the different orders that they would appear at the grand lodge meetings to help elect and "continue each other in office," the theory being that it would "set a bad example if the administration was not reelected." Thus, there obtained almost general perpetuation in office.

Subject only to a rather loose control by state authorities, these concerns were yet allowed to collect and to handle large sums of money; and, as a result, fatal abuses, mismanagement, and even in time corruption obtained in several of the states in which they operated.

Many were the items and excuses under which money was raised in the societies. Members were required to pay joining fees, local dues, grand lodge dues, supreme lodge dues, endowment assessments, extra assessments now and then, general expense taxes, pass-word taxes, educational taxes, building taxes, initiation fees, grand lodge degree fees, supreme lodge degree fees, and special fees which conferred "the *right* to run for any supreme lodge office."

Other sources of revenue were the sale of buttons, badges, pins, insignia, regalia, printed rituals, by-laws, pamphlets, and other forms and paraphernalia for opening and closing the lodge and for initiatory ceremonies.

Nearly all of the fraternal orders in the South had auxiliary insurance departments, erroneously called "endowment departments." These insurance departments rapidly became the major features of the societies, and it was in connection with them that abuses, mismanagement, corruption, and fraud obtained. The many failures of fraternal societies resulted from the insolvencies of their insurance departments.

Fraternal Failures

Many have been the causes assigned for the almost general failure of Negro fraternal societies. None, perhaps, is applicable to all cases. Inadequate assessments of the insurance departments probably caused more difficulties and dissolutions than all of the rest together.

Among other causes the following have been assigned:

a. Ignorance of the principles of life insurance
b. Mismanagement
c. Careless and incompetent selection of the risks
d. Political controversy, intrigue, and litigation
e. The numerous diversions and detractions of this modern age
f. The availability to Negroes of life insurance supplied by pure life insurance companies, without the loss of time and the trouble of attending lodge meetings
g. "Freezing" of the order's funds in big and unnecessary building
h. Fraud

Brief observations in relation to only the two last named, however, should suffice for this work.

Blunders in Buildings. The physical circumstances surrounding some of the buildings built by the officers of secret societies leave no doubt that the decisions to build them were not reached as a result of any survey of the prospects of profits on the investments nor of consideration of the possibility of ready liquidations, if necessary, to meet urgent or unexpected claim losses.

There has been no great demand for office space among colored people. No great number of colored professional and business men, on account of more limited patronage, have been able to pay profitable rents.

The business of Negro fraternal benefit societies was not real estate. That business was far afield from their professed objectives. Their officers were in duty bound to keep liquid the funds paid to them in the form of assessments for the payment of claims. They lost sight of the purposes for which the literature of their institutions said they were organized when they "tied up the funds in brick and mortar." The erection of an office building by a benefit society was never necessary to any greater extent than was required for transacting their own business.

Certainly the prospects of profits on the investments could not have been so promising as to make it seem necessary to levy extra or building taxes on the expectants of charity to raise funds to build buildings to make profits to dispense charity.

15

Most of these buildings have passed from the hands of colored people. Because most of them were taken over by receivers and their records have thus become unavailable, the figures here given as representative of their costs are, in many cases, approximations based upon the opinions of persons supposed to know something of their histories.

The late Dr. Sutton E. Griggs once said, "Some friends of mine entertained me all day in a certain city, showing me the buildings and property colored people *used to own,* except ten minutes, necessary to show me what they still own."

Buildings and figures mentioned below attest a high degree of accuracy in that statement.

FRATERNAL BUILDINGS LOST TO THE RACE, BY STATES

Building	City	Estimated Cost
ARKANSAS:		
Mosaic National Temple	Little Rock	$250,000
Mosaic State Annex	" "	50,000
Mosaic Hospital	" "	100,000
H. L. Bush Building and Hotel (Mosaic Connections)	" "	100,000
Pythian Building	" "	100,000
Taborian Building	" "	200,000
Sisters of Mysterious Ten and United Brothers of Friendship	" "	50,000
Century Life Insurance Company (Not Fraternal)	" "	110,00
Woodmen of Union Bathhouse, Hospital and Office Building[1]	Hot Springs	497,000
GEORGIA:		
Odd Fellows Building	Atlanta	303,000
Wage-Earners Building	Savannah	100,000
ILLINOIS:		
Pythian Temple Building	Chicago	over 1,000,00
LOUISIANA:		
Masonic Building	Shreveport	150,000
Court of Calanthe	"	200,000
Mosaic Templar Building	"	50,000
TENNESSEE:		
Masonic Building	Nashville	150,000
Masonic Building	Memphis	75,000
Taborian Building	"	10,000

[1] Foreclosed and possessed by the United States of America.

NOTE: According to Attorney J. L. Lewis $50,000 in state and county back taxes is owed on the Masonic Temple in Jacksonville, Florida, which cost approximately $300,000. The order has an approximate monthly income of $20,000, but it is reputed to owe $60,000 in unpaid death claims.

FRATERNAL BENEFIT SOCIETIES

TEXAS:

Odd Fellows Building	Houston	387,500
Pilgrims Building	"	285,000
	(Paid Cash	170,000)
True Men and Women of the World* Calvert		85,000

DISTRICT OF COLUMBIA:

Masonic Temple	Washington	950,000
TOTAL LOSS		$5,222,500

*This is one of the most interesting of all building mistakes. The three-story pressed brick building stands out with conspicuous inappropriateness in that little Texas town. Just what the officers of the True Men and Women of the World contemplated doing with such a building in a town like that is an enigma. Some years ago they had, ahead of current death claims, some $50,000. They thought they ought to erect a building with it. The plans they projected called for an expenditure of $85,000. They allegedly borrowed the additional $35,000 to give to the members of their order a fine building with both a roof-garden and a $35,000 indebtedness on top of it. Reports have it that the officers of the order were allowed to occupy it only about thirty days before the creditors took charge of it.

The following are among fraternal order buildings still owned either by the societies that originally built them or by other colored interests:

Building	City	Estimated Cost
Mosaic Temple	Pine Bluff, Arkansas	$ 40,000
Court of Calanthe	Little Rock, Arkansas	65,000
Pythian Bath House and Hospital	Hot Springs, Arkansas	150,000
Pythian Temple*	New Orleans, Louisiana	375,000
Odd Fellow's Building	Baton Rouge, Louisiana	121,000
Masonic Building and Mosque	Fort Worth, Texas	250,000
Pythian Temple	Dallas, Texas	100,000
TOTAL		$1,101,000

* Later reports state that this building has now been lost to the colored race.

In their heyday the United Brothers of Friendship and Sisters of the Mysterious Ten of Texas erected two fine buildings in the Negro down-town district of Houston. A few years ago when the order became insolvent, white creditors took over this piece of property "said to be the most valuable colored real estate in the Southwest."[2] In August 1939 it was returned to Negro ownership when purchased by the Watchtower Life Insurance Company through its president, T. M. Fairchild.

Fraternal Frauds

Next to inadequate or inequitably adjusted premium rates, fraud practiced on fraternal benefit societies probably takes rank among the major causes of their downfall. It was the losses from death claim frauds that contributed greatly to the impairments. These took form in four general classes: Misrepresentation of

[2] *The Houston Defender*, Sept. 5, 1939.

ages; misrepresentation of health conditions; misrepresentation of relationship as to insurable interest; fictitious claims.

The acceptance of members was largely left to the local officers after the lodges had been "set up" and started on their way by the "home-office deputies." There developed a system of collusion and reciprocal favors among the local lodge leaders. As a result of this, the old, decrepit, and the hopelessly sick relatives of all of the leading people in many communities became insured in some of the societies.

It was a natural and an easy step from this to the practice of seeking the names of old and feeble persons, misrepresenting the relationship, and having them insured, even without their knowledge, in one or more of the benefit associations. This led to a fairly general practice, in a number of communities, of the business of "carrying." "Carrying" people, or just the names of people, on lodge rolls became a very definitely profitable business in the first fifteen years following the beginning of the century by a few speculators in Attalla, Coahoma, Holmes, LeFlore, Sharkey, Warren, Washington, and Yazoo Counties, Mississippi.

One intelligent woman at Greenwood, Mississippi, confided that at times she had as many as forty "prospects made to her" (insured in her favor) in the different lodges there; and that she "aimed to have at least one 'come off' [become a claim] every month."

One shrewd colored ex-banker made arrangements with "the endowment secretary" of one of the large societies with its home office in the Mississippi Delta, in its declining days of difficulty, to give preference in payment to death claims he presented. He then borrowed money to go out and buy up claims from "carriers" anxious to sell at heavy discounts because of long delays in claim payments and the knowledge that the order had fallen into "financial straits." At last, however, he was caught in his own trap, when a representative of the State Insurance Commissioner took charge of the "endowment office" without notice and left the death claim broker holding a number of unpaid claims which he had "bought."

Uncle Joe Coleman of Greenwood, Mississippi, gained local fame as an "unprofitable prospect" for the several "carriers" who had "taken out" policies on his life. He was generally thought to have been about 85 years old in 1907. Without known relatives, he just wandered about town "making his living somehow." He appeared an ideal "prospect to carry," and several "carried him"; but he lived until 1914, by which time several of the "carriers" had preceded him in death, and some of the larger societies in which he was "carried" were betraying indications of early collapse. There were hundreds of other cases more flagrantly fraudulent and more successfully imposed upon the lodges in Mississippi as will appear from the following, related only to show the extent of these frauds:

In 1910 five of the colored fraternal orders operating in Mississippi—the Odd Fellows, the Woodmen's Union, the Sacred Order of Perfection, the Independent Order of Sons and Daughters of Jacob, and the Knights of Pythias—jointly employed M. S. Stuart to make investigations of suspicious claims filed. His compensation was based upon a commission of 10% of the amount saved; and during the years of 1911, 1912, and 1913 his average monthly commissions on the savings he effected amounted to $443, or a total of $15,948, making the gross savings to the five fraternals $159,480. The limited scope of these pages forbids the relation of the interesting and sensational details of the many cases uncovered and the prosecutions and convictions that grew out of them.

During the three years, the investigations uncovered twenty-three cases of flagrant and *wholly fictitious claims,* made up either by the use of "just names" which had been carried on the lodge rolls, or by forging so-called proofs containing the names of living persons. There were many others, less flagrant and fictitious, but, nevertheless, fraudulent.

Local lodge officers, undertakers, and sometimes doctors were involved in the many cases of fraud. In at least two cases investigated, white plantation agents were involved; and, in another case, a corrupt white man in Greenwood became indignant and attempted to take the life of the investigator for uncovering a fraudulent claim in which his yellow concubine was the beneficiary.[1]

Fraternal Conversions

It has already been observed that a number of the insurance units that began as church relief, benevolent or burial societies developed into important life insurance companies either as mutuals or stock companies; but there is no record of any of the larger

---

[1] Incidents related are from personal investigations of the author when employed as investigator by the lodges in Mississippi.

fraternal benefit societies having been saved from collapse by being either developed or converted into any other type of life insurance unit.

The outstanding attempt to do this did not work out successfully. J. L. Webb, Supreme Custodian of the Woodmen's Union of Hot Springs, Arkansas, held a heavy financial interest in the Century Life Insurance Company of Little Rock, Arkansas. About 1930 the increasing mortality rate of the Woodmen became a perplexing problem; and The Century at the same time was having financial difficulties. It appeared that through a merger expenses might be reduced and the combined organization operated on a safer basis. The plan, however, was only temporarily successful. With the coming of the depression years the large investments of the enterprise became ever less liquid, and in September 1932 the field business and the assets were taken over by Universal Life, acting as liquidating trustees.

Total Contributed to Fraternalism

Only the Insurance Department of South Carolina furnished any information of value on the question of the total amount paid by Negroes into fraternal benefit societies during the fifty years of their operation. While the figures given below are the result of approximation, it is safe to state that they do not exceed the true amounts. They are based on the known average annual collections of the Odd Fellows in Mississippi, the Independent Order of St. Luke in Virginia and the Knights and Daughters of Tabor in Mississippi, during ten specimen years.

It is estimated that Negroes paid into fraternal societies in the years from 1870 to 1920 the amounts listed for each of the states, as follows:

Arkansas	$ 8,000,000
Alabama	10,000,000
Florida	10,500,000
Georgia	16,500,000
Kentucky	1,000,000
Louisiana	6,000,000
Mississippi	10,000,000
North Carolina	6,000,000
Oklahoma	1,000,000
South Carolina	7,000,000

Texas	19,000,000
Virginia	25,000,000
Tennessee	8,000,000
All others	12,000,000
Total	$168,000,000

The greater part of this sum was paid to the beneficiaries of the deceased members.

Federated Insurance League[3]

In 1908 William S. Dodd took the lead in the organization of a "Federated Insurance League." This idea grew out of discussion of Negro problems at annual conferences held at Hampton Institute, Virginia.

The Federated Insurance League was organized in 1908 and all insurance associations and fraternals in the State [Virginia] were eligible for membership. [4]

In time most all of the fraternal concerns in Virginia connected themselves with the League. A report of the League in 1909 showed that 37 fraternal organizations in Virginia alone "did a business of $4,500,000." This, perhaps, is the first attempt at a general organization of Negro insurance units in the United States.

THE GRAND UNITED ORDER OF ODD FELLOWS OF AMERICA

The supreme or governing body of the Odd Fellows in America[5] is termed the "B. M. C."—Biennial Movable Committee. A smaller executive body, the "S. C. M."—Sub-Committee of Management in America —carries on the business of the order and executes the laws and regulations enacted by the supreme or legislative body.

On December 19, 1843, the Committee of Management of England passed a resolution empowering Philomathean Lodge No. 646 of New York City, New York (which appears to have been previously organized) to form a Sub-Committee of Management of America.[6]

Thus it was that the Grand United Order of Odd Fellows began operations in the United States; and, though composed of Negroes, it became the only authority in this country recognized by the

[3] Trent, W. J. Jr., *Development of Negro Life Insurance Enterprises,* 1932.

[4] Brown, W. H., *The Education and Economic Development of the Negro in Virginia,* p.124. Phelps-Stokes papers, 1922.

[5] Until 1880, it appears that the supreme or legislative body in America was known as the "A.M.C." There was a meeting of the Annual Movable Committee, held at Little Rock, Arkansas, October 7-10, 1879, and a meeting of the "B.M.C." in Boston, October 5, 1882, the change to the two-year meeting plan evidently having been approved in the meantime.

[6] *General Laws,* Grand United Order of Odd Fellows in America.

parent organization in England. "I. O. O. F.," the Independent Order of Odd Fellows, the organization of white people in America, is independent of English authority.

It was Peter Ogden, a New York Negro, who took the lead in securing authority from England to organize Odd Fellow Lodges in the United States; and he became the first American Grand Master.

The increase in the number of lodges in the United States appears to have been great in the period from 1843 to 1870. By the close of the latter year, 770 lodges had been "set up," and in 1879 lodges were to be found in Arkansas, Georgia, Illinois, Maryland, Pennsylvania, Tennessee, Virginia and, very probably, several other states. The growing number of local lodges provoked, at the meeting of the Annual Movable Committee in Little Rock,[7] Arkansas, in October 1879, a discussion of plans for the organization of State, or District Grand Lodges.

Later, E. H. Morris,[8] having written the laws for governing the District Grand Lodges, submitted them to the S. C. M. at its next meeting in January 1883. After the meeting of the B. M. C. in Boston in 1882, State or District Grand Lodges and Households of Ruth, the female units, were soon organized in all of the states having three or more subordinate lodges, and the "Endowment" or insurance departments soon were connected in most states in the South. A full history of this order in America is not here attempted.

A discussion of some of the experiences and final difficulties of the benefit departments of three of the larger district grand lodges, somewhat typical of the others, will convey a fairly adequate idea of the enormous sums of money annually paid into institutions of this type in the years of their popularity. If what is revealed of the transactions of these three be multiplied enough to cover the benefit bureaus not only of this same society in all the other states in the South, but of the numerous other fraternal orders as well, something approaching a full comprehension of the economic effect on the colored race may be gained.

[7] *General Law,* G.U.O.O.F.

[8] Edward H. Morris, shrewd, renowned lawyer of Chicago, Illinois, has almost completely dominated the meetings of the S.C.M. and the B.M.C. from 1882 until the present time, 1939. He has served as Grand Master more than forty of the fifty-seven years, holding that office continuously since 1910, after having the laws amended to make continuous succession legal.

Georgia

The Odd Fellows entered the State of Georgia with the organization of St. James Lodge No. 1415 in Atlanta in 1870.[9] District Grand Lodge No. 18, Jurisdiction of Georgia, was organized soon after the B. M. C., in 1879, adopted provisions authorizing state grand lodges.

The "Endowment Department" was organized in 1903 and by 1911 it was boasting a membership of 40,000, and collecting total assessments amounting annually to more than $300,000. The Grand Lodge treasurer, (not the "endowment department") collected yearly upwards of $20,000 in "grand lodge dues," each member paying 50 cents per year.

In 1912 the grand officers bought nearly an entire block, fronting on Auburn Avenue in Atlanta, paying $53,000 for the land alone, and erected on part of it a five-story office building at a cost of $250,000.[10] The next year they built an auditorium on the remainder of the lot at a cost of approximately $180,000. These concrete evidences of the "financial solidarity" of the Odd Fellows in Georgia still further accelerated the growth of the order, until about 1915, when trouble, which really had its inception at the B. M. C. convention in Richmond, Virginia, in 1906, and broke violently into the open at the meeting of the B. M. C. in Atlanta in 1912, began to affect the financial structure of the Georgia Grand Lodge.

The bitter difference engendered between former National Grand Master F. H. Morris and Benjamin J. Davis, District Grand Secretary of Georgia, at the meeting of the B. M. C. in Richmond, continued through the next B. M. C. meeting at Atlantic City in 1908 and to the following meeting of the B. M. C. at Baltimore in 1910. Here Edward H. Morris was again elected National Grand Master. It appears that B. J. Davis, leading the Georgia and other southern delegates, either was assured, or thought that he was, that if he made no opposition to the election of Mr. Morris and his ticket at the Baltimore convention, at the next meeting of the B. M. C., he, Davis, would have the support of Grand Master Morris and probably be elected National Grand Master without opposition. But, when, in September 1912, the B. M. C. convened

[9] Informant: Mr. B. J. Davis, former District Grand Secretary.
[10] Mr. B. J. Davvis, former D. G. Secretary.

in Atlanta, incumbent Grand Master Morris was significantly silent on the matter of not consenting to be re-elected.

At this meeting Georgia alone had more than 1300 representatives in the B. M.C., and the heavy representation from other southern states, most of whom were for the election of Davis, seemed to assure the election of the brilliant and aggressive Atlantan. But again, as at the Richmond convention, the shrewdness of the great Morris was not taken sufficiently into the account. Presiding, he again indulged in every kind of delay, and, in this, he was understandingly assisted by a number of his northern friends, masters in the art of filibustering. The election was started Friday night. The laws provided that "the incumbent Grand Master should hold office until his successor was elected and qualified."

The roll call of states was begun, and the leader of each state delegation arose and cast his state's vote, all proceeding smoothly until the name of Georgia was reached. Then, Henry Lincoln Johnson, the famous lawyer, arose and said: "I cast Georgia's 1365 votes for the election of Benjamin J. Davis as Grand Master."

Then, a delegate from Illinois shouted: "Georgia does not have 1365 legal representatives in this house, and I demand that the Georgia delegation be here and now individually polled."

Henry Lincoln Johnson replied: "Georgia asks no more and will accept no less than is required of all other states. If the Georgia delegation must be individually polled, I demand the same thing for all of the other states."

But, shrewd lawyer though he was, that was a great mistake. It was what the astute Morris wanted, knowing that the delegations could not be polled in that manner before the expiration of the contract for the auditorium at six o'clock Saturday morning.

At that time, Henry Lincoln Johnson, mounting the platform, declared B. J. Davis elected Grand Master along with other officers he named; and E. H. Morris replied, declaring that no election had been held and that the same officers would remain in office until the next meeting of the B. M. C.

Long litigation followed the Atlanta meeting. E. H. Morris and his associate officers, in possession of the national office in Philadelphia, sought to depose B. J. Davis, Henry Lincoln Johnson, and their friends in Georgia by recognizing another set of officers. On March 16, 1916, the organization was placed in receivership,

24

although records show that mortality claims were not, in the aggregate, more than $40,000 in arrears; and, in view of the great assets of the district grand lodge at the time, it seems, in retrospect, that the situation could have been mastered without the appointment of receivers.

However this may be, the following is, in round figures, the value of the assets which the receivers took in hand to liquidate, "for the benefit of the policyholders and beneficiaries":

Real estate in Georgia	$650,000[11]
Cash on hand	223,000
Government bonds	10,000
Municipal bonds	15,000
TOTAL	$898,000

To protect the order in the event of the loss by death of either District Grand Master Birl S. Ingram, or District Grand Secretary Benjamin J. Davis, their valuable lives were insured in favor of the Order in the Metropolitan Life Insurance Company for $25,000 each. The receivers immediately applied for and received the cash surrender values of $4,000 each on these two policies.

Early in 1917, before the receivers had paid any claims at all, the attorneys advising the receivers filed claim for and were paid $98,000[11] for their services to date. All told, the two receivers served twenty-five months and received $1,000 per month each for their services. Mr. B. J. Davis was assistant receiver and he received $500 per month for his services for the same period.

It appears that, by the end of 1918, the claims had all been paid and the receivers were dismissed; but, on account of further trouble, they were reappointed in 1920 and conducted the affairs of the Association until 1922, when the great Odd Fellows Grand Lodge and Benefit Association was dissolved.

The fine five-story brick office building erected by the Odd Fellows of Georgia still stands on Auburn Avenue, and is occupied by various Negro businesses, but the title to the building is not in Negro hands.

Mississippi

Lodges of the Grand United Order of Odd Fellows were organized in Mississippi in the early 1880's, and at the beginning of

[11] B. J. Davis, former District Grand Secretary and Assistant Receiver.

the present century there were one or more lodges and households in nearly every county in the state.

The Odd Fellows Benefit Association was organized under the authority of the District Grand Lodge in 1897, with Professor Ephriam H. McKissack of Rust College, Holly Springs, Mississippi, as Secretary-Treasurer. He was an honest, efficient officer, in whom most of the people of Mississippi had great confidence, even after the collapse of the department which he had conducted so well for the order for many years.

At first, the Odd Fellows Benefit Association operated on the safer plan of prorating the monthly assessments collected; and, at 75 cents per member for all ages up to 60, beneficiaries were being paid $780 each at the death of the policyholder in 1903. There was no thought of setting aside reserves for future protection.

At the meeting of the District Grand Lodge at Greenville, in August 1903, Professor McKissack in making his report stated: "We have enough money on hand to pay all beneficiaries due to be paid in September as much as we are paying those due in August. Therefore, I recommend that the September assessment be pretermitted." Wild applause and cheering greeted this statement, and the endowment secretary-treasurer was hailed as a "financial wizard."

For the next four years the membership increased greatly. In September 1906 the Reverend Edward P. Jones, District Grand Master, chartered a special train, carrying 315 delegates to the meeting of the B. M. C. in Richmond, Virginia. He was a candidate for election as "National Grand Master"; and, as in the case of Georgia, it is believed that differences growing out of the bitter political contest at the Richmond convention contributed greatly to the final downfall of the benefit department and the order in Mississippi. But, in this state, its reaction was somewhat different from that in Georgia.

It is interesting to note how this brotherhood, with its boasted maxim of "Friendship, Love and Truth," conducted an election. The incumbent National Grand Master, Professor J. McHenry Jones, of West Virginia (no kin to Reverend E. P. Jones), favored the latter as his successor. The wily Mr. Morris was supporting a brilliant young attorney, Mr. William L. Houston, of Washington, D. C., now Assistant United States Attorney-General and president of the National Bar Association. The southern forces, led by Davis,

26

Henry Lincoln Johnson, Jones, McKissack, Perry Howard, Topp, Stuart, and others, numbered more than twice as many delegates as the northern leaders could muster; and with McHenry Jones, a friend, presiding, it seemed only a formal matter of casting the votes to accomplish the election of the handsome, impulsive young minister from Vicksburg.

But Edward Morris was reputed to have said that neither Edward Jones nor any other man from south of Kentucky should or would ever be elected to the office of Grand Master as long as he lived. It was here that he first showed that he was a master strategist in dilatory convention tactics. On the roll call each individual delegate was required to arise and read his choice for the eight officers to be elected. There were more than 2400 delegates. Listed numerically, the older northern lodges were first on the roll; and quiet Jim Needham, Grand Secretary of Philadelphia, let no one hurry him in calling that roll. Northern delegates, obviously coached so to do, took plenty of time to call out their preferences, while still others interposed numerous and welcome interruptions. At eleven o'clock Friday night, less than fifty of the approximately 1700 southern delegates had voted, while more than half of the seven or eight hundred followers of the Morris faction had. The southerners' trains were scheduled to leave Saturday morning. The more intelligent Morris followers, at every opportunity, staged what they made to appear a "Band Wagon Stampede" to Houston, to discourage their illiterate brothers from the South.

From a vantage point way up in a corner in the gallery, the great Chicago barrister watched the strategy, and at psychological moments, prompted emissaries, under the guise of friends, to impress upon Jones the futility of staying in the race. At last they told him that if he would withdraw, Morris would support a motion to send him (Jones) as a delegate to the meeting of the Annual Movable Committee in England, pay all expenses and give him, in addition, $1,000. The southern leaders stoutly opposed the plan; but despite their pleadings, Jones accepted the Morris offer. That step on his part marred his name among the Odd Fellows in Mississippi and very definitely detracted from his influence in the Order.

See now how this led to the insolvency of the order in Mississippi. At the next Grand Lodge meeting in Vicksburg, in August

1907, there occurred a bitter political contest against Jones. A majority of the delegates opposed his re-election as Grand Master; but he prevented them from voting by bringing in the Vicksburg police to take charge while he swore out a writ of injunction against his opponents, and thereby secured the appointment of a white man, Police Judge Harris Dickson, the noted author of "Old Reliable" and other magazine articles, to preside over the meeting. With many of the leaders of the opposition arrested and others intimidated and run away, "Acting District Grand Master Dickson" had to suffer no strain of veracity at all to declare Jones the choice of the majority.

National Grand Master Houston was on the scene and advised the opposition to appeal to the Sub-Committee of Management. Perry W. Howard, Professor Daniel W. Gary, and M. S. Stuart went to Philadelphia in January 1908 to lay the appeal before the S. C. M. But there they were advised by Morris and Houston not to press the matter "for the present." So nothing was ever done about this contest; but dissatisfaction grew in Mississippi, and many members commenced to drop out.

To stem this rising tide of resentment, McKissack, Secretary-Treasurer, had the society adopt a policy providing $1,000 as a death benefit for an assessment of $1 a month for all ages up to sixty. Of course this was highly inadequate. At the next Grand Lodge meeting the assessment was increased to $1.50 per month. The decrease in membership became more pronounced. The assessment was then raised to $20 per year.

At the next meeting of the Grand Lodge at Biloxi, in 1915, the order owed $95,000 in unpaid death claims. The membership, at the end of 1916, had dropped from the peak of 23,000 in 1908 to less than 3,000.

The O. F. B. A., because of the persisting esteem in which McKissack was held, was not put into the hands of receivers. Jones resigned and moved away to Chicago; but McKissack, by compromising, scaling down, and advancing personal money, succeded in paying all claims before his death in 1924.

Soon, however, the Odd Fellows Benefit Association ceased operations. Thus, there passed an organization that, in the less than twenty years of operation, collected more than $8,000,000 from Negroes in Mississippi.

Louisiana

District Grand Lodge No. 21, jurisdiction of Louisiana, is exceptional among the southern state units of this fraternal order in that it is still operating. It, of course, like many other institutions, is now faced with perplexing financial difficulties, due probably to persistent unemployment growing out of depression years.

The Order entered the State of Louisiana when Butler Lodge No. 1336 was organized by Negro soldiers at New Orleans in 1873.[12] The endowment or insurance department was organized in 1896, and in 1919 still another bureau, styled the burial department, was organized.

Beginning in 1896, there was a per capita assessment of 10 cents per death, producing, of course, variable amounts for death benefits. In 1902 this was changed to 50 cents per month with a definite commitment to policies paying $500, and this plan continued until 1934 when the department commenced to issue policies in denominations of $100, $200, and $300, with a monthly assessment of 35 cents per $100 of insurance.

In 1935, in an effort to satisfy outstanding claims, Agreement Loan Certificates were adopted, under the terms of which beneficiaries agreed to accept a part of the mortality benefit due them and "lend" the Society the remainder with 3 per cent interest per annum. At the present time the total of the amount loaned the Order and oustanding is $61,000, and this amount does not include $30,000 of unpaid claims incurred since the adoption of the Agreement Loan Certificate plan.

A novel plan was adopted for the erection of the Odd Fellows Building in Baton Rouge. No assessment was levied on the members. It was paid for from interest earned on endowment deposits. While the building is unencumbered, the officers now seek a government loan sufficient to pay outstanding claims which probably would again restore confidence and start the institution on the road to prosperity.

[12] Mr. William Kelso, District Grand Master.

Note. The Texas Grand Lodge did not cease to operate until July 10, 1939, when its charter was revoked and John W. Rice, State Grand Master, and James T. Ewing, "Endowment Secretary," were removed from office. At the same time the insurance of the members in that state was transferred to the Modern Mutual Health & Accident, a white insurance company of Houston, Texas.

THE IMPROVED BENEVOLENT PROTECTIVE ORDER OF ELKS AND MASONIC GRAND LODGES

EXCEPTIONAL among the larger fraternal societies is the Improved Benevolent Protective Order of Elks, which has never attempted to operate an insurance department but has raised funds to make donations for relief by voluntary contributions of its members.

The late Arthur J. Riggs, of Cincinnati, Ohio, took first steps in February 1897 to establish the Order of Elks among Negroes. He associated with him in this work the late B. F. Howard and Mr. Frank H. Hunter, now an active member of the Greater St. Louis Lodge. The first lodge was set up in Cincinnati on June 10, 1899, and the following were on its roster of officers: Frank H. Hunter, Exalted Ruler; Dr. Frank Johnson, secretary; and H. T. Jackson, treasurer.

Almost from the beginning this fraternal as a whole encountered bitter opposition from white people, who were opposed to Negroes having an organization similar in name and practices to theirs. So intense became the persecution which Riggs incurred because of his leadership in this movement that he was forced to move his family to Springfield, Ohio, and assume a different name in order to find work. B. F. Howard also was made to feel the sting of pressure, and forced to move across the river to Covington, Kentucky. At various times throughout its history, state and local units have had to face serious difficulties of the same nature. In 1905 the Reverend Edward P. Jones of Vicksburg, Mississippi, and others were prevented by court injunction from establishing this order in Mississippi. The same thing happened to the Elks Lodge in Memphis, Tennessee, in 1912; but here in the year 1938 these objections were overcome and a prosperous local lodge organized through the energy and influence of Messrs. R. R. Church, G. W. Lee, and C. C. Valle, the National Organizer. The order was also established in Mississippi in 1934 and is now operating in that state without opposition.

Despite the frequent opposition by white interests and fierce internal dissensions, this order, since originating in Cincinnati, has expanded rapidly. The first Grand Lodge was organized in Ohio with B. F. Howard as Grand Exalted Ruler; and, as the number of local lodges increased, Grand Lodges were organized in several other states, until there are now lodges, temples, and affiliates in all forty-eight states and some even in the island possessions and territories of the nation. The membership of this organization is now said to be 400,000.

Notwithstanding the fact that mortality benefits depend upon the voluntary contributions of the members, the total amount paid dependents of deceased members exceeds $100,000.

In August 1925, at the National Grand Lodge Session held in Richmond, Virginia, an Educational Department was established; and in Cleveland, Ohio, in 1926, this department began to sponsor National Oratorical Contests which award various scholarships each year at an annual expenditure of more than $5,000. Through this means a keen interest is promoted in education and especially in the art of public speaking, as well as in the principles of the Constitution of the United States, some phase of which is stressed in the orations every year.

Other departments now sponsored by this organization are: Economics, Civil Liberties, Athletics, and Health. The Order of Elks stresses the brighter side of life, and its members maintain a keen interest in social diversions. Special pride is taken in its various finely equipped clubs and lodge halls throughout the country. Many of these clubs are housed in valuable real estate units owned by local lodges. The value of this real estate is in excess of $1,365,000.

The following are among the officers of the National Grand Lodge: J. Finley Wilson, Grand Exalted Ruler, Washington, D. C.; James E. Kelley, Grand Secretary, Birmingham, Alabama; Edward W. Henry, Grand Treasurer, Philadelphia, Pennsylvania; William C. Hueston, Grand Commissioner of Education; Perry W. Howard, Grand Legal Adviser; Dr. Charles B. Fisher, Grand Medical Director, of Washington, D. C., and C. C. Valle, Grand Organizer, New York City.

The following have served as Grand Exalted Rulers of this popular fraternal order:

Dr. James E. Mills (Deceased)	Norfolk, Virginia;
J. Frank Wheaton (Deceased)	New York City, New York;
Harry H. Pace,	Chicago, Illinois;
A. .H. Y. Judge	Charleston, West Virginia;
Armond W. Scott,	Washington, D. C.;
George W. F. McMechen,	Baltimore, Maryland;
George E. Wibecan,	Brooklyn, New York.

The Masons

The Masonic Order is one of the oldest and was one of the most popular fraternal organizations among Negroes. There were and perhaps still are several colored branches in America. Most of the state jurisdictions of the several branches rely upon voluntary contributions to raise funds for insurance benefits. A few in the South, however, adopted stipulated, periodical assessments and became committed to the payment of definite amounts for death benefits.

That branch known as the "Free and Accepted" became highly popular and financially strong in several southern states, especially during the first fifteen years following the beginning of the century. The Texas Grand Lodge of Masons is still in operation and reported on good authority to be in a prosperous condition. It is claimed that this is due to the skillful guidance of the wealthy and famous banker and politician, Bill McDonald of Fort Worth, the Grand Treasurer of that state. Also in Georgia one branch of this society is reported to be operating successfully.

Mississippi Masons—Cotton Sacks Full of Dollars

In Mississippi an elaborate so-called Endowment Department was organized about 1900, and for a number of years large death benefits were paid. However, it became a victim of the same type of financial troubles that caused the undoing of all the other large organizations in Mississippi in the years from 1900 to 1920. Following the death of Ellis Perkins at Edwards, Mississippi, in 1910, Charles Banks of Mound Bayou, banker, cotton mill magnate, financier, and famous politician, was elected endowment secretary, to succeed Perkins. Banks was a resourceful and daring man. At times he resorted to queer pretexts to quiet the clamor of claimants long deferred and unpaid.

At one of the Grand Lodge meetings at Holly Springs, Mississippi, to quiet rumors of impending failure, he, by pledging borrowed cotton warehouse receipts, secured from a Memphis bank for temporary use sufficient silver dollars to fill two cotton sacks, and these he shipped to Holly Springs and, spectacularly, during the Grand Lodge Session, had them brought in and piled upon a table in full view of the delegation. "There," said he, "is visible and concrete evidence that this order has plenty of money." But the ruse sufficed for only a short time.

This organization was introduced in Mississippi by M. W. Stringer, its first Grand Master. He was succeeded by Bishop E. W. Lampton, after whose death W. A. J. Morgan was elected and, in turn, he was succeeded by W. W. Phillips of Kosciusko. Mr. John L. Webb, the incumbent Grand Master, has succeeded in reviving the order in Mississippi, stressing only the ritualistic and fraternal phases as major features.

The Endowment Secretary-Treasurers were T. S. Littlejohn, Sr., Ellis Perkins, and Charles Banks, all now dead.

Among other operating organizations in Mississippi may be mentioned the Afro-American Sons and Daughters, and the Knights and Daughters of Tabor. The latter, after being dissolved in 1913, has been revived in recent years.

THE INDEPENDENT ORDER OF ST. LUKE

This fraternal benefit society was organized in Baltimore, Maryland, in 1867, by Mary Prout, a former slave. It was first known as *The Grand United Order of St. Luke.* Later, William M. T. Forrester severed connection with the parent organization and established *The Independent Order of St. Luke* in Virginia.

The endowment department was organized in 1881. A juvenile department was started in 1895. In 1899, Mrs. Maggie L. Walker was elected secretary-treasurer. She led the work of this society for more than thirty-five years. Due to her leadership and business genius lodges were rapidly set up in several of the states adjoining Virginia, and the membership increased to more than 100,000 before the end of 1925. The total collections for that year amounted to $405,450.40.

This, the oldest of the successfully operating fraternal benefit societies, has to its credit the following accomplishments, in addition to the great amounts paid for claims:

Enterprise	Year Established
St. Luke Printing Plant	1902
St. Luke Office Building	1903
St. Luke Penny Savings Bank	1903
St. Luke Regalia & Supply Co.	1904
St. Luke Emporium—opened	1904

Business in force Dec. 31, 1925 . . . . $8,145,880
Total amount of claims paid from organization through 1925 . . . . $1,289,078

The Home Office of the Independent Order of St. Luke is in Richmond, Virginia. It is enjoying successful operation; and its officers are justly proud of its history of useful services covering a period of seventy-three years.[13]

[13] Wendell P. Dabney, *Maggie L. Walker, Her Life and Deeds.*

Chapter III

IMPORTANT PHASES AND DEVELOPMENT OF NEGRO LIFE INSURANCE

LIFE Insurance, as we now know it, is a complicated financial business. In one form or another it has played an important part in the progress of the Negro race. Negroes have made their greatest commercial successes and have suffered their greatest financial failures in this field.

That the Negro race, without training and experience, with the varied American fields of business before it, should have chosen to enter in such a large way into this particular line is remarkable, and, in a sense, queer. Seventy-five years ago, even among American white people, the business of life insurance was in its infancy. Not more than twenty-five of the insurance organizations now operating in North America were incorporated prior to 1865. Not only had little progress been made in the number of companies organized and in the amount of business written, but the principles of the business and the best methods of operation were not nearly so well understood as they are now.

All this is noteworthy since Negroes, in the field of commerce, started focussing on this least understood and most complicated of all of America's big businesses. Needless to say this was not by premeditation. Like several other lines in which the Negro has engaged, he "just happened" to get into it; for there was in the early day of his freedom no planned program; no guiding hand to induct him into any particular field for which his peculiar qualities might have seemed best to fit him.

Probably, Negroes turned easily to life and disability insurance because it is a natural suggestion of relief from distress; and, necessarily, the Negro came out of bondage distress-conscious.

As already observed, several of the important Negro life insurance companies grew out of church relief societies or benevolent-burial associations. Their development was gradual; and the present high degree of financial importance to which they have risen in the economic life of the race was at first entirely uncontemplated.

The process upward through their earlier years was largely un-directed, and without any preconceived objective or ultimate form of organization. The magnitude of the successes which they achieved in their original forms, and the organization by other leaders of companies on the stock plan, definitely corporate and financial from inception, suggested to the controlling spirits of the earlier relief associations the feasibility of converting their organi-zations into mutual or stock life companies. The North Carolina Mutual Life of Durham, North Carolina, is the most prominent of the mutuals so converted.

The following are some of the outstanding stock life companies resulting from a similar development: The Atlanta Life, the Afro-American Life, the Southern Aid Society, the Pilgrim Health and Life, and the National Benefit.

The Mississippi Life, Standard Life, Victory Life, Liberty Life, and Universal Life were among the stock companies pre-mediately organized to be corporate and financial in character.

Industrial Insurance

The business of life insurance among Negroes has necessarily been and still is preponderantly industrial. Colored people are an industrial people; weekly wage earners. Hence, anything that pro-vides medicine and medical services in times of physical disability presents an almost compelling appeal.

But the weekly visits of white men to Negro homes to collect premiums soon developed the inevitable close relation between the social and economic life of people living in the same territory. In the South, the conduct of many white agents in Negro homes has not been commendable. Their haughtiness, discourtesies, and not infrequent abuses of the privacy of the home were resented, but to a great extent tolerated until the organization and entry of Negro companies into this field. Nothing has more greatly aided Negro agents in meeting the competition of their more experienced com-petitors than the abundance of examples of insults and abuses of Negro policyholders at the hands of white agents which could nearly always be pointed out in every community. Because of the participation of a white agent in the lynching of a colored man in a southern state, the debit of a struggling Negro company was increased more than 800 per cent within a month. In another instance, the collection book of a white agent was found "under the lynchtree" in Vicksburg, Mississippi. He lost 60 per cent of his debit and his company a large part of its Negro business in that city. Other instances of the deliberate violation of the privacies of boudoirs and bathrooms over the protests and to the embarass-ments of the female inmates have been bitterly and publicly resented by Negro leaders, and effectively used by Negro agents. The prac-tice of white agents of placing calendars with the pictures of white women on them in Negro homes had to be discontinued. Not the least among the valuable contributions made by Negro industrial life insurance companies to racial respect is the great improvement in the conduct of white agents in colored homes which the presence of Negro competitors is effecting.

Among other causes contributing to the rapid progress of indus-trial insurance among Negroes, the following are of great import-ance: the frequent, prompt payment of death claims, the more fre-quent payment of weekly disability claims, and the obvious fact that premiums paid into Negro companies claim the added value of creating employment available to Negroes.

One and One Quarter of a Million Dollars Every Week for Protection and Discrimination

The total weekly industrial debit of twenty-nine Negro com-panies was $248,910, December 31, 1938. This means that Negroes pay into their own companies almost this amount each week for industrial insurance. It is safe to say that this is not more than 25 per cent of the amount paid by Negroes into white com-panies for the same purpose. Obviously, then, the total industrial premiums paid into white companies each week by Negroes is not less than $995,640; and the total paid into all companies for this class of insurance is $1,244,550. Undoubtedly the total must have exceeded $1,250,000 per week December 31, 1939—surely a tribute to the thrift and forethought of a circumscribed group.

On the basis of a theoretical individual weekly debit of $100, it will require 2,489 agents to collect the total Negro debit in Negro companies; and 9,956 agents on the same basis to collect the $995,640, the total Negro debit in white companies.

Every one of the $248,910 paid into Negro companies is free to perform its natural function of helping to create employment to which the qualified among the group that spends it are eligible. Every one of the $995,640 paid by Negroes into white companies, as soon as paid over the line, becomes earmarked for discrimination against employment of the group that spends it; and the employment these dollars help to create is forbidden fruit to the sons and daughters of those who each week unthoughtfully pay this price to keep the doors of opportunity closed against their own.

Different Classes of Industrial Business

Industrial life and disability insurance was devised for the convenience and to meet the needs of people who receive their wages in comparatively small weekly or monthly payments.

The institution of accident and health insurance stands today as the result of a long evolutionary process. Instances of community efforts at indemnification for disability reach into antiquity. The modern accident and health insurance business dates back to 1848 when the Railway Passengers Assurance Corporation of London was chartered by the English parliament. It was organized at the instigation of the railway managers as a means of stimulating travel by train, then thought to be a hazardous undertaking. The business was introduced in the United States by James G. Batterson of Hardford, Connecticut, who had observed the operations of the Railway Passengers Assurance Corporation while traveling in England. In 1864 Mr. Batterson founded the Travelers Insurance Company of Hartford, which was the first successful accident insurance company established in this country.

The success and example of the Travelers encouraged many men to enter the field. In the twenty years from 1864 to 1884, several hundred companies were founded. Most of them failed because of improper management or inadequate capital.[1]

That form of insurance sometimes erroneously referred to as weekly "health and accident" seems to deserve the place of first importance among the several classes of industrial business in colored companies.

Among Negroes it first appeared as the product of burial or benevolent societies that undertook to provide some measure of

[1] *Selling Accident and Health Insurance,* The Health and Accident Underwriters Conference, Chicago, Illinois, 1938, pp.5, 6.

MISS ESTHER O. TIBBS
The Only Negro Female Actuary in the World.

Dunbar Mutual Insurance Society

DENNIS COURTLAND CHANDLER
Vice President and Agency Director.

relief for their disabled members and decent burials for their deceased. The raising of funds for these purposes depended at first largely upon the voluntary contributions of those connected with the organizations. As crude as were these early methods and as variable the resultant benefits, they yet were manifestations of the elementary principles of life insurance in operation. Moreover, the operation of these primitive units of community interest showed that even during slavery Negroes appreciated the advantages of organization and combination of even their meager resources.

From these early units a more scientific, exact, and reliable general industrial class of business was developed, and its practice commenced soon after the beginning of the present century. Several modified subdivisions of this general form have been added during the past twenty years; and now, among Negro companies, there can be found an industrial counterpart of nearly every branch of the so-called Old Line or ordinary life business.

A combination weekly Industrial Life and Disability policy is the most popular of all industrial forms among colored people. It provides both a small death and weekly disability benefit.

Fraud

From figures reported to the National Negro Insurance Association it is ascertained that Negro companies have paid to their policyholders more than $38,000,000 in discharge of disability claims during the past twenty years. From the same source a not extravagant approximation places the average number of holders of this class of policies at 416,000. In this score of years, then, companies of the Negro race have paid the equivalent of slightly more than $91 or about $4.55 per annum to each of these policyholders.

The Negro companies, during the same period, experienced an average morbidity rate of more than 8 per cent in excess of the theoretical 35 per cent of the premium collections computed to be sufficient to cover valid morbidity losses. Probably not all of the $3,040,000 excess above the theoretical can be assignable to fraud; but it is known that the greater part of it should be. Moreover, the opinion prevails among the experienced that only a comparatively small proportion of the total number of policyholders in this class received most of the benefits paid. Card records of some of the companies reveal a strikingly large number of the names of the same beneficiaries appearing persistently through many years as sufferers from a suspiciously great variety of complaints and injuries. This extraneous element of loss is a defect in this phase of the industrial business affecting the interest of all of the payers of premiums in the companies. It is a form of fraud which persists because it receives a far too liberal degree of tolerance from the public, and, frequently, assistance from physicians either indifferent or dishonest.

Industrial Whole Life

Next to the combination weekly Industrial Life and Disability business, the weekly Industrial Whole Life policies are probably issued in greatest numbers by member companies of the National Negro Insurance Association.

The premiums are calculated for the life of the insured and are adequate to provide legal reserve accumulations amounting to the face of the policy at the age of 96, beyond which, in actuarial theory, no one lives. This type of policy provides nonforfeiture privileges and cash-surrender values. In addition, under the laws of several states, after the premiums on policies of this class have been paid for a minimum of three years, even though the holder ceases to pay, the accumulated reserves must be used as a single premium and applied to purchase term insurance equal to the face value of the policy for such time as the said reserves may be adequate.

In recent years Negro companies have commenced to sell industrial limited pay life and industrial endowment forms mostly in the ten and twenty year terms. This is evidence of a tendency towards insurance of a scientific nature.

The graph indicating the mental trend of Negro leaders in the field of insurance may seem to bend steadily away from the old conception of charity. This evolution, however, is but an increasing recognition of the full value of the contrbutions in the form of premiums made by the policyholders. If the terms Cash Surrender, Extended Insurance, Nonforfeiture Privileges, Free Paid-Up Policy, and Matured Endowments seem foreign to the language of charity, let it be remembered that, quite to the contrary, they are values growing out of the premiums, made available to the insured under the improved forms of modern policies.

Ordinary Life

Of the $340,000,000[2] total business in force in Negro insurance companies December 31, 1937, $67,906,000, or about one-fifth, was in the several divisions of the Ordinary Life or so-called Old Line business; but, in considering the ratio of the Ordinary Life to the Industrial business, the amounts of insurance outstanding do not reflect the true picture. The relative proportion of premium income is undoubtedly of greater importance. The premium income from the Ordinary Life business at the end of December 1937 was slightly less than one-sixth of the total income of $12,488,681.

No separate Ordinary department of any Negro company has as yet proved satisfactory. On account of the smaller average amount of per capita insurance carried by Negroes in Negro Companies the latter sustain a much higher acquisition cost than white companies to maintain intact an adequate Ordinary agency force. The Ordinary in Negro companies is secured almost wholly through the same organizations as the Industrial.

Capital Stock

The total capital stock of Negro stock companies in 1924 was $763,982. By the end of 1937 it amounted to $1,477,584, lacking only $50,388 of being twice the amount it was at the end of 1924; and this notwithstanding that in the meantime there had been lost to the colored race the following large stock companies from among those operating at that time: Standard Life, National Benefit Life, and Victory Life.

The report of the statistician of the National Negro Insurance Association in Cleveland, Ohio, June 1938, showed ten mutual and eighteen stock companies.

Dividends

The total dividends paid since organization by seven of the eighteen Negro stock life insurance companies amounted to $1,011,-811.98 December 31, 1938.

Incomplete figures from the reports for the years 1932 to 1937

[2] On account of the lack of uniformity in the methods of reporting statistics to the National Negro Insurance Association it has not been possible to adhere to strict accuracy in the figures quoted herein. The number of reporting companies varies from year to year. Frequently no distinction is made between the Ordinary and Industrial in reporting the various phases and results, and it has been possible to secure only very incomplete reports for the years prior to 1931. Reports as of December 31, 1937, contain the latest available data on most of the important phases of the business, and most of these could not be secured until late in 1938.

inclusive reveal total stock dividends paid as amounting to $281,-417.20, an annual average rate of 2.04 per cent on the combined capital of the eighteen companies. But, at least the first three of these years marked the low of the great depression, and the last three were probably greatly affected by the results of it. The total stock dividends paid for 1937 amounted to $66,424.65, very nearly 4 per cent of the combined capital. This was $22,546.80 more than the previous year, and $34,008.49 more than for 1932, the first year of the period under consideration, thus reflecting constant improvement in profit earnings. The total dividends paid to policyholders on participating policies at the end of 1938 was $6,091.00.

Insurance in Force

The total insurance in force in the important Negro companies December 31, 1920, was $86,039,131. As of December 31, 1937, it had increased to $340,816,707.

To gauge the degree of responsiveness of the Negro to appeals of thrift and economic improvement it may be of interest and value to view the amount of life insurance carried by the group as a whole in comparison with that carried by some other groups. The amount here given for Negroes is on Negro lives and in Negro companies only, and is compared with the following foreign groups:

Group	Population[3]	Insurance in Force[4]
France	42,000,000	$2,891,422,000
The Netherlands	8,400,000	2,004,470,000
Italy	42,625,000	1,953,109,000[5]
Argentine Republic	12,000,000	500,000,000
Belgium	8,275,000	341,631,320
Negroes	13,891,143[7]	340,000,000
Brazil	41,500,000	179,186,000
Poland	33,500,000	136,389,000[8]
Mexico	18,000,000	102,966,000
Rumania	19,000,000	76,658,000[8]

[3] Latest available statistics. *Foreign Commerce Yearbook*, 1935, Dept. of Commerce.

[4] As of December 31, 1936. John A. Stevens, vice Pres. Penn Mutual Life address to 32nd Convention of Life Presidents, Dec. 2, 1938.

[5] Includes Government Insurance.

[6] Estimate by Department of Commerce probably too great—was only $106,000,-000 in 1929.

[7] Estimated for 1938.

[8] Includes insurance both on lives of domestic and foreign residents.

| Siam | 13,000,000 | 45,000,000 |
| Yugoslavia | 15,000,000 | 41,398,000 |

The $340,000,000 outstanding life insurance on the lives of Negroes in Negro companies represents only a minor part of the total amount of insurance on the lives of Negroes in all companies in America. However, no reliable statistics of the amount of insurance on Negro lives in white companies in the United States can be secured; and, of course, any statement is largely on estimation.

Luis Dublin, statistician of the Metropolitan Life Insurance Company of New York, said in 1923 that 1,800,000,[9] or about one-sixth of all of the Negroes in the United States, were policyholders in that company. If no lower ratio of the Negro population than this is insured in that company at the present time (and there are reasons for believing it is higher) it is reasonable to say that Negro holders of Metropolitan policies number not less than 2,300,000. It is not extravagant to assume that the average amount of insurance per holder is not less than $300. If these two assumptions be correct, then the amount of insurance in force on the lives of Negroes in this company alone is $690,000,000, or just about twice as much as in all of the Negro companies.

Although the total amount in force on Negro lives in the many other white companies that cater to Negro risks cannot be ascertained, it probably is several times the total amount in the Metropolitan.

A southern Negro educator addressed a simple questionnaire to forty-five white life insurance companies writing insurance on Negro lives, requesting information as to Negroes—the amount of insurance in force, and other data. Only eleven of these replied at all, and these furnished little information of value.

There is a widespread opinion in Negro insurance circles that the amount of life insurance in force in Negro companies is approximately one-fourth of the total in force on Negro lives in all companies. This opinion is based purely upon gross approximation; and is probably in excess of the correct proportion. But even on this basis, the total life insurance on the lives of Negroes would amount to $1,360,000,000, thus placing the Negro race ahead of

[9] Brown, W. H. "Educational and Economic Development of the Negro in Virginia," in Phelps-Stokes Papers, University of Virginia.

all of the smaller national groups except Canada, with $7,000,000,-000; Sweden, with $1,500,000,000, and Australia, with $1,390,-000,000.

Lapsation

A constant source of criticism of Negro life insurance companies has been their heavy lapsation. In 1936 business issued amounted to $181,997,068 and business lapsed amounted to $150,211,121.[10] For 1937 the issued was $179,846,356[11] on the lives of 1,201,614 policyholders and that lapsed was $157,198,163 on the lives of 1,135,227 policyholders.

The following indicates that for several years interested persons not connected with these companies have noted this heavy lapsation as a defect to be remedied:

A rather startling feature of Negro insurance is the enormous amount of lapsed policies.[12]

For 1929, seventeen Negro companies issued 502,626 policies for $87,069,019 and lapsed 529,553 policies for the sum of $84,139,827 which entailed among other losses about $75,000 for medical examinations and the printing of policies.[13]

Inevitably, the thought of great losses must arise in connection with the cost of soliciting this insurance, getting the applicants examined and the policies issued and serviced during the time they remain in force. This loss is, of course, borne, in part at least, by the premiums of policyholders who continue to maintain their insurance in force; and it is contended that the premiums are necessarily higher because of this unnecessary (so claimed) element of waste. It is further contended that, from this high lapsation, not only in Negro companies but in all industrial companies, an unfair profit is derived. Moreover, that for this large number of lapsed policyholders, life insurance falls short of performing the functions for which it was intended.

The best method of reducing lapsation has been a frequently

---

[10] Report of Cyrus Campfield, Statistician to the National Negro Insurance Association.

[11] Report of Miss Esther Tibbs, Jacksonville, Florida, Statistician for the National Negro Insurance Association.

[12] *Educational and Economic Development of the Negro in Virginia,* W. H. Brown, Phelps-Stokes Papers, 1922, (Courtesy of the University of Virginia.)

[13] "Cause of Negro Insurance Company Failures," Bulletin No. 15, United States Department of Commerce, 1937, p. 3.

recurring subject of papers read at several sessions of the National Negro Insurance Association. This indicates that the executives of Negro life insurance companies are fully aroused to the wisdom of reducing the high annual rate of terminations. Moreover, to state that the rate of lapsation in Negro life insurance companies is higher than that of other companies is only another way of saying that the general economic situation and opportunities for Negroes are more precarious than for other Americans. Lapsation of life insurance policies is one of the certain results of unemployment from which Negroes suffer more than other groups.

> "The defect in industrial insurance most costly to the policy-holder is the large number of lapses. . . . Lapses continue to be the major waste of the business. . . . The high number of lapses has released large sums carried as reserve liabilities by the companies.[14]"

Naturally, it is encumbent upon those especially interested in the welfare of the business of insurance to correct, as far as possible, all waste and other defects in the operation; but, that an undeserved prejudice of the public may not be aroused against the operators of this business, let us consider other phases of American economics:

Of all the financial installment devices practiced in American commerce, an industrial insurance policy is planned to extend over the longest period. Who has compiled statistics to show the percentage of defaults or lapsation in the attempts in other lines to complete installment contracts? How many individuals out of a given number have failed to pay for their automobiles, their furniture, their real estate? Is it an indictment against the correct principles of these other lines that changes in the economic conditions of the purchasers cause defaults of their contracts? Moreover, should not any statistics quoting the high number of lapses as defects in the operating policies of the business also display in equal prominence an analysis of the causes from which high lapsation arises?

Of course, there should be a tendency to curb high pressure selling of industrial insurance. Nevertheless, as long as there are constant changes in the economic situations of policyholders; as long as people have the privilege of changing their minds about

---

[14] Mr. Louis H. Pink, Superintendent of Insurance, State of New York, as quoted in the report of Asa T. Spaulding, Actuary, N.N.I.A., 1939.

spending their money, there is going to be a high ratio of lapsation in the industrial insurance business and a high percentage of defaults in other types of installment contracts. But this high ratio is not a condemnation of the methods of operation of the industrial life insurance business, any more than it is of other lines of installment businesses.

Income

The total income for Negro companies for the year 1921 was estimated at $2,525,000. In the next ten years it had grown to $13,966,839; then in the next year, 1932, when the full effects of the depression had become widespread, the income from premiums dropped to $8,587,954 and the total income to $9,685,564, a decrease of $4,281,275.

In the meantime, however, the National Benefit Life Insurance Company, one of the largest of Negro companies, had become involved in financial troubles and its premium income was not included in the report for the year 1932. Moreover, it is probable that even the premiums of the Victory Life of Chicago were not included since it also became involved in 1932.

At the close of business December 31, 1936, the premium income of Negro companies amounted to $16,567,482; and while the report for the year 1937 showed the total income as $13,667,027, it is known that this apparent decrease as between 1936 and 1937 is not real but due to the failure of several companies to make their reports to the national statistician in time to be included. The total premium income for 1937 was, in round figures, $12,500,000.

Disbursements

The total disbursements as of December 31, 1937, for Negro companies were $11,891,873.79. The heaviest single item of expenditure of life insurance companies is, as it should certainly be, the payment of claims to policyholders and to the beneficiaries of policyholders. Of the $12,500,000 premium income for 1937, the following total sums were paid for the items shown:

		Per Cent
To beneficiaries for death claims	$2,362,909	18.8
To policyholders for disability claims	1,756,753	15.05[15]

[15] Of the total premium income including ordinary and industrial whole life.

Total to Policyholders and Beneficiaries	4.119,662[16]	32.09
Commissions to Negro agents for collecting	3,249,784	25.09
Branch office expenses	509,294	4.07
Salaries of Home Office employees and Officers	978,774	7.8
Agency Supervision	574,436	4.5
Medical Examiners' fees	87,809	.7
Total for Administration	5,400,097	43.2

Assets

The total admitted assets of Negro life insurance companies as reported to the National Negro Insurance Association for the year 1920 amounted to $4,208,415. For the year 1937 they amounted to $20,125,870; and this was after the rigid tests of depression years.

Of these assets $5,487,565 was invested in real estate. These figures represent the book value, which probably is under the market value. On first mortgages $3,120,305 was loaned. Under the statutes of nearly all states, not more than 50 per cent of the appraised value may be loaned on first mortgages on real estate. The property, then, by which these mortgages are secured is probably worth much more than represented by the figures above.

The book value of the bonds amounted to $6,425,540, which probably was not in excess of the market value.

"Negro life insurance companies, during the hard years of the depression, proved to be financial reservoirs to which their thousands of policyholders turned for assistance."[17] The total amount loaned to policyholders at the close of 1937 was $1,722,902. It amounted to $1,430,364 for the year ending December 31, 1932.

Liabilities

Necessarily, the business of life insurance, whether operated under a mutual directorate or stock company control, is of a semi-public nature. Because of the long range into the future required to test the dispositions and abilities of the operators properly to conduct the business, the necessity of some form of governmental

---

In the total amount estimated for policyholders' benefit should be included the amount required each year for reserve additions set aside for policyholders' protection.

[17] Department of Commerce, *Causes of Negro Insurance Company Failures*, 1937.

supervision fortunately was recognized long ago. This resulted in the gradual creation of state insurance departments in most of the states of the Union. State statutes give many of these departments almost unlimited authority over the operation and affairs of companies doing business within their territories. The periodical examinations of their examiners grow constantly more scrutinizing and exacting. Great precaution is usually taken to disclose all liabilities.

The major liabilities of life insurance companies are the reserves required to be constantly deducted from the total annual collections of premiums and invested at interest to assure the payment of policies at maturity. Policy reserves are not, as many suppose, a part of the assets of life insurance companies. They are liabilities and belong to the policyholders.

It is an important part of the work of state insurance examiners to see to it that the companies set aside adequate reserves each year. The total of the net reserves required by law of all important Negro companies as of December 31, 1931, was $8,944,386.[18] At the end of the next year it was $8,039,486, a decrease of $904,000, a natural result due to a decrease in premium collections. December 31, 1937, net reserves for policyholders amounted to $14,719,178[18]; and, although the total premium collection for this year was slightly less than for 1931, the informed in insurance circles will understand the great difference between the total reserves for 1931 and 1937 as being largely due to the greater average of policies in force, or, expressed differently, to the larger number of old policies.

The total liabilities of Negro companies December 31, 1931, exclusive of surplus and capital stock,[19] was $11,479,275. December 31, 1932, it was $9,066,407, and $15,760,055, December 31, 1937.[18]

Employment

In the Introduction to this work reference has been made to the employing power of the spent dollar and the constant struggle of Negroes to bridge the chasm of prejudice that separates them in many phases of business from the employment created by the dollars they spend. No sales talk has proven more appealing and

---

[18] Report of Cyrus Campfield to the National Negro Insurance Association.

[19] Both the amount of the capital stock and the surplus are listed as items of liability in the statements of life insurance companies, because they belong to the stockholders as individuals and are also subject to the prior claims of policyholders in the event of liquidation.

effective in securing patronage for Negro businesses of all classes than presentation of the obvious fact that dollars spent "with race enterprises" encounter no interference in completing the economic cycle. The gradual increase in the number being employed in trade is probably due largely to this fact.[20]

Qualified Negroes find employment in Negro life insurance companies as agents, field managers, supervisors, inspectors, auditors, traveling solicitors, medical examiners, clerks, and home office executives. The following table will show the number of employes and the compensation paid them by Negro life insurance companies for the years 1931-7 inclusive.[21]

Year	Number of Employes	Agents' Commissions	Agency Supervision	Salaries	Medical Fees	Total Compensation
1931	7104	$2,116,842	$376,319	$913,027	$74,503	$3,480,692
1932	6388	2,078,138	280,133	773,445	46,140	3,167,856
1933	7656	1,959,452	478,111	843,599	53,620	3,334,783
1934	7874	2,341,602	529,391	860,215	61,864	3,793,072
1935	8150	2,606,099	654,811	858,992	66,891	4,186,795
1936	8964	2,859,054	682,188	953,500	78,348	4,753,093
1937	9010	3,249,784	574,436	978,774	87,809	4,809,803
GRAND TOTAL		$17,210,971	$3,775,389	$6,181,552	$2,649,185	$27,346,094

Personnel

Several companies controlled by white interests starting in the industrial life insurance business in the South, before or soon after 1900, employed a number of colored men as agents. The services of all of them were discontinued after only a few years. The reason given for this by the officials of such companies was that Negro agents were not competent.

These officials knew at the outset that there were no Negroes trained in the business of life insurance; but there was an absence of that degree of persistency that would have established a sincerity of purpose or desire to continue Negro agents in their employ. If it be remembered that of the nearly 500 life insurance organizations now operating in the United States and Canada not more than 25 were incorporated prior to 1865 and less than 60 others chartered before the beginning of the present century, it will become plain that there was no abundance even of trained white agents in 1900; and patently, these white companies must have been willing to pay the

[20] In 1910 there were 119,755 Negroes employed in trade; 141,119 in 1920, and in 1930 there were 183,809. *Negroes in the United States*, 1920-32. U. S. Department of Commerce, Bureau of the Census.

[21] Taken from the Reports of the Statistician to the National Negro Insurance Association.

price of training white agents by practice and experience—a price they declined to pay to use Negro agents.

Negro companies, of course, had to begin with raw novices, and if there were available any forms, books, or other literature on life insurance, few Negroes knew where to procure them. They had to pick up here and there such scraps of information as they could find. Some Negro companies were able to secure the services of some of the "incompetent" cast-offs who had worked for white companies. These proved valuable in providing the sparks of knowledge from which grew the flames of enlightenment to illuminate the entire situation.

Under the caption "Freedom of Enterprise," the United States Department of Commerce sheds light on this condition:

"It cannot be doubted that the unlimited right of individuals to enter legitimate businesses, regardless of personal qualifications, has been a contributing factor in the failure of Negro insurance companies. Prior to 1910 few Negroes were schooled in the requirements of the insurance business and there were practically no opportunities for apprenticeship with soundly operated life companies. For example, a business specialist who was associated with one of the defunct companies writes that: 'Two men unquestionably ran the company, and neither of them had had any previous insurance experience, and their education was limited. This company flourished during good times as most institutions did, but during the depression, the test of efficiency and leadership could not be met.' "

But in the thirty years since 1910, Negro companies not only have developed several thousand agents whose theoretical knowledge of the business and whose average practical efficiency compare favorably with the average of white field men, but they have trained several thousand competent district managers, assistant district managers, supervisors, and traveling agents.

Approximately three hundred home office executives direct the work of the hundreds of office clerks required for their business. Several of the home offices of these companies are equipped with the latest improved machines for accounting and clerical work, which are handled by highly trained forces and efficiency experts. Two of the larger Negro life insurance companies have their own

Negro actuaries whose work and reports are accepted and approved by the various insurance departments of the states in which these companies operate.

The insurance departments of some states subject insurance agents to rigid examination. During 1938 the North Carolina Mutual Life Insurance Company qualified to operate in the State of Pennsylvania. All agents appointed by the company to work in Pennsylvania successfully passed the examination and received state agency insurance licenses.

There is a movement on foot, encouraged by the National Negro Insurance Association, to induce Negro colleges to include a course in life insurance in their curricula.

Negro Actuaries

In the United States and Canada an actuary is an authorized and recognized statistician and computer of risks, rates, premiums, benefits, and other data required for the proper operation of the insurance business. Because reliable statistical tables of rates and other data for this business can be determined only by implementing deeply involved mathematical formulae, prolonged courses of study in the higher branches of mathematics are required to complement actuarial qualifications.

In the earlier days of Negro life insurance companies, the reputation for expertness of actuaries caused them to be regarded with a certain sense of awe by many officials and employees of colored companies. Moreover, Negro insurance executives of the time, unfamiliar with the high costs of experts, stood amazed in the presence of men who could command such great compensation for their daily services. This probably then was regarded as a field beyond the reach of Negroes; and only until comparatively recent years did any Negro attempt to qualify as an actuary. Naturally, therefore, the importance of those few of the race who have qualified is more heavily stressed in Negro insurance circles than white actuaries in the insurance business of that race.

The Actuarial Society of America was organized April 25, 1889, with Sheppard Homans as the first president.[22] In 1931 it had 302 members, of whom 8 were women. A great majority of these members are Americans and Canadians; but there are a few

---

[22] Cyclopedia of Insurance in the United States, 1932.

corresponding members in England, Belgium, Japan, and perhaps other foreign countries.

The membership is divided into two grades, Fellows and Associates. "Practically speaking no one can become a Fellow unless he passes the prescribed examinations for Associateship and for Fellowship. . . . Any Associate who has been such for at least ten months and is twenty-five years of age may apply to the Council for Fellowship, and if his application is approved and he passes the prescribed examination he will then become a Fellow."[23]

Fellows may append to their names the initials "F.A.S." and Associates, "A. A. S."

There is also an American Institute of Actuaries. It was organized in Chicago in 1909. "Its object is to advance the Science of Insurance Mathematics and the knowledge of the theory and practice of Life Insurance and related interests by associating together [white] persons of like interests."

There are three grades of members composing this Institute, Fellows, Associates, and Contributing Members. Actuarial students, if recommended by two fellows, may by meeting certain qualifications and passing the prescribed examinations become Associates.

On August 1, 1931, this organization had 462 members, consisting of 168 fellows, 158 associates and 136 contributing members. Students listed on that date numbered 390.

Neither of these organizations permits Negroes to apply for membership no matter what their qualifications.

It is reported that Miss Esther O. Tibbs, former actuary for the Afro-American Life, contemplating application for membership to the Actuarial Society of America, had, by correspondence, received and satisfactorily passed two of the required examinational subjects before her racial identity was discovered. She was then advised that she would not be admitted.

Mr. Maceo Walker, actuary for the Universal Life Insurance Company, is authority for the statement that one of his teachers in the University of Michigan informed him that it would be useless to attempt to gain membership in either the Actuarial Society or the American Institute of Actuaries.

[23] Loc. Cit.

Mortality Experience

Perhaps no phase of the history of life insurance companies is of more importance than their mortality experiences.[24]. The tables below, showing the per cent of *actual to expected mortality*, the per cent of *loading to premiums*, and the per cent of *expense to gross premiums*, include those Negro companies for which the data could be secured and a selected number of white companies somewhat comparable in volume to the Negro companies shown. For obvious reasons company names are not disclosed.

COLORED COMPANIES[25]

Company	Year	Per Cent of Actual to Expected Mortality	Per Cent Loading to Premiums	Per Cent Insurance Expenses to Gross Premiums
(A)	1936	65.4		
	1937	73.04	41.93	54.63
(B)	1933	90.8		
	1934	101.2		
	1935	100.99		
	1936	82.6		
	1937	67.7	43.55	50.48
(C)	1933	45.14		
	1934	64.75		
	1935	69.87		
	1936	59.8		
	1937	62.37	33.75	54.61
(D)	1936	89.5		
	1937	71.6	36.7	57.5
(E)	1936	91.1	69.0	47.3
(F)	1937	98.7	54.3	52.8
(G)	1937	72.3	45.2	45.1

WHITE COMPANIES

Company	Year	Per Cent of Actual to Expected Mortality	Per Cent Loading to Premiums	Per Cent Insurance Expenses to Gross Premiums
(A)	1933	67.5		
	1934	68.5		
	1935	66.6		
	1936	66.7		
	1937	38.3	30.0	43.4
(B)	1933	63.3		
	1934	68.9		
	1935	76.9		
	1936	73.3		
	1937	67.5	28.8	44.5

[24] Unfortunately data concerning the mortality experience of Negro companies are not sufficiently available to prove enlightening.
[25] *Dunne's International Insurance Reports,* New York City, 1938.

(C)	1933	63.6		
	1934	64.8		
	1935	63.6		
	1936	63.5	37.2	50.3
(D)	1936	83.7		
	1937	70.1	50.1	27.4
(E)	1933	56.5		
	1934	59.8		
	1935	65.1		
	1936	61.1		
	1937	53.6	33.5	52.6

Efforts to secure information on the mortality experience of Negro risks as compared to white risks in forty-five white companies resulted in almost no valuable information.

In a paper read before the Annual Conference of the National Negro Health Week, October 27, 1934, Mr. Louis I. Dublin, Statistician for the Metropolitan Life Insurance Company, presented comparative standardized death rates for more than fourteen million white persons and nearly two million Negroes insured in the Industrial Department. Mr. Dublin stated: "Taking the country at large for the latest year of which data are available; namely 1930, the standardized death rate of white persons was 9.9 per 1,000 of population; that of the colored was 18.0. This means that the colored death rate was 82 percent higher than the write."[26]

Mr. Dublin further explained that this excessively high mortality of Negroes was influenced heavily by the high infantile death rate of colored people, since the death of an infant with its long expectancy of life affects the total mortality rate much more than the death of an older person with shorter life expectancy.

Cyrus Campfield, Statistician of the National Negro Insurance Association, in his report for 1931, aptly describes the ten leading causes of death as "Captains of Death." In 1931, they ranked as follows:

1. Heart Disease   (All Forms)
2. Tuberculosis   "   "
3. Nephritis (Kidney Inflammation)   (All Forms)
4. Pneumonia
5. Influenza

[26] Report of Cyrus Campfield, Statistician, National Negro Insurance Association, Detroit, Michigan, July 1936.

CHARLES H. MAHONEY
President

Great Lakes' Officials and Home Office

MISS R. LOUISE HENDERSON
Chief Accountant

LOUIS CHARLES BLOUNT
Vice President, Secretary-Manager

JOHN W. ROXBOROUGH
Vice President

MOSES L. WALKER
First Vice President and Treasurer

HOME OFFICE BUILDING
Detroit, Michigan

6. Cerebral Hemmorrhage (Apoplexy)
7. Paralysis
8. Diarrhea and Enteritis
9. Other Diseases of the Stomach
10. Cancer (All Forms)

Heart disease is still holding first place, but, in 1934, pneumonia displaced nephritis for third place, and then moved up ahead of tuberculosis taking second place in 1936; while "violent deaths" hitherto counted insignificant among *the aides-de-camp* of the grim reaper, moved up to fourth place in 1936 and 1937, pushing nephritis down to fifth place.

From Bulletin No. 15,—*Causes of Negro Insurance Company Failures,* issued by the United States Department of Commerce, April 1927—the following is quoted:

The Rate of Mortality—Although the rate of mortality is gradually improving for both races, the rate for Negroes is still greater than that for whites. The death rate for male whites in the first year of life is 63.32 and for Negro males, 87.32; and in the 11th year of life, when the mortality rate is lowest for the males of both races, the rate for white males is 1.47 and for Negro males 2.11. In the 45th year of life, when the rate has increased for both races, the rate for whites is 78.61 and for Negroes 87.75.

The premise of making *race* the basis of comparison seems to be fallacious. At least it does not produce an accurate picture. Probably the mortality of no selected class of an equally subdued economic status and composed of as high a percentage of common laborers would rate any lower than the Negro.

"The death rate of persons insured under industrial life policies is 40 per cent greater than that of those insured under standard ordinary policies of similar age distribution."[27]

This observation by the Metropolitan Life Insurance Company has no racial significance. The same authority reveals that "studies of death rates among various groups of the population show that men in occupations associated with the lower income groups have, on the average, a shorter length of life than men in occupations

[27] *Industrial Life Insurance,* by the Metropolitan Life Insurance Company, 1938.

55

associated with the higher income group—i. e. the death rate of those in the lower income group is higher."

It is difficult to reconcile the view expressed above with the oft-repeated statement that the higher death rate among Negroes arises from some peculiarly inherent racial weakness. The obvious truth of the matter is that the death rate is higher for any group subjected to greater exposure of weather vagaries, to contamination media in various types of industrial work, and to the restrictions of medical service, sanitary conveniences, and bodily care which lower incomes necessarily impose.

The total numbers of deceased policyholders for whom Negro companies have paid death claims for the past seven years are as follows:

1931	17,361	1935	15,232
1932	12,450	1936	17,496
1933	12,678	1937	17,848
1934	15,704		

Taxes, Licenses and Fees

A heavy annual item of expenditure of life insurance companies is the taxation levied by the state on the premiums collected from policyholders. Only in the states in which they are chartered are the premiums collected by life insurance companies exempt from taxation. In making this provision, the authors of insurance legislation apparently labored under a misconception, for the premiums are paid by the policyholders or citizens of the several states, not by the officers or directors residing in some other state; then why should the premiums of one class of citizens who elect to buy insurance from a company not domiciled in the state of their residence be subject to a tax from which the premiums of other citizens residing in the same state are exempt merely because they buy their insurance from a "home company"?

In addition to the premium taxes there are in many states various departmental fees and company licenses, and each agent is taxed for the privilege of writing business.

The total taxes paid by Negro companies for the years 1931-7 inclusive were $1,916,343.[28]

[28] Statistician, National Negro Insurance Association.

PHASES AND DEVELOPMENT

Social Security Taxes

The Federal Social Security legislation levied an old-age pension tax for employees under Title VIII and an unemployment tax under Title IX of the Social Security Act, effective as of January 1, 1936, on the compensation of all employees of companies and other corporations. The total paid by Negro insurance companies under this Act for the year 1938 amounted approximately to $15,000 per million dollars of premium income.

The purpose of the unemployment tax is, of course, to provide a fund to pay laborers weekly insurance whenever they are laid off by their employers. Since life insurance companies do not, as do some corporations, temporarily suspend operations in periods of economic depression, and rarely ever reduce the number of their field agents, the officials, not only of Negro life insurance companies but of others, contend that the compensation of their field employees should not be subject to this type of taxation.

In an effort to secure relief from this taxation the executive committee of the National Negro Insurance Association called a special meeting of the Negro companies in Louisville, Kentucky, on March 11, 1938, for the purpose of attempting jointly to secure the desired relief either through a congressional amendment or by such legal steps as might seem to promise results. A Social Security Committee, composed of Harry H. Pace, chairman; M. S. Stuart, executive secretary; J. Leonard Lewis, and W. D. Hill, was appointed. At the eighteenth session of the association in Cleveland in June 1938, Mr. Simeon Cunningham was added to the committee and Mr. J. Leonard Lewis made chairman instead of Mr. Pace, who asked to be relieved of the chairmanship.

The report of this Social Security Committee at the Nineteenth Annual Session of the Association in Los Angeles in July 1939, showed that through the work of the committee petitions for exemption of twelve member companies had been prepared and forwarded to the companies for filing with the Internal Revenue Department of Washington, D. C., and that favorable rulings of exemption had been secured for eight of these in so far as the Federal Government is concerned. A conservative estimate places the annual savings to these eight companies at more than $57,000 as a result of these rulings.

The exemptions referred to above were secured on the grounds that industrial insurance agents serve their companies as *independent*

57

contractors; but in the summer of 1939 a congressional amendment sponsored by the Industrial Insurers Conference (a white organization) was passed. This amendment exempted the compensation of all agents working on a commission basis from the tax (unemployment tax) imposed by Title IX of the Social Security Act.

Operating Territories of Negro Life Insurance Companies

Negro life insurance companies operate in the District of Columbia and twenty-four of the forty-eight states of the Union. These states with the Negro population[29] and the companies which do business in each are shown below:

State	Company	Negro Population
Alabama	Atlanta Life	944,834
	North Carolina Mut'l Life	
	Pilgrim Health & Life	
Arkansas	Universal Life	478,834
California	Golden States Mut'l Life	81,048
Florida	Afro-American Life	431,828
	Atlanta Life	
	Central Life	
Georgia	Atlanta Life	1,071,125
	North Carolina Mut'l Life	
	Pilgrim Health & Life	
	Afro-American Life	
	Guaranty Life	
Illinois	Supreme Liberty Life	328,972
	Unity Ind. Life	
	Victory Mutual Life	
Indiana	Mammoth Life	111,982
	Supreme Liberty Life	
Kansas	Atlanta Life	66,344
Kentucky	Domestic Life	226,040
	Mammoth Life	
	Atlanta Life	
	Supreme Liberty Life	

[29] *Negroes of the United States* 1920-32, U. S. Dept. of Commerce.

Louisiana	Louisiana Industrial Life	776,326
	Unity Industrial Life	
	Universal Life	
	The Douglas	
	The Victory Ind. Life	
	Good Citizens Benf. Ass'n.	
	Liberty Industrial Life	
	People's Industrial Life	
	Safety Industrial Life	
	Standard Industrial Life	
Maryland	North Carolina Mut'l Life	276,379
	Southern Life	
Michigan	Great Lakes Mut'l Life	169,453
	Supreme Liberty Life	
	Western Union Ass'n.	
Missouri	Atlanta Life	223,840
	Supreme Liberty Life	
	Universal Life	
Mississippi	Universal Life	1,009,718
New York	Victory Mut'l Life	412,814
	United Mut'l Benf. Ass'n.	
North Carolina	North Carolina Mut'l Life	918,647
	Winston Mut'l Life	
Ohio	Supreme Liberty Life	309,304
	Atlanta Life	
	Mammoth Life	
	Domestic Life	
	Fireside Mut'l Life	
	Dunbar Mut'l Ins. Society	
Oklahoma	Universal Life	172,198
	Security Life	
Pennsylvania	North Carolina Mut'l Life	431,257
	Provident Home Benf. Society	
	Key Stone Aid Society	
South Carolina	North Carolina Mut'l Life	793,681
	Pilgrim Health & Life	
Tennessee	Universal Life	477,646
	Atlanta Life	
	North Carolina Mut'l Life	

	Supreme Liberty Life	
	Union Protective Assurance Co.	
Texas	Excelsior Mut'l Life	854,964
	Atlanta Life	
	Universal Life	
	Western Mut'l Life	
	Watch Tower Mut'l Life	
Virginia	Southern Aid Society	650,165
	Richmond Benf. Life	
	North Carolina Mut'l Life	
	Virginia Mut'l Benefit Life	
West Virginia	Supreme Liberty Life	114,893
District of Col.	Federal Life	132,068[30]
	Richmond Benf. Life	
	Southern Aid Society	
	North Carolina Mut'l Life	

The American Woodmen, prosperous fraternal order domiciled at Denver, Colorado, operates in each of the following states: Alabama, Arkansas, California, Colorado, District of Columbia, Florida, Georgia, Illinois, Indiana, Kansas, Kentucky, Louisiana, Maryland, Michigan, Missouri, New Jersey, North Carolina, Ohio, Oklahoma, Pennsylvania, South Carolina, Tennessee, Texas, Virginia, and West Virginia.

The states in which no Negro companies operate, with the Negro population of each, are shown below:

Arizona	10,749	New Hampshire	790
Colorado	11,828	New Mexico	2,850
Connecticut	29,354	New Jersey	208,828
Delaware	32,602	North Dakota	377
Idaho	668	Oregon	2,234
Iowa	17,380	Rhode Island	9,913
Maine	1,096	South Dakota	646
Massachusetts	52,365	Utah	1,108
Minnesota	9,445	Vermont	568
Montana	1,256	Washington	6,840
Nebraska	13,752	Wisconsin	10,739
Nevada	516	Wyoming	1,250

[30] The total population of the District was found from the same census to be only 486,869.

Total Negro population in states in which Negro companies operate 11,463,889.

Total Negro population in states in which Negro companies do not operate 427,154.

State Insurance Departments and Negro Companies

Of the twenty-four states and the District of Columbia in which important Negro companies do business, thirteen—Alabama, Arkansas, Florida, Georgia, Kentucky, Louisiana, Maryland, Mississippi, North Carolina, Oklahoma, South Carolina, Tennessee, and·Texas—are usually classed as "southern" with all the significance in policies, practices, and attitudes of race with which the term in this country has come to be associated; yet inquiries reveal that colored officials who have had contact with these white State Insurance Commissioners have been accorded almost uniform courtesies and fair consideration in all of their dealings with them. It is often necessary for state examiners to spend several weeks in the home offices of Negro companies. This requires constant daily contact with executives and clerical forces in the investigations of numerous, complicated details. With remarkably few exceptions, according to reports, these associations have been pleasant; and, moreover, out of them have grown some warm and lasting friendships.

Some State Insurance Commissioners in the South have manifested great pride and deep interest in the progress of Negro companies domiciled in their states, not only by giving them the benefit of their advice and experience; but also by acting vigorously in their defense in any matters of disagreement with representatives of other states when the circumstances seemed to justify it. Some have even invoked the interstate retaliatory law to insure fair treatment of Negro companies operating in states not of their domicile.

Of course, in the interests of policyholding citizens of their states, they have, as rightly they should, imposed upon colored companies the same rigid regulations required by their laws for all companies. There has been found, however, no instance in the past fifteen years in which the laws have seemed to be any more severely applied to the operation of Negro companies than to others. This general attitude of State Insurance Commissioners is all the more commendable if it be remembered that the admission of a

61

life insurance company to do business in states other than that of its domicile is a privilege and not a legal right in most states. The Insurance Commissioners may use their own judgment in refusing to admit or in disqualifying any company already admitted. Notwithstanding this latitude, Negro companies have experienced no difficulties on account of race.

A Table of Progress

The record of the surplus, real estate owned, first mortgage loans, and claims paid of Negro life insurance companies appears in the following table:

Year	Surplus	Real Estate Owned	First Mortgage Loans	Claims Paid (Death and Disability)
1931	$1,521,917	$2,808,700	$2,808,700	$4,464,201
1932	1,403,801	3,096,630	2,409,790	4,117,616
1933	1,475,988	4,365,594	2,632,756	3,651,277
1934	1,882,516	4,305,640	3,294,534	4,155,493
1935	2,225,977	5,148,087	2,939,928	4,029,981
1936	2,419,933	5,420,654	3,233,920	4,473,278
1937	2,955,315	5,487,565	3,120,305	4,337,244

Surplus in the statement of a life insurance company reflects additional security for the policyholders. Company executives are not inclined to distribute the entire surplus of their companies; nor would state insurance departments consent to such distribution.

The increasing amount of real estate owned results from foreclosures of defaulted mortgages. Life insurance companies rarely ever purchase real estate except for home office purposes.

Chapter IV

NORTHERN ORGANIZATIONS

THE DUNBAR MUTUAL INSURANCE SOCIETY, CLEVELAND, OHIO

M. C. CLARK, *State Insurance Examiner*

As paradoxical as it may seem to the uninformed, the promotion of racial business enterprises frequently encounters more difficulties in the North than it does in the South. North of the Mason and Dixon Line the phantom of liberty and equality is more deceptive. It takes on more the appearance of the real than it does in the less subtle South; and the masses of northern Negroes, in years gone by, to a greater degree than now, accepted and followed this realistic-looking "ghost" of equality, and consequently evinced only an indifferent interest in the success of enterprises owned and operated by their own people. "What's the use?" many of them asked. "We are a recognized part of all the people, receiving every courtesy and consideration necessary—why have Negro enterprises?"

In time, however, there was an awakening, and it began to be realized that these deceptive "courtesies and considerations" are only shadows; and that for a group to exist in comfort, whether in the North or South, it must have the substance along with the shadowy courtesies. It must have work. Its talents must be employed; and to no sustaining degree in the North more than in the South are Negroes employed in the general commercial fabric of the nation. With this awakening came the realization that northern Negroes, too must commence to create commercial opportunities for their young people whom our schools and colleges are training.

The Dunbar Mutual Insurance Society, of Cleveland, Ohio, though yet in its infancy, is an instance of an attempt to convert this idea into a concrete reality. This insurance society grew out of the fortunate political recognition of the ability of Negroes in Ohio.

Mr. M. C. Clarke, the first member of our group ever to be appointed to the position of Examiner in the Insurance Department of the State of Ohio, was called upon, in the discharge of his duties, to suggest a plan for rehabilitating four small Negro insurance organizations in that state. At first it appeared that his duty would lead him only to a dead-end up the dark alley of liquidation, rather than to rehabilitation. But there was more involved in the assignment given Clarke than the mere liquidation of four small insurance units. Mr. Clarke himself, in the position of Insurance Examiner, was an innovation; and what would Negroes of Ohio say about him if, among his first activities, he gave the impression that he would use the authority vested in him to go about the state destroying Negro enterprises? Might not wagging tongues be quick to charge that he was "playing to white galleries"?

The realization of this danger in his assignment aroused his determination that, out of the chaotic situation, he would wring something concrete and constructive. He therefore, in 1936, welded the remnants of the four small organizations, and thus created the Dunbar Mutual Society of Cleveland.

Throughout his efforts at organization Mr. Clarke had the wholehearted cooperation of the Insurance Department of Ohio; but, when his suggested plan of merger was accepted by that department, he faced a new obligation: that of at least nursing the new financial baby until it was well on the road to growth and expansion. This required that he accept the office of president to convince all concerned of his confidence in the organization thus established. Notwithstanding the sacrifices involved, he undertook the task; and, under his leadership, the Dunbar Mutual is a progressive reality.

The Dunbar is a member of the National Negro Insurance Association, and was co-host to the organization in its eighteenth annual session in Cleveland, in June 1938. The large number of delegates in attendance were unanimous in their commendation of the exceptional comfort and courtesies which the employees of Dunbar Mutual, led by Mr. Clarke, provided for them.

The officers of Dunbar Mutual are as follows: M. C. Clarke, president; C. S. Wells, vice president; Attorney Lawrence O. Payne, vice president; Attorney David D. White, secretary; Dr. Charles H. Garvin, treasurer; D. C. Chandler, agency director; Roy C. Shelton, auditor; Mable G. Clark, cashier; and M. H. Frye, assistant secretary.

DENNIS COURTLAND CHANDLER,
Vice President-Agency Director

Dennis Courtland Chandler, vice president and agency director of The Dunbar Mutual Insurance Society, Inc., of Cleveland, Ohio, was born December 21, 1893, to John Richmond and Margaret Malinda Chandler at Duluth, Georgia. He attended the Duluth Public School and Bryant's Preparatory Institute where he completed high school work, after which he attended the Morris Brown College of Atlanta, Georgia, and Ohio State University. Mr. Chandler has also taken a business course from the LaSalle Extension School.

During his first two years out of school, the young man worked as an assistant bookkeeper, and for the past twenty-three years, exactly one-half of his life, has been engaged in the insurance business. He organized a fraternal organization when only twenty-one years old; and, at the age of twenty-three, organized and became president of the Adelphi Building and Loan Company, which is still in operation. For the past four years he has been with the Dunbar Mutual Insurance Society, Inc., as its vice president and agency director, and the progress of the field department of this comparatively young company has largely been due to his capable work.

Mr. Chandler is deeply interested in all activities for the elevation of his race, especially of its young people. He has for a number of years been an active worker in the Congregational Church, in both its Sunday School and Young People's Society, chairman of the membership drive of the Phillis Wheatley Association, and president of the Insurance Managers' Council.

On June 23, 1915, Mr. Chandler was married to Miss Lena Etta Eubanks of Atlanta, Georgia, who has been his principal source of inspiration through the years of their wedded life.

THE GREAT LAKES MUTUAL INSURANCE COMPANY, DETROIT, MICHIGAN

IT was just before that boom year in the industry and commercial prosperity of our country, 1928, that Great Lakes Mutual Insurance Company was born. It was the outgrowth of what is now known as the Great Lakes Agency Company. The purpose of the agency was ultimately to establish a life insurance company. This fine work was led by Mr. Colbert Sobrian, a young man who had formerly been with Victory Life and Liberty Life, both of Chicago. The organization, under the name of Great Lakes Mutual Association, started business March 1, 1928. Its home office was housed in one room, in which everybody worked. Later, to accomodate the increasing business, five rooms were leased at 471 Gratiot Avenue, and still later another floor of five rooms in the same building was added.

L. C. Blount, with thirteen years of experience with National Benefit, resigned his position as State Manager of that company to join the official family of Great Lakes Mutual. He was elected secretary, and in March 1929 was made general manager. The first executive committee was composed of Charles H. Mahoney, president and general counsel; Moses L. Walker, vice president-treasurer; Albert E. Kinney, vice president; Dr. Robert Greenidge, medical director; Henry Holcomb, inspector; and L. C. Blount, vice president-secretary.

One of the problems of Negro companies is the "heavy agency turnover." The Great Lakes Mutual has been exceptionally fortunate in this respect, having the lightest turnover of any member company of the National Negro Insurance Association. Messrs. J. E. Thompson, Roger Pryor, and A. Frands have been with the company as agents since its organization.

This company writes only one type of policy—the straight life. The maximum mortality benefit is $500, but this benefit is also written in denominations of $100, $200, $250, $300, and $400.

In 1934 the company purchased a home office building at 301 East Warren Avenue. One hundred and five persons are employed, 90 per cent of them working in the city of Detroit, the others in Pontiac, Flint, and Ypsilanti.

Policyholders are furnished free nursing service through a contract with the Visiting Nurses Association of the city. They also receive pre-natal and post-natal care.

About two years after the association was organized it was changed to Great Lakes Mutual Insurance Company.

Officers and Directors of this company are as follows:

    1. Charles H. Mahoney; born in Michigan; president and

general counsel; practised law for 27 years; active in politics.

2. L. C. Blount, vice president-secretary; born in Washington D. C.
3. Moses L. Walker, vice president-treasurer; born in Mobile, Alabama; U. S. Custom Officer; ardent worker in the* N. A. A. C. P., church and politics.
4. A. E. Kinney, vice president; born in Cincinnati, Ohio; adviser to Pullman Company.
5. Dr. Robert Greenidge, v i c e president-medical director; born in Georgetown, British Guiana; Superintendent and proprietor of Fairview Sanatarium; proprietor of the Walgreen Building; X-Ray specialist and member of the staff of Parkside Hospital.
6. Julian Holder, director; born in Bridgetown, Barbados, British West Indies; Real Estate Leasee.
7. Henry W. Holcomb, chief inspector; born in Chattanooga, Tennessee.
8. John Roxborough, vice president; born in Plaquemine, Louisiana; manager of Joe Louis, Heavyweight Boxing Champion of the world.
9. William Osby, director; born in Springfield, Illinois; engineer at the Madison-Lennox Hotel.
10. Everett I. Watson, vice president; born in Woodstown, New Jersey; president of the Watson Realty Company.
11. Mrs. Agnes Bristol, assistant secretary; born in Lomora, Virginia; Detroit school teacher.

CHARLES HENRY MAHONEY, *President*

There were not many colored people living in the little town of Decatur, Michigan, back in the 1880's; and thus it was that Barney Mahoney and his good wife, Viora, found most of their friends and associates among the white people of this liberal community. Barney was a successful contractor, and in fine favor with his neighbors. He owned his own comfortable home, found work at his trade, and life for this industrious couple was moderately happy.

To them, on May 29, 1886, there was born a boy whom they named Charles Henry—destined to achieve for himself high places of usefulness and distinction in the services of his state and people. Even in his grammar and high school days at Decatur his natural magnetism made him a favorite among his schoolmates. The good-natured twinkle in his dark eyes, his deliberate and thoughtful manner of speech, the hint of a pleasant smile apparently always threatening to break over his countenance betrayed to others the lovable nature and fine disposition that in after years won for him popularity among his fellowmen. Traits of initiative and leadership were definitely marked in young Mahoney. He was a leader of his schoolmates, being captain of both his high school and college baseball teams, of which all other players on both teams were white.

Finishing the high school courses in Decatur in 1904, he entered Olivet Academy in 1905. He found himself a student of Fisk University, at Nashville, Tennessee, in 1908, from which institution he received his A. B. degree, and then his LL. B. from the University of Michigan in 1911.

Mr. Mahoney at once commenced the practice of his profession in Detroit. He soon attracted a large clientele and created a lucrative and established practice. The high distinction which he achieved in the field of law naturally focused attention on him, and soon he was the recipient of many other honors. He now holds and has for many years held the office of Grand Attorney for the Knights of Pythias of the State of Michigan, and is the representative to the Supreme Lodge of that order from his state.

It was his trained mind that guided the organizational processes of the Great Lakes Mutual around legal obstacles when the Association was first formed in 1928. It was he who mastered the difficulties and handled the technicalities of qualification under the laws of Michigan as a mutual life insurance company two years later. He was then elected president of the company, which position he has since held. His unassuming, approachable good nature is a major factor in commending the Great Lakes Mutual to the masses of people in its operating territory, accounting in a large measure for the unusual growth of this rapidly expanding enterprise.

The able president of the Great Lakes Mutual has for a number of years been a delegate to the sessions of the National Negro Insurance Association, and, of course, has taken a keen interest in the proceedings. His thorough training in law and his ripe experience have been of valuable assistance in the work of the committees and on the floor of the convention.

This distinguished barrister believes that Negroes everywhere should claim their right to vote, and that the condition of the group in America will be effectively improved in proportion to its participation in politics.

In 1918 Mr. Mahoney was appointed a member of the Planning Board in the City of Detroit by Senator Couzen, then mayor, and served on it for four years. In 1924 he became a member of the Board of Supervisors of Wayne County, which office he filled with distinction for ten years.

It was unlucky for him that he was the Republican nominee for Congress from the First District of his state in 1932. This year happened to be one of the few times when Michigan went Democratic. Probably the popularity of no Republican in the state would have been sufficient to win the election to Congress from the First District that year. However, the race of this popular attorney measured up fully equal to that of his associates on the Republican ticket.

It was indeed a rare but well-deserved honor which came to Charles Mahoney when in 1939 the governor of Michigan appointed him a Commissioner of the Department of Labor and Industry. The importance of this department in the economic fabric of Michigan may be readily visualized if its many large automobile and other manufacturing plants be remembered. The Labor Division of this Department inspects all steamboats, factories, hotels, elevators and all other types of industry. It has a large force of inspectors whose operations cover the entire state. Not only do these inspectors work under the five commissioners, but there are six deputies subordinate to them who hear labor disputes and workmen's compensation cases in a manner similar to courts of origin. The five commissioners themselves may be compared in this particular phase of their work to an appellate court. They sit and hear arguments on briefs and records, and if appeals are made from their decisions they must be made directly to the Supreme Court of the state.

Mr. Mahoney not only is the only colored man on this, perhaps the most important commission in the state, but he is the only colored Commissioner of Labor in the country. Each commissioner in the State of Michigan is furnished an office, a private secretary, a law clerk, and an automobile. In the case of Commissioner

Mahoney, he not only is provided an office in Lansing, Michigan, but also one in Detroit.

During the year 1939 there was held in Milwaukee, Wisconsin, a convention of the Industrial Accidental Commissioners from all over the United States. The presence of a colored commissioner not only provoked no unusual comment, curiosity or resentment, but quite to the contrary the colored Michigan commissioner was accorded every courtesy by the southern as well as by all other commissioners, the commissioners from North and South Carolina, particularly, asking to be introduced to Mr. Mahoney.

Mr. Mahoney was married in 1922, and he and his wife, Lula E. Mahoney, enjoy their happy home on Josephine Street in Detroit. They have no children.

LOUIS CHARLES BLOUNT, *Vice President-Secretary-Manager*

There is no doubt of the influence of background in the traits of individuals.

This is true of Louis Charles Blount. He was born in Washington, D. C., January 26, 1892, of Jannie M. and Robert B. Blount, a groceryman. The early experience of the younger Blount in the grocery business with his father appears to have greatly influenced the trend of his life. His parents wanted him to become a doctor, and in deference to the wishes of his mother he matriculated in a pre-medical course in Howard University. Soon, however, he realized that business was the field for which his talents and inclinations best fitted him.

Finishing his grade and high school training in the schools of Washington, D. C., he took a course in life insurance at the University of Pennsylvania, and then in 1914 entered the services of the National Benefit Life Insurance Company as an agent in his home city. In 1915 he was promoted to Supervisor of South Maryland, and the next year all Maryland and Delaware were placed under his supervision. He organized agencies and developed this territory for National Benefit and soon made of it one of the company's most profitable units. In 1918 he was called to service in the United States Army and was honorably discharged in January 1919. He returned to National Benefit and his record for the next nine years in the service of that company takes rank with the best field men of the colored race. During this time the company's business in Pennsylvania, Ohio, New Jersey, Delaware, Rhode

HARRY HERBERT PACE, President

THE LATE FRANK L. GILLESPIE
Founder-President

W. ELLIS STEWART
Secretary

TRUMAN KELLA GIBSON
Chairman-Treasurer

JEFFERSON G. ISH, JR.
Vice President and Agency Director

Island, Maryland, Michigan, Kansas and Missouri greatly improved as a result of his ability and industry.

In 1928 Mr. Blount left the services of National Benefit to join the official staff promoting the organization of the Great Lakes Mutual. He is now vice president, secretary, and manager of that company; and it is due to his exceptional executive ability and capacity for handling details that this company is making such rapid progress.

Despite the work of looking after the numerous details of a fast-growing insurance company, Mr. Blount finds time to participate in and to lead many community activities. He is a former president of the Detroit Branch of the N. A. A. C. P., and at the present holds the following important positions: treasurer of the Parkside Hospital; chairman of the Religious Work Committee; vice president of the Booker T. Washington Trade Association; chairman, Advisory Committee of the Brewster Street Recreation Center; vice president of the Great Lakes Land and Investment Company; chairman, Detroit Negro Opera Guild, and Polemarch of the Detroit Alumni Chapter of Kappa Alpha Psi. Mr. Blount has also held the honorable position of president of the National Negro Insurance Association, his term having expired in July 1939. This very busy, public-spirited business executive finds relaxation in his hobbies—photography, gardening, and walking in the rain.

In 1921 Mr. Blount was married to Miss Beatrice Cordove of Washington, D. C., and they, with their two attractive daughters, Mildred and Constance, live in their beautiful home at 430 Chandler Avenue, Detroit.

JOHN W. ROXBOROUGH, *Vice President*

John W. Roxborough, Vice President of Great Lakes Mutual Insurance Company, Detroit, is best known today as manager of Joe Louis. He has been with this company since its organization. He is also chairman of the board of directors of Superior Life Insurance Society, and vice president of Great Lakes Land and Investment Company.

MOSES L. WALKER, *First Vice President and Treasurer*

Moses L. Walker was born January 17, 1882, in Montgomery, Alabama. He attended the public school, completing the eighth grade at the age of 14. In 1902, through the influence and generosity of Dr. George W. Carver, who made arrangements and furnished matriculation funds, he entered the Iowa City Commercial College, working his way through while taking a commercial course. He completed the course in February 1903. In the Fall of the same year, through the intercession of Dr. Booker T. Washington, he was called to Clarksdale, Mississippi, to become secretary and general manager to Eugene P. Booze (now deceased). In 1904 he was called to the Muskogee Indian Territory to become general manager of the J. W. Adams Mercantile Company. In December 1905, he was appointed as a skilled laborer in the office of the auditor for the Post Office Department, Washington, D. C., being certified from a special Bookkeeper's examination, held in Muskogee, Indian Territory, in September of that year. Since then he has held various positions with the U. S. Government, having been an Inspector of Customs in Detroit for twenty-five years. In 1928 he became one of the original founders of the Great Lakes Mutual Association and was elected first vice president. When the organization was changed to the Great Lakes Mutual Insurance Company, Mr. Walker was made its treasurer, and is at present first vice president and treasurer.

SUPREME LIBERTY LIFE INSURANCE COMPANY
CHICAGO, ILLINOIS

FRANK L. GILLESPIE, *Founder*

OSCEOLA, Arkansas, in 1876 was just a small village in what is now Mississippi County, Arkansas, consisting of a post office, a few scattered houses and a small cluster of rough-board stores, in the flat, muddy bottom of the Mississippi River.

It was here that Frank L. Gillespie was born November 8, 1876. But his parents did not keep him long in the dismal surroundings of this river-landing. They soon took their son to Memphis, Tennessee, where he received his grammar school education. Later, they moved to St. Louis, Missouri, and there the boy attended Summer High School for three years, after which he was sent to study music at the Boston Conservatory. While studying there he also finished his high school course. But instead of completing his musical education, he entered the law school of Howard University. Financial difficulties, in which his parents became involved, caused him to give up his law studies, and abandon further pursuit of his formal education.

Like many other young colored men, Gillespie, out of school and starting his fight upward in life, could not wait to choose the path he most preferred, but of necessity had to enter the first opening that seemed to hold promise.

It was in Chicago that he secured employment as a private secretary to a Mr. J. C. Yeager, a prominent white capitalist; and, no doubt, it was in this capacity that he first became inspired with the possibilities of Negro financial enterprises. But after the death of his wealthy employer he had to seek means of self-support and secured a position as the first colored employee of the Automatic Telephone Company, a position which he held only a short time, before he entered the real estate business with former Congressman Oscar Depriest. He was engaged in this business for two years, but somehow it did not seem to fit in exactly with his ambitions.

It was in January 1916 that he joined the agency force of the Royal Life Insurance Company of Chicago. By August of the same year, Gillespie had been promoted to the position of Superintendent of that Company, thus becoming the first colored superintendent of a northern white, old-line legal reserve insurance company engaged in both industrial and ordinary business.

It must here be noted that Gillespie was traveling in fast company. Many of his associates and underlings were young white men; and undoubtedly he had to meet the stern and acid tests of results to overcome the prejudice of color, and to excel to earn the promotion he received.

His success as superintendent of the Royal Life almost approached the sensational. Because of this in the fall of 1917 he was induced to become an organizer and an officer of the Public Life Insurance Company of Illinois. This was the first time in the history of life insurance that a Negro had been elevated to a position of such responsibility. The young company made rapid progress, owing to the brilliant mind and leadership of Gillespie.

He remained two years with the Public Life, and then it began to dawn upon him that possibly even here the fact that he was colored would hinder him to some extent in reaching the greatest possibilities of his talent. Moreover, he realized that through his connections with Public Life he would be able to open the doors of opportunity to only a comparatively few colored men and women. So he handed in his resignation and commenced the organizational work of Liberty Life Insurance Company.

On June 30, 1919, he secured the charter and the authority to sell 10,000 shares of a proposed capital stock of $100,000. Under the laws of Illinois, the sale of this stock had to be completed within two years. June 30, 1921, therefore, marked the deadline. These shares were placed on the market at $30 per share; and in sixteen months Mr. Gillespie and his associates had sold Liberty Life stock in the astounding amount of $300,000.

But Gillespie's efforts to sell insurance in a Negro company to northern Negroes encountered, at first, stubborn skepticism and a cold reception. There had occurred in Chicago the terrible 1919 race riot. Chicago Negroes and northern Negroes generally had been greatly disillusioned. They had been brought face to face with the fact that in crucial moments, North or South, they must rely entirely upon their own resources and efforts. The bloodshed of the Chicago riot, as it was soon afterwards to be realized, was not the only grave feature of it. For some days, gnawing hunger and starvation stared across the threshold of nearly every Negro home in the Illinois metropolis; for all of the stores and food-places closed their doors and refused to sell the necessities of life to Negroes.

It was this fact to which Gillespie pointed with convincing eloquence.

Although the sale and subscription of the entire issue of stock was completed by November 13, 1920, promissory notes had been executed for a large part of the issue, and the actual opening for the writing of business had to await the maturity and payment of these notes. It was not until March 1, 1921, that the promoters of Liberty Life were able to deposit with the Department of Trade and Commerce of the State of Illinois the $100,000 in first mortgages on real estate, as required under the laws of that state. This done, the company was then licensed .to insure lives on the legal reserve basis.

In 1903 Mr. Gillespie was married to Miss Edreaner Poree of New Orleans, Louisiana. A son and a daughter came in due time to bless this union and to cheer the beautiful Gillespie home at 4524 Grand Boulevard, Chicago.

The city of Chicago was grieved on Friday afternoon, May 8, 1925, when the news was given to the city that the founder and president of Liberty Life Insurance Company had died.

He had given to the Middle West a business which was the pride of every forward-looking citizen.

For nearly five years he had presided over and directed with

74

brilliant success the institution he had founded, and many hearts were grieved that he could not longer be spared to lead the fine organization he had assembled.

HARRY HERBERT PACE, *President*

Any description of the life of this versatile and successful man will be uncomfortably restricted by the cold and technical accuracy required of history's pages. A proper picturing of his brilliance and his will-power to overcome difficulties might invite criticisms of exaggeration.

Harry Herbert Pace, the son of Nancy and Charles Pace, a blacksmith, was born at Covington, Georgia, January 6, 1884. His father died while he was still an infant. Harry was a prococious child and finished the elementary school at Covington by the time he was twelve. At nineteen he had received his Bachelor of Arts degree from Atlanta University, where he was valedictorian of his class.

Somehow before entering college, this versatile youth had learned typesetting. It was at this he commenced work to pay his expenses when he entered Atlanta University. He soon discovered, however, that the college authorities were paying a white union printer 30 cents an hour for doing no better printing than he was required to do at 7½ cents an hour; and so he refused to work under such conditions. Rather than submit to them, he accepted the humiliation of being sent out on the campus to do the most menial chores until the authorities agreed to pay him higher rates.

In childhood Harry Pace had formed an ambition to become a lawyer; but his first job after graduation was in a printing plant which he took the lead in organizing in Atlanta. Bishop L. H. Holsey, Benjamin J. Davis, head of the Odd Fellows Grand Lodge of Georgia, William Driskell, Grand Treasurer of the same organization, and A. F. Herndon, were the joint owners; but the venture did not succeed.

Pace then secured a position as instructor in the Haines Institute at Augusta, Georgia, in an effort to earn money to enter Columbia University to study law.

However, the young man remained at the Haines Institute only one year, when he was persuaded by Dr. W. E. B. Dubois to join him and Ed Simon in launching *The Moon,* a weekly magazine to be published in Memphis, Tennessee. With Pace as managing editor and Simon as publisher, *The Moon* rose above the horizon of the young editor's future with bright prospects. But as soon as the clouds of debts and expenses commenced to gather, Dubois and Ed Simon withdrew further financial assistance and left Pace alone to struggle with the venture. He spent everything he had to meet the expenses of getting out the magazine. Soon he found himself penniless, his last suit of clothes threadbare, and hunger, almost his daily lot.

It was on a Saturday night in November 1906 that Harry Pace sat in the back of his dirty little printing office at what is now 197 Beale Avenue, Memphis, Tennessee. Dark failure stared him in the face; and he saw only one way out. There was the Mississippi River, swift, and deep, right at the foot of Beale Avenue.

It was while these dark thoughts were gaining the ascendency over the stubborn will of Harry Pace that his reverie was broken by the entrance of two persons—one of them a Postal Telegraph boy with a telegram in his hand; the other, Ruben Ware, cashier of the Solvent Savings Bank, Memphis' first and only Negro bank. The messenger handed Pace the telegram, informing him that the collect fee of 80 cents was due on it.

"Take it back," said the impatient, dejected Pace. "I haven't a dime in the world; and the only news that telegram could bring me would be bad news, and I don't want any more of that."

"Wait a minute," said Ware, "leave it. I'll lend him eighty cents."

Ware paid the fee, took the telegram and handed it to Pace who, refusing to open it, only handed it back. Ware read the message and then burst out laughing. It was from President B. F. Allen of Lincoln University, Jefferson City, Missouri. It read: *Will you accept a position as Professor of Latin and Greek in this institution at $110.00 per month? If so, report immediately.* But Harry was not yet elated. Discouragement had gotten him down and it was still giving him a thorough walloping.

"Why, how can I take it?" he said, "I have no clothes, no means of transportation and no way to get any money."

Thomas H. Hayes, Sr., then, as now, head of one of Memphis' most successful undertaking businesses, happened to overhear Pace's wail of dispair. He it was who gave a Memphis merchant orders to let Harry Pace have all he needed in men's apparel. Inspired by this, Reuben Ware offered financial assistance, and thus it was that the erstwhile printer became a professor of Latin and Greek at Lincoln University, which position he held during the terms 1906-8.

In 1907, there was trouble in the Solvent Savings Bank in Memphis, and the directors decided to reorganize the official personnel. Milton L. Clay, a business man and a director in the bank, had noted Pace's devotion to duty under the difficulties of publishing *The Moon*. It was he who wrote Pace at Jefferson City to come to Memphis to consider accepting the position of cashier of the Solvent Savings Bank. Pace also received a letter from R. R. Church, Sr., then president of the bank.

It was with reluctance, however, that Professor Pace consented to return to Memphis to discuss the proffered position. He frankly informed the directors that he knew nothing about the banking business, that he had given no thought to this line of work, and that it was his intention soon to commence the study of law. "Why," he asked, "do you want me to take this job when you know that I know nothing about it?" It was then that he was informed by Mr. Clay that his earnest work with *The Moon* had made a fine impression on the colored business men of Memphis. His initial salary at the bank was only $83 a month as against $110 at Lincoln; but he finally yielded to the persuasion of the bank directors, who pictured to him a brilliant and profitable future in the banking business.

The assets of the bank at that time—1908—were, in round figures, $50,000. It had a deficit of $7,000. By the end of 1912, four years later, the assets of the bank, under Pace's wise and progressive steering, amounted to approximately $600,000 and Pace's salary had been increased to $200.00 per month.

It was just about this time that Heman E. Perry was moving about the country trying to sell the stock required to qualify Standard Life Insurance Company in the State of Georgia. He came to Memphis and interested Harry Pace, who sold fifty shares of the stock at $200 per share to the members of the board of directors of the bank. Mr. Perry was so impressed with the ability of young Pace that he immediately set about to persuade him to accept the position of secretary of Standard Life, which Pace finally did. But, here again, he was called upon to make a financial sacrifice, working for $2,000 per year as against $2,400 in the bank in Memphis.

But it was not about the salary that Pace received his greatest disappointment. In Atlanta, he found that Standard Life Insurance Company had on hand only $1,700 after the required deposit had been made with the state. Not more than half of the $100,000 capital stock had been paid in cash, and it was necessary to find $50,000 from some source before the company could meet the tests of a state examination.

It was in 1913 that Harry Pace became officially the secretary-treasurer of Standard Life Insurance Company. He soon installed business systems and the necessary departments in the offices of the company, many of which have been copied by other companies. But the exacting regulations of these systems were not altogether relished by the company's visionary president, Heman E. Perry, who was impatient of details and the regulations of accounting. Following his fantastic schemes, he was inclined to invade any fund or department and make use of any available means to realize his dreams. The irregularities and complications resultant from such procedure met with strong resistance from his business-minded secretary; and, inevitably, there was destined to be serious conflict between these divergent policies. However, Pace managed to work on with Perry and the other officers until the summer of 1917, when tiny ripples of petty friction presaged the approaching storm.

At the beginning of 1917 there were the appearances of harmony in the official circles of Standard Life. Pace, believing that the trouble had blown over, decided to settle down in the insurance business in Atlanta.

On June 20, 1917, he was married to Miss Ethlynde Bibb, one of the most charming and beautiful young women of Atlanta. First having prepared an attractive home, the popular young Secretary of Standard took his bride on a honeymoon trip to Jacksonville, Florida.

During his absence designing enemies were busy trying to widen the breach which they believed existed between Perry and Pace. The latter, hearing rumors of the activities of his maligners, cut short his honeymoon and hurried back to Atlanta. There he found Perry's attitude strangely cool. But he was yet unconvinced that he could not repair any breach that existed between him and his president; and what he thought was a fortunate opportunity to do so soon presented itself: Standard was subjected to a rigid state examination. The examiners found that the company lacked some $60,000 of the amount required for the reserves under the "select and ultimate type" of policies then extant. There was despair in the official ranks of Standard. It was the versatile mind of Pace that came to the rescue. He believed that the interests of the policyholders of Standard ran deeper than their financial contributions. He knew that the company was the pride of its policyholders as well as of the race.

"Why not," said he, "offer the policyholders a non-participating type of policy requiring less reserves."

Sixty days was the period granted to make up the deficit. With the assistance of an intelligent agency force under the direction of Pace, the policyholders, with only a few exceptions, were persuaded to accept the new policies.

Nevertheless, the credit which went to Pace for his masterly feat, instead of establishing him in the good favor of Perry, proved a boomerang. The suspicions and jealousy of Perry were all the more aroused; and before the beginning of 1920 Harry Pace knew that his usefulness as secretary of Standard was at an end. Tendering his resignation, he went to New York.

There in 1920, with W. C. Handy, the famous author of the *blues*, whom he had known in Memphis, he organized the Pace and Handy Music Company and the Black Swan Phonograph Company of New York City, in which he invested heavily. But, owing principally to the advent of radio and the decline of the music business, he sustained heavy losses in this concern. Yet he stayed with it as president until 1925, when he resigned; and with a number of influential and wealthy friends organized the Northeastern Life Insurance Company in Newark, New Jersey, becoming its first president.

Then in 1929 it was the resourceful mind of Harry Pace that worked out the plan of merging the Northeastern Life Insurance Company of Newark, New Jersey, and the Supreme Life and Casualty of Columbus, Ohio, with the Liberty Life Insurance Company of Chicago, Illinois. In this way there came into existence the Supreme Liberty Life of Chicago; and before the end of 1929 a bigger, better, and stronger Negro institution was operating in Chicago with Harry H. Pace as its president. With rare skill and executive ability Mr. Pace continues to guide this fine institution.

At last, in 1930, Harry Pace found the opportunity to gratify his ambition to become a lawyer. The busy president of Supreme

Liberty Life Insurance Company entered a law school and spent at least three hours of hard study every night for a period of three years. He graduated with fourth honors in a class of forty, most of whom were young white men, receiving the degree of Doctor of Jurisprudence and membership in the Order of Lincoln. He is now a member of the law firm of Bibb, Tyree, and Pace.

While filling the major positions in which he has been engaged, the services of this useful man have been sought and obtained in various collateral capacities. He founded the first Elk's Lodge in Memphis, Tennessee, Bluff City No. 96. At the age of twenty-four he had become Grand Secretary of this order and was its Grand Exalted Ruler at the age of twenty-seven, the only man ever to hold both offices. He voluntarily resigned from the latter position. During this same time, he also served as secretary of the Republican Committee of Shelby County, Tennessee, and as assistant secretary of the State Republican Committee.

From 1917 to 1926 Mr. Pace was district grand treasurer of the Grand Lodge of Odd Fellows of the state of Georgia; president of the National Negro Insurance Association from 1928 through 1929; its statistician, 1929-30; and from 1934 until 1938, its general counsel.

On February 6, 1935, he was elected a member of the Diocesan Council of the Protestant Episcopal Church in the Chicago Diocese, being the first and only colored man ever to be elevated to membership of the governing board of that church. For many years he served as a member of the national board of directors of the National Association for the Advancement of Colored People. He is a member of the local board of the Urban League, and president of the Citizens Civic and Economic Welfare Council of Chicago. Mr. Pace is also a member of the Sigma Psi Phi Fraternity and has held the position of Grand Sire Archon of that fraternal organization.

In 1911 Mr. Pace organized and became president of the Colored Citizens Association of Memphis, Tennessee, with Bert Roddy as secretary. It was then that the now powerful E. H. Crump was a candidate for election to the office of mayor of Memphis. Representing this political organization, Pace interviewed the candidates, to secure pledges of concessions to colored people. After interviewing both candidates Pace reported back to the organization and recommended that the colored citizens of Memphis endorse E. H.

Crump. "For," said he, "the other candidate promises everything and I fear he will do nothing; but this red-headed fellow frankly declines to promise some of the things we want, but convinces me that he will fulfill the promises that he did make."

In 1933 Mr. Pace was chosen by Secretary of Commerce Roper as a member of the advisory committee to the secretary regarding the activities of the National Recovery Authority among colored people. In 1935 he was appointed assistant counsel of the Illinois Commerce Commission, which position he still holds.

Harry Pace is the author of a book of inspirational essays entitled *Beginning Again,* published by Dorrance & Company of Philadelphia in 1934. He also wrote a serial novel, published by the Chicago *Defender* during 1934. He has also written various other books and pamphlets on the subject of insurance, all of which have had wide circulation.

Mr. and Mrs. Pace, with their two children, Harry Herbert, Jr. and Josephine, live a life of contentment in their beautiful home at 413 East 60th Street, Chicago.

Dr. M. O. Bousfield, *Vice President and Medical Director*

Midian Othello Bousfield was born August 22, 1885, in Tipton, Missouri, to Willard Haymen and Cornelia Catherine Bousfield. His parents were moderately prosperous, owning their home and some other property in addition to a well-equipped barber shop which his father operated for a white clientele. When Midian was four years old the family moved to Kansas City, Missouri, and his father bought a barber shop there.

The son's desire to be industrious and self-supporting became evident when he was but a lad. At the early age of eleven years he was assisting his father in their shop in the evenings after school. Even though his time for play and diversion was thus somewhat restricted, he had, nevertheless a normal, happy childhood.

He attended grade school in Kansas City, Missouri, high school in Kansas City, Kansas, and then entered the University of Kansas at Lawrence, from which institution he received his Bachelor of Arts degree in 1907. He was always a good, though not a particularly outstanding scholar. His early training and experience at work proved valuable in helping him pay his way through college, where he worked as a barber for other students in the evenings, in addition to serving meals and stoking the furnace in a white fraternity house.

Interested in the study of medicine, he entered Northwestern Medical School in Chicago in the fall of 1907, from which, after two years of diligent application to his studies, he graduated with the degree of M. D. His interneship was served at Freedman's Hospital in Washington, D. C., after which he established his practice in Kansas City, Missouri. He was one of the first four colored physicians to be appointed to the staff of the old General Hospital of that city, now known as General Hospital Number Two.

But Dr. Bousfield in his younger days felt that his opportunities were limited by the barriers of racial prejudices, and early entertained an ambition to escape them. In 1911 he decided to make his home and find his fortune in Brazil, and it was then that he set sail for that country.

He was then only twenty-six years old; and it is said that loneliness or homesickness caused his return to North America. He came back home broke—in fact, in debt—but he was not discouraged.

In order to pay his creditors the young physician, before resuming the practice of medicine, took work as a railroad barber and buffet man. He followed this work for more than a year, and during this time became intensely interested in the low pay and poor working conditions of railroad men.

He accepted the position of secretary to what later became the Railway Men's International Benevolent Association, and was thus instrumental in organizing 10,000 men into one big union. Undoubtedly this work contributed toward the ultimate success of the Brotherhood of Sleeping Car Porters, now the most powerful labor union among Negroes.

Dr. Bousfield's entrance into the insurance field was purely the result of his activities among railroad men. It attracted the attention of Frank Gillespie, who invited him to join him in organizing the Liberty Life.

It was in 1918 that the preliminary organization work was begun. In recognition of his fine, pioneering work in the organization of the company, Dr. Bousfield was made first vice president and medical director in the temporary organization in 1919, and was later elected to the same positions in the permanent organization.

After the death of Frank L. Gillespie in 1925, Dr. Bousfield was elevated to the position of president of the company, the duties of which position he ably discharged until the merger and reorganization in 1929 permitted him to accept a position as associate director of medical services with the Julius Rosenwald Fund. Since 1936 he has been the Director of Negro Health Services of this fund, meanwhile discharging the duties of medical director of Supreme Liberty Life; though declining to accept for this work any compensation except the nominal salary of $1.00 per year.

This popular physician is always a very busy man. He is an active member of the National Board of the Urban League, and president of the Chicago branch; a member of the Chicago Adult Education board of directors; of the board of management of the Chicago Wabash Avenue Y. M. C. A.; of the Chicago Advisory Committee on Housing; of the board of governors of the Metropolitan Housing Council; the Illinois State Advisory Committee of the National Youth Authority; chairman of the section of Health and Housing of the Bethune National Youth Authority Conference; and is a past president of the National Medical Association.

The last-named association sponsors a Commission on Hospitals and Medical Education. As chairman of this commission, Dr. Bousfield has been instrumental in directing the interests of the National Medical Associaiton in this much needed field.

The United States Department of Labor is taking advantage of the services of Dr. Bousfield as a member of the Advisory Committee of the United States Children's Bureau. He is one of the members of the Committee on Tuberculosis among Negroes, a branch of the National Tuberculosis Association of America.

Dr. Bousfield is held in high esteem by the white medical profession and by all of those white people interested in social welfare who have come in contact with him. His distinction in this respect is attested by the number of positions of honor rarely held by colored men which he has held and filled with such outstanding credit to himself and to his people. Among these may be mentioned the following: fellow in the American Public Health Association; fellow in American Medical Association; member of the Chicago Medical Society; member of the Cook County Physicians' Association; of the Illinois State Medical Association; of the Cook County Board of Public Welfare. He is also a member of the National Medical Association; of the National Hospital

Association; of the board of directors of the South Side Boys' Club Foundation; of the executive committee of St. Edmund's Episcopal Church; and president of the Men's Club of that church. In several of the above-mentioned organizations, Dr. Bousfield is the only colored man holding membership.

The Negro race has probably produced no man who has been more interested in the improvement of Negro health conditions than Dr. Bousfield. To this cause he has dedicated much of his life. His papers on this subject read to various sessions of the National Negro Insurance Association have been noted for the thorough understanding of facts that could only be obtained as the result of genuine interest and intense study.

On September 9, 1914, the young physician was married to Miss Maudelle Brown. This union has been blessed by a daughter, Miss Maudelle Bousfield, a beautiful and talented young woman, who holds B. S. and M. A. degrees from the University of Wisconsin, and is now teaching in Chicago.

For a number of years Mrs. Maudelle Bousfield has been employed as principal of the third largest school in the city of Chicago. She still fills the position with rare distinction. Notwithstanding the busy lives of both Dr. and Mrs. Bousfield, they have enjoyed an exceptionally happy home life.

Perhaps the crowning distinction of this man of many honors was his elevation to membership on the City Board of Education of Chicago, Illinois, in October 1939, thus becoming the first colored person ever to serve on a similar board in a major city. This achievement climaxed a twenty-five year fight of Negro leaders in Chicago for representation on that commission.

Dr. Bousfield attributes the exceptional progress of Negro people in the business of life insurance to a fortunate development of a better type of salesmanship than our other fields of commerce have been able to secure. This business, he says, will be further expanded and improved as we are able to bring into it and train for field service more of our college graduates.

TRUMAN KELLA GIBSON, *Chairman-Treasurer*

"Persistence and Patience"

The first eighteen years of the life of Truman Kella Gibson were spent in Macon, Georgia, with his parents, John Arthur and

Annie C. Gibson, to whom he was born in August 1882. The moderate circumstances of the Gibsons did not permit young Truman many of the diversions of childhood; and, whether inherited from some unknown ancestor or developed through the restrictions of a youth necessarily devoted more to work than to play, there was early evidence in the boy of the two characteristics that were to run like shining rails throughout his life and on which he was to drive himself to a substantial place in the business world of his people. Persistence in dogging the footsteps of success— patience to wait for the fruits of his labors: these are the traits which have elevated Truman Kella Gibson to a position of importance in the saga of Negro insurance.

Young Truman attended the Ballard Normal School in Macon, Georgia, working after school and during the summers at various odd jobs—messenger, clerk in a drug store, and other positions which a lad in his 'teens could fill. When he reached the age of eighteen, he left home and went to Atlanta, Georgia, where he entered Atlanta University; and, since the finances of his parents could not be stretched to embrace a college education for their son, it was by self help alone that the boy was able to spend four years in college, graduating in 1905.

Evidently the hard work and sacrifices, the denial of recreation and leisure which were necessary in order for a youth to work his way through school, did not dismay young Gibson; for, at the completion of his studies at Atlanta University, he felt the need of more preparation to become better equipped to overcome the peculiar problems facing a young and ambitious Negro; and he entered Harvard College where, for two years, he patiently worked to support himself while pursuing his studies.

In 1908, after leaving Harvard, Gibson secured a position teaching at St. Paul School, Lawrenceville, Virginia. Here he taught until 1910, when he was persuaded by the urgent appeal of a former teacher-friend ot enter the insurance field.

The entrance of T. K. Gibson into the field of insurance was not marked by any brilliant flare of instant achievement; but, in keeping with his methodic march toward his place in the sun, he entered through the agency route with the Atlanta Mutual Insurance Company of Atlanta, Georgia. During the nine years that he served this company, he advanced from the position of agent to that of manager, and increased his annual earnings from $600 to

$2,080. But even this did not satisfy the broad scope of his ambition.

In 1919, the Supreme Life and Casualty Company of Ohio made its debut; and one of the moving figures behind that organization was Truman Kella Gibson. Gibson served the new company for ten years in an executive capacity; and when that company developed into what is now the Supreme Liberty Life Insurance Company of Chicago, Illinois, in 1929, he entered its services.

As chairman-treasurer of the Supreme Liberty Life, T. K. Gibson gives that brand of steady, efficient service which has symbolized his activities throughout his life. His duties in handling investments and the care and custody of properties and securities for the company call for the particular type of level-headed business acumen with which he is so well endowed. His ability in this field has been so marked that, in recognition of his achievement in the business world, he was awarded the Harmon Medal in 1930.

In 1910 Mr. Gibson was married to a lovely young woman, Miss Alberta A. Dickerson of Jersey City, New Jersey. They have three children; two sons who are practising law in the city of Chicago, and a daughter who is studying at the University of Chicago. Mr. Gibson proudly exhibits, as the final crowning of his success, the fact that he has been able to rear and provide for his progeny so that they, in turn, may help to build more solidly and securely the bulwarks of racial achievement.

Like many of our leaders, he is a conscientious believer in separate racial businesses. Even in early life, he was impressed with the difficulties of our economic situation, and that he majored in economics in college. He thinks that the general economic condition of the Negro race will be affected by the policy of separate businesses to an extent dependent upon its race-conscious growth and development. He believes the race must be producers—originators, not merely consumers; and that there is a vast market which should be cultivated by Negroes for Negroes.

In the onward march of Negro life insurance, there will always be a place for men like Truman Kella Gibson.

W. ELLIS STEWART, *Secretary*
"I Will Make Ready and Maybe My Chance Will Come"

The following three points in the life story of W. Ellis Stewart, Secretary of the Supreme Liberty Life Insurance Company, mark

DR. P. M. H. SAVORY
Chairman, Board of Directors

Dr. C. B. Powell
Vice President

The Late James E. Mitchem
Former Secretary

Bishop R. A. Valentine
Vice President and Treasurer

him as a man of decisive judgment and steadfast purpose: First, his ability to decide in his early life the line of work he wanted to follow; second, his determination to rise above the common level in that work; and third, his resolve to thoroughly prepare himself for it.

He was born on March 10, 1892, in the small town of Columbus, Indiana. It was here that he attended the elementary schools and finished the high school courses.

Always industrious, he never missed any opportunity, even during his first twenty years at home with his parents, to show his appreciation for their love and protection, by supplementing the family income, performing such chores as cutting grass, caring for horses, and working at other odd jobs for his neighbors.

After graduation from high school, he entered the University of Indiana at Bloomington, hoping to find work sufficient to enable him to continue his college studies. But after one year at Bloomington he found his funds exhausted. He then secured a position as a servant and cook in a white family, intending to earn enough there to return to college. And so satisfactorily did he perform his services in this family that his weekly wage was increased to $18, which at that time was more than the salary paid the principal of the high school in Columbus.

But the ambition that stirred the breast of this talented young man would not allow him to be content with a job as a domestic servant, no matter if the pay did seem high.

In 1914 a copy of *The Crisis* had come into his hands, and beneath the picture of a group of students he read the words that appear at the beginning of this story. These words haunted him. While at work he found himself repeating them: "I will make ready and maybe my chance will come." And then he asked himself, "Make ready for what? What is there for a colored man to do?" While he pondered this self-posed inquiry he saw an advertisement of Standard Life Insurance Company of Atlanta, Georgia. A Negro insurance company? Why, never before had he heard of such a thing! Was not a life insurance company a matter of big finance, such as only white capitalists could handle? *One hundred thousand dollars!* What an astounding sum of money! It was almost incredible to him that Negroes had subscribed and paid in such a huge sum, and yet, here it was in print.

It was then that he decided to devote his life to the work of life insurance. He wrote Heman E. Perry, president, and Harry H. Pace, secretary of Standard Life. Promptly he was offered the management of the Covington, Kentucky, district, and he was on the verge of beginning work there when again the words of *The Crisis* stopped him. He remembered that these words said, "make ready." "Am I ready?" This question kept pressing for an answer. In his reply to the secretary of the Standard he asked whether or not he should make further preparation by continuing his college career before commencing work. Fortunately, it was to a college man, Harry Pace, that he addressed this inquiry; and, although Standard Life needed the services of this smart young man, Pace very promptly advised, "By all means finish your college course."

So in 1917, he gave up his job as a servant and entered the University of Illinois at Urbana; and here he found work at odd jobs to defray his college expenses.

Thus, after five years, he found himself again a student in college; but now he had a definite goal to reach, and was able, therefore, more highly to appreciate the concrete application of his studies to life's activities. He amazed his white teachers and schoolmates by entering the College of Commerce to major in life insurance. "Why," they asked, "does a Negro want to major in the business of life insurance?" "What is he going to do after finishing such a course?" "No white company is going to employ a Negro in any capacity commensurate with such preparation, so why?" They had never heard of a Negro life insurance company, so Stewart became a rather pitied curiosity to his white teachers and schoolmates. He was frequently interrogated on his reasons for pursuing this course; but he kept his own counsel and let them wonder. He knew of at least one Negro company, and *The Crisis* had said his chance might come if he made ready.

By 1920, Stewart was in his last year of college; and, seeking work, he wrote to Frank L. Gillespie of Chicago, asking for a job. Gillespie replied, inviting him to call to see him immediately. As a result of this conference W. Ellis Stewart left Gillespie's office with a contract as a stock salesman of Liberty Life.

In June 1920, this stock salesman, notwithstanding having been interrupted by services in the United States Army as a corporal and sergeant from August 1918 to May 1919, was graduated from the College of Commerce of the University of Illinois with his B. S.

degree in life insurance. He was the first person, white or colored, to graduate from that University in such a course.

In December 1920 Mr. Stewart was elected secretary of the Liberty Life Insurance Company, which position he has since held and discharged with unusually high credit to himself, to his company, and to the race.

Then, in 1933, further to qualify for corporate services he took a course in law and is now a law school graduate and licensed to practice in Illinois.

In 1925, at its annual session in Chicago, Mr. Stewart was elected secretary of the National Negro Insurance Association, and for twelve years he held this position and discharged its duties with great credit.

This popular executive is well liked in the city of his residence by his business associates and acquaintances, as well as by the many friends he has made through his contacts as secretary of the National Negro Insurance Association.

Before leaving Indiana Mr. Stewart was elected vice president of the state convention of the Baptist Young People's Union. In the fraternal world he has served as Grand Polemarch (president) of Kappa Alpha Psi Fraternity.

He has also served as chairman of the board of the Wabash Avenue Y. M. C. A., as chairman of the South Central Recreation Committee, and of the South Central Charter Jubilee Committee.

Mr. Stewart thinks that for many, many years to come, perhaps indefinitely, our efforts should be dedicated to the promotion of separate Negro businesses. He believes, in fact, in the ultimate success of such a doctrine, and that through it the economic condition of the colored race will be greatly improved, as more and more the manufacture and the sale of the necessities of life result in the gainful employment of the men and women of the race.

On October 7, 1915, W. Ellis Stewart was married to Miss Cora Taylor, and due time brought them a son, Frank Lehman, now the pride of their attractive home at 4524 South Parkway, Chicago.

JEFFERSON GATHERFORD ISH, JR., *Vice President Agency Director*

In the earlier stages of racial development, the few who accumulated wealth or rose to positions of importance found, in some cases, that their wealth and commanding positions proved handicaps or deterrents to the success of their children.

It therefore is not an unreasonable conclusion that quite as much credit is due the colored man or woman who overcomes and conquers the handicaps of wealth and high position of his parents as to those who fight their way up through the difficulties of poverty.

The life of Jefferson Gatherford Ish illustrates this point in a very emphatic way. In his early life he was denied the rugged factors that contribute so often to self-confidence and independence in those who have to rely entirely upon their own efforts. His parents were able to care for him and to provide the means for a finished education.

On January 4, 1888, there was born to Marietta Hardwick and Jefferson Gatherford Ish, Sr., a second son, and to him they gave the name of the father who was, and had been for a number of years, engaged as a teacher and principal in the colored high school at Little Rock, Arkansas.

The senior Ish was a careful and thrifty business man as well as a competent teacher. The same characteristics were also dominant in the mother of Ish, Jr.; and she, too, was an outstanding character in the teaching profession of Little Rock. By frugal living they accumulated real estate and other property; and in this way were able to care for their family in unusually comfortable circumstances, and to provide their children with the means for completing their education.

Jefferson Gatherford Ish, Jr., an exceptionally smart lad, finished the grammar and high school courses at Little Rock with high credits; and then his parents entered him in Talladega College at Talladega, Alabama, where, after three years, he received his B. S. degree. Entering Yale University, he received his B. A. degree from that institution after two years. Notwithstanding that his school expenses were taken care of by his parents, young Ish, by hard study, was able to win scholarships from time to time, and thus, by his own ability, was able to supplement the means of his parents.

Like the lives of many other colored boys, Ish's life was determined, it seems, not by deliberate choice, but, more nearly, by circumstances.

It appears that had he been permitted to follow the bent of his talents he would have become renowned either as an outstanding mathematician or as a chemist. These were the studies that attracted and held his deep interest throughout his school and college days. Those who have been associated with him during his maturer years in the life insurance business know him for his ability to think quickly and clearly through complicated problems and situations.

In 1911, two years after his graduation from Yale, he was elected professor of mathematics at Lincoln Institute, Jefferson City, Missouri, which position he held until he was elected professor of mathematics of the Branch State Normal School for Negroes at Pine Bluff, Arkansas. Here, he so ably discharged his duties that in 1915 he was made president of this institution, which was then a State College. He was then only twenty-seven years old and the youngest man, white or colored, ever to head an important state college.

For six years he presided over the affairs of the Arkansas State College; but, by the year 1921, more than one important Negro life insurance company was scouring the country for competent talent. Then it was that Standard Life Insurance Company offered young Professor Ish a salary and commissions, as state manager for that company, amounting to $100 more a month than he was receiving as president of the State College. He accepted, but remained with Standard only year.

In 1922, the Mosaic Templars, a fraternal order, offered him a salary and commissions amounting to $275 a month more than the $300 being paid him by Standard Life. He served this society until the end of the year 1926.

Then he assisted in the organization of the Century Life, and became its first secretary, in which capacity he served from 1927 until 1930, when the Century was merged with the Woodmen of the Union, a fraternal order.

Soon after this he was made assistant agency officer of Supreme Liberty Life Insurance Company, Chicago, where his work proved such an outstanding success that after a few years he was made vice president and agency officer, the duties of which position he has continued to discharge to the great improvement of the field department of that company.

As a director of the field forces of Supreme Liberty Life, Mr. Ish has been unusually successful because of the readiness with which his followers in the field have been willing to repose complete confidence in him.

Though quiet of demeanor and mathematically inclined, he is

possessed of a creative mentality in originating new and inspirational schemes to attract and hold the enthusiastic interest of the agency forces he so capably leads.

Mr. Ish beblieves that from year to year the colored race will be enriched, and its economic condition improved, by the continued development of separate business enterprises. He entertains scant hope that interracial businesses will open their doors to any great extent to accomodate the rapidly increasing business talent of Negroes.

On March 11, 1911, Jefferson Gatherford Ish, Jr. was married to Miss Florence Ross of Muskogee, Oklahoma; and she has been of valuable assistance and inspiration in the remarkable career upward which marks their lives.

Their union was blessed by the birth of a daughter, now Mrs. Marietta Ish Mickey, of Chicago. To brighten the picture of the advancing years of Jefferson Gatherford Ish there has come into the home of the Mickeys a little daughter, Florence, the pride not only of Mr. and Mrs. Mickey, but of the grandparents.'

UNITY MUTUAL LIFE INSURANCE COMPANY, CHICAGO, ILLINOIS

UNDER the insurance laws of Illinois, foreign companies(companies from other states) are not admitted to transact business in Illinois unless, among other qualifications, they have a paid-in capital stock of $100,000 for each class of insurance business proposed to be written. This, probably, explains why Dr. P. H. V. Dejoie, C. C. Dejoie, and W. H. Roberson had to organize the Unity Mutual Insurance Company of Chicago as an independent Illinois company, instead of qualifying the Unity of New Orleans in Illinois.

This institution was organized in Chicago, in May 1920, to transact only sick and accident insurance. Among the sponsors and active officers were C. C. Dejoie and the late Dr. P. H. V. Dejoie of New Orleans.

The enterprise operated as a sick and accident company until June 1928, when license was secured from the State of Illinois for the Unity Mutual Life Insurance Company, organized as an assessment life concern on the legal reserve basis and authorized to do a mixed business of all forms of life and sick and accident insurance. The Unity Mutual Life immediately reinsured the business of the

Unity Mutual Insurance Company and the latter was dissolved. Unity Mutual Life has continued to write and handle all of the forms of insurance for which it was organized. It is managed by the following board of directors and officers:

C. C. Dejoie, chairman; A. W. Williams, president-treasurer; Attorney Sydney P. Brown, vice president-general counsel; Mrs. L. E. James, secretary; W. K. Allen, agency officer; Mrs. Hazel Lampkins, director; Mrs. Frances Roberson, director; Mrs. A. W. Williams, director, and A. Dejoie, director.

Although C. C. Dejoie of New Orleans is chairman of the board of directors of the Unity Mutual Life Insurance Company of Chicago, this institution is in no way affiliated with or connected with the Unity Industrial, a stock life insurance company of New Orleans.

A. W. WILLIAMS, *President-Treasurer*

The early life of Mr. A. W. Williams, president-treasurer of the Unity Mutual Life Insurance Company of Chicago, was spent in Philadelphia, and he was educated in the schools of that city.

In 1919, at the instance of Mr. W. S. Hornsby, secretary-manager, he entered the services of the Pilgrim Health & Life Insurance Company of Augusta, Georgia. After one year, however, in the services of this company, he returned to Philadelphia and became connected with the National Benefit Life Insurance Company, serving on its field force. Having shown unusual talent and ability in the field of life insurance, in 1922 Mr. Williams was stationed at the Home Office of the National Benefit in Washington, D. C., where he could receive more careful and thorough training. This he did, serving from time to time in all of the departments of that company. In 1923, he was appointed a supervisor over the various states in which the National Benefit operated, and held this position until 1927, when he came to Chicago to manage the Unity. Since being with this company Mr. Williams has served in every office except that of general counsel.

THE VICTORY LIFE INSURANCE COMPANY AND THE VICTORY MUTUAL LIFE INSURANCE COMPANY

HU SHIH, the eminent philosopher, says in his essay, "The Civilizations of the East and the West," that "according to Confucius, all implements or institutions of civilization are spiritual in origin; they all came from 'ideas'. When conceived they are called ideas."

Less than fifteen years ago there was conceived in the brain of Anthony Overton an idea that he could create a successful insurance company which would encourage thrift, create estates, protect widows and orphans, and furnish high-type, lucrative employment to the young men and women of his race who had trained themselves for lives of constructive service. Within six months after its conception, this idea was made concrete in the organization of the Victory Life Insurance Company, in Chicago, March 3, 1924.

The company was incorporated under the laws of Illinois and commenced business with a paid-in capital of $100,000 and a surplus of $50,000. All the original capital was invested in first real estate mortages on Negro homes. The first home office consisted of one room in the Overton Building with a personnel of three persons. At the close of the year 1924 an examination of the company by the Insurance Department of Illinois disclosed admitted assets of $167,000, capital and surplus of $157,000, total income of $14,719, and insurance in force amounting to $680,000.

In its first year the company confined its operation to the state of Illinois, but in 1925 it entered upon a program of expansion and qualified in Texas, Missouri, Ohio, West Virginia, Kentucky, the District of Columbia, Maryland, and New Jersey. At the close of the year 1925, the statement compiled showed admitted assets of $170,000, net reserve of $30,000, capital and surplus of $132,000, and insurance in force amounting to $2,250,000.

At the close of the year 1926, two years and nine months after its birth, the capital was $285,000; 308 persons were employed in the home and branch offices as officers, clerks, stenographers, bookkeepers, and in the field as agents, medical examiners, and inspectors; the total income was $203,000 with admitted assets of $369,000, net reserves of $74,000, and $4,500,000 of paid-for business on its books.

Although the year 1926 evidenced a rapid and healthy growth of the company, 1927 was to stand out as the most remarkable year of its existence.

Until 1927 no such financial organization of Negroes had ever qualified to operate under the stringent laws of New York. Largely through the influence of Dr. P. M. H. Savory, Dr. C. B. Powell, and the late John W. Duncan, the company was admitted for business in that state, February 9, 1927; and in the words of the late J. Garland Wood, "It was the first time in the history of our commercial life that we had received recognition by the highest financial authorities in the world." This remarkable achievement on the part of Victory Life was heralded far and wide in the press of the country; it made Victory Life a household word, and created a degree of confidence in the minds of the public that would otherwise have taken years to develop.

Victory's breaking the ice in New York state was remarkable also because it was the only company chartered by the state of Illinois to accomplish such a feat, as well as being one of the few companies which had been admitted by that department in a period of some twenty-five years.

But this was not all that occurred during this memorable year; for, immediately after beginning operation in New York, news was received that the company had qualified for business in Indiana, being the first old line company of Negroes to be admitted into that state; and, immediately thereafter, it was admitted also into Virginia. Each of these newly acquired territories was rapidly organized, and operations were begun. In November 1927, the Company entered Michigan, established agencies, and commenced rapidly to develop that field. The statement as of December 31, 1927, showed an income of $283,000, admitted assets of $438,000, net reserves of $158,000, capital and surplus of $262,000, and $8,500,000 of paid-for business on the books. March 3, 1929, marked the fifth anniversary of the institution's birth.

During five years of operation, $246,000 had been loaned on Negro property, and $114,000 had been paid to beneficiaries of deceased policyholders.

During the years 1929, 1930, and 1931, still further progress was made by the company. The statement for 1931 showed income of $715,849; disbursements, $454,369; admitted assets, $1,216,730; liabilities, $994,443; capital and surplus, $222,287; insurance in force, $16,350,633. But despite these accomplishments, two factors that threatened trouble for the company were at work. One lay in the company's investment policy and the other in the company's connection with the Douglass National Bank.

It has been noted above that all the original capital was invested in real estate mortgages secured on the homes of colored people. This practice continued throughout the company's operaitons, and while all subsequent investments were not in real estate mortgages, the ratio of such other investments to total investments was entirely too low. There was insufficient diversification of investments.

From 1919 to 1929 there was a great boom in real estate in Chicago, and values rose to a level of inflation. Property was bought and mortgages placed in keeping with the prevailing inflated market until the latter part of 1929 when values started their rapid descent. The company suffered along with all other financial institutions. The market value of the entire mortgage holdings was far less than the amount shown on the company's books, and less than the state Insurance Department would appraise it. Repair was made all the harder because mortgages held by the company were in amounts entirely too large. There were also personal loans to members of Mr. Overton's family secured only by Douglass National Bank stock and second mortgage bonds. Mr. Anthony Overton was president both of Douglass National Bank and Victory Life; and there resulted perplexing entanglements of the affairs of the two institutions through the heavy interlocking interests of their president. Major errors of investment on the part of Victory Life in connection with Douglass National Bank were $75,593.00 in Douglass National Bank stock, which proved to be worthless; $49,250.00 collateral loans, with only Douglass National Bank stock as security for the major part of it.

In a short time, however, a plan was formed to reorganize the company. This was set in motion by Drs. Savory, Powell, Bell, and the late John W. Duncan by the formation of a voting trust which included many of the stockholders and had the full moral and financial support of the policyholders in New York and New Jersey. These men later organized a protective committee whose personnel included from Chicago, John Holloman, L. K. Williams, president of the National Baptist Convention and Pastor of Olivet Baptist Church, and A. L. Williams; and from New York City, Dr. P. M. H. Savory, Dr. C. B. Powell, and the late John W. Duncan. The work of reorganization from the beginning was propitiously blessed in that the receivership was in the Federal Court instead of the State Court, and the presiding judge, the Honorable Evan A. Evans, was favorable to some plan for the protection of the policyholders.

A plan unique in its nature was evolved whereby a new stock company was to be organized, capitalized at $100,000, the stock of which was to be paid for by the receiver with assets then on deposit with the Illinois Insurance Department, one share to be given to each of fifteen directors and the receiver to retain the remaining 985 shares. This new company, the Victory Mutual Life Insurance Company, was then to be mutualized by retirement of the stock, after which it was to enter into a contract with the receiver of Victory Life Insurance Company, reinsuring all outstanding risks, assuming all liabilities, and taking over all assets at a value to be determined by the court. The new company was chartered April 5, 1933; shortly after that it mutualized. It received its license from Illinois on June 8, 1933, and entered into the reinsurance agreement on June 9, 1933. Thus reorganization was completed; the company was saved for the colored race. Judge Evans placed the management of the company into the hands of Dr. Savory, who had been elected chairman of the board, and the Reverend Dr. L. K. Williams, who had been elected president.[1]

The other officers of the new company were: executive vice president, John Holloman, chairman of the board of Pyramid Mutual Life Insurance Company; vice president, C. B. Powell, formerly a director of Victory Life Insurance Company; secretary, J. E. Mitchem, formerly secretary of Underwriters Mutual Life Insurance Company; treasurer, J. I. Morehead, practicing attorney in Chicago; director of agencies, J. A. Howard; conservation agent and assistant to the president, I. J. Joseph; medical director, S. W. Smith; and cashier, R. A. Valentine. Other directors were: Haley Bell, Detroit; John W. Duncan, New York City; H. E. Hall, president of the Mammoth Life, Louisville, Kentucky; J. E. Hubbard, Cleveland, Ohio; and S. H. C. Owens, Detroit.

The officers and employees of the reorganized Victory Mutual set about their tasks of rehabilitation with earnest application, with the result that the company is having a very satisfactory experience.

THE REVEREND LACY KIRK WILLIAMS, *President*

Negro business owes a debt of gratitude to the Negro church. It has received great assistance from it. In the development of all types of commercial enterprises, the doors of the church have ever been wide open. It has more than supplied the lack of daily papers in which to advertise Negro businesses; for the voice of the ministry has been constantly raised and its influence exerted

[2] Informant: J. E. Mitchem, Chicago, Illinois.

in active advocacy and defense of Negro owned and operated enterprises.

In the vanguard of the economic march of Negroes, the eminence of the Reverend Dr. Lacy Kirk Williams of Chicago, the president of the National Baptist Convention, largest of Negro religious organizations, is an inspiring figure not alone in religious but in business circles. He has not been content with furnishing abstract influence and oral support, but his confidence in the ability of colored leaders to operate business institutions in the best interest of the masses has been emphasized by investing his personal funds in their capitalization.

Lacy Kirk, the son of Elizabeth and Levi Williams, was born at Eufaula, Alabama, July 11, 1871, and he lived and worked with his parents on a farm until he was sixteen years old. Moving to Texas, he attended the public schools and Bishop College in that state. Later he became a student at Arkansas Baptist College, Little Rock, from which he received both the degrees of Bachelor of Theology and Bachelor of Arts. In school young Williams early betrayed evidences of the natural talents which, in later years, won for him such great distinction in the ministry. His gift of vivid expression and logical discourse manifested itself in his preferences for language studies and logic. It was in these that he led and achieved his highest scholastic ratings. Especially was he proficient in the study of Greek.

The high positions that he now holds in the fields of religion and business are not the results of fortunate breaks or "pull". In school, while just a boy, the qualities of leadership so pronounced in his character manifested themselves in class work and in play. Because of his natural brilliance, and through circumstances which often delayed the educational progress of other colored boys, Lacy Williams often found himself in school in a class with full grown men. Thus, he was the captain of his baseball club at thirteen, while all the other members of the club were past twenty.

Out of school young Williams turned at first to farming and teaching, and devoted his spare time and Sundays to activities in the church. He entered the ministry and in a short time was elected president of the Texas State Baptist Convention. Following the death of the Reverend E. C. Morris in 1925, he was elected president of the National Baptist Convention. This position he has filled until the present time with great credit and without opposition. Dr. Williams moved to Chicago when he was called to the pastorate of the Mt. Olivet Baptist Church in that city. This is one of the largest Negro Baptist Churches in the world—perhaps the largest. Though now advanced in years, he is still fulfilling with high satisfaction the heavy duties incident to pastoring this large congregation, while at the same time he directs the voluminous work of the National Convention.

When Anthony Overton took the initial steps to organize Victory Life Insurance Company in 1923, he had no more enthusiastic supporter than Dr. L. K. Williams. Dr. Williams subscribed for a substantial block of the stock when it was first put on the market; and later was elected a member of the board of directors. His sane advice, wide influence, and conservative attitude were among the important factors contributing to the establishment and rapid progress of that company.

In 1931, when, as a result of financial complications, a receivership was applied for and the Victory ceased operation, Dr. Williams joined with Dr. Savory and others to plan for reorganizing the company and protecting the policyholders. In recognition of his constructive business ability, he was elected president of the Victory Mutual; and from his denominational work he yet finds time enough for the executive functions of this rapidly growing insurance company.

DR. PHILIP MAXWELL HUGH SAVORY,
New York, Chairman of the Board

In the life of Dr. Philip Maxwell Hugh Savory is found a lesson in the benefits of life insurance. At some time in the early days of his childhood, there was wisdom of a rare type in his family. Its fruits came at a time when most needed and they could be of greatest advantage in the life of young Savory. He was enabled to finish his college education because somebody, back in British Guiana, when he was but a child, secured an endowment insurance policy on his life; and the maturity of this insurance came when the young man was in college and could not have continued there but for the proceeds derived from the policy.

Philip Maxwell Hugh Savory was born September 30, 1889, in British Guiana, S. A., to Frederick K. and Louisa Savory, with whom he lived until he was nineteen years old. He finished his elementary and high school courses at Georgetown, British Guiana, and then further pursued his education in New York City and at McGill University in Montreal, Canada.

Earnings in summer as a compositor, printer, and porter, together with the proceeds of the endowment policy, enabled this ambitious young student to complete his college and medical education. He worked for as little as $3 per week, but his pay was constantly advanced as he moved from one job to another. In the summer of 1917, he was inspector in an ammunition factory, at a good salary. In the summer of 1918, there was a shortage of men trained in medicine and chemistry. The Laurentide Paper and Power Company, of Grand Mere, Quebec, requested McGill University to send its best senior student, and Mr. Savory was selected, receiving a salary of $40 *per day* with board and lodging. Since that time his income has always been over $5,000 a year.

However, Dr. Savory's exceptional devotion to the work he performed while in school in no way interfered with his scholastic achievements. The distinction of the highest aggregate honors in all subjects for the whole time he was in college was won by him, for which he was awarded the Holmes Gold Medal.

Even while in school, young Savory resented every manifestation of racial prejudice; and it was largely due to his courage and determination that discrimination against the matriculation and graduation of colored students at McGill University was abolished. His crusade in this cause was untiring and often carried on at great personal sacrifices.

Dr. Savory commenced the practice of medicine in New York City in 1919; and, as in everything in which he had engaged, he soon distinguished himself in this field, and was rewarded with a large and lucrative practice which he still enjoys.

His motive for entering the field of life insurance was far from any personal, financial profit. He gratefully remembered the great benefit he had received from the endowment policy that matured when he was in school. He saw in life insurance one of the best agencies for economic security for his race. Hence, when he was approached by a representative of Anthony Overton, who initiated the movement for the organization of the Victory Life Insurance Company of Chicago, he readily agreed to invest heavily in the enterprise. When the organization was completed, he was elected a vice president.

Dr. Savory, a man of unselfish independence, daring to differ when convinced that difference was proper, in time found himself in disagreement with some of the operating plans and policies of the active officers of the company. His difference, however, was constructive and in the interest of the policyholders. After the assets of the old Victory Life had been placed in the hands of receivers, Dr. Savory was first and foremost among those who took steps to reorganize the company in order to protect the policyholders. It was due, in a large measure, to his sterling worth and persistent interest, that the plan succeeded. He was made chairman of the board of directors of the reorganized company.

Dr. Savory is a member of several civic organizations and of the Omega Psi Phi fraternity. He belongs to the Baptist Church.

To the student of Negro economics, the opinions of this noted physician should prove valuable. He believes that the doctrine of separate Negro businesses should and must be adhered to until Negroes are given opportunities in proportion to the money they spend in white businesses. He thinks, moreover, that the general economic condition of the race can be improved through this doctrine "to the point where we can furnish employment to a greater number of our group along lines parallel with other racial groups." Dr. Savory believes that a system of interracial business is impractical; because even though such an economic structure were undertaken on a large scale and even though Negroes invested heavily in the enterprises promoted by such a scheme, the degree of employment which Negroes would secure thereby would not be in proportion to the investments and patronage furnished by colored people. He compels respect and consideration for his views when, in succinct language, he states the following as the five greatest difficulties to be overcome in building successful Negro businesses:

1. Acquisition of well-trained personnel
2. Acquiring adequate capital and surplus
3. Lack of appreciation of the value of advertising
4. Lack of confidence in Negroes by Negroes
5. Unwillingness to learn the details of the business

In 1922, Dr. Savory was married to Miss Gertrude Wilson. The couple reside at 119 West 131st Street, New York, and enjoy the serene contentment that accompanies success and many years of unselfish service. Active in civic life, the doctor is secretary-treasurer of the Powell-Savory Corporation, publishers of the

New York Amsterdam News; chairman of the board and treasurer of the Community Personal Finance Corporation, the only Negro owned and operated Finance company licensed under the banking laws of New York to make loans up to $300, and director and secretary of the Brown Bomber Baking Co., Inc. of New York.

JAMES EDGAR MITCHEM, *Secretary*

Some of the lower animals, finding themselves caged, docilely accept the situation. Others rebel at cage-bars and confinement, and never cease to fling themselves against the barriers that stand between them and full freedom. Men are also like that. Some placidly resign themselves to the conditions of restriction that encage their liberties and live their lives out thus subdued.

Early in boyhood the nature of James Edgar Mitchem left no doubt that he would never prefer to travel the path of least resistance if it meant curtailment of his manhood rights and privileges.

Born in the scrawny little village of Arlington, Tennessee, on the threshold of the red hills of eastern Shelby County, the son of James Henry and Ada Byron Mitchem, he was brought by his parents, when an infant, to live in Memphis. Approaching school age, he found himself in a kindergarten under the keen but kindly eyes of Mrs. Julia Hooks, a pioneer teacher in the Bluff City.

From this school he entered LeMoyne Normal Institute of Memphis, from which he graduated in May 1906. He completed the sophomore year at Fisk University in Nashville in 1909. Then followed a course and graduation from the School of Commerce of Northwestern University, Evanston, Illinois. He did post-graduate work in mathematics at the Armour Institute of Technology in 1926, and a year's special study in actuarial mathematics at Columbia University, New York City.

But throughout these school years young Mitchem was not having smooth sailing. His father, though finding steady work in the cooperage industry, needed his son's help in caring for the invalid wife and mother, whose illness continued through many years. For this reason James Edgar had a greater responsibility than that of shifting for himself. He found jobs, variously, washing dishes and waiting in hotels, where he was frequently in clashes with the white authorities, thus losing one such job after another.

In 1909, as one of the Sterling Jubilee Singers, sponsored by the Redpath Lyceum Bureau, young Mitchem had an opportunity

FOUR GENERATIONS OF THE HOUSE OF LEWIS
A. L. Lewis, J. H. Lewis, J. L. Lewis, J. L. Lewis, Jr.

WILLIAM H. LEE
Secretary

MRS. MARY McLEOD BETHUNE
Director

to travel and to make contacts which later proved valuable in making other connections.

From 1910 to 1914, he was engaged at different times and on different roads as a dining-car waiter. For a short while in 1914 he found work as a clerk in the Department of the Interior, Indian Service, in Chicago, Illinois.

Back in Memphis in schooldays he had learned something of printing at LeMoyne Institute, and had received further experience as a printer with E. L. Simon of Memphis, publisher of *The Moon*, a monthly magazine. This experience helped him in securing work in the printing business with Bernard W. Fitts of Chicago, where he served for a year.

In 1915, when Mr. Mitchem found work as an agent under Mr. Albert Clover of the Royal Life Insurance Company of Chicago, Illinois, he knew that his life's work lay in this field. It will be noted that the young man had evinced natural propensities for mathematics, and, in the business of life insurance, he not only found the field for which his talents best fitted him, but he found in Mr. Clover the first white employer who regarded and treated him with that courtesy and respect to which he believed every American citizen is entitled; and, for three years, the enviable record made by J. E. Mitchem as an agent of the Royal challenged the talents of the best agents in that company.

In 1918 he was called to the army and became a Second Lieutenant of the 349th Artillery, 92nd Division, in which connection he saw service in France.

Returning from overseas in 1919, immediately following his honorable discharge, he was engaged as secretary of the Underwriters Mutual Life Insurance Company of Chicago. While connected with the Underwriters Mutual he commenced to attend the sessions of the National Negro Insurance Association, where his active participation in the deliberations, his clear thinking, and the orderliness of his presentations marked him as a man of rare business qualities.

In 1933, when plans were under consideration for the rehabilitation of the Victory Life Insurance Company, it was realized that the complicated nature of its affairs demanded an executive of comprehensive clerical ability. The financial complications were such that they could not be handled by mere routine or mediocrity. Mr. Mitchem was elected secretary, and his mathematical genius and long experience in the financial affairs of the business stood him and his company in good stead in dealing with the situation caused by the entangled condition of the assets of the old Victory Life. He was not long in bringing system and order out of the prevailing chaos and confusion. In the ensuing years he has continued to direct the office work of Victory Mutual with gratifying satisfaction to his associates and the thousands of policyholders of this company.

Mr. Mitchem is a member of the Alpha Phi Alpha Fraternity, the Appomattox Club, and the Umbrian Glee Club. He engages in Y. M. C. A., Y. W. C. A., and N. A. A. C. P. work, as well as other community activities.

This experienced business man believes that a doctrine of separate racial businesses should mark the preliminary stages of the group's commercial progress, and that our ultimate goal should be to find an entree into the general economic fabric of the nation on a level of full and equal participation with other Americans.

Mr. Mitchem married in August 1920 Miss Katie M. Fowler, then a resident of Chicago, but who formerly lived in Atlanta, Georgia. He and his wife have a son, James Edgar, Jr., to whose education and home training they devote loving but firm and painstaking attention. The Mitchems enjoy a happy and attractive home at 6015 South Loomis Boulevard, in Chicago.[2]

DR. CLILAN BETHANY POWELL, *New York City, Vice President*

Not only heroes, but also men of less spectacular roles, often find their opportunities for distinction in the stress of emergencies. Some ride their opportunities to fame and fortune; others are content if only they have a chance to make unselfish contributions to some worthy cause. The lofty motives and noble conduct of Dr. Clilan Bethany Powell in connection with Victory Mutual Life Insurance Company place him unquestionably in the latter class.

Some of the characters in places of prominence and power in the field of Negro life insurance, caught in the current of the early trends of their lives, have been swept up to high stations on the crest of fortunate circumstances. Others have entered the field with frank premeditation of profit from investments. Dr. Powell is among the few who have been willing to contribute of their time

[2] Both Mr. and Mrs. Mitchem have died since this book was in manuscript; the former in Many 1940 the latter in December 1939.

and means solely to remedy a failure, to prevent lost confidence in and embarrassment of Negro business.

When he joined in forming a protective committee to reorganize Victory Life as a mutual company for the protection of Negro policyholders, he knew full well that he could expect no stock dividends in a mutual company. He knew, moreover, that the undertaking was fraught with the possibilities of failure and resultant personal embarrassment for him and his associates. He was fully aware that the plan which he and they were attempting was highly innovational in nature. Nothing like it had so far been attempted in the annals of the business of Negro life insurance. Besides, this organizational venture was launched in a period that marked the lowest ebb and the most chaotic condition in the history of American business. But the commendable zeal which actuated Dr. Powell to make an effective contribution in rescuing Victory Life was not deterred because of these conditions. They held for him a challenge which he met with courage. Even in those stringent times, he was enjoying a lucrative practice as an X-ray specialist in the city of New York, and did not need this connection with Victory Mutual for personal benefit.

Clilan Bethany Powell was born of Eliza and Everett Powell, August 8, 1894, at Newport News, Virginia. His father before him was an industrious and thrifty man, and, as a driller in a shipyard, he made and saved enough to assist in the education of his son. Young Clilan attended the public schools at Newport News and then finished from the Virginia State College at Petersburg, following which he took up the study of medicine at Howard University, Washington, D. C.

In school, like many other young men of brilliant minds, Mr. Powell did not find it necessary to bind himself down to rigid application to his studies. Ordinarily he was just a fair scholar, but at times when he was seized with the ambition to excel, he had no great trouble in doing so. He was a good scholar when he wanted to be, and his brilliance has asserted itself in every phase of his post-school life.

Dr. Powell is first vice president, chairman of the finance committee, and vice chairman of the board of directors of Victory Mutual Life Insurance Company.

It is to be noted that this busy man of medicine, with an active official connection with the company, has found time to take a course in Life Insurance Management. Is not this a challenge to many engaged full time in the business, who are attempting to prosecute it without the benefit of systematic training?

Further evidence of Dr. Powell's business ability and versatility is the fact that he was a co-organizer of the Community Personal Finance Corporation—a small loan company licensed under the New York State Bank Department to make loans up to $300—which has a capital of $100,000, with a loan balance of $40,000. He is president and editor of the New York Amsterdam News and a member of the Audit Bureau of Circulations. This newspaper has the largest audited circulation among the Negro population of New York, and is the third largest in the country in both circulation and advertising. In addition to these prominent connections, he also is a director in several smaller companies.

Dr. Powell believes that the policy of separate racial businesses is determinable by local conditions, and that this should be taken into consideration by Negro business men contemplating entering the business field.

In October 1938, Dr. Powell was married to Miss Lena Audrey Dukes of Boston, Massachusetts, and they make their home in New York City.

BISHOP R. A. VALENTINE, *Vice-President-Treasurer*

Perhaps the intellectual and economic poverty of the American Negro would now be greater but for the fact that, however fortunately removed from the peculiar general racial difficulties in this country, members of the race everywhere have most often been willing to share the lot common to Negroes.

The life of Bishop R. A. Valentine, vice president and treasurer of the Victory Mutual Life Insurance Company, illustrates this point and emphasizes the natural racial loyalty that has always been a moving force in his nature. He was born May 2, 1880, on the island of Antigua, British West Indies, of Emma Byrd and Casello Johnson Valentine. His father was an industrious carpenter and interior decorator, and highly respected. Although of moderate means, he assisted in the education of his son, which began in the St. Peters Parochial School under the supervision of the British Government. Young Valentine further pursued his education by taking a four year preparatory course at Teachers College. Then he became qualified to take the Leeward Islands competitive

106

examination; and in 1900 he was granted the Leeward Islands Government Scholarship, a much coveted prize. In the same year he entered the Mico Teachers College in the Island of Jamaica, where he spent three years. Returning to Antigua he was appointed principal of St. Peters School, which he had first attended when a boy. In 1906 he was promoted to the principalship of the St. Georges Parochial School in the Island of Montserrat. After two year's service here Mr. Valentine was granted a leave of absence to visit Montreal, Canada, where he found his associations so congenial that he remained during the next twelve years. Then, although enjoying the blessing of liberty and full opportunity for which Canada is noted, he yielded to a pressing sense of duty to share the conditions under which his race in the United States lives, and to participate in its contest against racial discrimination. In 1920 he moved with his family to Chicago, where he has since lived.

Investigations of Mr. Valentine's life reveal an early and deep interest in matters of religion; in fact, there are indications that at one time he was ambitious to devote his entire life to the ministry. He took special lectures and studies in the Anglican Theological College at Up Park Camp in Jamaica, after which he qualified as an authoritative Catechist. However, Mr. Valentine's natural love of liberty rebelled against the restrictions imposed by the Protestant Episcopal Church on its Negro membership; and so he renounced his allegiance to the Episcopacy of that Church and connected himself with the African Orthodox Church, which, although closely identified with the doctrines of Catholicism, is governed by Negroes. Soon after moving to Chicago, he organized the St. Matthews Church in that city and is still its rector. In 1929, at a meeting of the Synod in Philadelphia, he was elected to the Episcopate, and on May 30th of the next year was consecrated a bishop.

But the religious zeal of this distinguished prelate has only heightened his interest in the economic freedom and progress of his people. Impelled by the ambition to serve his people in the two phases that he believes most vitally affect their progress—the ministry and their economic improvement—Mr. Valentine early subjected himself to rigid and studious preparation for both lines of endeavor.

Soon after arriving in Montreal he took a commercial course at the Mount Royal Business College, after which he secured work

107

in the subscription department of *The Witness,* a Canadian newspaper. Due to his thorough preparation and qualifications, the Canadian Pacific Railroad soon secured his services as an auditor in its Freight Claim office. Meanwhile, he used his spare moments as a part time agent for the Manufacturers Life Insurance Company of Canada. This connection, however, exposed to him a subtle practice in discrimination practised by this company in limiting Negro applicants to a sub-standard form of policy. Immediately he severed his connection with the Manufacturers and went to work for the Confederation Life, first having it distinctly understood that qualified Negro applicants would be granted the same types of insurance as all others.

Shortly after moving to Chicago in 1920 Valentine became a stockholder in and an agent for the Public Life Insurance Company, in the employ of which several prominent Negro insurance characters first saw service. When Anthony Overton and others commenced the organization of the Victory Life Insurance Company, Mr. Valentine was among the first to purchase its stock, and, as a result, he became enthusiastic about insurance in the lives of American Negroes. When the old Victory Life passed into the hands of the receivers Bishop Valentine did not despair. A pet aphorism with him had always been "accept failure with a smile," and this he not only did but set about in association with John Holloman and Dr. Savory and others to protect the policyholders of Victory Life and save the confidence of Negroes in their leaders. This determination resulted in the organization of the Victory Mutual Life Insurance Company of Chicago, of which Bishop R. A. Valentine is third vice president and treasurer.

In 1906 Mr. Valentine was married to Miss Irene Ashby White and they are the parents of the following children: Vivian Lawrence, Clarence, Emma Violet, Robert Richard, and Cyril Johnson.

Chapter V.

SOUTHERN ORGANIZATIONS

AFRO-AMERICAN LIFE INSURANCE COMPANY, JACKSONVILLE, FLORIDA

ONE night in March 1901, there were gathered in the pastor's study in the parsonage of Bethel Baptist Institutional Church seven Negro men, pioneer citizens of Jacksonville, Florida.

These seven Negroes had observed the distressing conditions among their people, and felt the need of some plan by which this suffering might be relieved. They started the organization that was later incorporated as the Afro-American Industrial Benefit Association. One thousand dollars was raised and the Association first capitalized.

From the Afro-American Industrial Benefit Association with $1,000 capital there came in time the Afro-American Insurance Company with capitalization of $25,000, and then the Afro-American Life Insurance Company with a fully paid-up capital of $200,000.

Of the seven founders of the Afro-American, five have died, namely: Tilman Valentine, E. W. Latson, Reverend J. E. Gregg, President A. W. Price and Reverend J. Milton Waldron. Dr. A. W. Smith long since has severed his connection with the institution to devote his entire time to the practice of medicine.

The one remaining founder, A. L. Lewis, was promoted first to serve as secretary; and, upon the death of President A. W. Price twenty years ago, he was chosen president. The eighteen years of his administration were the most successful of the company's existence. The capital, surplus and assets increased steadily; employment was given to hundreds of additional men and women, and the company qualified for business in the State of Georgia.

On December 31, 1936, Mr. A. L. Lewis voluntarily retired from the presidency and was succeeded by his son, J. H. Lewis, the present incumbent, the father becoming chairman of the board of directors.

L. D. Ervin, cashier and vice president, has the distinction of being the first agent to represent the company, and by his ability and loyalty has won steady advancement, having filled every office except that of president.

The secretary, W. H. Lee, also came up from the agency ranks by reason of merit.

The officers and directors of Afro-American for the year 1939 were as follows:

A. L. Lewis	Chairman of Board and Treasurer
J. H. Lewis	President
L. D. Ervin	1st Vice President and Cashier
W. H. Lee	2nd Vice President and Secretary
J. L. Lewis	3rd Vice President and Assistant Treasurer
R. L. Brown, M.D.	Medical Director
S. D. McGill	Attorney
A. St. Geo. Richardson	Assistant Secretary
F. W. Barnes	Assistant Cashier

Other members of the board are:

Mrs. Mary M. Bethune	Rev. S. J. Johnson
Rev. K. D. Britt	Dr. Theodore L. Long
Prof. N. W. Collier	Dr. T. L. Lowrie
Rev. J. R. Evans	J. S. McLane
Bishop R. A. Grant	Kelsey L. Pharr
Rev. J. J. Heath	D. D. Powell
Mrs. M. E. Harris	Dr. W. S. Stevens

These men and women bring to the company a wealth of rich experience and far-reaching influence.

The assistant officers, auditors, bookkeepers, supervisors, superintendents, agents, and employees are graduates of various institutions of learning. They not only efficiently serve the company in their several capacities, but engage in the social, religious, civic, and business activities of the Negroes in their respective localities.

ABRAHAM LINCOLN LEWIS

Chairman of the Board of Directors and Former President

Abraham Lincoln Lewis was born in Madison, West Florida, in 1865, of sturdy, pioneer Christian parents, Robert and Julia Lewis. Of humble parentage, with meager surroundings, and extremely limited opportunities, he had the sober influence of a Christian home, modest though it was.

In the earliest period of his childhood, he was, by precept and example, led into the recognition of Christian worship. Barefoot, he would accompany his mother to the church of her choice more than three miles distant from their small home. Thus, his connection with and reverential love for the African Methodist Church began very early in his life, and have been more and more evident as controlling forces up through the changes of childhood, youth, manhood, and maturity.

He came to Jacksonville, Florida, in the year 1880, and for a few brief terms availed himself of such limited educational training as was offered through Oakland Public School under the tutorship of a Professor Gibbs. Before he could complete his graded course of study, acute economic difficulties forced the boy to seek employment. He succeeded in getting the job of water-boy for the employees of one of the largest sawmills and lumber plants, at that time, the chief industry of Jacksonville.

By nature industrious, Abraham Lewis early cultivated habits of thrift, and, even as a youth, adhered rigidly to his plan of saving something out of his earnings, no matter how small they were.

He proved faithful, trustworthy, and dependable as a water-boy, and as the years passed was given merited recognition by his employers, being advanced in work and wages until he was finally made foreman, receiving the highest wage paid any man of his color. He remained a trusted employee of this firm for a period of twenty-two years.

Mr. Lewis joined the Mt. Olive African Methodist Episcopal Church of Jacksonville in 1884, and has since been a member. Repeatedly, he has been a delegate to the general conference of his church, and has also served as trustee and treasurer of the Edward Waters College, which is supported by that denomination. For fifty-four years he has been superintendent of his Sunday school. He now serves as a member of the Episcopal Committee of the General Conference of his church. Wilberforce University recently conferred upon him the honorary degree of Doctor of Laws.

Like many other Negro leaders, A. L. Lewis clearly saw the need of organization in the early decades following the Civil War and reconstruction days. To him, as to others, the fraternal orders and secret societies seemed to offer the best opportunity for organized efforts among Negroes.

He was the founder of the Sons and Daughters of Jacob, and for many years steered its affairs with success and credit.

He served as treasurer of the Endowment or Insurance Department of the Masonic Order. It was chiefly through his business acumen that the lot was secured and the present imposing structure, the Masonic Temple, built, and paid for in a short time. This building is in the uptown business district of Greater Jacksonville, and is perhaps the most valuable structure and business unit owned by Negroes in Florida.

He still maintains an interest in Masonic circles and strives to keep alive the spirit of Masonry in these times of the waning popularity of fraternal societies.

The Negroes of Jacksonville, when the city was shocked many years ago by the lynching of two colored men within its borders, sought the advice of A. L. Lewis, and he advised them that the influence of Negroes would be sufficiently strong to prevent such dastardly crimes only when Negroes became factors in business and politics strong enough to force recognition. The colored people of Jacksonville believed what he told them, and that was the turning point in the sentiment of colored people for Negro business in that city.

Today, the Afro-American Life has a weekly industrial debit in excess of $8,000 in Jacksonville, the largest debit in a colored insurance company in any city.

A. L. Lewis is rated as one of the wealthiest members of his race. His holdings in city, suburban, improved business and residential properties are extensive and valuable. Whether a farm or cemetery it seemed always to turn to gold when it fell into his hands.

Mr. Lewis was elected vice president of the National Negro Insurance Association in August 1924, and on the death of Frank L. Gillespie in 1925 he became president. In recognition of the splendid services he performed during the unexpired term of Gillespie, he was re-elected August 7, 1925, and served the full term with great credit.

This wealthy man is among the few Negroes who have been able to accumulate a competence and then a surplus for leisure and travel. In 1935, he, with other prominent business and professional men, made a good-will tour of the Republic of Haiti. The survey and clarifying observations which they were able to make as a result of the trip are interesting in showing, by comparison, the more favorable condition of Negroes in the United States.

Then, in realization of a long cherished dream, in the summer of 1937, he spent a long vacation traveling in Europe, visiting the Holy Land and many other places of interest.

Mr. Lewis believes that more earnest efforts should be made by the leaders to influence the younger people of the race to follow definite plans of thrift and economy. He thinks that there are many great business opportunities, but that these cannot be embraced unless the youth of the race make ready for them by saving.

Mr. Lewis was first married in 1885 to Miss Mary Sammis, and to them three children were born, two of whom are deceased. The one remaining, James H., is now president of the Afro-American Life Insurance Company. This happy union lasted thirty-eight years, but was broken in February 1923, when the devoted wife passed away. He was again married in 1925, and he and Mrs. Lewis enjoy a happy life in their beautiful home in Jacksonville.

WILLIAM HENRY LEE, *Secretary*

William Henry Lee was born in Atlanta, Georgia, April 26, 1873. He was educated in the public schools of Atlanta and at Atlanta University.

He began life as a teacher in the public schools of Georgia and served in this capacity for a period of five years, by which time he was convinced that his talents fitted him best for service in the field of finance.

As a stepping stone, therefore, he took the civil service examination and was appointed to the position of post office clerk in Atlanta.

At the age of thirty-five he gave up his position in the post office to become an insurance agent. It was then that he seemed really to have found his life work, and he began a steady ascent in business. His exceptional service as an agent soon qualified him for a position as superintendent and then as assistant manager. Sixteen years ago, in recognition of his constantly valuable work on the field, the Afro-American Life Insurance Company chose him as its secretary, and later, made him also vice president and a member of the board of directors.

Mr. Lee has also other business interests and prominent connections in them. He is a member of the board of directors and secretary of the Fifty-Fifty Bottling Company of Jacksonville, and a member of the board of directors and secretary of the Afro-American Investment Association.

Mr. Lee is Brigadier General, commanding the Florida Brigade of the Uniform Rank, Knights of Pythias.

He is a communicant of Bethel Baptist Institutional Church; teacher of one of the largest men's Bible classes in the South; and has served over a thirty-year period as superintendent of the Sunday school and as a deacon and trustee.

In April 1932 he was elected president of the National Negro Insurance Association, serving a full term with outstanding credit and success.

Early in life he married Miss Jerusha Burnham, who was prominent in the public schools of Jacksonville, Florida, and in the civic and charitable activities of that city.

MRS. MARY MCLEOD BETHUNE, *Director*

It is with consciousness of inability to do justice to the qualities of this noble woman that the telling of her story is undertaken. To enter her presence is to become aware of an atmosphere of unusual executive ability. Her every movement radiates self-command and self-confidence. She seems to sway men and women as she moves among them.

Superb courage, driving energy, positive decisions, plans relentlessly pursued—the impression of these is inevitably made when this inspired woman is observed in action in any cause. But the moving forces behind these qualities are her deep sympathy for and desire to be of benefit to the unfortunate, and a strong faith in God.

Mary McLeod was one of a family of seventeen children. She was born of slave parents, Sam and Patsy McLeod, in a humble cabin on a rice and cotton farm near Mayesville, South Carolina.

When Mary was but eleven years old, a little school was opened near Mayesville by the Board of Missions of the Presbyterian Church. At the time her mother said: "We had to make some of the children go, but it seemed that Mary understood what it all meant."

In a few years the little school had done its best for Mary, and Miss Emma Wilson, her beloved teacher, told her one day that Miss Mary Crissman, a dressmaker in Denver, Colorado, wanted to pay

114

for a little girl's schooling at Scotia Seminary; Miss Wilson had chosen Mary to go, because she had done so well in school. With a heart overflowing with joy the child ran home with the good news, and started preparing herself for the journey to North Carolina.

Arrived at Scotia, awkward and shy at first, she was often the victim of foolish rebuffs and ridicule, but she met every slight and criticism with unfailing good humor, and soon won the hearts of teachers and students alike.

At the close of her work at Scotia, she received a scholarship that enabled her to continue her studies at the Moody Bible Institute in Chicago.

At the end of two years at Moody's, Mary McLeod hoped to see the fulfillment of a long cherished hope to go to Africa as a missionary, but a bitter disappointment awaited her. At the Presbyterian Board of Missions it was found that there would be no vacancies, and she was appointed a teacher at Haines Institute, Augusta, Georgia.

Within a short time, with her true missionary spirit, she had gathered a large group of little children from the streets, and was holding with them a little "mission school" on Sunday afternoons.

Her next point of service was Sumter, South Carolina. She taught there two years. It was there that she met and married Albert Bethune, a teacher, and moved to Savannah, Georgia. The next two years were spent in quiet home life, and during this period her son, Albert McLeod Bethune, was born. Then again came the call to service—this time to Palatka, Florida.

In Palatka, Mrs. Bethune taught at a mission school and rendered a most remarkable service—reading, visiting, and teaching the prisoners in the county jail. The end of five years found Mary McLeod Bethune on the way to Daytona, with her little boy. After paying her fare from Palatka, she had $1.50 in her purse; but there is no way of estimating the value of her faith, her courage, and her yearning to serve her people.

The great need for a school for girls in Daytona and the vicinity was painfully apparent to Mrs. Bethune, and she had a burning desire to establish such an institution. She was faced with difficulty, however, in securing a shelter for herself and such a school. Her energy and faith stood her in good stead at this point; for she soon had a little cabin, rented to her on faith by a good man. The house, being found, there was no furniture; but

115

with the resourcefulness that is characteristic of her, she procured dry goods boxes from neighboring stores, pieces of discarded matting or carpet, a bed or two, and proceeded to make and repair furniture.

At last, the little cabin was in readiness and on October 4, 1904, in a room where everything was simple and even crude, but scrupulously clean, Mrs. Bethune opened her school. Five little girls answered the ringing of the bell, and the first session opened with the thirty-second Psalm and the singing of an old hymn, "Leaning on the Everlasting Arms."

Trials and struggles have accompanied the growth of the Institution under the guidance of Mrs. Bethune. The thirty-two acres of land that comprise the main campus, were purchased with a down payment of $5 secured from the sale of cakes and confections. From its inception, the personnel of the little school— teachers and students— has been fired with Mrs. Bethune's enthusiasm. The first building, Faith Hall, was literally "sung up" by Mrs. Bethune and her students. The evolution from the little cabin to the present campus, composed of fourteen beautiful modern buildings and valued at almost a million dollars, seems more of a dream than a reality. And Mrs. Bethune says that it is "a vision come true." The confidence of the public has been won and kept.

The service of this unusual woman to her race and country has placed her in the highest ranks of living Americans. When, a few years ago, Ida Tarbell published a list of the fifty greatest women in the United States, she included the name of a Negro woman—Mary McLeod Bethune. Miss Tarbell's measuring rod of selection was the "ability to initiate or create, and ability to carry on." Honorary degrees of Master of Arts, Doctor of Laws, and Doctor of Humanities have been conferred upon Mrs. Bethune by outstanding universities. She has been awarded the Spingarn Medal for the year's greatest achivement of a Negro citizen of the United States.

But, notwithstanding the numerous and varied activities in the field of education and uplift work, Mrs. Bethune has not been indifferent to the necessity for the business development of her people. Years ago she became a stockholder and director in the Afro-American Life Insurance Company.

She was one of the founders and for a number of years also a director of the Central Life Insurance Company of Tampa,

Florida, but in recent years she has transferred her holdings to her son, who has succeeded her as a director of that company. She has also served as vice president and director of the commission on Interracial Cooperation and of the National Urban League.

When the National Youth Administration was established by President Roosevelt she was named with another of her race to serve on the National Advisory Committee. So effective was her work on this committee that she was called to Washington as the resident director of the Division of Negro Affairs of this organization. She was appointed to serve on the President's Committee on Farm Tenancy. In January 1937, she directed the organization of a conference in Washington to discuss and provide for racial needs, to which Negroes of every vocation were called.

Mrs. Bethune has traveled extensively in America and abroad. Her name now is a byword, synonomous with achievement. Schools, clubs, and organizations in every section seek permission to use her name for various purposes. Up from the cotton fields Mary McLeod Bethune has come into her own as one of the greatest of American women.

THE ATLANTA LIFE INSURANCE COMPANY
THE LATE ALONZO F. HERNDON
Greatest Negro Financier

PROMINENT in the organization of the Mutual Aid Association, which later became the Atlanta Life Insurance Company, appear the names of the Reverends P. J. Bryant and J. A. Hopkins. It was these two ministers who under the laws of the State of Georgia in 1904 organized an association for the relief of its members, in cases of sickness or accident, by the payment of small benefits, ranging from $1 to $5 per week for a limited number of weeks in each calendar year. Provisions were also made for defraying the burial expense of each member in amounts ranging from $10 to $50. A weekly premium or assessment from 5 to 25 cents was charged to assure the payment of the benefits promised.

The Mutual Aid Association operated under the management of these two ministers until some time in the year 1905. The laws of Georgia had until this time imposed no rigid restrictions upon the organization and operation of burial or benefit associations of this nature. Because of this laxness and the ease with which such associations could be organized, large numbers of them commenced

117

to operate in that state. Naturally, unethical practices, abuses, and mismanagement became pronounced. It was soon generally realized that some steps for the protection of the citizens who might be imposed upon by unscrupulous and incompetent persons, in the organization and improper operation of these associations, must be taken.

In 1905, Georgia passed a law requiring all such associations in the state to place on deposit the sum of $5,000 for the protection of policy or certificate holders.

The enactment of this law caused consternation in the ranks of the officials of the many benefit associations in the state. Not many colored men who were able to deposit $5,000 could be found. Most of the few who could did not have the vision or courage to venture this large sum of money in the development of a new and unproved field.

The life insurance business among American Negroes would not be what it is today if, in the crisis created in colored benefit association circles in Georgia by the enactment of the $5,000 Guaranty Law, there had not stepped into the breach a young man with courage, vision, and the money. That man was Alonzo F. Herndon.

A. F. Herndon was born a slave in Walton County, Georgia, June 26, 1858. He started life as a farm hand, working for almost nothing. But he stole away from the scenes of his boyhood before he was twenty-one years of age, and went to Senoia, Georgia. Again, he worked at the only thing he knew—as a day laborer on the farm. In this early day, everything he did, even the little jobs, whether on the farm or elsewhere, he did the best he could, and always wished that he could do better. On Saturday afternoons, he started cutting hair at Senoia. He had no shop or adequate tools; but in some way he picked up an old pair of scissors and an old-fashioned razor, on which, with a whet-stone and a little water, he always kept the finest edges. He rented a little corner in the colored section, and soon his reputation as a fine barber spread throughout the community. In a short time, he had to work until midnight every Saturday to serve his patrons.

Always thrifty, Herndon in about three months at Senoia had saved enough money to open his own first barber shop, which he did in Jonesboro, Georgia. In that little town his good reputation as a barber soon again became well known. Successful, his vision

118

THE LATE ALONZO F. HERNDON
Founder

EUGENE M. MARTIN, JR.
Secretary

LIEUT. GEORGE W. LEE
Director

now reached beyond the confines of a small, country town. He wanted yet larger and better things. In January 1882, not yet twenty-four years old, he made his way to Atlanta.

The unusual sights and complications of the big city somewhat awed him at first, but he soon overcame his timidity and sought and found a job as a journeyman barber. Receiving fair earnings, which he carefully saved, he was able in 1886 to furnish and open his own shop on Whitehall Street.

A rare blend of sincerity, honesty, and innocent good humor were apparent in the disposition of Mr. Herndon; and these qualities made a favorable impression on all who came in contact with him. Among those who were impressed by these traits was a white merchant and capitalist, named Silvey. When this man opened Markham House and fitted it up as a fine hotel, he provided space for a barber shop. A barber shop in a hotel at that time was somewhat of a novelty; but Mr. Silvey believed that Alonzo Herndon's popularity would greatly help in successfully establishing the venture. During the nine years the young colored barber worked in this hotel shop, hundreds of white men went to the hotel just to be served by Herndon. His personality became an attraction of the hotel. The shop had to be enlarged and several assistants employed to accomodate its patrons. Among those assistants was C. H. Faison, a constant friend throughout Mr. Herndon's life. Mr. Faison became one of the directors of the Atlanta Life Insurance Company.

But success, however great, in the employ of another man was not the height of Alonzo Herndon's ambition. He wanted a big shop of his own, and he had saved the money to fit it up. Mr. Silvey gave him no excuse for leaving his hotel. In fact, it was made so congenial for him that he probably would have remained longer had not the place been destroyed by fire on May 17, 1896.

Mr. Herndon then opened two shops of his own, meant only to occupy him until he could find the location and make preparation for a far greater venture in the barbering business. He realized that to maintain success he would have to measure up to the best that white competitors now entering the field could provide. He therefore resolved to have the finest shop in the world.

In the years intervening, between the burning of the Markham Hotel and the opening of his Peachtree Street shop in 1904, the young man traveled to all of the larger cities of the United States,

119

investigating barber shops. He found one in Los Angeles, California, considered there to have been the finest in the world. He then returned to Atlanta determined to equip one to excel the finest. Thus, in the year 1904, he opened his Peachtree Street shop. It became the most popular and most successful business of its kind in the country, and so continued for years. As late as 1937, it was still in the hands of colored barbers, but for white patronage.

Mr. Herndon's influence in the latter years of his life was able to defeat a bill introduced in the Georgia legislature making it a violation of law for white people to be served by colored barbers. Allegedly, this bill was inspired by competitors.

The courage and the vision of this man looms greater in retrospect when it is remembered that on the advent of white barbers in the South, he fitted up this fine barber shop at 66 Peachtree Street and invested a fortune in it, while, at the same time, remaining proprietor of two other shops. Here was a colored man daring to make a determined fight for white business against white competitors. Many said it was a foolhardy venture; but soon, in his three shops, he was giving employment to seventy-five men.

Successful in the barbering business, even beyond his expectations, he now turned his attention to organized services for the benefit of the masses. He bought the association started by the Reverends Bryant and Hopkins for the fabulous sum of $160, in the summer of 1905. In the office of the association at this time was an old "blind" typewriter, two secondhand desks, a table, a half dozen rickety chairs, a few lead pencils, and two or three rust-eaten pen staffs and points. The business in force did not exceed $100, and the full-time employees consisted of one agent and a clerk. The only office was one room in the Rucker Building, Auburn and Piedmont Avenues, in Atlanta.

He gave his newly acquired association the name of the Atlanta Mutual; and then, to establish confidence, he commenced to take over several of the small associations that were not able to comply with the Georgia law. The following are among the insurance associations and organizations that the Atlanta Mutual (later changed to Atlanta Life, has taken over and reinsured during the past thirty years:

Alabama Protection	Metropolitan Mutual
American Mutual	Royal Association

Atlanta Benevolent	Royal Benefit
Benevolent Union	Union Benefit
Booker T. Washington	Union Central
Empire Industrial	Union Mutual of Alabama
Great Southern Home	Union Mutual of Georgia
Liberty	

Under the competent direction of A. F. Herndon, the business of the Atlanta Mutual commenced almost immediately to increase rapidly. His reputation for fair dealing and his business ability were now established throughout Georgia, with the result that young men, ambitious to enter the field of insurance, sought to be connected with his company as agents or managers.

In 1910, the Atlanta Mutual qualified for business in the State of Alabama. In a comparatively short time the Birmingham district of the company became the largest Negro industrial unit in the country outside of Atlanta. In 1914, the company reinsured the business of the Union Mutual Aid, then one of the largest Negro industrial companies in the South.

Mr. Herndon soon realized that however popular the idea of mutual cooperation, some capital would be needed to finance the rapidly growing business of the organization. In 1916, capital stock amounting to $25,000 was subscribed and sold. All of this, except a few shares taken by his immediate friends, was purchased by Mr. Herndon himself.

Also, in 1916, a department of industrial straight life business was organized to write policies with a maximum single benefit not in excess of $500.

Again, in 1922, he increased the capital stock of the company to $100,000, all but a negligible part of which he bought. At this time he had the charter amended, the name again changed to Atlanta Life Insurance Company, and the company authorized to write all classes of life, and life-and-disability insurance from $10 to $10,000. The Atlanta Life Insurance Company, the pride of 12,000,000 Negroes, the wonder and admiration of thousands of white people of America, was now well on its way; and its founder was already contemplating plans to double the company's capital. During the succeeding years with this increased capital, its growth became no less gratifying than the increasing soundness of its methods.

The dauntless energy that had dominated the career of this

121

remarkable man stopped on July 20, 1927; and thus passed the greatest Negro financier produced in the little more than the half century during which he lived. His name will live among the names of those whose work has been of such enduring nature as to project itself across the grave to posterity. Never was his unusual career marred by the breath of suspicion. No one ever charged him with unfairness. The stability of Atlanta Life, so well established by him is beyond doubt.

Following the death of the great capitalist, the white and colored press and prominent acquaintances extolled his life and work in lavish eulogies, brief quotations from a few of which are given:

* * *

EXCERPTS FROM *Vision*

By Reverend W. J. Faulkner, Pastor, First Congregational Church, Atlanta, Georgia

He was a friend to man—among the lowly of earth as well as the favored. His sense of justice and right was exercised toward prince and pauper alike. He had faith in folks and worked among them to help them in their struggles upward. In his dealings with men he strove to keep his conscience free of guilt—of word of offense to God and man.

By Lieutenant George W. Lee, Author of Beale Street *and* River George

The Captain of our army has made his last stand. He fell on the battlefield of economic conquest with his boots on. His sword was unsheathed and held high, and, dying he flung back to his host: "Fight on, fight on until the cause has been made secure."

By Dr. George Cleveland Hall, Chicago, Illinois

Alonzo F. Herndon lived at No. 1 University Place. He should have had a home on the campus of every college in the city of Atlanta, as a living example of what a high purpose, a high resolve and a sterling character will do for one who makes life worth while. He held no A.M. or LL.D. He was educated in the great "University of Life."

By C. H. Faison, Director, Atlanta Life Insurance Company

When a boy of fifteen, I came to Georgia. I applied for

and obtained work with Mr. Herndon in his barber shop in the Markham House. From that time until 1904, I worked for him as a journeyman. In July of that year he and I entered into a partnership and opened a shop at 100 North Pryor Street. That cordial relationship existed until the present time. In all of these years, our friendship grew and ripened more and more. He loved young men and it was his pleasure to advise them along business lines.

By President M. W. Adams, Atlanta University

His conservative and wise management of affairs in the business world is well known to us all. So strongly did it impress me that when I was given the opportunity this spring to nominate candidates for the Harmon award in the field of business, I nominated Mr. Herndon as being worthy of that award. And only this morning I wrote to the Foundation to which I had sent my nomination, informing them of his death.

From The Barbers, *by J. C. Chapman*

We have gathered here this morning to pay a tribute of respect to a good citizen, and a Christian gentleman. I have been associated with him for thirty years or more, employed as a barber. He was honest, always gentle and kind, desiring that his barbers give the best services possible to his customers. Mr. Herndon never allowed any unfairness. We will miss him because of his good advice and the many things he has done for our Race. We loved and respected him.

By C. C. Spaulding, President, North Carolina Mutual Life Insurance Company, Durham, N. C.

Emerson said: "What you are sounds so loud I can't hear what you say you are." This is most applicable to the deceased, Mr. A. F. Herndon. His life, character and integrity speak so loud among Negro business men of the country that what we might say would not be necessary. The Negro business men of America regarded Mr. Herndon as one of the sanest and most successful men of the Race."

WHITE AND BLACK VIEW HERNDON IN STATE
by "Fuzzy" Woodruff, [Atlanta Georgian]

Alonzo F. Herndon, who was born a slave down at Social

Circle, Georgia, not three score and ten years ago, rested in state from 8 o'clock to 10 o'clock this morning at the First Congregational Church of the people of his Race. Through the two hours the bier remained in the church before the funeral services, literally thousands of Atlanta's colored citizens passed the pall and gazed with awe and reverence on the features of the man whose life had pointed them the way out of darkness.

Honored by Whites

And, interspersed with the thousands of Negroes, were hundreds of the best white citizens of Atlanta, there to mourn the passing of a man whose life had told the story of how a Negro could achieve eminence and retain the friendship and regard of every kind and class and creed in his community.

He was born a slave, and still the English he spoke was meticulously and unaffectedly correct. He grew up in the darkest hours his Race has ever known, and he achieved a dignity and an inborn courtesy that always made him a marked man himself.

He left a splendid record for charity. His gifts toward altruism, especially for the furtherance of the progress of his Race, were enormous, but they had always been quietly contributed; and, above all, he had always lived at peace and in harmony with the civilization of which he was an important part.

*   *   *

The fine staff, into whose hands fell the direction of the great Atlanta Life after the passing of its founder, soon after his death enacted into reality one of the great plans they knew he had had in mind. In 1929, the capital stock of Atlanta Life was increased to $250,000, and all of the additional issue was immediately subscribed in cash.

The complete roster of the officers and staff of Atlanta Life Insurance Company, January 1, 1939, follows:

President Treasurer	N. B. Herndon
First Vice President	Mrs. A. F. Herndon
Second Vice President	
Director of Agencies	L. H. Haywood
Third Vice President &	
Assistant Agency Director	H. W. Russell

Secretary	E. M. Martin
Auditor	F. A. Toomer
Assistant Secretary Cashier	W. H. Smith
Medical Director	C. C. Cater, M. D.
Assistant Agency Director	Cyrus Campfield
Assistant Agency Director	Charles W. Greene
Assistant Agency Director	C. N. Walker
Manager Ordinary Department	W. C. Thomas
Manager Printing Department	H. L. Conley
Sup't. Industrial Clerical Department	Miss Jessie E. Reid

Directors

N. B. Herndon	E. M. Martin
Mrs. A. F. Herndon	W. H. Smith
L. H. Haywood	F. A. Tomer
H. W. Russell	George W. Lee

A. F. Herndon, II

NORRIS B. HERNDON, *President*

Norris B. Herndon was born in Atlanta, Georgia, the son of the late renowned Alonzo F. Herndon, founder of the Atlanta Life Insurance Company. He is a graduate of Atlanta University and of the Harvard School of Business Administration.

In 1927, on the death of his illustrious father, he became president of the great company the latter founded; but, prior to this, he had seen service in various positions, both on the field and in the home office, so that he assumed the responsibilities of president of the company well prepared with a practical knowledge of all phases of the business.

Under his administration, the capital stock of the company has been increased from $100,000 to $250,000; the assets from $1,000,000 to $3,390,403.54; surplus to policyholders from $172,298 to $830,850.32; and the insurance in force from $24,096,946 to $50,007,399. The operation of the company has been characterized by the same sound and conservative policies that were so vital a part of the company under his father's masterly guidance.

Mr. Norris B. Herndon, representing his company, was a delegate to the first meeting of the National Negro Insurance Association in Durham, North Carolina, in 1921, and also to the Tenth Annual Session in Atlanta in 1930.

125

Mr. Herndon does not have much time to devote to collateral activities or personal diversions. The numerous heavy duties of the office of president, together with those required for his extensive personal holdings, demand his constant, close attention.

EUGENE M. MARTIN, JR., *Secretary*

Twenty years ago the Atlanta Life was an obsession with some of its officers and employees. Absorbed in its development, "after hours" meant nothing to them. They worked to complete tasks, not just to make time.

It was a cold, dreary evening, "after hours," at the offices of the company, in November 1919, when President Herndon called Eugene M. Martin, Jr. into his office and gave him the astounding information that he wished to elevate him to the position of secretary of the company. He had been entirely unaware that the shrewd and observant eyes of that master executive had marked his hard work, honesty, and devotion to the business entrusted to him; and, though this promotion came as a surprise, it aroused in him a renewed determination to prove worthy.

Mr. Martin was born in Atlanta, October 17, 1888. His parents were Mrs. Mary Elizabeth and Eugene M. Martin, Sr., the latter a letter-carrier. Young Martin was educated in the schools of the city and at Atlanta University. Even though he had the support of his parents while in college, he was no pampered child of wealth and luxury; nor was he content to rely wholly upon his parents for the necessary expenses in college. He secured work in the summer with the Guaranty Mutual Insurance Company of Georgia, and thus was able not only to earn an important part of the money he needed to complete his education, but to learn the rudiments of the insurance business and lay the foundation of a most remarkable career.

Graduating from college, the young man found more interest in an application for an insurance policy than he did in his diploma. He had no trouble securing work as an agent of Atlanta Life; and, almost immediately, the systematic traits, natural to his character, commenced to be reflected in the efficient manner in which he collected and handled his debit. As a result, he was soon advanced to the position of assistant district manager, and then, branch office inspector, district manager, home office auditor; and, in 1917, when the Atlanta Mutual organized its industrial straight life department, Mr. Martin was selected as its director of agents.

At once he revealed that degree of independence and confidence in his own ability that has marked his entire career. He gave up a position with a stipulated salary; and, spurning the offer of an increased stipulation for directing the industrial straight life department, he preferred to be compensated on a commission basis for the business secured. In less than three years his earnings from commissions were such that the company felt justified in offering him the exceptional salary of $4,000 per year to become secretary of the company.

There is no question now that Mr. Herndon, in selecting Mr. Martin to handle the clerical affairs of the company, chose the man best fitted in every way for that job. To appreciate his remarkable comprehension of the complicated problems involved in the business of life insurance, it is necessary to understand the magnitude to which Atlanta Life has grown and the precision with which each year's program is contemplated and the unerring success invariably obtained as a result.

Twenty years of exacting attention to numerous details have to no extent satiated Mr. Martin's appetite for hard work. Today he is the same energetic, careful, hard-working man that he was when he became the director of agents in the industrial department. His company has grown big, its character more corporate, but, with it all, E. M. Martin has always kept abreast of the times, familiar with every phase of the company's work, conversant with every detail of improvement in every department of the company's business.

This busy executive has manifested a keen interest in the progress of the National Negro Insurance Association since its organization. In recognition of his independent, incisive thinking and masterly ability, he was elevated to the presidency of the association at its thirteenth annual session held in Chicago in June 1933. Mr. Martin was not in attendance, and he bears the distinction of being the only person ever elected to that office while absent.

The popular secretary of Atlanta Life is an unassuming, matter-of-fact man; and far from any evidences of egotism, there is in his character modesty and self-effacement; and he lends himself but sparingly to diversions. Tennis is the only game in which he indulges.

He believes Negroes ought to cease focusing on the lighter veins of life, and more heavily stress the more substantial fields of activity. He believes that the economic condition of the group

127

would be much more rapidly improved if, for a period of fifteen or twenty years, the principal program of all of the colleges and high schools consisted of technical training in the fields of commerce and in the trades and manual arts.

It was an event of high social interest to colored Atlantans when, on June 30, 1926, the popular secretary of Atlanta Life was married to Miss Helen Edna White. Mrs. Martin is the sister of the famous Walter White of the National Association for the Advancement of Colored People, and of George White, an official of the American Missionary Association.

The Martins have two lovely little daughters, Madeleine Rose and Helen Gene, who contribute to the happiness of the quiet home life which they enjoy in their beautiful brick bungalow in Atlanta.

HOWARD WALTER RUSSELL,

Vice President and Assistant Agency Director

Howard Walter Russell was born August 18, 1865, at White Sulphur Springs, Georgia, the son of Reuben and Emmalie Russell, with whom he lived until he was twenty-one.

He is a veteran of the insurance field, and typifies that optimsitic, enthusiastic, bubbling energy so necessary to inspire drooping spirits when depressed by the long line of consecutive rebuffs which field agents often encounter. For twenty-five years "Dad" Russell has been the idol and leader of a large section of the field forces of Atlanta Life; and much credit for the high level of sustained increase of the great Georgia company is due to his hard work and natural tact.

Prior to entering the insurance business, Mr. Russell served as a messenger in the General Assembly of the State of Georgia for many years; and served for four years and eight months as the trusted servant of former Governor J. M. Terrill of that state.

During his adult life, he has been an ardent and prominent worker in the Baptist church, and especially in the Sunday school. At one time he was superintendent of a Sunday school of 800 scholars and 85 teachers.

In 1886, Howard Walter Russell was married to Miss Ella M. Martin, and to them have been born three children, Mrs. Maggie D. Carter, Howard R., and Joseph Terrill Russell, the latter deceased.

In his own words: " 'Dad' Russel, with his seventy years, can cover as much territory and write as many applications as any of the younger boys of the company."

Mr. and Mrs. Russell live at 100 Griffin Street, Atlanta, Georgia.

LIEUTENANT GEORGE WASHINGTON LEE,
Director and Manager of West Tennessee Division

If American slavery had cheated its victims only of the market values of their labors of drudgery, the evaluation of this theft, in dollars and cents, would amount to a staggering sum. And yet, even such a Gargantuan measure of human misery, in sordid gold, shrinks into insignificance when compared to the immeasurable values in talent and genius withered by the centuries of human bondage. But, while man's devices in viciousness sometimes defeat ambition and temporarily crush the inherent talents of the gifted, the strains of genius often break through the bonds, perhaps after generations of dormancy; and, manifesting themselves in posterity, make their triumphant contributions to world enlightenment.

In the minds of those who know him in the full maturity of his accomplishments, there is no doubt that Lieutenant George Washington Lee draws heavily from the founts of natural versatility and greatness springing from some strain of ancestry. The gift of vivid expression, both oral and written, the flame of imagination, have been heavily stressed in him; and unquestionably are his predominant characteristics. They are not acquired qualities. They are so natural they may crop out in floods of eloquence, even in ordinary conversation.

George Washington Lee was born January 4, 1894, of the Reverend George and Mrs. Hattie Lee, at Heathman, Mississippi, a mere flagstop between Indianola and Greenville on the Southern Railroad. His father died when George was hardly more than an infant, and the boy and his mother stayed on the plantation for several years, moving then to Indianola, where George had his first chance to enter school.

It was in Indianola that George Lee first felt the active sting of prejudice. He had lived in an area where racial prejudice was as "taken for granted as the sunshine." But the full realization of what it actually meant had not been forced upon him until a white merchant in Indianola discharged a dishonest white boy, and put this colored lad in his place. Friends of the discharged boy stirred up feeling in the town, and the merchant was compelled to dispense with George's services, although he protested vigorously that he was only acting on the theory that "a nigger wouldn't have the nerve to steal as much as a white boy."

In 1911, as a result of the most persistent thrift, Hattie Lee had saved enough to send her boy to Alcorn College. Augmenting his mother's aid with earnings from hotel work he performed in the summers, young Lee was able to complete his junior year at that institution. Then he was accepted for military work at the officers' training camp at Des Moines, Iowa; and there he was soon commissioned a second lieutenant of infantry. The authorities wanted to select Lee to go to Camp Mead, Maryland, to train colored soldiers; but, in the meantime, the Houston riot between a colored regiment and citizens of Houston, Texas, had occurred; and some question was raised in the War Department as to the wisdom of having colored army officers. The authorities sent the young lieutenant to Camp Mead where his masterly work justified the confidence reposed in him.

In September 1917, he was ordered to Bourbon-les-Bains, France, a great military training center. Soon he was at the front in the Vosges, where he led his company and the first combat patrol against the Germans. After being under almost constant fire for a month, his unit was sent to the Argonne sector and participated in the capture of Benarville, a famous German strategic center. It was at this battle that Lieutenant Lee was cited for bravery, by the commander of the 33d French Brigade, after he had carried important messages through the Argonne in pouring rain and under heavy fire. He was promoted to the rank of first lieutenant. After the armistice, the young officer returned to America and was honorably discharged.

Robert R. Church, of Memphis, Tennessee, having read of the brilliant record of Lieutenant Lee, wrote him to come to Memphis to accept a place on the city detective force. Lee, however, was embued with the ambition to enter the insurance business. The Mississippi Life sought and secured his services to manage its West Tennessee District with offices in Memphis.

George Lee is among the very few Negro insurance men who have been successful without having had previous agency experience. The Memphis territory, under his able direction, rapidly grew into one of the company's largest districts; and in 1920 he was elected vice president of the company, which position he held until 1923, when the business and assets passed over to the Southern. Lee took the lead in a bitter fight to prevent the Southern from taking charge of the field business. He organized agency opposition, largely as a result of which the business of the old Mississippi Life in Tennessee was never consolidated in the hands of the white company.

In January 1924, Alonzo F. Herndon, came to Memphis to secure the services of Lieutenant Lee to manage the interests of his company in west Tennessee. Lee has had a successful career with Atlanta Life; and in 1939 the stockholders elected him to a place on its board of directors.

The exacting routine of business has not been sufficient to keep in suppression George Lee's natural literary gift. In 1934, the American public was agreeably surprised by the appearance of *Beale Street,* his first book. Almost overnight, it attracted the interest and comment of literary critics throughout America and marked attention in England and Canada. It attained large circulation; was selected as an alternate by the Book of the Month Club, and definitely placed its author in the ranks of the outstanding contributors to the literature of his race. The public demanded more from his pen; and in 1937 *River George* was published, a work which, although classified as fiction, portrays a true picture of Negro life in the Delta, and which takes more than a few of its colorful incidents from the life of its author. Mr. Lee has written numerous short stories, papers, and newspaper articles. He is an engaging orator, and has achieved national renown in this phase of his activities.

An intimate and firm friendship ripened between Lee and R. R. (Bob) Church, the distinguished Republican politician; and the young ex-soldier-insurance man developed a deep interest in politics. In 1924, he was made vice chairman and second in charge of the western Republican division in the Coolidge campaign. In 1927, he was chairman of the West Tennessee Civic and Polictical Club and waged a vigorous and successful campaign for the election of Mayor Watkins Overton of Memphis, who was opposed by the then power-ful Ku Klux Klan. In 1928, the Republican National Committee selected Mr. Lee to be chairman of the Colored Veterans Division in the Hoover campaign. Again, in 1932, he was one of the seven on the National Planning Board of the second Hoover campaign.

In 1936, he was again chairman of the Colored Veterans Division in the campaign that year.

This versatile man has never married. He lived with his mother until her death June 28, 1939; and his constant devotion and care to assure her every comfort was long the subject of favorable comment by his fellow citizens in Memphis.

Lieutenant George Washington Lee has not only been an official success for the concerns he has served, but his life has been a model of conservative thrift. The best authorities now count him among the wealthy men of his community.

THE CENTRAL LIFE INSURANCE COMPANY, TAMPA, FLORIDA

T. W. BRYAN's associates never quite understood what it was that exploded in his dispostion after fifteen years as a peaceful, even-tempered superintendent of agencies of the Afro-American Life Insurance Company of Jacksonville, Florida. It was a creditable job he did in building up an efficient staff of district managers and agents for that company.

Mr. Bryan retired from the Afro-American in 1919, and immediately became active in the organization of the People's Life Insurance Company of Jacksonville. But he did not long enjoy smooth sailing with the People's. Retiring in 1921, he went to Tampa, and there he was successful in interesting a number of prominent colored citizens in the organization of a new company, the Central.

With a capital of $10,000 subscribed and fully paid, the company was organized with Dr. G. P. Norton, president; Dr. M. J. Anderson, vice president; G. S. Middleton, Secretary; Dr. L. A. Howell, treasurer; T. W. Bryan, general manager; and W. H. Bryan, assistant general manager.

In the five years from 1921 to 1926, the Central increased to an annual premium collection of $245,000, and continued to pay stocks dividends until 1929. In 1930, differences over methods of system and routine were magnified into an imagined major trouble which resulted in Mr. Bryan's retirement as general manager. It seems that, notwithstanding the adoption by the Board of Directors of an improved clerical system, Mr. Bryan refused to install and follow it.

Resigning, he led in the organization of a new company which he named the Keystone, and then there resulted a bitter insurance war between the leaders of Central Life and Mr. Bryan of the Keystone.

Mr. N. H. Martin, who had succeeded Mr. Bryan as general manager of the Central, had had long experience in the insurance business, having served with the Southern Aid Society of Virginia; the National Benefit of Washington; the Century of Arkansas; and the Pyramid of Chicago. This ripe experience stood Mr. Martin in good stead in this heated contest for insurance agents with the militant Mr. Bryan. This strife was intermittently continued until 1932.

Then Dr. Norton, the former president of the Central, who had followed Mr. Bryan's lead in the organization of the Keystone, died, and was succeeded as president of the latter company by his son, Dr. Carl Norton. But again, in that same year, the hand of fate took part in settling the inter-company strife. Mr. Bryan, the emotional leader in the controversy, also died; and then the business of the Keystone was reinsured by the Afro-American.

Mr. G. S. Middleton served as secretary of the Central from its organization until his death in 1933, and in the last two years of his life, as secretary-treasurer, the two offices having been combined when Mr. Edward Stone, Treasurer, was killed in an automobile accident in Washington in 1931.

Mr. C. Blythe Andrews, son of W. W. Andrews, a former vice-president of Central, was elected to the Board of Directors in 1930. He succeeded G. S. Middleton, deceased, as secretary-treasurer in 1933, which position he now holds.

The Central owns its own home office building on Harrison Street, valued at more than $50,000. Although operating only in the state of Florida, it employs three executive officers, a staff of thirty home office and district clerks and two hundred agents to supervise its prosperous industrial debits.

GARFIELD DEVOE ROGERS, *President*

Obviously the general economic status of any group as a whole affects directly the opportunities and the careers of its individual members. The normal difficulties which any young man beginning life may expect to face are made more complicated and vexing if he is identified with a group victimized by an indefinite or artificially limited economy.

Outstanding natural talents in fields of life narrowed by unnaturally imposed difficulties may, and frequently do, remain subdued or entirely dormant. Young Negroes, clinging precariously to the slim ledges of opportunity, always on the threatening brink of disaster, must too frequently be content to pick the mere fragments of existence out of the crevices of the rocks of adversity in any and all situations. That ambition in the human breast does not always submit to such abnormal obstacles is proved by the life of Garfield DeVoe Rogers.

He was born January 23, 1885, in the discouragingly sterile, piney woods country surrounding Thomaston, in Upson County, Georgia, and had only the bare necessities of life in his early boyhood. Finishing the eighth grade in the Cedar Grove Elementary School when he was twelve years old, he had to give up further formal schooling to work on the farm with his parents, who were sharecroppers. But, having sipped slightly from the fountain of knowledge, each night, by the light of an oil lamp, he continued to seek knowledge through the inconvenient medium of correspondence schools. From these he received the equivalent of a high school education by the time he was sixteen years old; and, in the meantime, he had given up the dreary work of a sharecropper to become engaged variously as a laborer on the railroads, in the sawmills, in the turpentine industry, "grubbing" land and ditching, in none of which occupations did he receive more than $1.25 a day.

Young Rogers ability to engage in and to handle successfully many varied undertakings at the same time seem almost amazing; but no less so than the persistent manner in which he applied himself to acquiring further knowledge while following several kinds of work.

When he had reached his majority in 1906, he left his home in Upson County with only 90 cents in his pocket; and, walking barefoot, found his way to Florida, seeking work. It was while doing public work as a day laborer that the young man came into contact with great numbers of the rougher and more profligate types of colored people. Their indifference to their condition and outlook on life troubled him. He felt moved to do something to improve their lot.

It was while giving much thought to just what he could do that

GARFIELD DEVOE ROGERS
President

N. H. MARTIN
Comptroller and Manager

C. BLYTHE ANDREWS
Secretary-Treasurer

Home Office Building
Louisville, Kentucky

a copy of a Negro newspaper came into his hands. From its columns he saw that there were many Negroes who had achieved success in various lines. He was surprised but elated to note that there were even Negro authors of widely read books. It occurred to him that if some of these books could be put into the hands of his indifferent associates they might be impressed by the contents. This led him to become a book agent, selling the books of Negro authors; and while his inspiring motive was to help others, at the same time he was laying the foundation of a most remarkable career in salesmanship. His success in selling books convinced DeVoe Rogers that he could sell other things; and, without dropping his book work, he became a merchant-tailor, and made enough money in this line to finance a truck-farm and a transfer and transportation business to haul freight and the United States mails.

The book agent was now, in 1924, a business man with a gross annual income of more than $50,000 from his various enterprises, and employing constantly from five to fifty people in various ways. It was in this same year that the great Florida real estate boom began to assume noticeable volume. Mr. Rogers, it appears, did not relinquish his interests in his numerous other businesses, but took on two additional lines: insurance, and real estate; and in the six years between 1924 and 1930, his real estate sales amounted to more than $1,000,000. Working on commission, he realized a sizeable fortune; but he was no different in one respect from many others who thrust their fingers in the glitter of fantastic booms. He kept his hands in the game too long; and, on the decline, lost all that he had made.

Rogers was not discouraged. He had not only held on to his insurance agency during these six years, but had also organized a chain of undertaking establishments, setting up parlors in Bradenton, Fort Myers, Palmetto, and Cross City, all of which are successfully operating at the present time. The units of this chain of funeral homes are managed by colored men and women, all college graduates, one of them being a son and one a daughter of G. D. Rogers.

Mr. Rogers must have been an extremely busy man in these years; and yet, while giving sufficient attention successfully to supervise his numerous concerns, all along he was finding enough spare time to take additional correspondence courses. By this method he completed courses in embalming and in law, but never entered the practice of either.   After his course in embalming, in an examination before the State Board of Embalmers with forty-eight other applicants, all of whom had the benefit of schoolroom courses in embalming, Rogers made the highest mark of the five white and three colored applicants who passed.

It was in 1933, in the most dismal depths of the depression, that the directors of Central Life Insurance Company decided they needed the resourceful ability and progressive talents of G. D. Rogers as their president through those doubtful times.   He had been first vice president since 1930; and an original stockholder and a member of the board of directors since the organization of the company.   He was elected president to succeed Dr. L. A. Howell, who retired to devote his full time to the practice of medicine. Central, under his leadership, is making commendable progress and rendering valuable services to the people of Florida.

In 1909, Mr. Rogers married Miss Minnie Lee Thompson. Sixteen children have been born to them.   However, that dread sorrow, which only parents who have lost children can really understand, visited the Rogers' home seven times in the twenty-four years of his married life.   Of the nine living children, there are three boys and six girls, the oldest of whom is twenty-seven and the youngest three.

Despite poverty, obstacles and domestic sorrows, this busy man has always found time to take an interest in the civic, political, and educational activities of his people.   In 1912, at Bradenton, Florida, he organized a "Law and Order League," and followed this with the organization of more than thirty-five locals, scattered throughout the state.   Also in church and fraternal work, Mr. Rogers is an outstanding leader in his state.

A colored man seldom makes another fortune after losing one. Not so in the case of Garfield DeVoe Rogers.   The Florida boom broke him, but now he is reputed to be worth more than $50,000 in liquid stocks, bonds, and improved real estate.   He attributes this financial success to constant thrift and the help of a good wife, and to "sticking to my business, loyalty to my people, to my church, and to my God."

THE DOMESTIC LIFE AND ACCIDENT INSURANCE COMPANY, LOUISVILLE, KENTUCKY

THE Domestic Life and Accident Insurance Company was

incorporated May 17, 1920, commenced business September 8, 1921, and is among the exceptionally few Negro insurance companies that had the benefit of a fully paid capital stock of $100,000 before it opened its doors for business.

G. P. Hughes, the organizer, founder and first president, was no novice in the insurance game. For a quarter of a century he had served in various capacities in the business. Associated with him was Vice President J. E. Smith, who has not yet been able to wean himself from his love for the field work. His experience, too, at the time of the organization of the Domestic, was ripened by twenty-four years of activity in the training of field men and the organization of agencies.

Another associate in the organization and founding of the Domestic Life and Accident was W. F. Turner, with twenty-nine years of insurance experience. Mr. Turner was elected secretary, and, throughout the seventeen years of the company's operation, has discharged the duties of the clerical phases of the company with progressive ability and faithful care.

The Domestic, like most other Negro companies, commenced business writing only combination life, health, and accident insurance. It soon, however, established an industrial straight life department; and, in 1923, it added an ordinary department, and in this field has made rapid gains.

The company now boasts of total business in force amounting to $6,000,000, and its more than $500,000 in assets are invested in commercial stocks and other liquid securities and improved real estate, including its home office building, conservatively valued in excess of $250,000, and located near the heart of the business section of Louisville.

The Domestic is an exception to many financial institutions in that, throughout the severest years of the depression, it did not find it necessary to borrow money or resort to moratoriums to satisfy its obligations.

W. W. SPRADLING, *President*

Prominent in the organization of the company in 1921 was W. W. Spradling who had spent all his adult life in fields of successful businesses, having had experience as a banker, real estate broker, and president of the Louisville Cemetery Association. Mr. Spradling was chairman of the board of directors of Domestic

Life until the death of G. P. Hughes in 1930, when he was elected president. The steady increase in premium collections and high solvency of the company have continued under the conservative leadership of its reigning president.

The other officers of the company are: Mary V. Parrish, second vice president; Reverend R. D. Stoner, third vice president; Reverend M. B. Lanier, fourth vice president; W. F. Turner, secretary manager; O. P. Mack, assistant secretary; Clarence Young, treasurer; and Dr. C.W. Snyder, medical director.

In addition to these executives, the company employs approximately 300 men and women on its field debits and in its district offices throughout Kentucky and Ohio.

The Domestic Life and Accident Insurance Company, with its home office in the border-line territory on the banks of the Ohio River, finds it necessary to shape its operating policy to meet the frequently divergent views of colored people north of the Mason and Dixon Line, and those to the south of the river that, traditionally, divides the land of so-called liberality from the ultra conservatism of the South.

EXCELSIOR LIFE INSURNCE COMPANY, DALLAS, TEXAS

HENRY STRICKLAND, *President*

Henry Strickland was born January 12, 1874, at Athens, Georgia. His parents were Solomon and Matilda Strickland, with whom he lived until he was twenty-one years old. The parents were farmers, and Henry worked with them on their farm until he attained his majority.

Although the home of the Stricklands was near Athens, it was too far away for Henry to attend the town school, even if he could have spared enough time from the rigid requirements of his farm work. It was, therefore, through his irregular attendance during the short terms of the rural school near Athens that the youth was able to pick up the rudiments of reading, writing, and arithmetic. Questioned about his childhood activities, Mr. Strickland, in his characteristically deliberate manner, explained the factors which have contributed to his great financial success in the following words:

From childhood I was very ambitious, and the wish always dearest to my heart was that I might do any task assigned me better than anyone else. Whether farming, digging ditches or what not, I always tried to do the job better than any one else. A strong ambition with an eager temperament prompted me, when I became a man, to imitate that which I admired, and to strive to build something worth while.

After he was twenty-one years old, young Strickland was engaged in farming until 1907, when he found work as a common laborer on public works; and in this service he spent three years; but it did not offer the opportunities in life for which his ambition craved.

In 1910, having found his way to the great state of Texas, he was employed as an agent of the American Mutual Benefit Association, with home offices in Houston; and he became enthusiastic about its possibilities among Negroes.

It was in 1916, that, with Silas Cofield and other associates, he laid the plans for the organization of the Excelsior Mutual Benefit Association. Mr. Strickland was naturally elected its first president, and Silas Cofield, its secretary-treasurer.

The Excelsior Mutual Benefit Association operated successfully and profitably under the leadership of Mr. Strickland as president until 1937, when its board of directors decided to convert it into an old-line legal reserve life insurance company. The proper details of the organization being arranged, a capital stock of $25,000 was authorized and soon subscribed and paid for; and the name was changed to the Excelsior Life Insurance Company of Dallas, Texas, with Henry Strickland, president. As a life insurance company, the organization goes forward at an accelerated pace, rendering approved services to colored people in Texas.

Mr. Strickland is active in church work, being a faithful member of the New Hope Baptist Church of Dallas. He is a member of the Dunbar and Idlewild Social Clubs, and affiliated with the Y. M. C. A. in his home city. He takes an active interest in the Chamber of Commerce, the Community Chest, Red Cross, and the National Association for the Advancement of Colored People.

He believes that the lack of confidence and cooperation among Negroes is the greatest commercial difficulty with which we have to cope.

ECONOMIC DETOUR

MRS. CHARLES ETTA JONES, *Secretary-Treasurer*

The charge has been made that the opportunities for Negro women in the field of life insurance are very limited, and that they are not accorded that full measure of recognition to which their services and abilities entitle them. Among the several outstanding women in this business, whose successes refute this charge, is Mrs. Charles Etta Jones, secretary and treasurer of the Excelsior Life Insurance Company of Dallas.

It was not as a result of any special favors that she rose to her place of high importance in the insurance world. She was born December 9, 1893, of Charlie and Kate Emory, of Sherman, Texas. Her father was a common laborer, and her mother did domestic work. They were not able to make much financial headway, for their earnings were scarcely enough to cover their living expenses; yet, by careful management, they were able to keep their daughter, Charles Etta, in school until she had finished the Dallas High School. Then they placed her in school at Langston University, Langston, Oklahoma.

Throughout her school years Miss Emory made up for any lack of brilliance by her constant diligence and faithfulness to the tasks assigned her. Even in elementary school, traits of future leadership and independence manifested themselves. The approaches to the Fred Douglas Elementary School at that time were always converted into sloppy mud-trenches whenever it rained. The principal of the school had no funds with which to correct this condition. Charles Etta, overhearing him lament this fact, suggested that she could make fine sandwiches, and that, if allowed, she would make and sell enough sandwiches to raise the money to pay for paving the sidewalks. Her success and example in this little effort encouraged other students; and soon the school had a number of competitive sandwich clubs, raising the revenue for the pavement of the sidewalks. But Charles Etta made better sandwiches than the others; and the profits from her sales steadily increased. She won the contest.

It was this childish commercial venture that set her thinking about business. It created in her an ambition to enter the fields of business and, by exceptional services, to win distinction. That she has done.

The young woman, however, realized, even in those early days, that she would have to prepare herself for the technical require-

140

ments of commercial work; and, applying herself diligently, she constantly excelled in her classes in mathematics and spelling.

Out of school in 1912, she secured work as a clerk of the American Mutual Benefit Association, at a salary of $5 a week; but, this being not sufficient to cover her living expenses, she decided to teach school until she could find a more promising opening in commercial work. From 1914 to 1916 she taught school at a salary of $47.50 a month. When the Excelsior Mutual Benefit Association was organized in 1916, Mr. Henry Strickland, remembered the faithful work that Miss Charles Etta Emory had performed for the American Mutual Benefit Association in 1912. She was called to accept work as a clerk for the Association.

Steadily, by meritorious services, she continued to advance; and in 1933 she was elected secretary-treasurer. On the reorganization and conversion of the association into a legal reserve life insurance company in 1937, no one else but this efficient and reliable woman was thought of for the posiiton of secretary-treasurer. From sandwich salesgirl to secretary-treasurer of a progressive life insurance company is a long step, but Mrs. Charles Etta Emory Jones accomplished it by persisting in meritorious service and honesty.

Mrs. Jones is an active member of the Salem Baptist Church, Royal Art Club, Ladies Reading Circle, Y. W. C. A., Red Cross and the N. A. A. C. P. of Dallas.

LOUISIANA INDUSTRIAL LIFE INSURANCE CO.
NEW ORLEANS, LOUISIANA

DR. RIVERS FREDERICK, *President*

In the early days of changing flags and allegiances, when the natural trends of men were but loosely restricted by the artificial devices of prejudice and politics in the old southwest territory along the southern reaches of the Mississippi River, the blood of several important races met and mingled. It was a fertile field for genius, where the robust freshness of New World ruggedness poured its invigorating stream into the languor of Old World culture to produce new and daring types of intellect and skill.

It was out of such a fortunate blend of unmolested nature that Dr. Rivers Frederick, president of the Louisiana Industrial Life Insurance Company, sprang. He was born on May 22, 1874, at New Roads, Pointe Coupee Parish, Louisiana, of George and

Armintine Dalcourte Frederick. His early childhood days were spent in this Creole area, and his associates were of the same proud racial strain as he.

He received his grade and high school training in the schools of New Orleans, after which he further pursued his education at Straight and New Orleans Universities, and graduated in medicine from the University of Illinois in 1897.

Then those ancestral traits of love for homeland so marked in people of French extraction asserted themselves with peculiar force and results. This young man of rare talents surely was aware of the wider fields and greater possibilities in the larger cities, yet he elected to begin the practice of his profession at the place of his birth, a little town of not more than one thousand people.

In the midst of subdued mediocrity, spectacular eminence and glittering genius sometimes provoke contrasts so harsh as to invite their own discomfiture. It was so in the case of Dr. Frederick. The ease with which his exceptional ability as a physician accomplished for him over-shadowing success at New Roads forced upon him the realization that the limited opportunities of that small neighborhood would forever enslave his great talents, bridle his restive energy, and deny to his inherent qualities their spheres of greatest usefulness. He noted with growing concern the increasing stringency of racial customs in Louisiana; and the yearning for a field where his success would be measured only by his own ability became more and more irresistible, until he bade farewell to his native state and sailed away to Spanish Honduras. Here, contrary to the information he had received, he found that the examinations to test medical qualification were given only in Spanish and must be answered in that language, which he could not speak. When, however, he was almost at the point of despair, the chief surgeon of the government hospital, who spoke English and had become impressed with the obvious ability of this young Creole Negro doctor, selected him to answer and attend an emergency call from a prominent Honduran, who had been seriously injured in a rural settlement. Frederick found the slim chance of saving the life of the man lay in a delicate operation, which, if undertaken, must be performed under the crude and limited facilities and in the heat of that backwoods area. The two local doctors opposed the attempt; but, confident of his own skill, Dr. Frederick performed the operation with great success. Then, in recognition of this daring feat of surgery, he was awarded the authority to pracitce in Honduras without having to submit to the examinations.

Though handicapped by strange customs and language, he soon won great distinction as a physician. In less than two years he was selected as chief surgeon of the government hospital at El Riotan. For four years he filled this position with great credit. Retiring to private practice he rapidly became wealthy, and probably would have remained in Honduras; but he soon found himself in sympathy with the cause of a revolutionary movement which attempted to overthrow the incumbent government of that country. He was made chief surgeon of one of the large army divisions, in which capacity he served until the defeat and disorganization of the forces of which he was a part. Upon his return to New Orleans for rest and vacation, his reputation as a great surgeon somehow became known in that city. Agreeing to do an operation as a favor for a friend, he soon found himself pressed into service in first one and then another case of grave emergency until he literally became enmeshed, despite his own inclinations, in the practice of surgery in the Crescent City. In this way was he almost forced to make the decision to reside in that Louisiana city.

In New Orleans, he has served as professor of surgery of Flint Medical College and on the staffs of the Provident and the Old Flint Goodridge Hospitals. In 1932, when the New Flint Goodridge Hospital was being organized and established, the medical advisory committee of five white New Orleans physicians was authorized to appoint the staff. On all staffs, except surgery, the chiefs were white physicians and the associates colored doctors during the preliminary period required for proper experience. Dr. Rivers Frederick was the chief of the staff of surgery and his associates white surgeons. He still is filling this position. For twenty years he has been on the surgical staff of the Southern Pacific Railroad, and for ten years he has conducted the Clinics of the Southwestern Council in the Good Hope Sanitarium at Lafayette, Louisiana. Here he has performed more than fifteen hundred successful major operations.

With a mortality loss of less than 5 per cent, Dr. Frederick during his career of thirty-five years in surgery has performed more than 31,000 operations.

This revered citizen of Louisiana is a man of magnetic

143

personality and poise; and in the courts of his state his testimony and opinions are accorded the highest of respect and credence.

Accomplished and wealthy and perforce a man of many business affairs, he yet has always found time to take a deep interest in aspiring young men. He has been a great teacher in his field, and hundreds of young physicians throughout the South and Southwest cherish the name of this skillful expert in surgery.

A charter member of the board of directors of the Louisiana Industrial Life Insurance Company, he was prevailed upon to accept the presidency of this corporation in 1936. He had helped to establish the institution, and, under his able guidance, the company's unbroken record of profitable operation is being continued and enhanced.

DR. PERCY PENNINGSTON CREUZOT, *Secretary*

President, National Negro Insurance Association

It is extremely difficult to achieve success without making enemies. Yet the successful life of Dr. P. P. Cruezot, president of the National Negro Insurance Association, seems to be an exception. In New Orleans where he resides and at the many other places in the nation where he is well known he is greatly admired and highly popular. The fact that he has no known enemies is frequently commented on by the host of friends he has made.

Percy Penningston Creuzot was born October 27, 1886, at Marksville, Louisiana, of Louis and Marie Creuzot. When he was four years old, his parents moved to Alexandria, Louisiana, and he lived there with them until their deaths in 1919. He was educated in the primary public and parochial schools of Alexandria; at Straight University, New Orleans; Fisk University, Nashville, and Northwestern University, Chicago, taking his A. B. degree at Fisk and the degree of doctor of dental surgery at Northwestern.

Dr. Creuzot's father, Louis, was an industrious man, engaged variously as a farmer, proprietor of a brickyard, country storekeeper, a bricklayer, and contractor. From him young Creuzot inherited the traits of thrift and industry. At twelve years of age he was proficient in brickmasonry; and, working at this, he earned some of the necessary money to defray his school expenses. While at Northwestern he became associated with a valuable friend, Mr. Joseph Rousseau, and together they formed the contracting firm of Rousseau & Creuzot, which connection he maintained until some time after his graduation in dentistry. Also before finishing school he found work as a bookkeeper and retail shoe salesman in the Negro town of Boley, Oklahoma.

In 1919 Dr. P. P. Creuzot commenced the practice of dentistry at 2252 Dryades Street, New Orleans. As in other work, his practice was successful and profitable to an exceptional degree almost from the beginning, and the young man's financial worth increased rapidly.

In 1920 when the Louisiana Industrial Life Insurance Company was organized he was one of the founders, and invested in it heavily. In 1924 he was elected secretary, a position that he has since held and filled with high efficiency and great satisfaction.

He has taken a keen interest in the programs of the National Negro Insurance Association ever since the fifth annual session at Louisville, in 1925. At the seventeenth session of the association in 1937, which convened in Augusta, Dr. Creuzot was elected a member of the executive committee. At the eighteenth annual session held in Cleveland, in 1938, he was unanimously elected first vice president; and again unanimously elevated to the presidency of the association at the nineteenth session held in Los Angeles, in 1939. Dr. Creuzot demonstrated his keen interest in the general welfare of the business of life insurance among Negroes at the beginning of his administration by personally donating a substantial sum in cash to be offered as prizes to agents of all companies to inspire special efforts to make high collections during the National Collection Month, which the National Association celebrated in October 1939.

This eminent insurance executive believes that business progress for the Negro race is most handicapped by the still too high percentage of general illiteracy, the high level of poverty and the lack of a sufficient number of technically trained men and women. He especially laments, moreover, the high per cent of illiteracy among the ministers of some of the churches.

On December 30, 1918, young Dr. Creuzot was married to Miss Angele A. Charbonnet of New Orleans, and this union has been blessed with the following children: Alexa M., Percy P. Jr., Hortense E., and Martina J. M. Creuzot. Devotion to his fine family is an outstanding and much noted characteristic of this very successful insurance executive and dental surgeon.

145

ECONOMIC DETOUR

FRANK ARTHUR YOUNG, *Agency Director*

The careers of colored men who have achieved any degree of prominence seem to refute the old belief that young men should choose their life's work according to their predominant talents and characteristics. Men and women of the Negro race, particularly, often have to submit to economic trends and necessities, and out of the material situations thus created wring their fortunes and fame. Frank Arthur Young, the agency director of the Louisiana Industrial Life Insurance Company, in early life found himself forced into a groove of unyielding circumstances and compelled to step from one thing to another as the opportunities arose; but, whatever his associations or connections, he made hosts of friends by his magnetic personality.

Frank Young was born November 17, 1881, in New Orleans. His parents were James I. and Amelia Young. While still an infant, he was taken to Medford, Massachusetts, where in due time he finished grade and high schools, and then the Ringe Manual Training School at Cambridge; after that he spent one year at Harvard studying dentistry. Unable to secure the necessary further financial assistance to continue in school, he, for a short while, assisted his mother in the catering business.

Then, while yet a young man, he returned to New Orleans, the place of his birth. Here, unable to find other work, he did not disdain to accept employment unloading barrel-staves for 5 cents an hour for a cooperage firm. However, he did not long continue this work. Passing the Railway Mail Service examination, he was appointed a clerk in 1899. Here he made a record of almost errorless efficiency during his thirteen years in that branch of the service. Meanwhile, becoming interested in the development of insurance as conducted by the then popular fraternal orders, he voluntarily resigned as mail clerk and was elected Grand Secretary of the Pythian Grand Lodge in Arkansas in 1908, which position he held for five years. In 1913, the National Order of Mosaic Templars, with headquarters in Little Rock, secured his services to train state officials and their local forces in the systems and technique of that fraternal order throughout its extensive territories of operation. Following this, he was chosen to head the field organization of the Woodmen of Union Fraternal Order of Hot Springs, which position he filled for two years.

Perhaps Mr. Young's most brilliant services were rendered

146

Standard Life as Agency Director for the State of Arkansas. During his five years tenure in this position, his organization produced an average of more than $1,000,000 of insurance per year on the lives of an exceptionally high type of risk, as evidenced by the fact that the mortality experience of Standard Life in Arkansas during its operation there was the best of any state.

When Standard Life ceased operation in Arkansas, Mr. Young was elected to head the field force of the Woodmen of Union, which work he prosecuted with characteristic vigor and effectiveness until the Woodmen of Union was merged with the Century Life Insurance Company of Hot Springs. He became agency director of that company, where he continued the same type of work until the business of the Century Life was reinsured by the Universal Life in 1932.

In 1933, he was elected agency director of the Louisiana Industrial Life Insurance Company of New Orleans; and even though he took charge in the darkest of the depression years, his administration has been marked by progressive increase and profits for that company.

In recognition of his fine, long record of supervisory field services, the National Negro Insurance Association, at its 1939 session, elected him chairman of the National Negro Insurance Week Committee. The National Negro Insurance Week campaign has come to be recognized as perhaps the most important function of the National Association, and selection as head of this committee is regarded in Negro insurance circles as a testimonial of the highest efficiency.

In 1911, Mr. Young was married to Miss Huldah Kraft, of Alexandria, Louisiana; and this happy couple has been blessed with six children: Mrs. Helen Howard, a graduate of Fisk University, and industrial secretary of the Y.W.C.A. of Chicago; Frank A., Jr., agent of the Louisiana Industrial and graduate of Dillard University, New Orleans; Theo K., a graduate of the Little Rock High School; Madeline Fay, a sophomore at Philander Smith College; Gloria A, a senior high school student in Little Rock; and Julius A., also in school in Little Rock.

This is the record of a man who, though serving several different organizations since reaching adult life, has never had a day of unemployment; and who has never had to seek a job; for, always, when on account of circumstances for which he was in no way responsible, any job he held ceased to exist, there was another waiting for him.

DAVID DEVON SHACKLEFORD, *Auditor*

Although those who work behind the scenes are denied the thrill of the spotlights and plaudits of the audience, yet, without efficient work on their part, the show could not go on. In every worthwhile business organization somewhere behind the scenes there are careful, quiet, hardworking men and women but for whose painstaking work in keeping accurate records chaos and confusion would ensue. Compact, cogent financial statements and reports, reflecting in brief form all of the conditions and progress of various business units, are the results of long, hard hours of labor, assembling, classifying, entering and reconciling volumes of details.

Prominent in the class of these unspectacular workers is David Devon Shackleford. He was born in Memphis, Tennessee, of David D. and Ida M. Shackleford, December 28, 1884. His father was engaged in railroad work, and a lasting impression was made on the mind of young Shackleford by the way in which railroad companies dispatched and kept track of their great numbers of trains and the tremendous amount of traffic which they handled. He learned in early youth that the accuracy and promptness with which this great work was handled was due to the smooth performance of regulated systems of business; and thus there was aroused in his childhood the ambition to study and become a proficient business man.

Finishing the public schools of Memphis, Tennessee, and Gulfport, Mississippi, he entered Tuskegee Institute, after which he took actuarial mathematics in Columbia University. Since then he has taken extension courses in mathematics, higher accountancy, income tax, business administration, and office management from the Alexander Hamilton, LaSalle, and Walton Schools of Commerce. He has also had private courses in mathematics and actuarial science from the International Accountants' Society.

From this it will be seen that Mr. Shackleford has gone to exhaustive lengths to prepare himself as an accountant; in fact, thorough and scientific preparation for business is almost an obsession with him. However, notwithstanding his thorough preparation, he has encountered in this line of work, as have many men of the race in other lines, unusual difficulties. When Shackleford presented himself for the examination for certified public accountants in Georgia he was informed that no Negro was qualified for this type of work. However, he has met requirements imposed by the American Institute of Accountants for the degree of C. P. A., and has passed three of the five subjects required by Georgia for the same title.

In his chosen work, Mr. Shackleford's career has been marked by steady advancement. Starting in 1911, as an assistant cashier in the Tuskegee Institute Bank, he has with great success filled the following positions: assistant postmaster at Tuskegee Institute; auditor of the Supreme Lodge of the Knights of Pythias; auditor for Standard Life Insurance Company, Atlanta, Georgia; auditor and office manager of the Mid-West Life Insurance Company; auditor, assistant secretary, office manager of the Century Life Insurance Company; and auditor of the Louisiana Industrial Life since 1932.

Besides his work in life insurance Mr. Shackleford has always taken an active part in church affairs and the various programs of the local Y. M. C. A. and in fraternal orders.

ALFRED WESLEY ZILTON, *Founder and Former President*

Alfred Wesley Zilton was born in Terrehomme Parish, Louisiana, May 31, 1874, to Joseph and Catherine Zilton, who were engaged in farming. He attended the public schools and Houma Academy near his home town. Early, however, young Zilton developed a bent for insurance, and feeling that he needed more training he took a course in insurance salesmanship from Sheldon Institute, Chicago.

Mr. Zilton has served in three capacities in the insurance field— first, as district manager, then as manager, and finally as president of the Louisiana Industrial Life Insurance Company from 1930 to 1932. He led in organizing this company.

DR. LEONIDAS T. BURBRIDGE, *Former President*

Leonidas F. Burbridge was born October 25, 1870, on a farm near Lexington, Kentucky. He received his academic education at Straight College, New Orleans, graduating in May 1889, with a B. S. degree. He then entered Meharry Medical College, from which he graduated in February 1893. He has practiced medicine, principally in New Orleans, since 1898.

In 1920, Dr. Burbridge helped to organize the Louisiana Industrial Life Insurance Company, and served as its vice president. In September 1921, he became president and remained in that capacity until February 1933. In 1926 he promoted and supervised the building of the home office of the company at Dryades and Josephine Streets. The cost of the building and grounds was approximately $100,000, with $5,000 in furnishings, all of which was paid for in cash. In 1926, he also raised the original capital of the company from $25,000 to $50,000. During his administration, the assets of the company were increased from $25,000 to $228,000; and its premium income from $65,000 to over $500,000.

At the tenth annual session of the National Negro Insurance Association in Atlanta in 1930 Dr. Burbridge was elected president and served one year.

THE MAMMOTH LIFE AND ACCIDENT INSURANCE COMPANY, LOUISVILLE, KENTUCKY

THE Mammoth Life and Accident Insurance Company was founded by Henry E. Hall and William H. Wright, as the first officially recognized insurance company organized by Negroes in the State of Kentucky.

H. E. Hall, a native Kentuckian, was born in Henderson, Kentucky, November 22, 1876. It was here that he received his public school education. When he was not in school, he worked in tobacco factories to assist in supporting himself and the rest of his family. At seventeen he matriculated at Hampton Institute, Hampton, Virginia. Here he completed his formal education in 1896, and returned to teach school in Henderson County. This was a rural, five months school. Each year, at the close of the school term, he would return to the factory as a stemmer or day laborer.

In 1900, a fraternal organization from Lynchburg, Virginia, began operating in his home town. He secured a position with this company as agent, with compensation on a commission basis. He rose from the position of agent to assistant state manager, and from this position to state manager of Kentucky. This latter position he held until the Virginia company was forced to withdraw from the state in 1904.

He kept the business under his supervision intact, and organized

Domestic Life and Accident Insurance Company

The Late G. P. Hughes
Founder

W. W. Spradling
President

W. F. Turner
Secretary-Manager

Dr. C. W. Snyder
Medical Director

J. E. SMITH
Vice President-Agency Director

CLARENCE YOUNG
Treasurer

O. P. MACK
Assistant Secretary

Excelsior Mutual Life Insurance Company

HENRY STRICKLAND
President

MRS. CHARLES ETTA JONES
Secretary-Treasurer

DR. P. P. CREUZOT
Secretary

FRANK A. YOUNG
Agency Director

DR. L. T. BURBRIDGE
Former President

the National Benevolent Union of Kentucky, which he developed until 1911. At this time he was threatened with arrest for operating an insurance company without license, or conforming to the insurance laws. Facing this emergency, he sent out a call to all companies known to him that were operated by Negroes. The Atlanta Mutual, of Atlanta, Georgia, came to his rescue, conformed to the laws of Kentucky, and acquired the business as its own. After this acquisition the Atlanta Mutual employed Mr. Hall as state manager. He held this position from 1911 until the Standard Life Insurance Company of Atlanta was launched, with an agreement that the Atlanta Mutual should operate its health and accident department in Kentucky in the name of the Standard Life Insurance Company. On being placed in immediate charge of the Standard Life's business in Kentucky, he assumed the state management for both companies.

In 1914 the health and accident department was forced to withdraw from Kentucky; and, as this department was his principal income, Hall and W. H. Wright organized the Mammoth Life and Accident Insurance Company. The Insurance Department of Kentucky refused to license or approve the organization. The company resorted to court action and secured a favorable decision from the State Court of Appeals. This decision forced the Insurance Department to issue a license to the company.

W. H. Wright was born in Livingston, Alabama, in 1877. He attended school in Selma, Alabama, and later continued his education at State University, Louisville, Kentucky, afterwards known as Simons University. Inclined to follow the legal profession, he enrolled in the Law School at Howard University, Washington, D. C., where he earned his degree in law. On completion of his law course he began to practice in Louisville in 1904. Here he maintained a successful practice until his death, June 29, 1926.

He became the friend, associate, and legal adviser of H. E. Hall soon after he opened an office in Louisville, and ably handled all matters pertaining to the legal phase of organizing the Mammoth Life and Accident Insurance Company.

On July 12, 1915, the late W. H. Wright, the late Rochelle Smith, the late B. O. Wilkerson, and H. E. Hall organized the Mammoth Life and Accident Insurance Company with office space at Sixth and Liberty Streets. The first officers were H. E. Hall,

151

president; George L. Cheatham, secretary; and B. O. Wilkerson, treasurer.

H. E. Hall and a few agents developed the business in Louisville. It grew to such a surprising extent that it became necessary to enlarge the office force and space. Field representatives were sent to work in Kentucky's largest towns. This resulted in districts being established in Lexington, Paducah, Bowling Green, and Hopkinsville.

Some of the men who are pioneers of the company and who helped the development in Kentucky are: I. B. Thomas, J. A. Buford, W. C. Buford, J. P. Black, J. F. Moxley, and J. F. Payton.

With the business in Kentucky developing so rapidly, and seeing that rental space was needed by other Negro businesses, the company built a three-story brick building at 422 South Sixth Street, with home office space on the first floor, consisting of a reception room, president's office, clerical office space, and a large agency assembly room, accomodating fifty or more agents.

1924

The company was a mutual company until 1924, when stock was sold to hundreds of people throughout Kentucky, making the institution a stock company. A stock issue of $100,000 was over-subscribed in ninety days. It was then that the officials decided to increase the capital stock to $200,000. All of this was shortly sold and the company began operations this year as a $200,000 stock company. W. H. Wright was elected chairman of the board of directors. Other officers elected at this time were: H. E. Hall, president; J. M. Smith, secretary; and B. O. Wilkerson, treasurer. The following stockholders were elected directors: Ira T. Bryant, Mrs. J. E. McDowell, Mrs. Albert Collier, A. J. Pullen, W. H. Wright, John Holloman, B. O. Wilkerson, W. E. Johnson, H. E. Hall, A. B. Ridley, C. M. Hayes, W. T. Merchant, Mrs. J. M. Smith, S. H. George, and I. B. Thomas.

A dividend of 7.5 per cent was declared.

1925

It was in this year that the company, realizing the further need of buildings with modern conveniences for Negroes, erected a new six-story home office building at 604-12 West Walnut Street, at the cost of $377,000. This building consists of a beautifully decorated theatre and four store fronts on the ground floor. The president's office, a large space for the home office clerical force, offices for physicians, attorneys, The Urban League and other insurance branch offices are on the second floor. On the remaining four floors are twenty-four modern and up-to-date apartments. This building is located almost directly across the street from the City Armory, and within a stone's throw of the City Hall, the United States Post Office, and the Fourth Avenue shopping district.

J. Rice Porter was elected to the board of directors this year. The company entered the State of Arkansas, and reinsured the business of the Enterprise Mutual Insurance Company.

1926

Dr. R. W. Oliver was elected to the board of directors and Dr. W. T. Merchant became its chairman.

The financier of the company, W. H. Wright, became ill. Every possible comfort and care was given Mr. Wright but to no avail. On June 29th, he died. Not only did the company feel his passing keenly, but many others paused to pay last respects to a worthy citizen.

After Mr. Wright's passing, the entire responsibility of this great organization rested upon the shoulders of President H. E. Hall. He was equal to the emergency. He knew he had a great work to do; an obligation to the people who had put their trust in a race-building institution. There could be no failure for this pioneer concern; and so, through many difficulties, he successfully directed the course of the company.

1927

L. F. Wright, J. L. V. Washington, W. C. Buford, and A. B. Ridley were elected to the board of directors. In a meeting of the board, the president emphasized the strong financial condition of the company, evidenced by a surplus nearly as large as the capital stock.

1928

License was issued to do business in Ohio, August 20th, and in Indiana, September 5th. District offices in Ohio were opened at Cleveland, Toledo, Youngstown, Portsmouth, and Cincinnati. It was in this year that the company purchased the Community Mutual Life Company of Indiana.

1929
On February 1st a dividend of 2.5 per cent was paid to stockholders.

1930
H. L. Street was elected to the board of directors. The company's business in Arkansas was sold to Southwestern Insurance Company of Pine Bluff, Arkansas. Mrs. Julia M. Smith, secretary died April 7th. As Mrs. Smith had filled this position in a highly satisfactory manner, the board of directors appointed another woman—Mrs. Jennie E. McDowell, secretary.

1931
The success with which the company weathered the financial storm when the banks closed their doors on November 7th was the subject of general comment in Louisville and throughout Kentucky.

1932
The Company reinsured the health and accident business of the Gibraltar Insurance Company of Indiana.

Dr. W. T. Merchant, chairman of the board of directors, died. Dr. Merchant was one of the outstanding physicians of the country, instrumental in the building of the Red Cross Hospital, and a business man. He was succeeded as chairman of the board of directors by J. Rice Porter.

1933
The company showed a big increase in income over that of 1932. Efficiency on the part of the claims department showed a large decrease in the claim ratio.

1934
Mr. A. B. Ridley, a member of the board of directors, one of the outstanding undertakers of the city and a credit to his race, died.

1935
The company established depositories in more districts, to distribute its cash so that it would be nearly all covered by government insurance. Reports for the year showed remarkable improvement in all departments.

Mr. B. O. Wilkerson, treasurer of the company since its beginning, died in August. He had been connected with the organization since 1915. He was a postal employee until the company demanded all of his time as treasurer, when he resigned his governmental position. Mr. W. E. Johnson, a member of the board and a retired postal clerk, was elected as treasurer. Mr. S. W. Whitley was elected to the board of directors.

1936

On June 23rd, Dr. S. H. George, prominent physician of Paducah, Kentucky, and for twenty-one years a member of the board of directors, died. Mr. E. J. Ellis was elected to the board of directors. Then, on July 16th, Mrs. Jennie E. McDowell, who had served as an agent, director, member of the executive committee, and secretary of the company, died.

Ohio and Indiana enacted laws requiring all life insurance agents to pass an examination before receiving a license to do business. The company, therefore, in order that its agents might receive proper instruction in the fundamentals of insurance and salesmanship, appointed Mr. W. C. Buford to prepare a suitable course and direct the proper training of the entire field force. When Mr. Buford's completed course was presented, it was agreed by the Indiana Insurance Department that all agents who were able to complete the course with creditable rating would be exempted from the state examination and that licenses would be issued to them.

On September 1st, Mr. W. E. Johnson, treasurer of the company, who had served as a member of the board of directors for twenty-one years, died. Mr. H. L. Street, who had come from the ranks of agents to be field representative, manager of the claims department, and member of the board of directors, was elected secretary-treasurer.

1937

The company declared a dividend of 2.5 per cent to the stockholders.

During the flood that swept the country in January, the company housed without charge several hundred refugees in the district office building at 422 South Sixth Street and the home office building at 608 West Walnut Street.

1938

Dr. Russell V. Rice, a prominent physician and medical director of the company, died in January. He had held this position for six years.

The company declared a dividend of 3 per cent.

1939

The company again declared a dividend of 3 per cent.

The present officers of the company are as follows:

H. E. Hall, president; H. L. Street, secretary-treasurer; J. Rice Porter, vice president and chairman of the board of directors: J. L. V. Washington, member of the executive committee.

The members of the board of directors of the company are:

H. E. Hall, H. L. Street, J. Rice Porter, J. L. V. Washington, S. W. Whitley, A. D. Doss, W. C. Buford, E. J. Ellis, and Miss L. F. Wright.

THE PILGRIM HEALTH AND LIFE INSURANCE COMPANY OF AUGUSTA, GEORGIA

"Nothing in the past to regret; nothing in the future to fear."

BECAUSE a delivery boy in a grocery store on Gwinnett Street, Augusta, Georgia, saw beyond the immediate benefits outlined in a policy carried by him in a white company and envisioned the rich returns to his people such a business, operated by them, would yield, there now radiates from a central office on this same street in Augusta, the beneficent influence of a great insurance institution. Solomon W. Walker was that delivery boy, and the Pilgrim Health and Life Insurance Company is the embodiment of his vision.

Young Sol shared his illuminating idea with three lads of about his own age; and the boys decided to launch out into its development. The other youths were W. S. Hornsby, T. J. Walker, brother of Solomon, and J. C. Collier, who later became a physician and medical director of the company. As a stabilizing influence and in moral support, the Reverend T. J. Hornsby, a respected Baptist minister of Augusta, became the first president. The organization took place at the home of the Reverend Mr. Hornsby, 1741 Milledgeville Road, Augusta, May 2, 1898, under a Richmond County charter. The fledgling company was called the Pilgrim Benevolent Society.

The growth of the company as a benevolent society was steady and substantial; but the founders had in mind a broader conception for the culmination of their plans. There was a law that required a life insurance company to post a deposit of $5,000 with the state in order to do business in Georgia. There were a few other societies that had been organized after the Pilgrim. None of the societies alone was able to raise the necessary $5,000, and their official families, therefore, decided to pool their resources and merge activities under one banner. Thus, in 1915, the Pilgrim Benevolent Society, the Cooperative Industrial Society, and the Benevolent Relief and Benefit Association, all of Augusta, became the Pilgrim Health and Life Insurance Company.

In the years following, the progress of the Pilgrim has been marked by significant milestones. In 1923, Alabama was entered. Five years later the company qualified for business in South Carolina.

In 1930, the ordinary life department was added. In the same year, it became an old line legal reserve life insurance company.

In 1931, the Pilgrim took over the Georgia Mutual Health and Life Insurance Company, which had fallen into insolvency; and thus preserved good will toward Negro insurance companies.

Since its beginning, the company has been served by five presidents. The first was Reverend Thomas Jefferson Hornsby, who served for ten years. He was succeeded by Mr. A. B. Powell, who in turn was followed by Mr. H. C. Young.

H. C. Young, son of slaves, born in 1864, an active and influential part of the religious and civic life of the Augusta community, died in April 1917; and the direction of the affairs of the Pilgrim was again entrusted to the wise hands of a minister, the Reverend Charles Williams.

Charles Williams was born in Burke County, Georgia, December 21, 1856. He served the company well and unselfishly until his death in September 1931.

After the death of Reverend Williams, the cycle was completed when the direction of the company came into the hands of the man who, as a youth, had dreamed it into being. Solomon W. Walker, originator and co-founder, followed Reverend Williams as president and now holds that office.

The Pilgrim Health and Life Insurance Company is now forty years old. Those forty years have been rich and full; complete in the knowledge of service rendered and future good to be done. It now employs 500 people; has total admitted assets of $758,309.19; has paid to members and beneficiaries during its life time the sum of $16,128,959.41; has a surplus for policyholders of $125,556.92;

has legal reserves of $556,891.98, and owns stocks and bonds amounting to $662,094.09.

The company's development has been conducted along conservative and well-planned lines, and today it is considered among the most substantial of its kind in the three states its territory embraces.

THE LATE REVEREND THOMAS JEFFERSON HORNSBY,
First President and Founder

The Reverend Thomas Jefferson Hornsby was born at Blythe, Georgia, in the County of Burke, October 22, 1852. His parents were Samuel Moody Hornsby and Rachel Glover Hornsby. His formal education was pursued at the Augusta Institute, which later became successively the Atlanta Baptist Seminary, Atlanta Baptist College, and finally, Morehouse College.

On leaving school he taught school and later entered the ministry in the Baptist Church. He was very active as a pastor and community leader wherever he served. He was a church and convention organizer and moderator. It was his capacity for organizational work that in a large measure helped to bring into fruition the dreams of his youthful associates in the Pilgrim idea. His pastorates included Antioch, Augusta, Springfield, Gainesboro, Waysgrove, Appling; all Georgia pastorates in the Baptist denomination. He was moderator of the Walker Baptist Association, president of the Augusta Minister's Union, secretary of the General Missionary Baptist Convention of Georgia, chairman of the trustee board of Walker Baptist Institute, and a civic leader of distinction.

He was a historian and theologian of accomplishment, and one of the most profound preachers of his day; noted for his nobility of character, and consecration, and withal a good business man. He owned valuable property and was always a voter. He married twice, and was the father of seven children: Louise Anna, Lizzie Magdalene, Rachel Bethesda, Walter Spurgeon, Eugene Davis, Clifford Alvin, and Tommie Louise. After a life of distinguished achievement the Reverend Hornsby died November 10, 1901.

SOLOMON W. WALKER, *President and Founder*
And Resident Manager of The Atlanta District

Solomon W. Walker, president and founder of Pilgrim Health and Life Insurance Company, while working as a delivery boy in a grocery store, grew tired of paying his insurance premiums into a white company in which his dollars were robbed of their power to employ colored men and women. The Pilgrim Health and Life Insurance Company is the direct culmination of Mr. Walker's vision and his determination as a youth to establish a Negro insurance company.

Mr. Walker, the son of Reverend Henry and Mrs. Martha Walker, was born at Blythe, Georgia, in Burke County. He received his formal scholastic training at Nellieville Academy and Walker Baptist Institute in Augusta. His higher education was received in the great university of life, for he is the very embodiment of the quotation: "All life is a school, a preparation, a purpose; nor can we pass current in any higher college unless we are willing to undergo the tedium of education in this lower one."

Regardless of the lack of academic degrees, Mr. Walker is essentially a scholar and a student of men. He has long believed that men are always moved by examples of courage, confidence, and inspiration; hence, he was undaunted when he realized that he had only $2.50, saved from his meager earnings as a delivery boy, to pay down on the charter of the Pilgrim Benevolent Society, which cost $25. He proposed that it be purchased on the installment plan. It was. Many obstacles had to be overcome, mainly the lack of money, but through all of these Mr. Walker's courage and determination were the guiding principles that led Pilgrim Life upward to its present position among the leading insurance companies owned and operated by Negroes.

In Atlanta, Mr. Walker, leading a large force of willing workers, has built an industrial debit of more than $5,000, at one time the largest weekly district debit collected by any Negro life insurance company in the world.

Mr. Walker is active in the Reed Street Baptist Church and chairman of the board of deacons; for several years he has been treasurer of the Sunday school, and a member of the executive committee of the Baptist State Convention.

He is a member of the committee of management of the Butler Street Y. M. C. A., Atlanta; a member of the executive committee of the Atlanta branch of the N. A. A. C. P.; vice president of the Boy's Law and Order League of America; a member of the board of directors of the Atlanta Urban League; a member of the advisory committee of the Federal University Housing Project; a member of the trustee board of Spellman College; and a member of the committee on recreation and camping of the National Youth Administration.

Family Life

In 1901, Mr. Walker married Miss Julia Donnigan. There are four children, Alvetious J., James H., Agnes L., and Willie Marion Walker.

WALTER SPURGEON HORNSBY,
Vice President and General Manager

The success and glamour which attended the activities of the many prominent ministers in and around Burke County, Georgia, in the two decades preceding, and the two following the beginning of the present century, did not, in the case of Walter Spurgeon Hornsby, as with many other men of the day, inspire him to enter the ministry as his life's work. Innate in his nature were definite trends towards business and commerce.

He was born at Blythe, Georgia, February 22, 1882, to the Reverend Thomas Jefferson and Mrs. Charlotte Campfield Hornsby.

He was graduated from the Walker Baptist Institute of Augusta in 1901. In school he was fond of mathematics, "because," he said, "it required hard work." He did some work as a janitor to defray his expenses while attending school; but even before his graduation he was learning the business of life insurance by serving as a soliciting agent, while at the same time occupying all his odd moments selling newspapers, peddling vegetables, serving as a coachman, butler, painter and grocer.

When only sixteen he insisted on having a part in the organization of the Pilgrim Benevolent Society, which later became the Pilgrim Health and Life Insurance Company, of which he is now the guiding genius.

Mr. Hornsby's talents in business run along a variety of lines; and while impressed with the enduring character of life insurance, he nevertheless has been active in the fraternal world, serving as a leader in the Independent Order of Temple Builders, Odd Fellows, Knights of Pythias, and Masons. He was the prime mover in the organization of the successful Hornsby-McCoy Realty Company and the Pilgrim Tonsorial Parlor.

But while Walter Spurgeon Hornsby never felt that he was called to preach, he has from early childhood been a firm believer, a staunch member, and an active worker in the church. He has served as head of the Walker Baptist Junior College Alumni; president and director of Shiloh Orphanage; president of the choir, and trustee of Antioch Baptist Church as well as vice president of the Baptist Laymen's League of America.

Mr. Hornsby is regional vice president of the National Negro Business League; trustee of Haines Junior College; former chairman of the Court of Honor, Colored Boy Scouts of America; and an active leader in the Y. M. C. A.

When the organizational meeting of the National Negro Insurance Association was called to meet at Durham, North Carolina, in October 1921, Walter Spurgeon Hornsby was an active and valuable member, contributing, by his level-headed advice, much to the enactment of laws and the formulation of plans that have made this organization the most effective Negro economic agency.

It was inevitable that at sometime the National Negro Insurance Association would demand as its leader this character, who so persistently has proven his business acumen and worth as a man. When the Association met in Detroit, in July 1936, he was unanimously elected president.

The 1937 annual session, held in Augusta, Mr. Hornsby's home town, was noted for the many thoughtful provisions for the comfort and pleasure of the delegates and plans for the future progress of the business of life insurance among Negroes.

Twice married, first to Miss Mamie Dugas, December 25, 1912, and then to Miss Hattie Beatrice Driscoll, June 25, 1930, he is the father of five children, Walter Spurgeon, Jr., Thomas Dugas, Charlotte Josephine, Jean Lenore, and Harriet Waltena.

Mr. Hornsby is recognized in the financial circles of Augusta as one of its most substantial citizens, regardless of race; and his racial identity does not interfere with the freedom with which his advice on business matters is sought by the citizens of his home town.

J. S. PERRY, *Secretary-Treasurer*

Mr. Perry was born at Sandersville, Georgia. He attended the grade school in the town of his birth and later went to Atlanta to further his education in a private institution.

Some of the activities he engaged in prior to becoming connected with Pilgrim were as teacher, electrician, barber, cobbler, printer, merchant, and banker.

Since joining the forces of the Pilgrim Life he has also served the company in many capacities. Starting as a debit man he worked his way up, becoming assistant secretary and a member of the board of directors. Upon the death of Secretary-Treasurer T. J. Walker in 1937, Mr. Perry was the unanimous choice of the authorities for that important post.

Mr. Perry is widely known in religious and fraternal circles. He is a trustee and treasurer of Bethel A. M. E. Church of Augusta, and teaches the men's Bible class at the same church.

Mr. Perry is happily married to the former Miss Marie Louise Brokins, and they are the proud parents of four devoted children: Theus, J. S. Jr., Laurosa L., and Freddie D. Perry.

T. WALTER JOSEY, *Medical Director*

Dr. T. Walter Josey, medical director of Pilgrim Health and Life Insurance Company is one among many who attribute their success to the guidance in early life of Miss Lucy Laney, affectionately known as "the mother of the children of the people," at Haines Institute.

Born in Augusta, Dr. Josey received all his early school training at Haines Institute. After graduating from Haines young Josey matriculated at Atlanta University. Later he entered the Medical School of Howard University, from which he received his degree. He then established himself in the practice of his profession in Augusta.

Even before he went to medical school Dr. Josey was interested in the growth and development of the Pilgrim Insurance Company. He worked constantly with the Hornsbys, the Walkers, and young Collier. After he became a physician, they prevailed upon him to accept a position with the company as medical director. This position assumed greater proportions when the ordinary life department was added in 1930. At the present time Dr. Josey heads a staff of approximately one hundred medical examiners, who look after the risk selections for Pilgrim.

DR. J. C. COLLIER, *Medical Director*

One of the young men whom Solomon W. Walker interested in the benevolent society in 1898, and one of the three now surviving founders, is J. C. Collier, a prominent physician in Augusta and a medical director of the company.

Dr. Collier is a native of Augusta, the son of Madison J. and Frances Collier. He received his early school training in the Mauge Street School in Augusta; pursued his college work at Paine College, Augusta, and completed his medical course at Leonard Medical College of Shaw University, Raleigh, North Carolina. It was largely through his own industry and thrift that he was able to finish medical school; during the years of his professional training he worked on the Hudson River Day Line in the summer months to earn money for his next year's school expenses.

After completing his medical education, Dr. Collier taught school a short time before seriously taking up the practice of medicine.

In addition to his duties with Pilgrim Life as medical director and attending to his splendid practice in Augusta, Dr. Collier is actively engaged in the fraternal and civic life of his city. He is the grand secretary of the Independent Order of Good Samaritans and Daughters of Samaria and is a member of the Stoney Medical Society of Richmond County, Georgia.

On December 22, 1916, he was married to Miss Vivian Carr. They have no children.

J. THOMAS WALKER, *Second Vice President and Agency Director*

Pilgrim Life is fortunate in having as one of its officers and directors the son of one of the company's founders, whose life was from his early youth imbued with the interests and principles of life insurance. This young man is J. Thomas Walker, the only child of Mr. and Mrs. Thomas J. Walker, born January 15, 1901, at their family home in Augusta.

Young Walker first attended school at Haines Institute under Miss Lucy Laney, and was later transferred to Walker Baptist Institute where he completed both his grammar and high school training. He was later graduated from Morehouse College in Atlanta with the A. B. degree. While at the Institute and at Morehouse, he distinguished himself as an athlete and an orator, and was always well toward the top in scholarship. In athletics he won the coveted "M" in baseball and football at Morehouse; and was made a member of the Kappa Alpha Psi Fraternity there.

Having at an early age made up his mind to follow in the footsteps of his father in the life insurance business, young Walker, upon graduation from Morehouse, did graduate work in the School of Business Administration of Temple University at

163

Philadelphia. Wisely, he started at the very bottom of the ladder to learn the insurance business from the ground-work up. He earned his promotions by meritorious services in each of the capacities and departments in which he has served his company; from the debit, up through the duties of special man, home office clerk, auditor, and field supervisor, until his executive ability was recognized by his election to the board of directors and director of agencies. That he has succeeded in this post is proved by his having recently been named second vice president in addition to his agency directorate.

S. B. THOMAS, *Director and Supervisor of Claims*

S. B. Thomas, a director and supervisor of claims of Pilgrim Health and Life Insurance Company, was born March 18, 1897, at Guyton, Georgia. He is the son of the Reverend and Mrs. J. T. Thomas. He attended the public schools of Blackshear and Waycross, Georgia, until he finished high school. He then entered Morris Brown College where he took two years of college work.

Shortly after coming out of Morris Brown, Mr. Thomas decided that he would enter life insurance work. He was first employed in 1917 by Pilgrim Life as an agent in the Albany district, and he has remained with this company uninterruptedly since that date.

Mr. Thomas has served the company satisfactorily in many capacities. At various times he has been manager and supervisor in all three states in which the Pilgrim operates. He led Pilgrim forces in opening up South Carolina. He has been a member of the board of directors for six years, and on February 11, 1937, he was promoted to the position he now holds, that of supervisor of claims.

On April 5, 1925, the marriage of Mr. Thomas to the former Miss Mary Alice Hargrove of Montgomery, Alabama, was solemnized. This happy couple now reside in their charming home at 1444 Gwinnett Street, Augusta.

W. S. HORNSBY, JR., *Investment Officer*

Walter Spurgeon Hornsby, Sr., the vice president and general manager, and one of the founders of Pilgrim Life, is blessed by having his first-born son follow his footsteps.

Walter Spurgeon Hornsby, Jr. was born in Augusta, November 11, 1914. His formal education was received at the Walker Baptist Institute Kindergarten, the Mauge Street Grammar School, the

Walker Baptist Institute High School, and Hampton Institute, Virginia, where he took a business course. Upon leaving Hampton, young Hornsby took courses in life insurance, from the investment angle, under private tuition.

He first entered the services of Pilgrim Life as an agent, was promoted to special man, and was home office attache for some time. He was recently made a director with the status of investment officer.

COLONEL T. J. WALKER, *Late Secretary-Treasurer and Founder*

Colonel Walker was born at Blythe, Georgia. His parents were the Reverend and Mrs. Henry Walker. His formal education was received at Walker Baptist Institute, Augusta, Georgia. Early in his life young Walker became a printer by trade. In 1898 he became associated with his brother Solomon, Walter Hornsby, J. C. Collier, and the Reverend T. J. Hornsby in the establishment of what is now the Pilgrim Health and Life Insurance Company. At the outset Colonel Walker was named secretary-treasurer, which position he held until the time of his death in December 1936.

Colonel Walker was active in religious, civic, and fraternal affairs. He was a loyal member of Tabernacle Baptist Church. He was also active in the Sunday school. He served on the trustee board of his church. He was high in the councils of the Knights of Pythias, being particularly interested in the Uniform Ranks, in which he rose to the station of a colonel. He was prominent as a Mason and an Odd Fellow.

In 1898 he was married to Miss Susie Odum. To their union one child was born, Joseph Thomas Walker.

THE UNITY INDUSTRIAL LIFE INSURANCE CO., NEW ORLEANS, LOUISIANA

THE Unity Industrial Life Insurance Company of New Orleans, Louisiana, was organized in 1907 by Dr. Paul H. V. Dejoie, in association with the late George Geddes and others. Unity Industrial was, until its transfer to white interests, the oldest Negro insurance company in Louisiana. Dr. Dejoie served as president of the company for many years and until his death. He was succeeded by his brother, Connie C. Dejoie, Sr.

The company was founded with a capital stock of $10,000,

nearly all of which was at first owned by connections of the Dejoie family, of whom there are many in the Crescent City. The operations were always confined to Louisiana.

Under the administration of Connie C. Dejoie, Sr. there was steady and rapid progress for a number of years. In 1929 the annual income reached a peak of over $600,000; but since that time it has steadily decreased, being only $273,261 at the close of business, December 31, 1937. The general economic condition of the country accounted to a great extent for this shrinkage in the company's business. However, during the depression, the management decided to discontinue writing the health and accident business and attempted to substitute industrial whole-life policies for all the industrial life and disability business in force. The decline in business was probably due even more to this step than to the general depression.

Although the controlling interest in this company was in the hands of the Dejoie relatives, in the summer of 1939 bitter differences among the directors, which had for some years been kept under cover, became public. Henry L. Wilcox, general manager of the company and long an intimate friend of President C. C. Dejoie, Sr., shot Prudhomme J. E. Dejoie, vice president and treasurer of the company and son of the late Dr. Paul H. V. Dejoie, the founder. Prudhomme Dejoie had successfully opposed the election of C. C. Dejoie, Jr. to a place on the board of directors. It was about this that the shooting occurred. Prudhomme Dejoie was not fatally wounded; and C. C. Dejoie, Sr., probably despairing of workable relations with his nephew, on Saturday, September 9, 1939, sold the controlling stock of the company. Whether or not the sale was to directors of a white company as alleged, it is true that white men took charge of the home office at 535 South Rampart Street during the following week. A new board of directors, a majority of whom are white men, had been elected.

The extent to which the colored people of New Orleans and of Louisiana generally were aroused by the alleged sale of this old Negro institution to white interests will be seen from the following quotations from *The Sepia Socialite,* a weekly newspaper published at 4719 Erato Street, New Orleans:

* * *

Tuesday, September 12, in an advertised meeting of the stockholders, this "leader," this "has been" patriot of his own

166

HOME OFFICE BUILDING
Louisville, Kentucky

H. E. Hall
President

H. L. Street
Secretary-Treasurer

W. C. Buford
Attorney and Director

A. D. Doss
Director

SOLOMON W. WALKER
President

WALTER S. HORNSBY
Vice President and General Manager

THE LATE REV. T. J. HORNSBY
First President and Founder

S. B. THOMAS
Supervisor of Claims

race, "sold out or caused to be sold out" to nine members of the white race his control of this pioneer company that Negro nickels and dimes built. The worst tragedy of this act lies in the fact that Mr. Dejoie dealt this black-eye to all that racial cooperation could ever mean, deliberately, and with cold calculated intent—even at the disparagement of his own family blood.

The meeting was called by C. C. Dejoie's white lawyer. The Prudhomme Dejoie faction objected to his officiating in the absence of the President, when Prudhomme Dejoie, the Vice President, according to the charter, had this right. This objection and other subsequent objections were over-ruled steamroller fashion with the usual "bluff" and fanfare of white dominance and supremacy, according to reports of those in the meeting.

Upon adjournment—after approximately an hour and a half—thirty-two years of racial upbuilding was torn down in a single whack of white supremacy.

It is a serious indictment to brand Mr. C. C. Dejoie a traitor to the race; but unless he speaks for himself and offers some explanation, the 46,000 policyholders, yea the 170,000 Negroes in New Orleans, the hundreds of thousands in the State of Louisiana, should henceforth despise him and consider him the TRAITOR THAT HE IS.

*   *   *

The majority faction's explanation of the sale will be seen in the following quotations from *The Louisiana Weekly* of Sept. 16, 1939, published in New Orleans by C. C. Dejoie, Jr.:

*   *   *

Climaxing irreconcilable differences between members in the Dejoie family which has controlled the Unity Industrial Life Insurance Company since organization, resulting in a split within the family, the C. C. Dejoie faction sold their stock (the majority) to an unnamed insurance company Saturday afternoon. The minority faction was represented by P. J. E. Dejoie, nephew of C. C. Dejoie.

In an effort to adjust their differences the majority faction offered to purchase the minority's interests. This offer was refused. Rather than endanger the interests and rights of the policyholders or disrupt the field and office force of the Company by continued court litigation the majority stockholders disposed of their interest at a great sacrifice.

UNIVERSAL LIFE INSURANCE COMPANY, MEMPHIS, TENNESSEE

The Race's Greatest Financial Deal

UNIVERSAL Life Insurance Company, a stock company, was organized as a Tennessee corporation and commenced business in Memphis, September 6, 1923. Dr. J. E. Walker, in April 1923, formed a stock sales agency to sell the stock. By September of that year, under his leadership, the entire authorization of $100,000 had been sold. During the next two years authority to operate in Arkansas, Kansas, Missouri, and Texas was secured.

In 1926, when Dr. Walker heard that M. S. Stuart, head of the Stuart-Anderson Agency, was attempting under their option to reinsure the business of The Mississippi Life Division with the North Carolina Mutual, he asked for a conference. In the discussion that followed it was pointed out that Universal already had a charter and capital stock of $100,000 fully paid; but that it had not been able in so short a time to secure a sufficient volume of business for profitable operation—its premium income as of December 31, 1925, being $93,000; that the Stuart-Anderson Agency had an annual premium income of $836,999.30 (December 31, 1925) but no charter, capital stock or license; and that, therefore, a combination of Universal Life with the Stuart-Anderson Agency would immediately create not only one of the most important Negro life insurance companies, but would practically return the Mississippi Life business to colored people; for here was 80 per cent of its old debits still profitable; here was much of its former organization still intact.

More than $150,000 Saved

The Interstate Life Insurance Company of Chattanooga reinsured all the industrial business of the Southern except that written by the Stuart-Anderson Agency; and it is reported that it paid the Southern "twenty-two times the industrial debit." Under the contract between the Southern and the Stuart-Anderson Agency it was provided that the sales price of that industrial business should be "ten times." At the same rate that the Interstate paid, the Universal, instead of paying $150,000 in round figures, would have been required to pay more than $300,000. Thus it was that Universal, through the Stuart-Anderson Agency contract, saved more than $150,000.

In several respects, the successful reinsurance of this unit and the return of this large annual collection of more than $800,000 in premiums back to the hands of Negroes was the largest and most important financial transaction in the history of the race. It was of great importance in restoring confidence in the financial ability of Negro business leaders. It was a magnificent victory for that loyal, brave field force of Mississippi Life, which had served so unselfishly to build up their company only to see it slip from their grasp through the wild manipulations of a visionary financier.

But all was not yet easy going. The burden of paying for this great amount of business heavily taxed the resources of a company so young as Universal. In spring 1927, a great part of the company's operating territory was flooded and so remained for more than three months, during which time not only was it impossible to collect premiums, but the officers felt obliged to pay all disability and death claims in the area. Then, late in December 1927, the Fraternal-Solvent Bank, with about $39,000 of the company's money on deposit, much of which was never recovered, closed its doors. Hardly had the company absorbed these losses before the general economic depression fell on the entire country.

In the early summer of 1932, it became known in business circles that the Woodmen Union Life Insurance Company, of Hot Springs, Arkansas, was involved in financial difficulties. In an attempt to prevent the great assets of this company from meeting a fate similar to that which had befallen other Negro companies taken over by receivers, officers of Universal Life entered into a reinsurance agreement with John L. Webb, president, and B. G. Olive, secretary. Under the terms of this agreement Universal acted as liquidating trustees, for the purpose of collecting the premiums of Woodmen Union, liquidating its assets and paying all claims against the latter company in so far as they should be able to with the premiums collected and the liquidated assets. Under this arrangement all occurring claims under Woodmen Union Life policies were paid in full; a dividend of 9 per cent was paid on all the claims outstanding when Universal took charge, and there were grounds for hope that full, ultimate protection of the policyholders would be effected under the plan.

But, in 1934, the new insurance commissioner of Arkansas applied to the courts of that state for the appointment of a receiver. One was appointed, and the history of these assets since that time is not available.

Universal also reinsured the business of the Great Southern Insurance Company of Arkansas in 1927, and of a number of small mutuals and associations since its organization.

The following are among the substantial and prominent characters who assisted Dr. J. E. Walker materially in the organization and capitalization of the Universal Life:

> M. M. McKissack, architect and contractor of Nashville, Tennessee
> Dr. M. L. Ross, of Topeka, Kansas
> Dr. F. E. Pinson, of Vicksburg, Mississippi
> The late Reverend Preston Taylor, of Nashville
> The late Dr. J. T. Wilson, famous surgeon of Nashville and Chicago
> The late C. W. Willis, wealthy planter and financier of Decatur, Mississippi

Dr. J. T. Wilson, from the beginning of the company until his death, was the largest stockholder. Other important stockholders who later invested in the company are Mr. M. E. Anderson of Jackson, Mississippi, and Chicago; and Dr. J. B. Martin of the famous Martin family of Memphis.

DR. JOSEPH EDISON WALKER, *President*

Fortunately, qualities of greatness in human beings may as confidently be expected to spring from conditions of poverty and restrictions as from the high privileges of wealth and power. They can neither be assured by the latter nor defeated by the former, especially in America.

The picture of dreary hopelessness presented by the surly, red hills and virulent race prejudice of southern Claiborne County, Mississippi, forty-five years ago when Joseph Edison Walker reached adolescense, might easily have produced despair or contentment in penury in a mind less determined. But when young Walker grew old enough to think, his nature rebelled at the prospects of drudgery in his rural surroundings, and plans of escape from them obsessed him.

Joseph Edison Walker was born at Tillman, Mississippi, of George and Patsy Walker, on March 31, 1880. He received his primary and grade school education in Claiborne County. His parents were not able to furnish him sufficient financial assistance to defray the expenses of further education; however, he matriculated at the Alcorn A. &. M. College, Lorman, Mississippi, in January 1896; and kept himself in school with the money he earned working on the college farm, and by teaching during the summer months. Money earned as a teacher enabled him to complete his medical education. During these years he had to subject himself to many privations and sacrifices to accomplish his ambitions; but then, as ever in his life, he followed with great determination the purpose to which he had set his mind. Graduating from the Alcorn College with a B. S. degree in June 1903, he entered Meharry Medical College, September 1903, and, by hard study, received his degree in medicine in April 1906.

On May 24, 1906, Dr. J. E. Walker opened his office in Indianola, Mississippi. Conditions there at that time were not very reassuring for a Negro professional man. Three years before, some of the white people had made it so unpleasant for a Dr. Fulton that he had to give up his practice and move away. It therefore required a full measure of courage to begin life in a community so prejudiced towards colored people as was Sunflower County in 1906. Dr. Walker had to meet the many difficulties that arise from race prejudice.

However, from the beginning he was highly successful as a physician. He grew rapidly in popularity, and through thrift increased his financial worth to major importance. He became associated with W. W. Cox and others in the Delta Penny Savings Bank, of which he was ultimately elected president.

He was prominent in the movement to organize the Mississippi Life Insurance Company in Indianola in 1909; was one of the charter members and elected vice president of that institution. Due to his untiring energy and exceptional optimism even under the most adverse circumstances, a spirit of confidence and buoyancy was kept alive by him in the early years of struggle of that company.

In 1917, on the resignation of A. J. Howard, he was elected president of the company. There was an actual impairment of some $13,000 in the company's capital. In this situation, Dr. Walker astounded his official associates by proposing to sell at a premium all of the remaining original issue of $100,000 of the capital stock. It was a daring venture—to attempt to sell stock at a premium in an impaired company; but this was only the first of several notably brilliant ideas which during his life time he has converted into realities to master difficult financial problems. The young physician at this time temporarily laid down his practice of medicine and assumed the role of a traveling stock salesman. Through his personal efforts all the remaining stock authorization was sold; and then, in the company's financial statement, instead of an impairment there appeared a surplus.

During Dr. Walker's administration the annual income of Mississippi Life was increased from $201,168 to $943,671; the assets from $85,832 to $467,671; surplus from $62,591 to $116,229; and the business in force from $1,970,280 to $14,896,848. His clear business mind and almost unerring judgment in investment affairs were established beyond doubt when the Mississippi Life, even through the hands of receivers, paid dividends of 185 per cent to the stockholders.

Differences of opinion in the official circles of the Mississippi Life having become acute, Dr. Walker resigned February 22, 1923, in the interest of "peace and harmony," and soon organized Universal Life; but these were not easy days for a young Negro life insurance company. Keener competition than that of the prior decade was now to be encountered, not only from other Negro companies, but from large white companies that were aroused to meet the threat of Negroes competing for business among their people. Despite all of this, however, Universal Life maintained itself regardless of its stronger competitors until September 6, 1926, when it reinsured the Mississippi Life debits.

This was an enormous deal to consummate. It cost $156,000 to buy this business, and the financial genius of Dr. J. E. Walker was again subjected to perhaps its severest test in arranging the necessary credits to complete this great transaction.

The attempt to purchase debits costing $156,000 with the limited resources of this young company at the time would have appeared to many as sheer folly; but not so to the marvelously optimistic mind of Dr. Walker. His confidence in his ability to accomplish things was and is measured only by his desire for them.

Dr. Walker has been an enthusiastic member of, and participant in, the National Negro Insurance Association. He appeared first in the second meeting of the Association in Atlanta in 1922. He was elected president of the Association at New Orleans in 1926; and had the distinction of being the only president, except C. C. Spaulding, the first president, to serve two full terms. At the time of Dr. Walker's elevation to the presidency of the Association, interest in it was at a low ebb, and many Negro companies were unrepresented at its meetings. As a result of his energetic work, several of these companies were induced to apply for membership. The Association probably experienced its greatest growth under the administration of Dr. J. E. Walker. Notwithstanding that he was the president of a company, he endorsed the fight at the Atlanta meeting in 1930, and again in Hot Springs in 1931, to break the precedent of electing only company presidents to the office of president of the Association.

As far back as 1916, Dr. Walker was a delegate from the Third Mississippi Congressional District to the Republican Convention in Chicago. At the present time, he is chairman of the Democratic Club of Memphis; and in that capacity is ever alert for an opportunity to make substantial contributions to the good of the community.

Another evidence of the national prominence of this insurance executive was shown in the session of the National Negro Business League held in Oklahoma City in August 1939. There Joseph Edison Walker was elected president of the League by unanimous vote. The Business League was organized by Booker T. Washington; and since his day the office of president has been held by only five men, the first of whom was Dr. Washington.

Dr. Walker has not been too busy with his various activities for affairs of religion. He was the organizer of two local Christian churches, one at Indianola, Mississippi, and one at Memphis, Tennessee, both of which have large, active, congregations. He is a dominating influence in his church; and in 1935, was elected by the Church at Large in America to represent it in the World's Convention of Disciples of Christ which convened in Leicester, England, being the only American Negro in the delegation. He addressed the convention and received the greatest ovation of the entire session at the conclusion of his eloquent and thoughtful speech on "Race Relations."

Dr. Walker married Miss Lelia O'Neal in 1906. They have two children, Mrs. Johnetta Walker Kelso, the wife of Dr. Julian Kelso, and Mr. A. Maceo Walker. The Walkers are devoted and spend a happy, quiet life in their beautiful residence in Memphis, Tennessee.

A. W. WILLIS, *First Vice President*

Progress and profits would probably both register low records in the business of industrial life insurance if in the official personnel of operating companies there were not executives actuated by such a high spirit of cooperation and genuine interest that they gladly forego the more spectacular roles to devote untiring patience and constant executive vigilance to the unending stream of drab details which their routine requires.

Probably in no one is the disposition and ability to do this exacting type of work expressed in a higher degree than in A. W. Willis, first vice president of the Universal Life Insurance Company. He shows that he realizes that no fickle votary of caprice can best serve the interests of this business. He contributes long hours of hard work to its dull routine. No item of detail is too small or vexing to receive thorough consideration and analysis at his hands.

Archie W. Willis was born at Decatur, in the "hill-billy" section of central Mississippi, of Ellen Murrell Willis and Charley W. Willis. He was educated in the grammar schools of Newton County, Mississippi, and in the Alcorn A. & M. College, Alcorn, Mississippi. Finishing the academic course at the latter institution at the expense of his wealthy father, he exhibited characteristic independence of nature by spurning further financial assistance from his parents to work his way through college. In 1919, he found his way into the services of the Mississippi Life as agent at Birmingham, Alabama. From the very beginning, his work was marked by a high degree of clerical accuracy and efficiency; and he excelled as a producer—two accomplishments not frequently found in the same individual.

The excellence of his work won him promotion to the position of district manager of the Birmingham district in 1920, in which capacity he early attracted the favorable attention of the field officer of the North Carolina Mutual Life and was appointed jointly with Dr. J. Z. Barghy as special ordinary agents for Alabama. Their record of $365,000 of ordinary life produced in nine months stood unbroken in Negro companies for several years.

In 1923, Mr. Willis' brilliant salesmanship was noted by Dr. J. E. Walker; and, after assisting materially in the sale of the necessary authorization of stock of Universal Life, he was elected second vice president. In 1931, he was elected first vice president. In addition to the usual duties of this office, he is in charge of the auditing department.

The first vice president of the Universal Life was, at the time of his election, one of the youngest colored men to be elevated to a position of such high importance. Realizing this fact, he became a diligent student of the technique of office management. He is an authority on this phase of business.

Mr. Willis, with all of his exacting company duties, finds time to support and participate in religious and civic activities, being a staunch member of the Methodist Episcopal Church and the local Negro Chamber of Commerce and the National Negro Business League.

Mr. Willis was married to Miss Mamie E. Cammack on May 19, 1924; and they have two boys, Archie W. Jr. and Thomas J., and one girl, Cecilia Dyanthe.

A devoted husband and father, Mr. Willis is yet a prudent disciplinarian, taking particular care that his children develop a sane, practical view of life. The family lives in their beautiful bungalow home at 881 Mississippi Avenue, Memphis, Tennessee.

MARK WILLIAM BONNER, *Secretary*

Some characters seem to wear a natural shield of serenity, against which the sour winds of misfortune beat with baffled fury. Unruffled, they pursue the even tenor of their lives in calm defiance of the bitterest blasts of adversity. The life of Mark William Bonner, secretary of Universal Life Insurance Company, affords a cheering example of that philosophical optimism and composure which extract from all conditions of life the utmost of contentment. In the unsheltered tenderness of infancy a cruel fate deprived him of childhood's fondest symbol of protection—his mother, whom he lost by death when he was only one year old. Four years later, his father was fatally wounded by accident while hunting; and the orphaned boy was taken to live with a married sister.

Mark Bonner, the tenth child of Cyrus and Annie Bonner, was born May 24, 1884, in the scrimpy lands of Warren County, Tennessee, near McMinnville, where lived the older sister to whose

175

home he went for shelter after his father's death. The hopes of his relatives for better opportunities for education for the boy in McMinnville were short lived; for soon again the grim reaper struck, taking this time the husband of the sister in whose home he lived, forcing the latter, with her children and young Mark, not yet seven years old, to return to their old farm home to try to wrest a meager existence from the hard grip of its stingy acres. Mark William, even at this early age, was forced by stern necessity to learn that he must work to eat; and until twelve years old he toiled with his brothers and sisters on this old farm, eking out a bare living. Then an uncle took him to live with him in Nashville, Tennessee.

He greeted this new life in a large city with excited joy and contemplation of playful leisure. In this, however, he was soon to be disillusioned. His uncle thought that a boy of his age, to be kept out of mischief, should only go to school and work. In a short time young Bonner had a job as a bank porter, which required that he report at 3 o'clock every morning, work until 7:30, then go to school; and, returning at 3 in the afternoon, work until 8:30 at night. The pay for the ten hours of daily hard work performed by this youth was 50 cents per week. Still the slumbering conscience of humanity was not disturbed by the great need for child labor laws. It was under these hard circumstances that Mark William completed the public school course. He had just commenced to make plans for further education when misfortune again stalked across his pathway. The health of his uncle failed, and support from him could no longer be expected.

While serving as porter at the bank, young Bonner met and attracted the favorable attention of A. M. Burton, a white capitalist. whose kindly interest started him on his life's career. While still forced to work, Bonner, encouraged by Mr. Burton, took at one of the Nashville schools a general business training course. When after nearly two years this class disbanded, the young man, determined further to prepare himself for business, learned through a brother, a lawyer in Louisville, Kentucky, of an opportunity to continue his studies there. Completing an eighteen months course in life insurance in Louisville, he returned to Nashville. Again he found work at the bank, now as porter-messenger, and at better pay.

But his white friend, Burton, had, in the meantime, organized the Life and Casualty Insurance Company, and announced the opening of Nashville District No. 2, the entire operating personnel of which was colored. Bonner filed application for work as an agent, and for doing so was ridiculed by relatives. Perhaps he would have continued at the bank but for an occurrence, which is symptomatic of race prejudice.

Bonner and the two other messenger-porters, youths of about his age, one of whom was white, were one day called in by an officer of the bank; and the two colored boys, in the presence of the white boy, were told that "this young white man is going to be promoted, and hereafter you two fellows must say "Mister" and "Yes, sir" and "No, sir" in talking to him." The three boys had played in idle moments in the basement of the bank, with never a thought of difference; but now this cutting humiliation provoked sharp resentment; and, as a result of either the real or imagined arrogance of the white youth, when they again met in the basement, Bonner's ire vented itself in a fist-fight at the expense of the more fortunate white messenger. That hastened his decision to become an insurance agent.

But there were still obstacles in the way. He had to pass an examination, and the cost of required license was $25, a staggering sum for one of his limited resources. He did not despair, however, but got a job as laborer in a factory. From a minimum weekly wage of $2.50 to a maximum of $9, he managed in time to save $25; and the lesson in sacrifice and thrift which he says he learned from this was the most valuable in his entire life. Thereafter he never found it hard to save some of his earnings.

Mr. Bonner started work with great enthusiasm as an insurance agent; but, very shortly, clashed with his superintendent, who resented the young man's suggestion that he hire more colored agents. For "getting out of his place" he was ordered to appear at the home office. Heavy-hearted and scared, he faced the white official there, who said to him: "Suppose you take on the task of finding more Negro agents." To the white man's surprise Bonner took up the challenge, organized a night class in insurance, and in a few weeks offered the company ten applications for agency work. By the end of the first year he had built a weekly debit amounting to more than $100. Then, on the death of the Nashville superintendent, he was offered the management of that district, which, at first he declined, but later accepted. Under the direction of

Superintendent Bonner, Nashville District No. 2, within his first year, from $850 reached a combined debit of more than $1,200.

In 1910, the Life and Casualty entered Mississippi, and M. W. Bonner was selected to make a survey of the prospects for colored business in that state. He was so impressed with the large Negro population in the Delta, that he asked to be allowed to open a district in Greenville, Mississippi. In four years the Greenville district of the white company under his management had a combined weekly debit in excess of $1,000. Then there commenced to appear evidences of that type of small town race prejudice so unfortunately characteristic of some sections of this country. Certain white people of Greenville first filed with the home office of the company protests against "this nigger holding a white man's job," and then wrote letters threatening violence unless the company removed him. A. M. Burton, the president of Life and Casualty, at first would not consent to Mr. Bonner's removal. But the intimidations continued. On one occasion the colored superintendent was "picked up" by the police, loaded into a wagon with common laborers to be sent to work on the levee, and was only rescued when the mayor intervened.

Then the white Mississippi state manager of the company decided that "for Bonner's personal safety" he would transfer him to Fort Smith, Arkansas, a town which had a small Negro population and was one the hardest Negro insurance spots in the Union. Of course, behind all of this was the determination to transfer to the supervision of a white man the fine debits Bonner had built. But the scheme omitted consideration of one important factor in the equation—Bonner's ability to decide for himself what he wanted to do and to do it. He was not *sent* anywhere. He *went* over to the Mississippi Life, then in its struggling infancy, and took with him the entire agency force. In a few weeks more than 85 per cent of the Negro policyholders of the white company in Greenville followed Bonner and his agents into the colored company.

That put Bonner in a difficult situation. Suit for damages to the amount of $10,000 was filed against him for "switching business"; and the Mississippi Insurance Commissioner threatened to cancel the Mississippi Life's license unless it dismissed him; but was persuaded to withhold action pending the outcome of the lawsuit. The charges could not be sustained. Negro policyholders, called as witnesses by the prosecution, all testified in substance that they had become insured in Mississippi Life at their request and in full knowledge of all of the circumstances.

In less than three years the Greenville district of the Mississippi Life was among its largest and most profitable; and in 1917, Mr. Bonner was made state manager for Arkansas. In 1920, when the Mississipi Life moved to Memphis, he was promoted to the office of general inspector, working out of the home office.

In 1923, when Dr. J. E. Walker organized Universal Life, Mr. Bonner was elected secretary, in which position he has continued to serve. During his administration in this important executive position, the company's clerical systems have kept pace with its rapid development and increase in all departments.

Thus, from the sterile, hard-pinched farm lands in the scraggy scrub woods of Warren County, has the stony path of this orphan boy led always upward to his present high place in the business affairs of Negroes; and ever, whether in the grip of poverty or on the high crest of triumphant success, the tranquility of his deportment has remained unruffled.

Mr. Bonner was married in 1911 to Miss Etta Mae Hayes, a cultured young teacher of Hopkinsville, Kentucky. To this happy couple the years have brought two lovable girls, now young women of high attainments. The older daughter, Corrine, is the wife of Dr. J. B. Martin, Jr., of St. Louis, Missouri, and the younger, Miss Kathleen, is a directress of social work in Cleveland, Ohio. The parents live at 719 Walker Avenue, Memphis, Tennessee.

MERAH STEVEN STUART,

Vice President-Director of Governmental Relations

From the beginning of the nineteenth century until the Emancipation in 1865 there was a mingling of the blood of several races in Adams and Pickering (later Jefferson) Counties, Mississippi, the first two counties organized in the old Southwest Territory. The intersocial relations obtaining when colored slave women were sometimes the playthings of white masters did not, of course, abruptly end with the termination of the Civil War. Some of these white masters then discovered that their free indulgnces with their slave women had developed attachments that were even more difficult to sever than their chattel ownership of these women. It was from such a strange combination of human relations that Merah Steven Stuart sprang.

He was born June 27, 1878, in the former slave quarters on the Stampley Plantation at Stampley, Jefferson County, Mississippi, of Henrietta Stampley and Blount W. Stuart, a white man of Fayette, Mississippi. Henrietta was the mulatto daughter of Steven Stampley, the white Irish slave-owner of the large Stampley Plantation. Merah is the fifth of her six children. His childhood was spent on a farm managed by his mother near the scene of his birth, his father having died when Merah was only seven years old. His mother was a thrifty provider, and therefore the lot of her children, while in many respects similar to that of the children of relatives and neighbors, was, in the necessities of life and rural comforts, a little above the low average of the community.

Merah attended a rural public school in Jefferson County, Mississippi, four months in a year for ten years. The school building, a one-room log house, was often cold and uncomfortable. Through the three-inch cracks between the logs, only partly plastered with a mixture of clay and the native Spanish moss, the winter winds blew freely. The students, divided into four groups, were admitted to the warm seats nearest the one iron stove by shifts of one hour each.

In his fifteenth year young Stuart's mother allowed him to cultivate an "outside patch" (about two and a half acres of land not connected with the principal farm) and to retain the entire proceeds. He took a cousin into partnership with him, and they "made" a bale of cotton and sold it in the fall of 1893 for $40. Merah's share amounted to $25 of which he was permitted to spend $2 for Christmas. In January 1894, he was hustled off to Alcorn College, a state-supported school near Port Gibson, Mississippi, and his balance of $23 was used for matriculation and board.

In college he was paid 7 cents an hour for work on the college farm after school hours, payable then in cash; and in this way he earned all of his school expenses and returned home after school with a surplus of $28. This and other similar cases caused the authorities thereafter to limit the students' earnings to an amount not greater than their expenses. In subsequent years young Stuart paid for his schooling by milking and attending cows at the college dairy, serving in the mess hall, and working in the college shoe shop.

After leaving college, Stuart taught school in Wilkerson County, Mississippi, for $28 a month, which munificent salary he received for five years. He was then elected to the town school at Centreville, Mississippi, where his earnings were increased to $35 a month.

In the autumn of 1906, "Professor" Stuart was discovered by the Reverend Edward P. Jones, Grand Master of the Mississippi Grand Lodge of the Odd Fellows and Supreme Master of the United Reformers, who persuaded him to move with his family to Greenwood, Mississippi, to become president of the George P. Jones Institute, a boarding school sponsored by the United Reformers.

In 1907, disagreeing with Grand Master Jones on the program of the Odd Fellows, he tendered his resignation as president of the school and moved to Indianola, where he found employment as teller in the Delta Penny Savings Bank.

In 1909, he accepted the position of cashier of the American Trust and Savings Bank of Jackson, Mississippi. After serving awhile in this position he became convinced that the capital of the institution was not sufficient for profitable operation, proposed liquidation, and resigned. Soon afterwards the bank closed its doors and paid all depositors and stockholders in full.

In 1910, Mr. Stuart was appointed a sub-railway postal clerk, but resigned after six months, and investigated fraudulent claims for several Mississippi fraternal orders, until December 31, 1913.

In 1914 he accepted the position of general manager of the industrial department of the Mississippi Life Insurance Company of Indianola, Mississippi, in which position he served untl 1923. During this time the company's annual income increased from $60,000 to more than $1,200,000. In April 1924, the Southern Life, a white company of Nashville, Tennessee, appointed Mr. Stuart with two associates to take charge of all the business of the Mississippi Life that it had reinsured in Arkansas, Mississippi, and Texas.[1]

In September 1926, when the Universal Life Insurance Company reinsured the business of the old Mississippi Life, Mr. Stuart was elected vice president and general manager of Universal, filling this position until 1937. During this time Universal's annual income increased from $93,000 to more than $900,000. In 1937, he was elected vice president and director of governmental relations, taking charge of the technical and complicated social security

---

[1] The debits in these states came to be known as the Stuart-Anderson Agency, operated as a separate unit under the charter of the Southern, with annual collections amounting to about $800,000. In 1924, this agency made a profit of $43,485 of which each of the two partners received $10,871.25.

department made necessary when Congress enacted the Social Security laws.

Mr. Stuart was one of the moving figures in the organization of the National Negro Insurance Association in 1921; was chairman of the committee on organization; the association's first secretary; and the first man not president of a company to be elected president of the National Association. This honor was conferred upon him in April 1931, over the bitter opposition of a faction lead by Anthony Overton.

This active insurance executive has maintained a keen interest in the progress of the National Association since its organization. When the fourth, fifth, and sixth sessions were held in 1924, '25, and '26, he was technically in the employ of a white company; and, as a result of a constitutional provision—of which he himself was the author—confining membership to employees of Negro companies—he was barred from these sessions. However, he has been an active participant in fifteen of the nineteen annual conventions. At the fifteenth session in Durham, North Carolina, in 1934, he was elected to the office of historian, created at that time.

He has all along contended for the right of the field employees of the companies to be represented in the National Association on a basis of equality with the executives.

Mr. Stuart, who has married twice, has been the victim of heavy sorrows and prolonged griefs due to lingering illness and loss of children. Four of his seven children have been taken by the grim reaper. Of the three living, Elvert, the son, is employed by the American Woodmen in Denver; Evarie is the wife of Professor A. L. Thompson, of Memphis, and Clivetta is a student in the Booker T. Washington High School of the same city.

JOHN ALEXANDER SWAYZE, *Assistant Secretary*

The famed old silver spoon was nowhere around when Johnny Swayze was born. There was only one spoon, an iron one, in the Swayze family. It was matched by a single old general-purpose iron knife, which all of the members of the family took turns using. Such was the almost incredible poverty of the Swayzes, who in the days of the so-called "Reconstruction" lived in the hilly eastern section of Yazoo County, Mississippi. It was here that J. A. Swayze was born July 31, 1876. He missed slavery by the narrow margin of thirteen years; but many of the customs originat-

UNIVERSAL LIFE INSURANCE COMPANY

Dr. J. E. Walker
President, National Negro Business League

UNIVERSAL
LIFE
INSURANCE
COMPANY

A. W. WILLIS, First Vice President

M. W. BONNER, Secretary

J. A. SWAYZE, Assistant Secretary

Universal Life Insurance Company

A. Maceo Walker
Actuary

B. G. Olive, Jr.
Agency Director

Dr. Julian W. Kelso
Medical Director

The Late C. W. Willis
Director

Watchtower Mutual Life Insurance Company

Thornton M. Fairchild
President

Charles A. Shaw
Vice President and Secretary

ing in and resulting from slavery and the Civil War still obtained even after he had reached adolescence. His parents were tenant farmers whose economic plight was far worse than that of the typical sharecropper of today; and yet, in the dense gloom of this poverty, the flames of ambition flickered in the breasts of these underprivileged children of toil.

At eleven, Johnny Swayze was a skilled teamster, carried "the lead row" chopping cotton, and could pick 150 pounds of seed cotton in a day, until the index finger of his left hand was severed in a molasses mill accident.

When Johnny Swayze reached the age of seventeen, cotton was selling for 5 cents a pound, and day labor on the farm was getting only 50 cents for fourteen hours of hard work. Even so, an older brother was a senior at Alcorn College, and that was where young Swayze was ambitious ot go. His father had no money to help him, but he granted him a leave of four months' absence to work on a white neighbor's farm. This neighbor, B. K. Swayze, a second cousin, hired him for $6.25 a month. In four months he had earned $25, of which he had to spend $2 for shoes and other necessities.

It was Christmas morning 1893, when, with $23 in his pocket, he made his way to Yazoo City, where he paid $5 for a second-hand suit, and boarded the train for Alcorn, which cost him nearly $4 more. He arrived at the college with $11.15. This was not enough to pay for matriculation and the first month's board; but the college authorities allowed him time to pay the balance by working. The afternoon of his first day at Alcorn found young Swayze with an axe in hand cutting sprouts on the college farm. He attracted the interest of the professor of agriculture; and in four months was appointed "assistant cow-milker." In a short while he was in charge of the college dairy, which position he retained throughout his days at Alcorn.

Later, he attended Wiley College at Marshall, Texas, and further added to his education by correspondence courses.

Between school sessions, he found work on the Texas and Pacific Railroad, first as an engine-wiper. Naturally apt, he worked into a position known as handy man, from which he was promoted to traveling timekeeper between Marshall and New Orleans.

After finishing college, Mr. Swayze became the professor of mathematics at Langston High School, Hot Springs, Arkansas; and at odd times was a musician, instructing brass, orchestral, and vocal units in Marshall, Texas, Malvern, Hot Springs, and Little Rock, Arkansas.

In 1908, Mr. Swayze took the Civil Service examination at Dallas, Texas, being the only colored person among forty applicants. He was shocked when informed that he was the only Negro who had ever applied and probably would not be permitted to serve if appointed. He persisted, however, and stood highest on the list of those who passed. The Republican postmaster advised him that he could "not afford to appoint a nigger to serve here." Undaunted, he took the matter up with the district secretary in New Orleans, and was granted permission to take a special examination in his home town, Marshall, on April 9, 1909. As he sat down to this examination he was handed an anonymous special delivery letter telling him that he was wasting time, for "the whites here will not stand for a Negro letter-carrier." The postmaster, though friendly, advised Mr. Swayze that it would be useless anyway as Marshall would not need any additional carriers for quite a long time.

Disgusted, he moved with his family to Hot Spring, Arkansas, where he had to wait one year to establish citizenship. Then he took the Civil Service examination again, in 1910, and again not only stood at the head of the list of the successful, but so far ahead that the postmaster, skeptical of the results of ignoring him, made no appointments for twelve months, after which Swayze's eligibility expired.

He took the examination again in 1911, and again was first on the list. In 1912 he was appointed a letter-carrier in Hot Springs.

When he became chief college dairyman at Alcorn in the '90's, he appointed M. S. Stuart assistant dairyman. Nineteen years later this former assistant dairyman persuaded Mr. Swayze to enter the business of life insurance. He started in as district agent at Hot Springs, Arkansas, and in six months he was district manager of the Mississippi Life at Little Rock. Under his management the collections increased more than $1,200 a week in five years.

In 1923, he was called to the home office to succeed M. W. Bonner as general inspector. When the business of the Mississippi Life was reinsured by the Southern in 1924, Mr. Swayze became secretary of the Stuart-Anderson Agency; and when, in 1926, the agency was taken over by Universal Life, he became vice president and assistant secretary, which positions he has since held.

The principles of thrift and economy having in his early years of poverty become a part of his nature, he has been able to finance and establish other enterprises from his savings. He is the proprietor of the Swayze Service Station in Memphis.

It is a far cry from $6.25 per month to an executive position in a corporation that collects more than a million dollars annually; but, over this stretch, J. A. Swayze has by patient industry, good nature, and ability, climbed ever upward.

He counts among the happiest memories of his life his being invited back in 1935 to deliver the commencement address to the high school graduates in Yazoo City, where forty-one years before he had boarded a train clad in a $5 second-hand suit. Among those who met him with warmest greetings was a white relative of Mr. B. K. Swayze, in whose employ he had earned the first $25, which started him on his upward career.

Mr. Swayze was married on October 28, 1898, to Miss Ida Bowens of Marshall, Texas, with whose superlative devotion and motherly care they have reared to maturity four children. Edwin, a son, achieved great distinction as a cornetist in the famed "Cab" Calloway orchestra with which he made four successful European tours.

Mr. John A. Swayze is a devout Christian and an ardent church worker in the Mississippi Avenue Christian Church.

BENJAMIN GARFIELD OLIVE, JR., *Vice President-Agency Director*

Benjamin Garfield Olive, Jr., was born February 21, 1890, at Lexington, Mississippi, of Benjamin Garfield, Sr., and Anna Olive. After attending the primary schools of Holmes County, he continued his education at Tuskegee Normal and Industrial Institute at Tuskegee, Alabama, and finished his technical education at Alcorn College, Alcorn, Mississippi.

Mr. Olive, Sr., is an efficient contractor and builder, and the son had the benefit of training in the art of construction, which his father was eminently able to bestow upon him. He further prepared himself in construction work at Tuskegee Institute and then entered Alcorn College. Mr. Olive therefore began life as a contractor, but was attracted to the possibilities in the field of life insurance in 1917 when the Mississippi Life Insurance Company qualified for business in Arkansas.

His first occupation in insurance was that of a debit agent; but he soon attracted attention and won promotion as state manager of

Arkansas for the North Carolina Mutual when that company qualified for business in that state in 1919. Soon Oklahoma was added to the territory under his direction. The business in these two states, under Mr. Olive's energetic and competent direction, grew rapidly during the next six years. In 1926 he became the moving spirit in the organization of the Century Life Insurance Company of Little Rock, Arkansas. It was through his contact and influence with the North Carolina Mutual that the Century was able to purchase and reinsure all of the business of the North Carolina in Arkansas, Mississipi, and Oklahoma.

He was elected agency director of the Century and continued to serve in that capacity until that company was merged with the Woodmen of Union Fraternal Order in 1931, when he became secretary-manager of the combined institutions, in which capacity he served until 1932. Then the assets and field business of the Woodmen of Union were taken over by the Universal Life Insurance Company, acting as liquidating trustee; and the former secretary manager of the Woodmen of Union Life Insurance Company became the agency director of the ordinary department of Universal Life and was elected agency director of the entire company in 1937, which position he still holds.

Mr. B. G. Olive was married in May 1914, to Miss Bessie L. Wright, an accomplished young woman of a very prominent and substantial family of Jackson, Mississippi. The quarter of a century of happy married life of this union was broken by the sudden death of Mrs. Olive on July 28, 1939.

A. MACEO WALKER, *Vice President and Actuary*

Mr. A. Maceo Walker, vice president and actuary of Universal Life Insurance Company, was born at Indianola, Mississippi, on June 7, 1909, of Dr. and Mrs. J. E. Walker. He moved with his parents to Memphis, Tennessee, when he was about eleven years old. He attended the primary schools of Indianola and completed the grammar and high school courses at LeMoyne Institute (now LeMoyne College). He recived his B. A. degree from Fisk University in 1930; the degree of Master of Business Administration from New York University in 1932, and completed the course in actuarial science at the University of Michigan in 1935.

Mr. Walker is exceptionally well prepared in the practical phases of the business of life insurance, having served as a field auditor for

Universal Life during school vacations for several summers prior to 1935. After finishing his actuarial work at the University of Michigan in 1935, he was appointed actuary of Universal Life, in which position he still serves.

Under his direction there has been instituted in the home office of Universal Life the most modern clerical machinery for the transaction of the company's large and rapidly increasing business. Intensely interested in all phases of the company's activities, in addition to his actuarial work he finds time to make occasional visits to the company's field offices where he instructs the field employees in many necessary technical phases of operation.

Mr. Walker is one of the three active Negro actuaries, and the calculation of reserves and compilation of the annual statements under his direction are accepted without question by the various insurance departments of the states in which Universal operates.

He has taken an active interest in the progress of the National Negro Insurance Association. His discussions and papers to the seventeenth and eighteenth annual sessions of the associations were noted for their depth of thought and their clear, concise expression. He is also an ardent worker in the various departments and programs of the Christian Church, and a member of the Kappa Alpha Psi Fraternity.

When little Maceo Walker was old enough to begin talking, his parents discovered to their dismay that he was afflicted with a very handicapping impediment of speech. This embarrassing stammer seriously marred the pleasure of his life until after he reached maturity. Then the outstanding trait of determination which he inherited from his father asserted iteslf. He decided that this handicap would detract from the success of his life, and he resolved to conquer it. It was a stubborn foe that he attacked and one that could not be mastered in a few months; but young Mr. Walker persisted and in a few years, to the delight of his parents and his many friends, he accomplished a normal manner of expression. In the frequent public addresses which he makes he proudly says: "I didn't see anything in life in which a man could excel without the ability to talk normally; and certainly I knew that I would be a misfit in the business of life insurance, no matter how much I knew, unless I could express myself to others." He states, moreover, that overcoming this difficulty increased his confidence in his own ability to surmount other handicaps.

On June 8, 1938, Mr. Walker was married to Miss Harriet Ish, the cultured and popular daughter of Dr. and the late Mrs. G. W. Stanley Ish of Little Rock, Arkansas. Already this young couple has been blessed with the birth of a little girl, Lily Patricia. They reside in their beautiful home at 824 McLemore Avenue, Memphis.

DR. WILLIAM JULIAN KELSO, *Vice President-Medical-Director*

The popular idea that excellence and earned success are produced only by alternate generations is very definitely refuted in the exceptional ability and brilliant record of Dr. William Julian Kelso, vice president and medical director of Universal Life Insurance Company. This young physician comes of educated, cultured parents whose lives have been blessed with success and comforts above the average for colored people; yet neither this fact nor that he is an only child has at all detracted from his sterling qualities and determination to merit by his own efforts the highest measure of success.

Born at New Iberia, Louisiana, November 25, 1903, of Mabel White and William R. Kelso, he was in infancy, taken by his parents to Alexandria, where he attended grammar school and the People's High School, a private institution of that city. He then entered Wiley College at Marshall, Texas, from which in due time he graduated with the degree of B. A. He completed the medical course at the Meharry Medical College, Nashville, Tennessee, in May 1929, and received his Certificate of Interneship from Flint-Goodridge Hospital, New Orleans, Louisiana.

Dr. Kelso began to practice medicine in Alexandria in 1930. From the beginning, his success was outstanding. Scholarly, quick of perception, of great intiution, he is peculiarly gifted as a physician. The public in Alexandria was not slow to avail itself of the benefits provided by the rare type of services this skillful young physician was capable of rendering; and, as a result, in eight years he found even his exceptional energy and industry overtaxed to give to his large and lucrative practice that careful attention which he bestows upon every matter of duty.

Universal Life Insurance Company, impressed by the exceptionally low mortality of ordinary applicants examined by him, at the directors' meeting early in 1938, unanimously elected him vice president and medical director.

As a result of improvement in the methods and manner of

selection of risks which he has instituted, reduction in the mortality rate of the company is becoming more and more evident.

At the eighteenth annual session in Cleveland, in June 1938, he was elected national medical director and fourth vice president of the National Negro Insurance Association. By virtue of this office, he had charge of the direction of all activities connected with National Negro Health Week, under the auspices of the Association, in 1939, and of the reports and health programs at the nineteenth session of the association in Los Angeles, in July of that year. Very readily, at this session, it was recognized that in Dr. Kelso the association had made a valuable addition to its official staff.

Dr. Kelso was married December 2, 1929, to Miss Johnetta Walker of Memphis, Tennessee, the popular daughter of Dr. and Mrs. J. E. Walker.

THE LATE CHARLES W. WILLIS, *Director*

To James K. Vardaman's diatribe that "Education is wasted on the Negro," Bishop Galloway, a noted churchman of the South, retorted that, "If the Negro could survive in modern civilization without the benefit of education, that would prove him superior to other human beings."

While the life of Charles W. Willis of Decatur, Mississippi, did not include the advantages of education, it does show that the natural greatness of some characters surmounts the lack of technical training to such an extent as to make it seem almost unnecessary. Mr. Willis could barely write his name; yet he accomplished in his lifetime, in the way of material comforts, far more than does the average educated American.

Charles W. Willis was born at Macon, Georgia, in 1859. While an infant, he was brought by Jim Willis, his master, to a plantation near Decatur in Newton County, Mississippi; and here he was destined to spend seventy-nine years of a life that measured up to every requirement of success. At seventeen he started out for himself, and secured a job for four months at $8 a month. During these four months, he saved $24 out of the $32 he earned; then, securing work for six months more at the same rate, he saved $32. The youth idolized and guarded closely that little nest-egg of $56; and he says that never again during his long life was he without a little surplus cash on hand. Early in his life he commenced to buy the timbered land about him, but made it a rule never to spend all of his cash for anything. This shrewd business man bought the land, and always watched his opportunity to sell both timber and land at a profit. In time he owned as much as 4,800 acres, conservatively appraised at more than $200,000.

Even before he was fifty years old, Mr. Willis became known as the most substantial farmer, white or colored, in east Mississippi. To him and his good wife, Ellen, there were born twelve children— six boys and six girls—all of whom received college educations. But more priceless than this formal training was the training in thrift and economy that they received from their father.

When, in 1923, Dr. Walker was organizing Universal Life, Mr. Willis not only invested heavily in the organization of the company himself, but advanced his son, A. W. Willis, $5,000 in cash for the purchase of stock, without security or written evidence. Unlike many sons, however, Mr. A. W. Willis repaid the entire amount on the date promised. It was the ready cash of C. W. Willis, advanced in large sums, in the struggling days of the company, that often eased the financial tension which all young companies of this type encounter.

Mr. Willis was highly respected by white and colored people throughout the section in which he lived. Straight-forward, brusque of speech, and fearless, he radiated rugged independence that commanded the high regard of his neighbors, regardless of their station in life.

Charles W. Willis was a man of handsome mien, energetic of movement, tall, erect, well-proportioned, and highly indicative of physical power and endurance.

At his death on May 8, 1939, he left a large estate of cash, land and stocks. At Decatur, Mississippi, near the scene of his long, busy life, surrounded by hundreds of neighbors and acquaintances, both white and colored from the adjacent country-side, he was laid to rest, having survived his faithful wife by only three months.

WATCHTOWER MUTUAL LIFE INSURANCE COMPANY, DALLAS, TEXAS

THORNTON MCNAIR FAIRCHILD, *President*

THORNTON McNair Fairchild was born December 14, 1875, of Robert and Amanda Fairchild, who were engaged in the teaming and hauling business at Houston, Texas; and who, being thrifty and industrious people, accumulated a modest amount of city property, and were able to give their son the advantage of a good education. Young Thornton received his primary and intermediate schooling in the grammar schools of Houston. His parents then sent him to Prairie View College where he distinguished himself as a scholar, and earned a scholarship which defrayed the expense of his last two years at college.

Thornton Fairchild started teaching school at the age of seventeen. He taught for six years, and then entered the Railway Mail Service, which occupied him for eleven years. In 1911, he became a real estate agent; and in 1915, he first entered the life insurance business, being also engaged as a funeral director. He made his entrance into the field of life insurance as an ordinary agent for a white company.

Mr. Fairchild has been president of the Watchtower Mutual Life Insurance Company since its organization. His interest in the success of the life insurance business is deep and sincere. He believes that our universities, colleges, and high schools should adopt courses to include full instructions in the business of insurance.

CHARLES AUGUSTUS SHAW, *Vice President-Secretary*

Charles Augustus Shaw was born to Charles A. and Anna F. Shaw in Brunswick, Georgia, December 2, 1891. His father was engaged in the real estate business and was proprietor of a barber shop; and young Charles was therefore able to enjoy a normal, happy childhood surrounded by comfort and care. He attended a parochial school and Selden Institute in Brunswick, and there received his elementary and high school education. He then entered Howard University, where he remained for four years; and he then spent two years at Northwestern University. His college education was financed partly by his father and partly by his earnings as a newsboy, bootblack, working on boat lines, and as cashier in his father's business. He was valedictorian of his class, and a leader in class activities and athletics.

There seems to have been no doubt at any time in young Shaw's mind about the course he wanted to follow in life. In school he devoted his major studying to business; and, except for a period when he served in the army, his employment has always been connected with the business of life insurance. He entered the field of life insurance in 1915 through the position of agency secretary

191

of the Standard Life Insurance Company, Atlanta, Georgia. This occupation was interrupted in 1917, when he was called to serve in the army, where he held an officer's position until he was honorably discharged in 1919. He then returned to the Standard and remained with that company until 1925 in the capacity of assistant secretary and office manager. In 1925, he became connected with the Vitory Life Insurance Company, Chicago, Illinois, in the position of secretary and assistant to the president. When the dissolution of that company loomed, young Shaw threw all of his resources and energies into a noteworthy but vain effort to save the assets. He now holds the positions of both vice president and secretary of the Watchtower Mutual Life Insurance Company of Houston, Texas; and his splendid foundation of training, in addition to the years of varied experience he has had in the insurance business, are proving valuable assets to that company.

Charles Augustus Shaw is sincerely interested in all projects and undertakings connected with the uplift and progress of his people. He is especially active in civic life, and has held many positions of responsibility. Among these may be mentioned: secretary of the Atlanta Negro Business League; president of the Atlanta Business League; vice president Atlanta Anti-Tuberculosis Association; secretary, National Negro Insurance Association; director, Atlanta Urban League; secretary, Atlanta Branch N. A. A. C. P.; member of Committee of Management Atlanta Y. M. C. A.; senior warden, St. Paul's Episcopal Church, Atlanta; president, Men's Club, St. Edmund's Episcopal Church, Chicago; lay reader, St. Luke's Episcopal Church, Houston, Texas; executive secretary, Houston Negro Chamber of Commerce; member of Committee of Management Houston Y. M. C. A.; and first lieutenant, U. S. Army, and assistant to the chief of staff.

WESTERN MUTUAL LIFE INSURANCE COMPANY, DALLAS, TEXAS

THE Western Mutual Life Insurance Company is a very young company which confines its operations to the State of Texas. It was incorporated May 11, 1933, and was licensed for business August 9, 1933.

Although comparatively a newcomer in the field, the company shows great promise. It is backed and conducted by responsible and influential citizens of Dallas. Its officers are: Dr. L. G. Pinkston, president and treasurer; Attorney D. B. Mason, vice president and general counselor; A. Maceo Smith, secretary; M. M. McGaughey, 2d vice president and general manager; and Dr. W. K. Flowers, medical director. These officers also make up the board of directors.

In December 1937, the business in force of the Western Mutual was $776,407.00. In December 1938, its total business in force was $1,173,770. It now stands at more than $3,000,000.

Chapter VI.

SOUTHEASTERN ORGANIZATIONS

MILESTONES IN THE PROGRESS OF THE NORTH CAROLINA MUTUAL LIFE INSURANCE COMPANY

* * *

(From the 40th Anniversary Number of THE WHETSTONE)

1898—The North Carolina Mutual and Provident Association was organized in Durham, October 20, John Merrick, president; A. M. Moore, treasurer; D. T. Watson, secretary-manager, under the laws of North Carolina by a special act of the legislature, February 28. Dr. T. O. Fuller, prominent minister and author of Memphis, Tennessee, then a member of the N. C. legislature, introduced the enabling act.

1900—July 1 the company reorganized and all of the original incorporators except John Merrick and A. M. Moore withdrew. John Merrick, president; A. M. Moore, secretary-treasurer; C. C. Spaulding, general manager, continuing his duties as agent and janitor.

1906—Purchased the People's Benevolent and Relief Association, Charlotte, North Carolina, November 16.

1908—Reinsured Capital Benevolent Association, Columbia, South Carolina.

1909—Had first examination by an Insurance Department, that of North Carolina. Voluntarily had its business valued and set up reserves on it. Assets $93,540. Insurance in Force $1,535,568.

1913—Charter amended and assessment feature eliminated, business put on old line legal reserve basis.

1916—Entered District of Columbia. Assets $232,964. Insurance in Force $8,259,549.

1918—Entered Maryland and Tennessee. Subscribed to $300,000 in Liberty Bonds (America now at war with Germany). Said Secretary of the Treasury McAdoo: "The Treasury Department has never received a more substantial expression of the patriotism of the Negro Race." Assets $476,695. Insurance in Force $16,096,722.

1919—Name changed from North Carolina Mutual and Provident Association to North Carolina Mutual Life Insurance Company. Entered Mississippi, Arkansas, and Florida.

1920—Entered Alabama and Oklahoma.

1921—Dedicatory exercises held December 17 of new $250,000 six-story office building, erected on site of first home office. Assets $1,517,922. Insurance in Force $33,763,816.

1922—Reinsured Afro-American Mutual Life Insurance Company, Rock Hill, South Carolina.

195

1927—Withdrew from Florida, Mississippi, Arkansas, and Oklahoma. On January 1st transferred over $10,000,000 insurance in force in these states and over $500,000 assets covering the reserves to Negro companies operating there. Assets end of year $3,004,604. Insurance in force end of year $36,963,096 (after withdrawal).

1932—Appointed first actuary of race: A. T. Spaulding. Established Merrick-Moore Memorial Scholarship Fund, supported by company's employees, to aid worthy students pursuing business courses.

1937—Insurance in Force $41,521,952.

* * *

THE LATE JOHN MERRICK, *Founder and First President*

The founders and first presidents of the colored race's two largest life insurance companies—John Merrick of the North Carolina Mutual, and Alonzo Herndon of the Atlanta Life—both started adult life as barbers with white clienteles. Neither had the benefit of a college education; and yet both were highly successful as barbers, in the accumulation of real estate, and as organizers and leaders in the operation of the two great financial institutions.

The barber shop of John Merrick must have been to him a schoolroom, and some of his white patrons teachers of the "every day," economic affairs of life. Among his prominent, wealthy white patrons there were the Dukes of tobacco fame, the Watts, the Carrs, the Fullers, and many other business men prominent in the affairs of North Carolina. He was the personal barber of Washington Duke, organizer of the American Tobacco Company; and this required that Merrick go to the Duke residence every Sunday morning to give this wealthy man daily service.

William Jennings Bryan, while on a visit to Durham, probably in 1895, when he was a candidate for the presidency, gave Mr. Merrick a silver dollar bearing the date of 1882, and requested that he not spend it until he, Mr. Bryan, became President of the United States. The dollar is still a treasured souvenir in the hands of the Merrick family.[1]

John Merrick was born September 7, 1859, in Clinton, Samson County, North Carolina. At the dawn of freedom when he became of school age there were no schools to which he could go; and it was some years before the make-shift educational units typical of such rural communities were established. When he was twelve years old it was necessary for him to secure work to support

[1] R. McCants Andrews, *John Merrick, A Biographical Sketch*, p.37.

196

a dependent mother. At this early age he commenced to do the work of a full grown man in a brickyard at Chapel Hill. However, young Merrick did learn to read and write and to understand arithmetical calculations well enough to transact such affairs of business as he had during his early manhood. He was never able to give any very clear explanation of how he picked up this limited degree of textual knowledge. He always said that he learned it "somehow." But, notwithstanding his lack of technical training, his educational ability in the broader sense kept apace with his rapid progress in business; and his understanding of men and the worldly affairs of which he was a part was constantly broadening

At the age of eighteen John Merrick went to Raleigh looking for work. He found a job as a hod-carrier and soon became a brick-mason; and, working on the campus of Shaw University, he helped to erect college buildings which Fate never permitted him to enter as a student. Then, by some queer turn of circumstances, young Merrick found a little job as bootblack in the barbership of W. G. Otey in Raleigh. In a short time he was elevated from blacking boots to a barber's chair. That aroused his ambition to have a shop of his own. In 1880 he moved to the thriving town of Durham where he went to work in a shop for a Mr. Wright. Within six months he bought a partnership in the business; and, when in 1892 the latter left Durham, Merrick undertook the entire responsibilities, debts, and expenses of the shop. As sole owner he soon had it operating on a profitable basis; and, in a few years, he had opened and was operating three other prosperous shops for white patrons and two for colored patrons, all in Durham.

The thought has been expressed that college training handicaps some men; that thereby they are made too cautious, and will attempt nothing that they cannot figure out beforehand by mathematical formulas and equations. This may explain why Merrick so readily undertook several projects in different lines; he was successful in all of them, save one.

In 1883, he bought the Royal Knights of King David; and, as Supreme Treasurer, successfully directed its financial affairs until his death. By that time it had become of wide scope and had great volumes of business in North Carolina, Virginia, Pennsylvania, Georgia, South Carolina, Florida, and the District of Columbia.

Also, it was about this time that he bought his first piece of real estate, a lot in that part of Durham known as Hayti. On that

197

lot he erected a small three room cottage for a home. Here it was that his second daughter, Mabel, and his son Edward were born. In 1887, he bought a larger and more comfortable cottage on Fayetteville Street; and in this home were born his third daughter, Martha, and his son, John Merrick, Jr. In 1895, his barbering business having become profitable, he plunged into the real estate business on a large scale. He commenced to build cottages for rent. But he first turned carpenter and became his own building contractor. The country boy who "just picked up" his knowledge of books and figures was able to figure out his bills for lumber which he bought at the mills, hauling it in his own wagons, to save money; and he directed every detail of work in every one of the several buildings he built.

In 1890, the versatile brick-mason, fraternal-officer, carpenter, real estate man decided that something ought to be done about dandruff. No doubt he had seen plenty of it on the hundreds of heads he had cropped; and so, although probably he had never been inside a chemical laboratory, he began experimenting with various concoctions for the cure of dandruff. Not much is known about the extent of the success or of the virtue of the preparation; but Merrick's Dandruff Cure was put on the market. It is interesting in showing the man's confidence in his own ability to do almost anything and his spirit of commercial venture.

* * *

"An old Webster Student's Note Book, found after his death, contains some advertisements he wrote for the newspapers setting forth the virtues of this tonic. These advertisements and a speech written in the other side of the same notebook, are among the few compositions written in his own hand that he has left. As an ad-writer, the barber shows his customary originality. A notation above one of the announcements calls for 'A cut standing at chair arplying tonick to head of customers,' after which follows the article:

Hair when in a unhealthy condition needs treatment like the sistum. dandruff is a clear demonstration that its unhealthy. Something aught to be done and must be if you would save you selfe from baldness
(Merrick's cure for Dandruff)

HOME OFFICE BUILDING
Durham, North Carolina
Inset: Left, THE LATE JOHN MERRICK; right THE LATE DR. A. M. MOORE, Founders

W. J. Kennedy, Jr., Secretary

Edward R. Merrick, Treasurer

R. L. McDougald, Vice President

Dr. Clyde Donnell, Medical Director

W. D. HILL
Assistant Secretary and Comptroller

M. A. GOINS
Assistant Secretary

D. C. DEANS
Assistant Director of Agents

G. W. COX
Vice President and Director of Agents

J. L. Wheeler
Asst. Director of Agents

A. T. Spaulding
Assistant Secretary and Actuary

Mrs. Bessie A. J. Whitted
Cashier

J. S. Hughson
Assistant to the Treasurer

Here are other samples:

> Now for a few facks there have been so many failues in cureing the scalp of Dandruff lots of them are due to the fack that one or two applycations will not do the work nether will one applycation cure a stomach trouble ore a case of fevor or consuïntion. . . Remember the Old addick a stich in time saves nine

> *treat your head at once* with Merrick's Dandruff Cure We don't clame to bring hair back on a ball head that nature has made and has been of long standing as its beyon mans Power no more than the Dentis can bring a tooth back when axtracted but he can save the original in many cases.

> No Dandruff cure has ever been put upon the market that has found such favor with the Tonsorial Profession as Merricks Dandruff Cure No greec no fussy oder its quick erfeck its cooling and clensing Power make it wonderful.

> Now dont let it be a consiteration of what have failed Prior to this but try Merricks Dandruff Cure or money refunded one dollar Per bottle

> hantled by all drugest
> and your Leading barbers
> or by addressing

John Merrick & Co
104 W Main St
Durham, N. C.[2]

*   *   *

There are minds that seemingly need only the slightest suggestion to arouse to activity their latent powers of originality. So it was with John Merrick. He must have, during the first ten years of his connection with the Royal Knights of King David, formed some doubts of the ultimate capacity of fraternal orders to provide adequate insurance service for the colored race. It was in 1897 that he commenced to talk about the organization of an insurance association. The Royal Knights was then in a flourishing condition;

[2] R. McCants Andrews, *John Merrick, A Biographical Sketch*, p.35.

and a man of narrow views or limited vision not only would not have proposed a competitive organization, but, supreme treasurer as he was, would most probably have opposed it. Not so with John Merrick. He took the lead in the organization of the North Carolina Mutual and Provident Association; and, even when the prospects seemed gloomy after one year's operation, he was not discouraged. He and Dr. Moore persuaded C. C. Spaulding to join them in the venture; and it is unnecessary to relate how well they succeeded.

It is worthy of note that Merrick, the uneducated, erstwhile hod-carrier, was chosen president from among other capable and educated associates. To stress the exceptionally high natural ability of this wonderful man it is necessary only to state that for twenty years, a period in which the company grew from an annual premium income of $840[3] to $1,224,541, he held the position, directed every phase of its rapid but sound development, and mastered the necessarily increasing complications of the financial systems required for this large volume of business. This appears the more remarkable when it is remembered that this was no stock company in which he might have retained office by stock control; but a mutual in which he was constantly surrounded by a directorate of educated men before whose exacting minds his efficiency had to be constantly tested.

Mr. Merrick ably supported Dr. Moore in founding the Lincoln Hospital, and he became the first president of the board of trustees. It was through his contact and influence with rich white men of Durham that Dr. Moore was able to secure large contributions for the support of the institution.

Due to the confidence that his connection with the venture inspired, the organization of the Mechanics and Farmers Bank was successfully completed and the bank became a permanent reality July 1, 1907. He was elected vice president then, and president in 1910.

John Merrick's versatile passion for commercial ventures was not satisfied even after he had added the banking business to his long and varied line of activities. In organizing the Durham Drug Company, Dr. Moore had been moved by an altruistic desire to provide a place where colored pharmacists might practice. But it was not conveniently located for the majority of the colored

[3] Ibid., p.108.

people of the city. It was not like John Merrick to overlook any opening for profitable business. In 1908, he organized around him a small group—Dr. Moore, C. C. Spaulding, W. G. Shephard, and S. T. James, the latter a pharmacist—and formed the Bull City Drug Company. Two drug stores, having been established and operating successfully, were later sold to their managers.

In 1910, the Merrick-Moore-Spaulding Real Estate Company was suggested by Mr. Merrick and organized with him as president.

The Durham Textile Mill for the manufacture of hosiery, organized in 1914, was the only unsuccessful business of the many units started by John Merrick. This was due to the fact that no trained Negro talent could be found; and the management had to be entrusted to an inexperienced man.

It was his friend, John Merrick, who came to the rescue of Dr. Moore when he sought to find a suitable building for the colored library. He not only sold the building to the library management at a very low price, but then donated $1,000 to the support of the project.

At this point, 1914, a period of thirty-four years of busy activity in the life of this unusual man had exacted its toll of his strength. Now, at fifty-five years of age, surely he should have rested. But he did not. The North Carolina Mutual was still growing rapidly, and he insisted on keeping close supervision over every phase of all of its departments. Exacting years were the next five, and they took more of his strength. Everything was upset by the Great War. Mr. Merrick was kept under high tension trying to hold the debits of his company intact, as many of his best agents were then called away, to the recruiting camps, to be sent overseas. This constant strain commenced to have its effects in weakened bodily tissues; but he continued to work, walk about, and stand on an ailing foot and further irritate what at first he had regarded as only a slight infection, until it had developed into a malignant ulcer. It was not until near the end of 1917 that he realized that he would have to stop for treatment. But notwithstanding radium treatments at John Hopkins in Baltimore, Maryland, and several weeks of baths and treatment at Hot Springs, Arkansas, the progress of the painful malady could not be arrested. At last he was advised that it would be necessary to amputate the affected foot. Frankly he was told that even that was of doubtful virtue. Here was a terrible decision for him to make; but he faced it with that same high courage and fortitude with which, through his early years of struggles and hardships, he had met and conquered so many adverse situations. There was a short period following the first few weeks after the operation when the beloved executive seemed much better. He managed to get out of doors and on crutches hopped about the neighborhood of his home, greeting friends with his normal good cheer and joviality. Soon, however, it was found that the malady had been only temporarily retarded; and, when again he was confined to his home it was realized that a dreaded misfortune to all of Durham and the colored race was inevitable. After weeks of excruciating pain, which he bore with courage and calmness, the end came on August 6, 1919.

The following brief quotations are among many left to posterity by R. McCants Andrews in his *A Biographical Sketch,* published in 1920:

*   *   *

From His Honor M. E. Newsom, then Mayor of Durham

Quietly but surely, during his early life, he won the confidence and good will of his white friends without releasing the influence he had with his own Race.

From J. B. Duke, multimillionaire tobacco manufacturer of New York, London, and North Carolina

John Merrick was a remarkable man. He was one of the few men of his Race I have known who had the ability to build up a large business through the cooperation of many other men. It was because he had traits of character that made it natural for other men to trust him and to work with him.

From Benjamin N. Duke, President of the Fidelity Bank

Perhaps no man of his Race in North Carolina ever won more conspicuous business success than he. But this fact alone does not account for the high esteem in which he was held by Durham people of all classes and races. He was unspoiled by success. He never lost the "common touch."

From Bishop John C. Kilgo, President Emeritus of Trinity College

"Christian gentleman" is high language to apply to any man, yet it is not extravagant to use as the description of this man's personal character.

*   *   *

202

Mr. Merrick was a man of fine address and pleasing appearance. He displayed a bearing of natural culture and poise under all circumstances. In the presence of the wealthy and the great he was as calm as in the company of the more humble. Constant association in his barbershop with the influential white people of North Carolina developed in him no semblance of egotism or pompous affectation. He never lost the warm esteem in which he was held by the less privileged masses of his people. The fact that he could always get the most favorable consideration from important white people caused him to be rated as a wizard by a great many colored people; and he never refused to use his influence in behalf of the worthy of his own people.

Mr. Merrick was a man of quick perception and keen insight. Especially in the matter of investments was his judgment almost unerring. He came to be regarded as an authority on real estate investments, both by white and colored people. But John Merrick was no speculator. He never visualized or desired fabulous profits.

Mr. Merrick was a quiet, faithful member of the St. Joseph A. M. E. Church of Durham. In his religious, as in other phases of his life, there was no ostentation. He was known more for his deeds than for oral protestations.

While still an unknown boy at Raleigh he was married, and throughout his married life he was a loving companion; and was regarded as "a pal" by his children. His first thought always was for the comfort and protection of his family with whom he found his greatest happiness.

In closing the all-too-brief account of this fine character, no greater tribute can be paid to him than to emphasize his lifelong devotion to his mother, and, in this connection, the following is quoted from R. McCants Andrews:

> On a woody knoll, near the side of a hill, he was laid in the peace and quiet of the Violet Cemetery, the burial ground which he had opened for the people of Durham and had named for his little mother. He sank into her arms and she took him on her breast for his last, long repose.

DR. AARON MCDUFFIE MOORE, *Former President*

Through the shadows of the retreating years the virtue of unselfish service in the life of the late Dr. Aaron McDuffie Moore shines with increasing luster. Though a man of medicine, yet in his zeal for his people's welfare he flung away all precaution for his own body. Like a few other Negro leaders of his time, seeing so much to be done and so few to do it, the multiplicity of burdens that he undertook in behalf of his people took too great a toll of his physical resources. He fell short of his "allotted three score and ten," but into his shortened span he crowded an over-full measure of good deeds for others.

Dr. Moore was born at Rosindale, North Carolina, September 6, 1863. Between planting and harvesting he attended the country school there; and, after getting all the "learning there was to get there," he taught school himself for three years in the same county. He then attended normal schools at Lumberton and Fayetteville; and in 1885 entered Shaw University intending to prepare himself to be a college professor; but the head of the Medical School there persuaded him to study medicine. He completed the medical course at Leonard Medical College in three years. In 1881 he appeared before the Board of Medical Examiners of the State of North Carolina with forty-six other applicants, thirty of whom were white. He was second in rank of those who passed.

In 1888, Durham was a young but rapidly growing little town. It was here in that year that the young physician, A. McDuffie Moore, entered the field of practical medicine. He was highly successful from the beginning, and by 1895 the income from his practice was sufficient to warrant his thinking of the development of business enterprises. It was then that he conceived a plan for the organization of a colored drug store. He told his associates in the venture that he never thought the Durham Drug Company would make any profit. That was not his intention. His idea was that Negro druggists ought to have places where they could gain experience and learn the business; and when it met this expectation he was satisfied.

In 1898, he joined with John Merrick and others to found a Negro Insurance Company. It did not, in that first year, achieve the success which five of its too eager organizers had expected. They withdrew. It was not because he was any better informed on matters of insurance than they that he persisted. It just was not a part of his nature to be so quickly discouraged. He and Mr. Merrick went out and persuaded young Charlie Spaulding to leave his grocery store and join them in the reorganization of the North Carolina Mutual and Provident Association. Dr. Moore gave up part of his office to make a "home office" for the new venture; and agreed to serve as Medical Director without compensation until the association was established.

In 1901 this energetic young physician, assisted by the generosity of the wealthy Duke family, founded the Lincoln Hospital. By doing this he defeated a plan to add a separate wing for colored people to the city hospital, from the facilities for practice and training of which Negro doctors and nurses would have been barred. The subscriptions for the completion of the $150,000 structure were secured almost wholly as a result of his personal efforts.

In 1907, Dr. Moore was elected vice president of the newly organized Mechanics and Farmers Bank; and, until his death in 1923, he continued his most valuable support of it.

Prior to 1913, no public need of the colored people of Durham gave the popular young doctor more concern than the lack of a library. Unable to secure funds either from the city or from philanthropy, he started a library in the basemnet of his church, the White Rock Baptist, and, using for the most part his personal funds, supplied a creditable number of books and other reading matter. But he overlooked the fact that colored people at the time were keenly denominational. The library was regarded as a Baptist Library, and the people of other denominations did not take advantage of it as Dr. Moore had hoped. Then he spent much time raising by public subscriptions the necessary funds to secure another building for a library where all denominations would feel equally welcome. He was elected president of the board of managers, and, in that position, continued to raise funds for the support of the library until his death in 1923.

By his unselfish contribution to Negro education Moore caused the State of North Carolina to improve the Negro schools. This great physician never forgot the hardships and suffering from exposure he experienced both as a student and teacher in the public schools of Columbus County in his native state. He believed that many of the defects in the Negro public schools would be corrected if the conditions in them were reported to the public and to the proper authorities. Prompted by this noble motive, in 1914, at his own expense, he paid the salary of a State Public School Inspector for Negro schools in North Carolina, whose duty it was to visit all the rural Negro schools, report conditions, and make recommendations for improvement. So successful was his work in improving the conditions of the schools that the next year the state took over the work and the expense, and Dr. Moore was made secretary-treasurer of the Rural School Extension Department of the State Teachers' Association.

When, in 1919, following the death of John Merrick, Dr. Moore yielded to the demands of his associates that he accept the heavy duties of the office of president of the North Carolina Mutual Life Insurance Company, there was plenty of office work for him to do at the home office; but the energetic spirit of the man would not be content with sitting in an office. He frequently traveled in the extensive operating territory of the company; and there is no doubt that the irregularities and inconveniences of constant travel helped to impair his health.

During the last two years preceding his death he was not a strong man physically; and yet he never relinquished any of his varied church work. He was Sunday School superintendent of his church for twenty-five years, and for several years president of the Baptist Sunday School Convention.

As Secretary of Haitian Work for the Lott Cary Foreign Missionary Convention, he made a trip to Haiti at his own expense to learn first-hand what might best be done in that field.

He it was who was responsible for the organization of a Y. M. C. A. in Durham. His interest in it kept it going successfully until the building burned. At the time he was too weak physically to raise more money for another building.

Dr. Moore, up to the last, maintained a keen interest in Shaw University, serving as president of the trustee board for ten years; and was one of the largest individual donors in support of the institution for a much longer period.

It is said that he never refused financial help to any worthy cause or person. Numerous were the students whose education he helped to complete. At the time of his death he was maintaining six students in school and paying their entire expenses. He never asked or accepted compensation from any of the various organizations he served, except the North Carolina Mutual; and he worked for it as medical examiner many years without pay. Pure unselfishness marks Dr. A. McDuffie Moore as one of the great characters of the colored race. It was his distinguishing characteristic. The halo of its light encircles his memory.

THE LATE JOHN MOSES AVERY, *Vice President and Secretary*

A bright morning in September 1899 found John Avery, a lad of twenty-three years of age, standing at Kittrell Station with 7 cents in his pocket, a homespun suit on his back and a straw bag in his hand containing all his worldly possessions. He had heard of Kittrell College and was coming to seek knowledge there.

Previous to this time John Avery had worked on his father's farm at Morgantown, North Carolina; in the local newspaper office; served as a porter in the town hospital, and, finally, as special representative of the Royal Knights of King David, a fraternal order. He had become dissatisfied with the little learning obtained from the county and district school. So he set his mind on Kittrell; and, by diligent self-denial, saved enough money to buy a ticket to Durham. When he arrived at this point, however, he was penniless. Mr. Merrick, whom he had previously met while engaged in the newspaper business, lent him his bicycle, and John Avery pulled through the muddy roads to Chapel Hill, where a former playmate and friend, Reverend A. J. Wilson, lived. The Reverend Wilson emptied his purse to Avery, counting out $1.44, which bought a ticket from Durham to Kittrell, and left the sum of 7 cents with which John Avery found himself when he approached Kittrell.

Professor John Hawkins, principal of the school, made him welcome and provided a means by which John could work in the day and go to school at night. In spite of this handicap, John Avery finished the normal course with the day class that entered with him; and, moreover, with second highest honors.

Equipped with a Kittrell diploma, a little learning, a healthy body, and a determined will to accomplish something worth while, he set out to face the world. One of his first and most successful accomplishments was his wedding, in 1903, with Miss Lula Aiken, also a graduate of Kittrell College, who was ever his constant partner, as he most affectionately termed her, through the rain and sunshine. They have two fine daughters, Janet and Vivian Bryant.

After graduating from Kittrell, John Avery returned to his native part of the state. He first served as principal of the grade school at Hickory and then held the same position in his home town, Morgantown. Finding a great need for a higher school in the mountains of North Carolina, where there were so many children who could secure only an elementary school education, Mr. and Mrs. Avery organized Waters' Academy in a mountainous village which they named Adako.

The need that this school filled in the lives of the people of western North Carolina will be remembered by them for years. He served here until 1905, when he was employed as a traveling agent for the North Carolina Mutual Life Insurance Company. His success in this field resulted in his being called to the home office of the company in 1907, where he was made assistant manager.

John Avery was made vice-president in 1919 and given charge of the agency force. In 1923, he was made secretary of the company. Twenty-five years before he had stood less than fifty miles from Durham with 7 cents in his pocket. By the dint of constant application and unswerving faithfulness, he rose from farm hand, porter, country teacher, traveling agent to the secretaryship of one of the largest Negro life insurance companies in the world. What an inspiration the story of his life must surely be to agents on the field!

Mr. Avery was, throughout his adult life, a faithful member of the A. M. E. Church.

CHARLES CLINTON SPAULDING, *President*[4]

Economic Leader of American Negroes

> *He that dwelleth in the secret place of the Most High shall abide under the shadow of the Almighty.*
> *I will say unto the Lord, He is my refuge and my fortress: my God, in Him will I trust.*

When asked to name the factors that he thought had contributed most to his success, that great business executive, Charles Clinton Spaulding, unhesitatingly answered: "The Ninety-first Psalm". The first two verses of that chapter are quoted because they seem to epitomize the theory of his life as he is known to have lived it. His conduct has always been in accord with the sentiments these words reflect.

[4] See picture, Chapter, *National Negro Insurance Association.*

Charles Clinton Spaulding was born on the farm of his parents, Benjamin and Margaret, in Columbus County, North Carolina, near Whiteville, August 1, 1874, the third in a family of fourteen children. His early life was not dissimilar to that of the average Negro boy reared in the rural section of North Carolina. There was the daily routine of chores about the farm and, during the winter seasons, short periods of training in the district school. Notwithstanding the inadequacy of the school facilities available, this contact supplied the foundation on which were built and extended immeasurably the ambitions dormant in this lad.

Although Mr. Spaulding will not agree even now that he is a leader, as early as the days back in Columbus County he evinced unmistakable qualities of leadership. It was he to whom his father looked to do the most difficult tasks about the farm. It was "Charlie" upon whom he depended most frequently.

When he had mastered all that was available in educational possibilities in the community where he lived, the lad made his way to Durham. He had heard that Durham had a future. It was a rapidly growing village; but when the farm boy reached his destination he did not immediately find the golden opportunities of which he had dreamed. The only thing he could find to do was washing dishes in the local hotel at a salary of $10 a month. Though disillusioned and somewhat disappointed, he was not discouraged; and he set about to improve his condition. Soon he was head bell boy and soon after, side-waiter. He saved every dime he could, denying himself many pleasures; and, his young mind still thirsting for knowledge, he arranged to work afternoons and nights so that he could attend the public schools of Durham during the day.

Spaulding finished the courses provided in the public schools of Durham in 1898 and at once turned to Negro business. A colored grocery store had just been organized and he secured the management of it. Its owners, however, were sadly lacking in business foresight; and Spaulding, with his customary thriftiness, diligently and steadily saved, little sum by little sum, so that when the time came, as he had foreseen it would, that the owners of the business could no longer keep it going, he was able to buy them out and take over the store himself.

The possibilities for making history in a grocery store are, to say the least, somewhat limited; and young Spaulding could scarcely hope to astound the world from behind a grocery counter. But he did make a success of it; and, more important, he learned much about business and the business point of view of the masses of Negroes. There, too, he first became known for his outstanding characteristics—strict honesty and reliability.

His successful acquisition and management of the little grocery business attracted the attention of the popular and wealthy barber, John Merrick, and of a prominent physician, Dr. A. M. Moore. Their adventure into the organization of a life insurance company the year before had gone somewhat awry, and some of the promoters had withdrawn; but Mr. Merrick and Dr. Moore believed that Charlie Spaulding, the energetic young grocer, could put new life into the struggling enterprise and start it on the road to success.

But Spaulding viewed the proposed alliance with some misgivings. He knew nothing about the insurance business; and the two men might be placing too much confidence in him. Finally, however, he agreed; and thus was formed the famous triangle of Merrick, Moore, and Spaulding, which endured for many years.

At first young Spaulding was the one and only agent of the company. Then he was made general manager; but, of necessity, he was at the same time office boy, clerk, office manager, and traveling promoter. He continued as general manager until the death of John Merrick in 1919, when he was elected secretary-treasurer. Four years later, upon the death of the president, Dr. A. M. Moore, he was elected president of the, by then, great North Carolina Mutual Life Insurance Company. The company had grown rapidly under his direction as general manager; had continued its growth with him as secretary-treasurer; and now that he held the presidency opportunity was given him to prosecute even broader and greater plans. When he assumed office, the great institution which he still heads entered into a period of growth and expansion never before experienced. It now is the pride of the Negro race.

At the 1921 session of the National Negro Business League, when the representatives of Negro insurance companies decided to organize a national association, no one thought of suggesting any other person save C. C. Spaulding to head it. There was some thought that the movement might be looked upon as a gesture of disloyalty to the National Negro Business League and that, therefore, Mr. Spaulding would not become a part of it. It was in this situation that his keen sense of balance and values asserted itself.

He readily agreed that the problems of Negro insurance could not receive the full consideration they deserved in the few hours possible as a section of the Business League.

He is the only president of the Association who has served more than two terms. He could have served many more, but he voluntarily resigned at the Fourth Annual Session, saying that, "The presidency of this organization is too great an honor to be monopolized by one man."

In 1926, Charles Clinton Spaulding was awarded the Harmon Award for distinguished achievement in business. In 1921, Shaw University conferred upon him the degree of Master of Arts, and in 1936 the degree of Doctor of Laws.[5] In 1931, his associates in the North Carolina Mutual Life Insurance Company wisely decided that the strain of directing the rapidly expanding company was proving too great for the vitality of its president. He was urged to take a rest and to visit the countries of Europe; but if his friends thought Spaulding was going to rest, even on a trip abroad, they were mistaken. He was too intensely interested in the development of Negroes; so, while others rested, he devoted his time to making investigations of the economic conditions of different racial groups in the countries he visited.

Aside from personally directing the activities of the North Carolina Mutual, through his unusual ability to master and coordinate his activities, time is found by Mr. Spaulding to serve in the following capacities:

1. Member, Durham Chamber of Commerce (white)

2. Chairman, Board of Trustees, White Rock Baptist Church

3. Trustee and Treasurer, Shaw University, Raleigh, North Carolina

4. President, Mechanics and Farmers Bank

5. President, Mutual Building and Loan Association, Durham

6. President, Mortgage Company, Durham

7. Vice President, Bankers Fire Insurance Company, Durham

---

[5] Yet he received no college training. In his own words: "The first time I ever went to a college it was to deliver the Commencement Address."

8. Member, Board of Trustees of Southern Education Foundation
9. Chairman, National Emergency Advisory Council for Negroes
10. Member, Committee for Community Relief
11. Secretary-Treasurer, North Carolina Commission on Interracial Cooperation
12. Trustee, Howard University, Washington, D. C.
13. Treasurer, National Negro Bankers Association
14. Trustee, North Carolina College for Negroes, Durham, North Carolina
15. Trustee, State Colored Orphanage, Oxford, North Carolina
16. Chairman, North Carolina Committee on Negro affairs

In 1936, Mr. Spaulding was elected president of the National Negro Business League, the organization founded in 1900 by Booker T. Washington, who served as its president until his death. Dr. R. R. Moton, president of Tuskegee Institute, was the next president and Mr. Spaulding succeeded him, being the first man not a president of Tuskegee Institute to head the great national organization. The titular head of the National Negro Business League is regarded as the leader of Negroes. Mr. Spaulding is in every respect the leader.

Thus, in the life of Charles Clinton Spaulding is found the story of a man hurdling the limiting handicaps of rural life in the South; and fighting his way, by sheer force of will and determination, to the position of national leadership. That "success is carved out by the chisel of efficiency, integrity, and hard work" is an expression often used by him. Men follow and obey him because they love and admire him. His presence never creates even a suggestion of fear in the minds of subordinates; yet he is invariably accorded the highest of respect and cooperation. It may truly be said of him that he is, instead of a great business magnate, a great human magnet, drawing men unto him because of his kindly qualities.

The degree of success attained by Negroes is not a true test of their abilities to endure hardships and make sacrifices to attain the goal of their ambitions. No matter what the inherent traits of character, men and women of color know that their ambitions travel a road that leads almost invariably to an inevitable dead end. They know there is a limit above which even great merit and excelling talents cannot rise.

The greatness of Abraham Lincoln has with justice been extolled. Much has been made of the lowly state of his birth and the pinnacle of success to which he ascended. How far could he have scaled the heights of fame had he been born colored? Would not his wonderful talents have been greatly subdued if not completely obscured? Scores of colored men have started life under conditions fully as hard as those of Abraham Lincoln; and many of them have evinced comparable traits of character and the fortitude to overcome hardships that beset their early days.

Charles Clinton Spaulding climbed to the highest pinnacle of usefulness and honor in the economic realm of Negroes; but, even so, were not his fields of usefulness to humanity narrowed by American racial limitations?

EDWARD R. MERRICK, *Treasurer*

On June 12, 1888, in a little three-room cottage in the "Hayti" Subdivision of the growing town of Durham, North Carolina, there was born to John and Martha Merrick a son, Edward.

Some of the successful things that had already been accomplished by the father loomed large and important, and they inspired high ambitions in him for the future usefulness of the baby boy which good fortune had brought into their home. And he was destined not to be disappointed, for, even in his younger years, Edward showed promise of fulfilling the fondest hopes of his parents.

To have a great father and a good mother does not prove necessarily to be a blessing; but, to Edward Merrick, it did; for these parents were too wise to rely upon the material things they were able to bequeath to him, or even to depend wholly upon Providence to develop in him the qualities of real manhood. John Merrick remembered that the hard road he had traveled had been a blessing in disguise; and he was anxious that the mettle in the character of his son be also tempered by hard work and self-reliance. Edward Merrick attended the public schools in Durham; and as soon as he was old enough, instead of wasting after school hours in the streets, he was required to go to his father's shop where he was taught to "clean shoes clean" and to learn the art of correct barbering. While still a boy he was placed in charge of one of his father's shops.

At this time, both the Royal Knights of King David and the North Carolina Mutual and Provident Association were displaying prospects of becoming highly successful; and it seems that the logical ambition John Merrick might have entertained for his son would have been a career in one of these institutions. Probably that was his ultimate ambition. Nevertheless, he wished his son first to become an accomplished barber so that, in any eventuality, he would be able to make his own way by his own efforts. The more remarkable fact, however, is that the youth himself entered into the plan with great enthusiasm, and soon became as proficient in the art as any of the other barbers employed by his father.

Graduating from the schools of Durham and his father's barbershop, Edward entered the A. and T. College at Greensboro, North Carolina, where, throughout the full course, he acquitted himself with high scholastic credit. Finishing college, Edward made application to the North Carolina Mutual Life Insurance Company, of which his father was founder and president. The officers of the company permitted the fact that he was the president's son to weigh neither for nor against him. His application was considered entirely on its merits, and in 1907 he was given a rather minor job as a clerk in the Sick and Accident Department of the company. His natural business talents and his diligent application to his duties attracted favorable attention within a year; and, although only nineteen years old, it was apparent that he was ready to assume heavier tasks.

At twenty, young Merrick started out as a traveling field agent "to learn the work from the bottom up." For five years this young man, whose father by this time was wealthy and influential in the affairs of the Company, endured without complaint the inconveniences and uncomfortable irregularities which every colored man traveling in the territory he worked must bear. It was not young Merrick's good fortune to "make" only the larger cities, where tolerable hotel and other facilities could be secured; but he had to go into all of the small towns and out of the way corners of Georgia, North and South Carolina, riding dirty, crowded Jim-Crow cars, having to wait for hours in filthy, uncomfortable waiting-rooms; and frequently finding himself in towns where either the colored

RICHMOND BENEFICIAL LIFE INSURANCE COMPANY

C. BERNARD GILPIN
Secretary and Manager

Top left: 222 South First Street, Richmond, where promoters met in 1893 and organized the company. *Right:* First Home Office Building, 527 North Second Street, Richmond, and the present Home Office Building, Third and Clay Streets, Richmond.

SOUTHERN AID BUILDING
erected in Danville, Virginia, in 1917.

Building Erected in Washington, D. C., in 1921.

BUILDING IN NORFOLK, VA., PURCHASED AND REMODELED IN 1918.
The Company has also erected and owns modern buildings in Petersburg, Lynchburg,
Portsmouth, Newport News and Hampton; and owns other valuable properties in Richmond.

hotels were intolerable or there was none at all. Yet, notwith-standing all this, within five years young Merrick had established the business of the North Carolina on a profitable and progressive basis in every worthwhile city and town in these three states.

In 1912, in recognition of his services, he was elected a director of the company; and in 1913 he was recalled to the home office and assigned to direct the clerical work of the Industrial Department and to introduce such improvements in the home office as his experience on the field indicated to be necessary. While so engaged the young man's innate ability for appraising property and for handling other matters in connection with the real estate business manifested itself in such an emphatic way that gradually a large part of this phase of the company's business was placed in his hands.

In 1915, he was elected assistant secretary. Although only twenty-seven years old at this time, young Merrick clearly foresaw the great expansion to which the North Carolina Mutual was heading and the necessity of scientific training to handle the great volume of investments that must necessarily become a part of the company's affairs. Securing a leave of absence for three months, he went to New York and took a special course in Methods of Investments. Upon his return, he took over much of the work involved in the making of investments and the collection of loans, thus relieving Mr. Spaulding of numerous details. For eight years he served in this capacity with great distinction and value to his company.

In 1923, upon the rearrangement of the official personnel, as the result of the death of Dr. Moore, Edward Merrick was elected treasurer of the North Carolina Mutual Life Insurance Company. It was during his eight years tenure as assistant secretary that he lost his father, and for four years of that time he was without the benefit of the advice and direction of this noble man.

Edward Merrick has arisen by reason of his own merit and relish for hard work. For sixteen years he has painstakingly supervised the vast financial system of the North Carolina Mutual; and he handled, through the testing years of the depression, the large invest-ment of this company with such masterful skill and precision that never, in the gravest hours of this economic disturbance, did the directors and officials of the company have any fear for its future stability and solvency. Notwithstanding his heavy duties at the home office, from time to time he has found opportunity to make

Occasional trips to the field to meet and fraternize with the field forces with whom he spent five happy years in his earlier days.

On November 21, 1916, Mr. Merrick was married to Miss Lyda Vivian Moore, the daughter of Dr. A. McDuffie Moore, the lifelong friend of his father. They have two beautiful girls, Vivian McCotta and Lyda Constance Merrick.

Men who have met and associated with Ed Merrick like him. He is a jolly, sociable companion, has a keen sense of humor, likes to hear good jokes and enjoys telling them.

He has attended several sessions of the National Negro Insurance Association and has always taken a lively interest in the proceedings. Particularly was his sound advice valuable to representatives of member companies who talked with him at the Twelfth Annual Session in Jacksonville, Florida, in April 1932. This was in the midst of difficult times, when securities hitherto regarded as almost gilt-edge were being quoted in the market at distressing depreciation of their former values; hence the delegates of all the member companies were anxious to find out just how Ed Merrick was handling the holdings of the North Carolina Mutual.

WILLIAM JESSE KENNEDY, JR., *Vice President and Secretary*

If, among the field forces of Negro life insurance companies, there are those who grow impatient of hearing opportunity's faint tap at their doors; if there are those whose hopes for advancement seem to wane, to them the story of the ascent of W. J. Kennedy, Jr. to fortune will surely commend itself. The uninterrupted smoothness of his path upwards, without the assistance of influential connections, is perhaps the most striking of all of the several remarkable phases of his life. That he had no bitter experiences nor factional opposition is eloquent testimony to the high efficiency and unmarred record of his services wherever he served.

William Jesse Kennedy, Jr. was born June 15, 1889, at Andersonville, Georgia, the son of William J., Sr. and Mrs. Katie C. Kennedy. He is a graduate of Americus Institute, Americus, Georgia, one of the leading American Baptist Home Mission Academies in that state. Being the eldest son of a large family, he found it necessary to seek employment immediately after completing his academic work in 1912. Realizing the great advantage of higher education, though unable to attend college, he continued his studies through special text books and a correspondence course from LaSalle University.

Mr. Kennedy's experience and activities in the insurance field have been full and varied. He began at Athens, Georgia, as an agent of the Guaranty Mutual Health and Life Insurance Company. During his first year he became district manager, then traveling inspector, and, finally, district manager of the company's largest branch office at Augusta, Georgia. It was in Augusta that Mr. Kennedy came in contact with the three Negro insurance "trail blazers," Merrick, Moore, and Spaulding, of the North Carolina Mutual of Durham, North Carolina, who were touring the state in the interest of their company. He was so impressed with their message, given at a banquet in their honor and fostered by all of the Negro insurance men in the city, that a burning zeal for insurance as a life's work was aroused; and, as he often states, "that zeal has never abated." He immediately commenced a study of the life insurance business, using Brown's, Huebner's, Young's, and other outstanding text books on the subject.

In September 1916, Mr. Kennedy was employed by the North Carolina Mutual to become manager of its district agency at Savannah. At that time the Savannah weekly district debit was only $275. The amount of ordinary in force was only $7,500. In two years it was the leader of all of the company's districts, with a weekly debit of $1,245 and nearly $100,000 of ordinary business.

Because of this record Mr. Kennedy was called to the home office, October 18, 1919, and appointed Manager of the Ordinary Department. In January 1920, he was elected a director of the company, and was made assistant secretary in 1923, following the death of Dr. A. M. Moore. In 1924 he was appointed office manager, and in 1931 was elected vice president and secretary, succeeding the late, beloved J. M. Avery.

Mr. Kennedy is the author of *The Negro's Adventure in the Field of Life Insurance,* which he describes in the Foreword as "a Brief History of Life Enterprises . . . Operated by Negroes." The volume has been widely read.

His paper on "Investments of Member Companies," read before the session of the National Negro Insurance Association at Richmond, Virginia, in July 1934, takes rank as one of the most thoughtful, helpful, and comprehensive documents of its kind ever heard in any of the meetings of the association. His advice and observations were most appropriate at that time, when business men were asking each other if depression's bottom had been reached. Also, his address before the association at Little Rock, Arkansas. in April 1929, made a lasting impression and revealed that, without a college education, he had by sheer dint of application prepared himself most thoroughly in all phases of business.

Notwithstanding the magnitude and success of the North Carolina Mutual, its popular secretary believes in the doctrine of a distinct racial business only as a means to an end. He thinks that the broader view should comprehend a non-racial economy and that non-racial business should be the ultimate goal of Negroes. He says, "There have been and are at present several examples of non-racial businesses operating and successfully competing under the supervision of Negro management and personnel, thus proving the possibilities of ventures of this type."

On December 27, 1917, he was married to Miss Margaret L. Spaulding of Clarkton, North Carolina, and they are the proud parents of two girls and one boy.

Mr. Kennedy is a World War veteran, having spent seven months in a battalion headquarters as corporal-clerk at Camp Holabird on the Chesapeake Bay.

Mr. Kennedy is a devout Christian, being a trustee and the treasurer of White Rock Baptist Church, assistant superintendent of his Sunday school, and teacher of the A. M. Moore Bible Class with an enrollment of over 150 young men.

CLYDE DONNELL, M.D.,

Medical Director, Vice President, and Director

Dr. Donnell was born August 4, 1890, at Greensboro, North Carolina, to Smith and Lula (Ingold) Donnell. He graduated from A. and M. College in Greensboro, North Carolina, in 1907; received an A. B. degree from Howard University, Washington, D. C., in 1911, and the degree of M.D. from Harvard University Medical School, Cambridge, Massachusetts, in 1915. He took post-graduate work in X-ray and Physiotherapy at Harvard in 1922, 1924, and 1926.

In 1916, he became part-time medical director of the North Carolina Mutual Life Insurance Company, assisting the late Dr. A. M. Moore, then medical director; and in 1920, he was elected medical director and also a director of the company.

He is vice-president of the Mechanics and Farmers Bank of Durham and Raleigh, North Carolina; of the Mutual Building and Loan Association; and the Mortgage Company of Durham; president of the Durham Academy of Medicine; secretary and treasurer of the Old North State Medical, Dental and Pharmaceutical Association; ex-general secretary and business manager of the National Medical Association; visiting physician and treasurer of Lincoln Hospital, Durham; a member of the Alpha Phi Alpha fraternity, the National Association for the Advancement of Colored People, the Interracial Commission, Urban League, National Negro Business League; and chairman of the committee on Health Problems of the Division of Cooperation in Education and Race Relations.

RICHARD L. MC DOUGALD, *Vice President and Director*

Born April 11, 1896, in Whiteville, North Carolina, Richard McDougald completed the business course at the North Carolina College for Negroes in Durham. In 1919 he was married to Miss Mattie Louise Moore, and to them were born two daughters. Virginia and Aarona. After being widowed, he married Miss Dorothy Everett of Hackensack, New Jersey. There is one daughter, Dorothy, by this marriage.

In January 1923, Mr. McDougald was elected vice president and a member of the board of directors of North Carolina Mutual Life Insurance Company. He is also cashier and vice president of the Mechanics and Farmers Bank of Durham.

He is a member of Omega Psi Phi Fraternity and of White Rock Baptist Church of Durham.

W. D. HILL, *Assistant Secretary-Comptroller*

William D. Hill was born July 9, 1890, at Richmond, Virginia, the son of Reuben T. and Irene Robinson Hill. He is the brother of the eminent T. Arnold Hill, Director, Department of Industrial Relations of the National Urban League.

He completed his academic work and some college work at Virginia Union University of Richmond. Later, he completed courses in business organization, accountancy and life insurance at Columbia University, New York.

Mr. Hill clerked in the True Reformers Bank and in the office of the True Reformers Fraternal Order, both of Richmond; he taught school in Wise County, Virginia; had charge of the Ladies Dining Room at the historic Westmoreland Club of Richmond for three years; and assisted in organizing, and worked with, the Richmond Urban League; and after that, in the same city, did not disdain to take an agent's collection book and carry a debit for the North Carolina Mutual Life Insurance Company.

But he would not permit himself to be forgotten or overlooked in that crowded field. He says it is possible for any agent's work on the debit to be such that no fair official superior can or will ignore it. In a short while, Mr. Hill was promoted to a general agency at Petersburg, Virginia.

Then came the great war, drafting fine young men from every line. Mr. Hill volunteered for Y.M.C.A. work, having had experience in a kindred line, the Urban League. Though later drafted, his value as a Y.M.C.A. worker was recognized, and throughout the war he continued with the "Y" organization.

After the Armistice, William Hill returned to the North Carolina Mutual and was sent to organize the field forces in Tennessee. Then he went to Maryland, the District of Columbia, and Virginia, to reorganize the agencies in that territory.

In 1922 Mr. Hill was made assistant agency manager, working out of the home office. In this capacity, he performed signal service in assisting vice president Avery in organizing and developing the agency department, and perfecting a standardized system for branch office records and accounts. The budget plan on which the company operates was introduced in 1927 and perfected by Mr. Hill.

In 1923 he was appointed director of agents in charge of the Northeastern Division. In 1930 he was elected to the position of assistant secretary-auditor; then to membership of the board of directors in 1932 and comptroller in 1936. He is a member of White Rock Baptist Church and of the Omega Psi Phi Fraternity. and treasurer of the American Tennis Association.

His hobby is his interest in the social and economic welfare of the group, as shown in the organization of the Algonquin Tennis Club of Durham and his activities as a member of the Durham Committee on Negro affairs.

On September 17, 1927, William D. Hill married Miss Ethel Russell of Charlotte, North Carolina. They have one child, a son, born in 1932.

SOUTHEASTERN ORGANIZATIONS

M. A. GOINS, *Assistant Secretary, Director*

M. A. Goins was born October 9, 1884, at Richmond Indiana, the son of Mr. and Mrs. Martin A. Goins. He finished grammar and high school at Richmond, then Earlham College, Indiana Business College, and took post graduate work in business administration and commercial law at Northwestern University.

He has served as bill clerk for the Pennsylvania Railroad at Richmond, Indiana; secretary of A. and T. College of Greensboro, North Carolina; and then, going to the North Carolina Mutual Life Insurance Company, he has seen service in the following capacities: manager of the statistical department; manager of the ordinary department (1922); assistant secretary; assistant investment officer in the executive board (1932); and in 1934 was elected a member of the board of directors.

On August 1, 1923, Mr. Goins was married to Miss Eva L. Whitted, a former employee of the North Carolina Mutual. They are the proud parents of two fine boys, M. A., Jr. and Elwood.

Mr. Goins is a member of the St. Joseph A. M. E. Church and of the Omega Psi Phi Fraternity.

ASA T. SPAULDING, *Our First Actuary*

During some of the earlier years of Negro life insurance companies, the word *actuary* had a significance of awe and mystification to many colored insurance executives. The belief was prevalent that the standard of actuarial qualification was so rigid it could only be reached by persons of extreme mathematical genius. Actuaries were regarded as rare and infallible mental supermen. In time, however, there was born the suspicion that some of those current were using their superior knowledge to the disadvantage of Negro companies.

At various times from 1919 to 1927 Asa T. Spaulding, working for the North Carolina Mutual, heard discussions growing out of these suspicions; and he decided that Negro life insurance companies should be able to have the services of Negro actuaries. That there had never been a Negro actuary served only as a challenge to Asa Spaulding. His constant triumphs in schoolroom tests had created in his mind the conviction that he could master any course of study in the English language.

Determined that there should be at least one Negro actuary, he entered the School of Commerce, Accounts and Finance in New

221

York University, from which he graduated with the degree of Bachelor of Science in Accounting. He then entered the University of Michigan and completed his actuarial studies with high honors and received his M. A. in Mathematics.

To acquaint himself with the practical phases of actuarial science, he then served an apprenticeship under the renowned actuarial firm of Haight, Davis, and Haight; and for a short period was associated with Mr. F. B. Dilts, actuary of the Home Security Life Insurance Company, and former actuary of the North Carolina State Insurance Department.

On January 9, 1933, young Mr. Spaulding was officially appointed actuary of the North Carolina Mutual Life Insurance Company and placed in full charge of all the actuarial work of this company. This action by the company received the unqualified approval of the Insurance Department of North Carolina. The calculation of the reserves, valuation of the company's business, premium rates, policies, and the annual statements by Mr. Spaulding have been accepted without exception or objection by the states in which the company operates. Prior to his qualification as an actuary he had long, practical experience in various clerical and accounting departments of the company; and this familiarity with the work and development of the business the more easily enabled him to institute many reforms and great improvement in its financial programs.

The first, full-fledged, practising Negro actuary has been far from selfish with his actuarial services and advice. He has been a regular attendant at the sessions of the National Negro Insurance Association since 1934, when he was elected the first actuary of the association. His prepared papers and talks from notes, as well as his impromptu remarks, have been of inestimable value to all of the member companies. It was especially fortunate that such expert counsel came along just at the time when the accumulating weight of depression problems had become most perplexing to the officials of many of the companies. The soundness of his advice is reflected in the constant improvement in the methods of operation which become more evident from year to year.

Mr. Spaulding is especially talented for the peculiar role in which he has been cast. There is a far greater opportunity for altruistic duties for him than for other actuaries. The pioneer in this racial field, it is, in a sense, incumbent upon him to lead the

222

way for Negro companies and help to pave the way for other Negro actuaries—to blaze the path, even as have the pioneers in more physical fields. It is to his everlasting credit that he performs, almost gratuitously, these broader tasks with enthusiasm. Always the student, he delights in research and illuminating comparisons. Unlike some mathematically bent, he is gifted in clarity of expression in the every-day language of the common worker in the office or on debit. He has the happy faculty of disentangling the most complicated mathematical theorems, dressing them up in linguistic work clothes, and applying them to the daily routine of the business.

When the North Carolina College for Negroes at Durham was known as the National Training School, Mr. Spaulding spent four years there in pursuit of high school studies, graduating May 24, 1923. The trustee's scholarship for maintaining the highest scholastic record of the entire school was awarded to young Spaulding every one of the four years he attended. At Howard University, for one year, he was an honor student and a member of the student council. He was the first Negro graduate *magna cum laude* from the School of Commerce, Accounts and Finance, New York University; and the first to receive the Gary Foundation Scholarship on his scholastic record. He. was the second colored person to be elected to Delta Mu Delta, National Honorary Society, and the first to be elected as a member of its executive committee. While at the University of Michigan, he became a member of Omega Psi Phi Fraternity and served as Basileus of his chapter.

Asa T. Spaulding was born July 22, 1902, in Columbus County, North Carolina. His parents were Armistead Spaulding and Annabell Lowery Spaulding. He was married on June 24, 1933, to Miss Elna Bridgeforth of Athens, Alabama. They have one child, a son, Asa T. Spaulding, Jr.

Mr. Spaulding is quiet of manner, democratic of approach, and wears his honors and distinctions with a natural, easy grace that makes him beloved and admired by hosts of friends and acquaintances throughout the land.

Mr. Spaulding is a director of the North Carolina Mutual Life Insurance Company, of the Mutual Building and Loan Association; chairman of the Housing Authority of Omega Psi Phi; and a member of governors of the National Society of Accountants.

GEORGE W. COX, *Vice President and Director of Agencies*

If physical proportions only had been the accepted standard of measurement of men in the early days of civilization, there is no doubt but that many fine contributions to the advancement of mankind would have been lost. While unusual smallness of stature is sometimes a *prima facie* handicap, many men not only permit it to be only of a temporary nature, but their mental calibres are such that they turn it to great advantage.

Thus it was in the case of George W. Cox, the dynamic Director of Agencies of the North Carolina Mutual Life Insurance Company. Born at Indianola, Mississippi, October 6, 1890, and growing to manhood there in the home of his famous uncle and aunt, Mr. Wayne W. and Mrs. Minnie Cox, he was so small of stature that he continued to be known by all in that small town as "Little George"; and persistently regarded as just a boy long after he had attained his majority. When he sought the hand of the girl he afterwards married, her father told him: "I believe in eugenics, and you are too small to be the father of my grandchildren." But in affairs of romance, no less than in building men and debits, George Cox was determined and well-nigh irresistible. In Indianola, even after he had taken his wife there; even after he had been appointed assistant general manager of the Industrial Department of the Mississippi Life Insurance Company, he became disgusted because, in his vigorous language, "I can't get these doggone folks 'round here to take me seriously."

One day in 1918 he mysteriously disappeared from Indianola, and when he turned up three days later he astounded the officials of the Mississippi Life Insurance Company and the Delta Penny Savings Bank, with which he was connected, by announcing that he held a contract of appointment as Southern Regional Supervisor of Alabama, Arkansas, Florida, Mississippi, and Oklahoma, from John Merrick, president of North Carolina Mutual Life Insurance Company with whom he had conferred at Hot Springs, Arkansas, where the great business executive had gone in search of health. The confidence that "Little George" had in his own ability is attested by the fact that he voluntarily abandoned an official position with a stipulated salary in the Mississippi Life, to which he had contributed such valuable services in debit-building, to accept a commission proposition with the North Carolina Mutual to develop, at his own expense, four new states in which the company had not yet qualified for business. Moreover, at that time, the stubborn reluctance of the insurance departments of several states to qualify Negro companies was well known.

Undeterred by the long waits for audiences, the cold receptions, the often unnecessary red tape and technicalities which he encountered in some of these state departments, he, by his natural, jovial disposition and tact, soon overcame all of these, and was the happy recipient of qualification papers in all of the states of his territory. Mr. Cox lost no time in establishing efficient agencies in all of the principal centers of Negro population in the states he supervised; and the force of intelligent young men whom he secured rapidly became enthused with the magnetic energy for which this physical mite of a man soon became famous in the insurance circles of Negroes.

Within four years the insurance in force to the credit of North Carolina Mutual in the George Cox agency amounted to nearly $13,000,000 dollars, with annual premium income of $525,000; and, from an annual salary of $1,200 with the Mississippi Life, Mr. Cox had increased his annual earnings from commissions to more than $12,000.

The success and rapidity with which "Little George" organized and built up his southern agency was without parallel among Negro insurance companies. No longer was the cognomen of his boyhood locale applicable to him. By sheer power of intelligent industry he had won signal distinction. It was not difficult now for him to be accorded "grown up" consideration; and in appropriate recognition of his valuable services his company called him to the home office at the close of 1923 and appointed him associate agency director. In 1930 he was elected agency director in charge of all field forces. In 1932 he was elected to the board of directors of the company and also a vice president and director of the Mechanics and Farmers Bank of Durham. In 1934 he was elected a vice president of his company, while retaining his title and position as agency director.

Since the organization of the National Negro Insurance Association, no man has evinced keener interest in its progress nor contributed more valuably to its accomplishments. He it was who suggested, in the organizational meeting at Durham in 1921, that it take the name by which it is now known to the nation as the most effective general economic organization of Negroes.

The office of historian, the medical section, National Negro Insurance Week, and the Sales Training Section are all children of his brain, and were made permanent parts of the work of the association through his legislative energy. He is author of the enactment by which membership and full rights and privileges of the association, once lost, were restored to the field representatives of the companies. He led the movement that abolished the unwritten rule that only presidents of companies could be elected to the office of president of the association. On July 27, 1934, he was elected president of the association; and the associational work of his administration was pursued with that same type of energy which he puts into everything he undertakes.

Notwithstanding the numerous constantly pressing duties required of a director of agencies of a company of the magnitude of the North Carolina, Mr. Cox finds time for activities in various other fields. He is a member of the boards of directors of the Mutual Building and Loan Association, the Mortgage Company, and the Home Development Company, all of Durham, in which city his effective ability has also been frequently requested in connection with various civic auxiliaries. His practical attitude in race relations came to the notice of Governor Ehringhaus, who appointed him a member of the Committee on Interracial Affairs of North Carolina.

He is an active member of the A. M. E. Church, of the Omega Psi Phi Fraternity, a thirty-second degree Mason, and a member of various social clubs.

On July 23, 1914, Mr. Cox was married to Miss Nola J. Stuart of Rodney, Mississippi, a former classmate and rival for class honors at the Alcorn State College of Mississippi, from which both are graduates. He is a devoted husband and father; and he and Mrs. Cox find constant happiness in the unfolding lives of their three children: Miss Nola Mae Cox, George W. Cox, Jr., and Mrs. Erma Carter.

JOHN LEONIDAS WHEELER, *Assistant Agency Director and Director*

Mr. John Leonidas Wheeler was born July 8, 1869, at Nicholasville, Kentucky. He was graduated from Wilberforce University with the highest honors in 1897, and spent one summer at the University of Chicago, 1900.

After graduation, Mr. Wheeler entered the teaching profession at Kittrell College, Kittrell, North Carolina, and rose to the vice-presidency and then to the presidency of that school, which he served ten years in all.

On September 25, 1901, he married Miss Margaret Hervey; and there were born to them three children: Ruth H., John H., and Margery J. Wheeler.

Mr. Wheeler resigned the presidency of Kittrell College at the General Conference at Norfolk, Virginia, in 1908, and through John M. Avery entered the services of the North Carolina Mutual Life Insurance Company. He was first an agent in the Raleigh, North Carolina, district, and after a short time became manager. In 1910 he was called to the home office to head one of the departments, where he served until 1912, when he was sent to Georgia to supervise that state and the Atlanta district in particular. In 1922 Mr. Wheeler was elected a member of the board of directors of his company. In 1927 he became regional supervisor and in 1933 assistant agency director, which position he now holds.

He is a member of Big Bethel A. M. E. Church which he has served as trustee and as superintendent of Sunday school, of the Board of Directors of the Butler Street Y. M. C. A., of the Church Cooperation Committee; The Atlanta Civic League; Negro Chamber of Commerce; Negro Business League; N. A. A. C. P. and the Omega Psi Phi Fraternity.

D. C. DEANS, JR., *Assistant Director of Agents*

D. C. Deans, Jr. was born September 8, 1888, in Essex County, Virginia, the son of Reverend and Mrs. D. C. Deans, now of Montgomery, West Virginia.

After finishing his academic course at West Virginia Colored Institute, now West Virginia State College, he returned to further his education by taking a three year commercial course, graduating with highest honors as valedictorian of his class.

His first position after leaving school was a stenographer in the campaign headquarters of the Republican party during the campaign of Dr. H. D. Hatfield who was elected governor of West Virginia. On completion of the campaign, Mr. Deans went to Atlanta, Georgia, where he served as stenographer to Ben Davis, District Grand Secretary of the Odd Fellows.

Coming north, he was employed by the Southern Aid Society of Virginia, in the capacity of head bookkeeper. When the call to arms

227

came, he joined the group headed for the shores of France. There he served as first sergeant and stenographer to the captain of his company, seeing eleven months' service abroad. On his return to America, he returned to the Southern Aid Society of Virginia as assistant manager of the Petersburg district.

In 1920 he decided to cast his lot with the North Carolina Mutual Life Insurance Company, and was given a contract as manager of the Richmond district. So outstandingly successful was he in the management of the district, that in 1924 the whole state of Virginia was put in his charge as state agent.

In 1927 his development of that state was rewarded by the addition of Maryland and the District of Columbia, and the title of regional supervisor. In 1933 he was made assistant director of agents, and North Carolina was added to the territory in his charge. In 1934 he was elected a member of the board of directors of North Carolina Mutual Life Insurance Company, a recognition well merited.

Mr. Deans also served for a number of years as a director and auditor of the Commercial Bank and Trust Company of Richmond, which was merged with the Consolidated Bank and Trust Company.

In 1921, he was married to Miss Carrie L. Turner of Richmond; and now, in 1939, the family numbers three. He is a trustee of the Ebenezer Baptist Church, a member of Omega Psi Phi, and the Astoria Beneficial Club of Richmond.

BESSIE ALBERTA JOHNSON WHITTED, *Cashier*

The business of life insurance, and especially a combination of life and industrial life-health-accident insurance, is a complicated financial enterprise.

In an insurance company of the magnitude of the North Carolina Mutual Life, the official who handles successfully the departmental supervision of this involved financial fabric leaves no doubt of unusual ability to act on individual initiative as the circumstances may require. It has been observed that a young woman watching the wheels turn over in a factory might not become concerned about why they turn, but that a young man would likely be moved to investigate the reason and origin of the activity; but the mind of Mrs. B. A. J. Whitted, cashier of the North Carolina Mutual Life Insurance Company, is bound by no such limitations. She has native originality and executive ability.

She is a native of Charlotte, North Carolina, graduated from Scotia Seminary in Concord, North Carolina, in 1905, and was employed in the same year by the People's Benevolent and Relief Association of that city. In 1906 this company was reinsured by the North Carolina Mutual, and Mrs. Whitted came to Durham to work for the reinsurer. However, she went back to Charlotte the next year and was employed there by the Royal Benefit Society, but returned to the North Carolina Mutual in 1907, and has remained with the company continuously since then.

In 1916 she was made the company's cashier and since that time has kept account of every penny of the millions of dollars that have been handled by the company. In 1931 she was elected an officer, it being the first time in the history of the organization that this honor was accorded a woman.

Mrs. Whitted organized a glee club of the company's employees, which, through broadcasts and other public appearances, has done much to advertise the company and create good will for it.

She is a member of the St. Joseph A. M. E. Church, and member of its choir, besides being active in many phases of community life. She is president of the Rho (Durham) chapter of Iota Phi Lambda Sorority for business women.

J. S. HUGHSON, *Assistant to the Treasurer*

Mr. J. S. Hughson was born January 19, 1898, in Fluvania County, Virginia. He is a graduate of Morris High School of New York and of Howard University, Washington, D. C.

After experience in the business world in the banking field, Mr. Hughson became connected with the North Carolina Mutual Life Insurance Company in 1930 as auditor. In January 1933, he was appointed assistant to the treasurer.

Mr. Hughson is unmarried, and a member of the Phi Beta Sigma Fraternity.

THE RICHMOND BENEFICIAL LIFE INSURANCE COMPANY, RICHMOND, VIRGINIA

The Richmond Beneficial, next to the oldest of Negro Life Insurance Companies, was organized by a group of forward looking men of the city of Richmond. Its charter was obtained July 14, 1894. It began business operations July 28, 1894.

The first officers and directors were: Reverend W. F. Graham, president; E. F. Johnson, vice president; John T. Taylor, secretary-manager; A. T. Grimes, treasurer; and S. J. Gilpin, J. E. Byrd, C. C. Cunningham, Jefferson Miles, Wise Ellis, and John Smith. Later Mr. E. F. Johnson was elected its president and Mr. S. J. Gilpin was chosen as vice president. Shortly thereafter Mr. A. T. Grimes died and Mr. J. J. Carter was elected to succeed him as treasurer of the company. Again in 1911 there was a change in the officers. Mr. S. J. Gilpin was then elected president and served in that capacity until his death in October 1934. Reverend M. H. Payne was elected vice president and is still serving in this capacity. The first clerk employed was Miss H. Belle Fitzhugh.

The company's first offices were at 506 E. Broad St. When it grew larger it purchased property and moved its offices to 728 North Second St.

In its beginning twenty men purchased a small amount of stock, and after a few years declared a stock dividend, and increased the capital to $25,000.

In March 1929, Mr. John T. Taylor, who had managed the company's affairs since its beginning, died; and the directors selected C. Bernard Gilpin to fill the post Mr. Taylor had occupied a great many years. Mr. Gilpin has successfully managed the institution through the great depression, the most crucial period of the company's existence.

In January 1935, Dr. George W. White, prominent physician, was elected president. The present officers of the company are: George W. White, president; M. H. Payne,[1] vice president; C. Bernard Gilpin, secretary-manager; J. E. Harris, assistant secretary-manager; J. J. Carter, treasurer; Sheridan Jackson, Jr., director of agents; directors: Quinn Shelton, Percy Wilson, James H. Shelton.

THE SOUTHERN AID SOCIETY OF VIRGINIA, INCORPORATED
(The Oldest Negro Life Insurance Company)
The Acorn of 1893 is the Spreading Oak of Today

IN Richmond, in 1893, when the growth of Negro fraternal orders was beginning to show promise of its later brief blossoming, there were few who had the vision to see the possibilities of an insurance

[1] Died in 1939.

PRESIDENTS OF SOUTHERN AID SOCIETY

THE LATE Z. D. LEWIS
First President

THE LATE ARMISTEAD WASHINGTON
1899-1905

THE LATE A. D. PRICE, SR.
1905-1921

JAMES T. CARTER
1921-

OFFICERS

B. A. CEPHAS
Vice President

THE LATE B. L. JORDON
Secretary and Manager

W. E. BAKER
Treasurer

THE LATE THOMAS M. CRUMP
Secretary and Manager 1899-1918

JOHN E. HALL, JR.
Assistant Secretary and Manager

W. A. JORDON
Secretary and Manager

THE LATE LOUIS R. BROWN
First Vice President

THE LATE EDWARD STEWART
Vice President

THE LATE DR. MILES B. JONES
Medical Director

THE LATE JAMES O. WEST, SR.
Home Office Superintendent

Southern Aid Society

Directors

Charles N. Jackson

William E. Randolph

Percy Wilson

A. D. Price, Jr.

society that lacked the specatcular features of the favored orders and societies. Among these few was a small group of men, headed by a minister.

This handful of pioneers met one night early in the year 1893, in the home of one of their number, to discuss the problems confronting a people but recently escaped from physical slavery. Young Negroes, freshly armed with whatever educational preparation they could secure, were beginning to appear on the economic scene in ever-increasing numbers; and, with so many doors of opportunity closed to them, these fathers of a race were faced with the necessity of providing self-sustaining employment for their own.

A solution to the problems confronting them did not present itself at this initial meeting, but the seed was planted—the acorn had fallen on fertile ground—and at subsequent meetings, from out of the welter of ideas, discussions, and plans, there slowly but clearly developed the vision of a venture that would open more avenues of employment to the youth of the race and, at the same time, furnish adequate insurance protection to both the classes and masses at the lowest cost for safe insurance. This was the Southern Aid Society of Virginia.

On February 25, 1893, the Southern Aid and Insurance Company was chartered. Its Articles of Incorporation included the following:

NAME

The corporate name of the Association shall be Southern Aid and Insurance Company.

PURPOSES FOR WHICH FORMED

The purposes for which this corporation is formed are the conducting and carrying on of a life insurance association and weekly benefits to sick members.

DIVISION OF SHARES

The Capital Stock shall be divided into shares of $10.00 each, and payable in such installments as the Board of Directors may direct, with a minimum capital of $500.00 and a maximum of $5,000.00

PRINCIPAL OFFICE

The principal office of this association shall be at Richmond, Virginia.

REAL ESTATE

The Real Estate proposed to be held by this Association shall not exceed the sum of One Hundred Thousand Dollars ($100,000.00).

Dr. Z. D. Lewis, already a leader in the church life of the community, was chosen to head the ·corporation. R. Louis Brown, whose doors had been thrown open to the pre-organization meetings, was chosen vice president. The other officers were W. G. Carter, secretary-manager; Charles Johnson, Jr., treasurer; and the officers, together with W. A. Payne, John E. Taylor and W. R. Coots, the remaining members of the little crew, comprised the board of directors.

In 1906, the name of the company was changed to the Southern Aid Society of Virginia, Inc.; but although the new title was somewhat similar to that of organizations in fraternal or lodge systems of insurance, the Society did not then and has never conducted its business in that manner. It is supposed that, since this was truly the heyday of the fraternal orders, this organization saw the wisdom of attracting the masses by the new name, yet selling them much more of value than ceremonies and badges.

During the first year of its existence, the company's gross business amounted to about $7,000, and it employed ten people. Less than a half century later, in 1937, it employed over 300 young men and women, and its annual collections were in excess of $500,000. It is now a Legal Reserve life insurance company, but limits its business for the present time to all modern forms of intermediate and industrial insurance coverage. At the close of 1937, it had a paid-up capital of $150,000; policy and contingent reserves of $437,137; surplus of $222,777.50 and admitted assets of $872,131.38. Claims paid to policyholders, to December 31, 1937, amounted to $7,569,151.76.

Its field of operation is limited to the State of Virginia and the District of Columbia; and there is a strong suggestion that this results from a strain of that provincialism that characterizes the Virginian, whether white or black. It is interesting to note that a policy adopted in its early days has been practiced uninterruptedly throughout the years of its existence—it has almost without exception drawn upon native sons to direct its affairs.

The Southern Aid Society of Virginia, Incorporated, is the oldest existing insurance company owned and operated by colored people in this country. The Acorn has become an Oak!

Presidents of Southern Aid Society of Virginia

THE LATE REVEREND DR. Z. D. LEWIS, *First President*

The Reverend Dr. Z. D. Lewis, first president and one of the organizers of Southern Aid Society of Virginia, was born at Perryville, Campbell County, Virginia.

He was pastor of the historic Second Baptist Church of Richmond, served as a trustee of Virginia Union University, on the executive board of the Independent Order of St. Luke and as vice president of the St. Luke Penny Savings Bank.

ARMISTEAD WASHINGTON, *Second President*

Armistead Washington, second president and one of the organizers of Southern Aid, was born in Goochland County, Virginia. He was an organizer and engaged actively in developing the following fraternal orders: Grand United Order of Odd Fellows, Knights of Pythias, Independent Order of St. Luke. He served as president of Southern Aid from 1899 to 1905 and is now senior vice president and a director of the company.

THE LATE A. D. PRICE, *Third President*

The late A. D. Price, third president of Southern Aid, was born near Ashland, Hanover County, Virginia; was a director of the Mechanics Savings Bank, the St. Luke Penny Savings Bank, the Capital Shoe Company, the Commercial Bank and Trust Company, all of Richmond. He was active in the operation of the American Beneficial Insurance Company, and at the time of his death a member of thirty-two fraternal orders. He was elected president of Southern Aid in 1905 and served until 1921.

JAMES T. CARTER, *Fourth President*

James T. Carter, fourth president of Southern Aid Society, was born in Richmond, Virginia. He attended the public schools of the city and then finished special courses in short hand, typewriting, and business under the tutelage of white specialists in the white schools and colleges of Richmond. He was employed as a typist for a white law firm, and used the opportunity to study law. When he took the bar examinations he was one of the six successful out of fifty-seven applicants, and the only one to receive honorable mention.

Active in several fraternal societies, he was for fifteen years treasurer of the Improved Benevolent Protective Order of Elks. He is vice president of the Consolidated Bank and Trust Company; a director of the Bankers' Fire Insurance Company of Durham, North Carolina; chairman of the board of directors of the Richmond Community Hospital and superintendent of the Second Baptist Church Sunday School of Richmond.

He was one of the incorporators and among the first directors of Southern Aid, and he has been identified with it during the forty-five years of its successful operation. Elected president in April 1921 to succeed the late A. D. Price, he is still the beloved leader of this progressive organization.

Officers of Southern Aid Society of Virginia

B. A. CEPHAS, *Vice President*

B. A. Cephas, vice president, was born in New York in 1875 and educated in the public schools of Richmond, Virginia. He was active in the Grand United Order of True Reformers before entering the insurance business. He is a successful real estate man and a director of the Consolidated Bank and Trust Company, serving on both the auditing and appraisal committees. In addition to his duties as vice president of Southern Aid, he is a director and chairman of the auditing committee of the company.

THE LATE B. L. JORDAN, *Secretary-Manager*

The late Booker Lawrence Jordan, secretary-manager of Southern Aid, was born in Louisa, Virginia, August 14, 1874. He attended public school there and in Richmond; completed secretarial and commercial courses at the Business College of Buffalo, New York; and a course in accountancy at Rochester. He then pursued the study of law in Chicago, completed the course and made 100 per cent in his final examinations. Mr. Jordan further qualified himself by completing a course in architecture, and it was he that designed and supervised the construction of the several fine buildings of the Southern Aid.

He commenced as an agent of the company on May 1, 1893, built a fine debit, bought stock and was elected to the board of directors. He was made secretary of the auditing committee, later had charge of the home office, and was then promoted to be field supervisor. He next became assistant secretary-manager, serving in this capacity for sixteen years. In August 1918, he became secretary-manager, in which position he served until his death, March 4, 1938, having experienced the longest period of service as an employee and executive of the corporation.

Mr. Jordan was a director of the Consolidated Bank and Trust Company of Richmond and of the Bankers Fire Insurance Company of Durham, North Carolina, treasurer of the Richmond Community Hospital, and an active Sunday school and church worker.

W. E. BAKER, *Treasurer*

Mr. Baker was born in Richmond, Virginia, and was among the first pupils to enter the first public school there. In his early life he worked his way to the management of the business of a white merchant by whom he was employed. He was one of the pioneers of the Southern Aid and is its present treasurer and a member of the board of directors.

THE LATE THOMAS M. CRUMP, *Secretary-Manager*

The late Thomas M. Crump was a native of Richmond, Virginia, and a product of the old Richmond High and Normal School. He was active in church, musical, civic and fraternal affairs. He was the Grand Keeper of Records and Seals of the Grand Lodge of Virginia of the Knights of Pythias; and one of the organizers of the old Mechanics Savings Bank. Mr. Crump served as secretary-manager of the Southern Aid Society for nineteen years until his death in 1918.

JOHN E. HALL, JR., *Assistant Secretary-Manager*

Mr. Hall was born in Manchester, Virginia, November 25, 1899; was graduated from Virginia Business College, June 1907. He began work with the Southern Aid as clerk and stenographer April 3, 1911. In his line of promotions he has served as assistant superintendent of the Richmond District, as traveling superintendent, superintendent of the Washington and Richmond Districts, after which he was promoted to the position of assistant secretary-manager, in which capacity he still serves the Company.

W. A. JORDAN, *Secretary-Manager*

W. A. Jordan has been connected with the Southern Aid Society since May 1893. Prior to 1900 he assisted his brother, B. L. Jordan.

When the Richmond District was separated from the home office, W. A. Jordan became its superintendent. The history of the development of the Richmond District under Mr. Jordan is replete with creditable achievements for the company. In 1918 he was appointed assistant secretary-manager and auditor, in which capacity he served until 1938. Upon the death of his brother, he was elected to fill the position of secretary-manager.

THE LATE LOUIS R. BROWN, *First Vice President*

It was in the home of Mr. Louis R. Brown that the Southern Aid Society was organized. Aside from his connection with this pioneer insurance company, Mr. Brown devoted much of his life to hotel and club activities, and through these connections, he enjoyed the acquaintance and friendship of many of the leading citizens of Richmond and Virginia. He served as vice president of the company until his death.

THE LATE EDWARD STEWART, *Vice President*

Edward Stewart was born in Richmond, Virginia, and educated in its public schools. In early manhood, he was a member of the famous U. S. Tenth Cavalry. Later he was engaged in the mercantile business for 42 years. He served as trustee of the Second Baptist Church for many years, and was connected with various other organizations and businesses. He was a member of the board of directors and vice president of the Southern Aid until his death, December 28, 1937.

PERCY WILSON, *Director*

Mr. Wilson is a native of Richmond, Virginia, and was educated in the public schools of that city. He has important holdings in a number of companies and enterprises, is director and claim adjuster of the Richmond Beneficial Insurance Company, and a member of the board of directors of the Federal Life Insurance Company of Washington, D. C., in addition to serving on the board of directors of the Southern Aid Society of Virginia, Inc.

WILLIAM E. RANDOLPH, *Director*

Like so many of the officials and directors of Southern Aid, Mr. Randolph is a native of Richmond, Virginia, and was educated in the public schools of that city. Entering the insurance field, upon the invitation of the late Thomas M. Crump, as an agent for Southern Aid, he was soon promoted to be assistant superintendent of the Richmond District. Investing heavily in the company's capital stock, he was one of the field men chosen for membership on its board of directors. He is also active in church and civic work.

THE LATE DR. MILES B. JONES, *Medical Examiner*

The late Dr. Miles B. Jones was born in Amelia County, Virginia; educated in the schools of Richmond, Howard University, and the Post Graduate School of Medicine, in Chicago. He taught school for ten years, and served as chief of finance of the Grand United Order of True Redeemers. For 21 years, Dr. Jones was superintendent and surgeon-in-chief of the Richmond Hospital, which was later called Sarah G. Jones Memorial Hospital, in honor of his wife, Dr. Sarah G. Jones, also an outstanding member of the medical profession in Richmond. He was also a faithful churchman, serving as superintendent of the Sunday school of the Second Baptist Church for 40 years.

THE LATE JAMES O. WEST, SR., *Director-Home Office Superintendent*

The late Mr. James O. West, Sr., was born in Hanover County, Virginia, and received his education in the public schools of Richmond. Giving up his partnership in an independent business to work for the Southern Aid, he first served as an inspector, then as assistant to W. A. Jordan, and then as superintendent of the Richmond District. At the time of his death, June 5, 1938, he was home office superintendent and a member of the board of directors.

CHARLES N. JACKSON, *Director*

Mr. Charles N. Jackson is also a native of Richmond, and was educated in the schools of that city, after which he served an apprenticeship with a jewelry firm. He was employed at the American National Bank in 1899 and by 1910 had advanced to the position of manager of all its office buildings, in which capacity he still serves. He is a director of the Consolidated Bank and Trust Company as well, as of the Southern Aid Society of Virginia, Inc.

A. D. PRICE, JR., *Director*

Mr. A. D. Price, Jr., is the son of the late Georgia A. and A. D. Price, Sr. Young Mr. Price showed an early interest in business, and devotes his major time to the undertaking business. He also maintains the various other business activities of his father, including membership on the board of directors of the Southern Aid.

VIRGINIA MUTUAL BENEFIT LIFE INSURANCE COMPANY, RICHMOND, VIRGINIA

WHEN the National Benefit Life Insurance Company was adjudged insolvent on September 9, 1931, and it became apparent that the general receivers would not take any steps to reorganize the company; when the other twenty-five states in which the National Benefit operated took no action in protest of the unsympathetic attitude of the general receivers; and when even the majority of the policyholders seemed resigned to the ultimate loss of their company—in this vista of gloom—there appeared only one star of hope, and that was in the sky of Old Virginia, when it was announced that the policyholders there had taken independent action to protect their interests by organizing the Virginia Mutual Benefit Life Insurance Company to reinsure the business in that state.

The National Benefit employees in Virginia, the loyal policyholders and a sympathetic local receivership came together, agreed upon a plan; and, with that type of dogged determination characteristic of Virginians, went to work to prove to the world that National Benefit could be saved and that at least the hard-earned savings of Virginia policyholders would not be sacrificed to the waste, excessive expense, and undeserved charges of receivers. The strength of the plan lay in the fact that the State of Virginia insisted on an absolute receivership, rather than an ancilary one; and on the further fact that the receivers were directed by the Circuit Court of the City of Richmond to continue the business as a "going concern." This prevented the general receivers from collecting and taking further funds out of the state, and permitted the reorganizers to construe the funds so acquired, plus the current premium income, as premiums on new insurance. Hence, with the required number of policyholders, who had paid in over $10,000 in premiums, a mutual company was not only permissable under the laws of Virginia, but was necessary and proper to protect the vested interests of the policyholders.

On January 24, 1933, the Virginia Mutual Benefit Life Insurance Company, Inc., was chartered, and, on March 18, 1933, it was licensed to commence business. $10,000 in government bonds was deposited with the state treasurer of Virginia, leaving a working capital of less than $2,500. December 31, 1937, it had $58,532 in assets, of which $56,316 was in government bonds and cash. It had legal reserves amounting to $38,490.27. The progress of the company in surplus during its first five years of operation is as follows:

1933	$3,432.03
1934	5,593.87
1935	8,968.88
1936	12,301.82
1937	13,882.44

Since organization, Virginia Mutual has paid $71,751,18 in sick and accident and death claims, or an average of $40.25 per day.

It was due to the courage, initiative, and genius in leadership of two brilliant young men that this state unit of the business of what was then the Negro race's largest insurance institution was saved. They are Mr. B. T. Bradshaw, president-treasurer, and Mr. C. L. Townes, secretary. Stories of their lives, with that of Mr. H. A. M. Johns, vice president, appear in these pages.

BOOKER TALMADGE BRADSHAW, *President-Treasurer*

Booker Talmadge Bradshaw was born February 26, 1904, in St. Louis, Missouri, of Mr. Marion H. and Mrs. Priscilla M. Bradshaw, with whom he lived until he was twenty years old.

Young Bradshaw, finishing the grammar and high schools of St. Louis, graduated with the B. S. degree in Life Insurance from the University of Illinois, and later took two post graduate courses on the same subject.

Traits of self reliance manifested themselves in the character of Mr. Bradshaw early in his life. Notwithstanding the fact that his father, working as a Pullman porter, would have contributed materially to the education of his son, the young man preferred to make his own way through school, filling such jobs as waiting table, selling insurance for Standard Life and National Benefit, working in a packing house, clerking in a store, and doing stenographic work. But Mr. Bradshaw does not consider necessities of such nature as difficulties in the student life of young men. He rather regards them to have been valuable aids in his early training. It was perhaps due to these tests of his own ability, which these early tasks imposed, that he was encouraged to take the lead in defying

239

the general receivers of National Benefit Life to take over and destroy the business of Negro policyholders in Virginia when that company ceased to operate in 1931. The preliminiary part time insurance work that Mr. Bradshaw performed while in school and the inspiration furnished by his brother who was already engaged in the work, were the deciding factors in determining for him his life's career.

There is a happy, but unusual, combination of two valuable qualities in the character of this aggressive young business man. He likes mathematics, accounting, and clerical work generally, and yet, unlike many people of such tendencies, he is by no means inclined to be an office recluse. He likes to meet and to mix with people; and he has found abundant opportunities for exercising both of these predominant talents in the business of life insurance. His record in salesmanship while managing the state of Virginia for the National Benefit Life Insurance Company has not been equalled by any Negro life insurance salesman in that state; and his ability in this respect no doubt is responsible for the rapid progress being made by the Virginia Mutual Benefit Life.

Aside from the many exacting duties required of him in the development of a young life insurance company, Mr. Bradshaw finds time for active participation in many collateral fields. He is connected with the National Negro Business League, Richmond Community Fund, Urban League, Citizens Association, Democratic Club, Capital Trade Association, the Y.M.C.A., Negro Forum Council, the Red Cross, N.A.A.C.P. and is president of the Virginia Trade Association, chairman of the Better Business Division of the Negro Organization Society of Virginia, and chairman of the Virginia Committee of Insurance Executives. Kappa Alpha Psi Fraternity also proudly numbers him among its active and outstanding members.

Mr. Bradshaw was married in April 1931, to Miss Emma Forrester, and this young couple reside at 1226 Wallace Street, Richmond.

H. A. M. JOHNS, *Vice President*

Mr. Henry Anderson Matthews Johns was born in Baltimore, Maryland, of William and Rosa Johns, on December 4, 1886. He was educated in the public schools of Gloucester County, Maryland, Cappahosic High School and Hampton Institute, and has further equipped himself with a correspondence course in law. In later years he took advantage of a special course in insurance offered by the University of Pennsylvania.

Mr. Johns did not have material assistance from his parents while in college but, undeterred by these circumstances, he not only paid his own way through school but earned four scholarships. Reaching maturity, this brilliant young man commenced life as a teacher and served as principal of a number of schools, after which, in 1923, Mr. Thomas M. Crump urged him to enter the services of Southern Aid. Later, he became a traveling auditor for the National Benefit Company, in which capacity he served until that company ceased operation in 1931.

Upon the organization of the Virginia Mutual Benefit Life Insurance Company he was elected vice-president and also serves as a district manager. Twenty-five years of service in the field of life insurance marks Mr. Johns as a veteran in the business. Through his ripe experience he is enabled to select and train the very best of agency material for his company.

Mr. Johns is an active church worker, being the superintendent of his Sunday school, president of the B.Y.P.U., choir director and a deacon. He serves on the committee of management for the Y.M.C.A., is president of the High School Parent-Teacher Association, and chairman of the Negro Municipal Hospital Committee.

Mr. Johns was married September 3, 1912, and he and his wife, Mrs. Nancy F. Johns, have two lovely children, Helen A., and Henry A. M. Johns, Jr.

CLARENCE LEE TOWNES, *Vice President-Secretary*

Mr. Clarence L. Townes, Sr., was born in Richmond, Virginia, June 24, 1902, the only child of Robert and Annie M. Townes. Having lost his father in infancy, young Townes naturally encountered many obstacles in early life. His education was interrupted on several occasions when forced to stop school to help his mother. Despite these handicaps, he was determined to succeed. After finishing the elementary work at Navy Hill School, and completing his high school course with honors at Armstrong High, he studied at Van de Vyver Business College and Virginia Union University.

Mr. Townes entered the life insurance business as a stenographer in the home office of the Southern Aid Society. After serving in this capacity for two months and observing the exceptional oppor-

241

tunities offered in the field, he requested a transfer to the agency division. He was given a debit at Newport News, Virginia, and in a short time had distinguished himself as an outstanding producer. In six months his progress on the debit had merited him a promotion to the position of special assistant to the secretary-manager, Mr. B. L. Jordan. Here he served with signal ability for nearly three years, until offered a position as traveling supervisor for the National Benefit Life Insurance Company of Washington, D. C. He continued in the services of this company, serving in various important capacities, until it was declared insolvent and finally liquidated.

In 1933, not being content at seeing his years of effort with the National Benefit go to naught, Mr. Townes, in association with Messrs. B. T. Bradshaw, H. A. M. Johns, S. W. Robinson, Jr., A. W. Ruffin, R. C. Scott, J. E. Robinson, R. L. Coots, C. D. Patience, and others, ably assisted in the organization of the Virginia Mutual Benefit Life Insurance Company. Mr. Townes served as the secretary of the original policyholders' committee, and was eleced vice president and secretary of the new company upon perfecting its organization. In addition to his duties as secretary he is also agency officer of the company and has charge of its field forces.

Mr. Townes became an active figure in the National Negro Insurance Association in 1934 when it held its annual convention in Richmond. He served with credit as secretary of the local entertainment committee of this convention. In 1933 at Durham, North Carolina, he was elected assistant secretary of the association and re-elected to this same position in 1936 at Detroit, Michigan. His service to the organization attracted real attention in 1937 when he served as secretary of the National Negro Insurance Week Committee.

In recognition of this work and because of Mr. Townes' keen interest in all of the association's activities, he won the distinction of being elected secretary of the association in 1937 at Augusta, Ga., to succeed Mr. W. Ellis Stewart who had served in this important position for twelve years. He is the association's fifth Secretary and is serving his third consecutive term with competency and satisfaction. During the first three years he held this office the membership grew from twenty-three companies and local associations to forty-two. Among the outstanding accomplishments of his administration was the efficient organization and supervision of the tour of eighty-five delegates from St. Louis to the Los Angeles Convention in July 1939.

Mr. Townes was married to Miss Alice F. Smith, a stenographer of the Southern Aid Society, on January 24, 1926. They have one son, Clarence Lee, Jr., and live at 1412 Idlewood Avenue, Richmond. He is an active member of the Second Baptist Church, an officer of the Phi Beta Sigma Fraternity, member of the Astoria Beneficial Club, and has taken keen interest in dramatic clubs and civic leagues. He is a former secretary of the Independent Progressive Educational Association of Richmond and a director of the B. Y. P. U. of his church.

Chapter VII.

WESTERN ORGANIZATIONS

THE SUPREME CAMP OF THE AMERICAN WOODMEN, DENVER, COLORADO

UNLIKE other Negro fraternal orders, the American Woodmen was not originated by Negroes. It was organized by the late John C. Kennedy, with the assistance of Edward F. Lake, John K. Shiram, and C. R. Parker. On April 5, 1901, they obtained a charter from the Insurance Department of Colorado for the American Woodmen, a fraternal institution, "to be operated in a modern and up-to-date manner in strict compliance with the laws of the Insurance Department and for the benefit and protection of Negroes." Two interesting observations seem in point here: First, why were white men moved to organize an institution for the protection of Negroes at any place? Second: Why in Colorado, the Negro population of which, in 1901, was less than nine thousand?

During the next five years of the society's existence it experienced hard times. At the end of the initial five years the sponsors were almost ready to abandon the idea; and a meeting was held to determine whether or not to merge with some other concern or to dissolve. They decided to do neither; the conference ended with a resolution to try once more to overcome the difficulties. They negotiated for operation in Texas, and for another five years the "ugly duckling" society struggled along, while in other parts of the country fraternal societies were enjoying success.

At the end of ten years, the membership of the American Woodmen was less than 2,000 and its total assets less than $8,000. Another conference was held in 1910. In this conference a very unusual situation developed, born, perhaps, of desperation. The white leaders in the organization confessed their inability to carry on. They grasped at what seemed to them a graceful way to withdraw. They prevailed upon C. M. White, a colored man, then clerk of the Local Camp in Austin, Texas, to accept the position of Supreme Commander, giving him the authority to select such other persons as he might desire to fill the other offices. Mr. White selected

245

A. R. Sanders, vice-supreme commander; Lawrence H. Lightner, supreme clerk; G. W. Norman, supreme banker; J. C. Eusan, supreme auditor; S. A. Rutherford, supreme watchman; D. J. Simpson, supreme sentry; William Lee, supreme prelate; E. W. D. Abner, supreme physician, and Samuel Eustace, supreme escort.

The year 1910 actually marked the beginning of the successful operation of the institution now commonly referred to as the Fraternal Giant. The Supreme·Commander assumed control of the extension work. The Supreme Clerk took charge of the management of the Home Office, as yet quite a one-man job. At the same time, the rates were adjusted and the Constitution revised better to serve the needs of the society as a whole.

From the time the control of affairs of the American Woodmen was placed in the hands of the little band of Negroes, led by C. M. White, the steady march of progress began. By the close of 1915, marking a third five-year period in the history of the society, the membership had increased to 17,509 and the assets to $78,307. At the close of 1920 the membership was a little less than 50,000 and assets more than one-half million dollars; and this notwithstanding that the years 1918 and 1919 were the years sullied by the raging epidemic of influenza that swept the country.

By 1923, Cassius M. White, the sage of Woodcraft, had just about exhausted his strength. He died on March 21, 1923. The Supreme Executive Council selected Dr. E. W. D. Abner, Supreme Physician, to serve the unexpired term as Supreme Commander.

When the Sixth Quadrennial Convvention was held in Denver in 1925 it was soon evident to the delegates in attendance that there would ensue a bitter political contest for the office of Supreme Commander. Major General John L. Jones, Major General of the Uniform Ranks, had already announced his candidacy for the position. There was no doubt of the influence and popularity of the dashing, debonair young Woodman from the Lone Star State. Thousands of uniformed members from all parts of the country had encamped in Denver at his command; and their well-trained, trimly garbed ranks, marching to the rhythm of martial music, attracted marked attention from the citizens of the Colorado capital and the large delegation in attendance. The coming struggle for the highest position of the Order was a topic of transcending interest during the first two days of the session. Dr. Abner had the advantage of being already the presiding officer and he lost no time

VIRGINIA
MUTUAL
BENEFIT
LIFE
INSURANCE
COMPANY

BOOKER T. BRADSHAW, President and Treasurer

C. L. TOWNES, Vice President and Secretary

H. A. M. JOHNS, Vice President

L. H. LIGHTNER
Supreme Commander

THE LATE C. M. WHITE
Supreme Commander

THE LATE G. W. NORMAN
Supreme Banker

DR. T. T. McKINNEY
Supreme Physician

B. H. GRAHAM
Supreme Clerk

GOLDEN
STATE
MUTUAL
LIFE
INSURANCE
COMPANY

WILLIAM NICKERSON, President

LIEUT. N. O. HOUSTON, Secretary & Treasurer

GEORGE A. BEAVERS, JR., Vice President

in organizing influential leaders from all the states in which the American Woodmen operated.

When the time for the election came, Dr. Sutton E. Griggs of Memphis, Tennessee, a veteran in political battles in the National Baptist Convention, silver-tongued and forceful, rose and made a motion that the rules be suspended and that the Supreme Clerk cast the unanimous vote of the convention for Dr. E. W. D. Abner as Supreme Commander. The motion was ruled out of order. Dr. Griggs then offered a motion that "inasmuch as Major General John L. Jones was holding an appointive office for life or during good behavior he should resign this office before entering the race for Supreme Commander." That motion prevailed; and it placed Major Jones in a difficult situation. Finally, after much hesitancy, he decided to withdraw from the race, and Dr. Abner was elected.

At the 1929 session of the Quadrennial, the incumbent officers, with the exception of Dr. T. T. McKinney, supreme physician, were without opposition. Dr. E. L. Watkins of Georgia was placed in nomination as an opponent of Dr. McKinney, but he declined and moved to make the election of Dr. McKinney unanimous. His motion prevailed.

The Eighth Quadrennial Meeting, August 13-19, 1933

At this session there occurred the most bitter political contest in the history of the Order. Many members of the American Woodmen had noted with regret the failing health of Supreme Commander Abner. Moreover, there were indications that it was having its effect on his erstwhile keen and comprehensive intellect. There was no doubt that the heavy burdens of the office were proving too heavy for his advanced age. Foremost among those who advocated a change in the office of Supreme Commander were: Roscoe Dunjee, editor of the *Black Dispatch* of Oklahoma City, Oklahoma; J. H. Allen of Texarkana; Reverend Dr. J. W. Haywood, Baltimore, Maryland; Reverend M. M. Haynes, Austin, Texas; W. G. Cain, Waco, Texas; Mrs. Fannie Robinson, Houston, Texas; M. S. Stuart, Memphis, Tennessee, and J. E. Robinson, Houston, Texas.

These leaders tried to have an agreement that Dr. Abner retire on an annual life pension of $3,750, one-half of the annual salary he was receiving as supreme Commander. To this proposition Dr. Abner did not, during the first three days of the session, agree.

Then on Friday there was a tremendous demonstration for L. H. Lightner to fill the office, after which Dr. Abner withdrew and was elected to the created position of Past Supreme Commander, with an annual life pension of $3,750, in which capacity he served until his death. L. H.Lightner was then unanimously elected Supreme Commander. Other officers elected were:

J. E. Robinson, Houston, Texas - Vice Supreme Commander
B. H. Graham, Los Angeles, California   Supreme Clerk
G. W. Norman, Austin, Texas   Supreme Banker
E. E. Carrington, Denver, Colorado   Supreme Auditor
T. T. McKinney, Denver, Colorado   Supreme Physician
Earl R. Sams, Pittsburgh, Pennsylvania   Supreme Escort
H. P. McAllister, Cleveland, Ohio   Supreme Watchman
R. J. Kenney, Jr., Richmond, Virginia   Supreme Sentry
J. W. Haywood, Baltimore, Maryland   Supreme Prelate

At the Ninth Quadrennial Session, held in Denver, Colorado, in August 1937, the same officers were re-elected except R. J. Kenney, Jr., Supreme Sentry, who was succeeded by Rosa F. Hargrett of Newark, New Jersey.

The American Woodmen is unquestionably the greatest Negro fraternal society in the world. This statement rests on the history of its efficiency of operation, its accomplishments, services rendered to its members, and its sound financial condition. It operates in twenty-five states of the Union. It owns its home office building in Denver, Colorado, which, though just adequate for its own home office needs, is yet of commendable physical appearance; and it cost the society not more than $15,000.

Since its organization the society has paid total benefits amounting to $4,915,272.00. Its total insurance in force is $17,391,000.00. Its reserves December 31, 1938, were as follows:

On Certificates, as per Actuarial Valuation	$2,432,774.00
For Investment Contingencies	175,000.00
For Mortality Fluctuation	175,000.00
For General Contingencies	123,779.20
TOTAL RESERVES	$2,906,553.20

The history of its constant and amazing increase in assets is as follows:

1910	$ 9,021.01	1925	$1,452,263.77
1915	78,307.85	1930	2,349,917.16
1920	646,832.26	1935	2,867,649.96
	1938	$3,232,731.99	

The Order's total cash on hand at the end of December 1938 was $573,759.72.

C. M. WHITE, *Late Supreme Commander*

Men who build in mortar and brick, in steel and stone, may erect structures of impressive magnitude and glowing beauty, but the stealthy waters of time encroach upon even the mightiest of these, and the fickle winds of changing modes blur their splendid outlines sometimes in the space of a lifetime. But the architects who build on the rock of faith in their God, their people, and themselves, who draw relentlessly upon their resources of health and strength to transform the fabric of dreams into the solid reality of great institutions to serve generations to come — these are the men whose brief lives flash in meteoric splendor across the horizon of a people's history, but whose accomplishments endure in the everlasting heartbeat of a nation.

The father of Cassius M. White was one of the horde of slaves who refused to accept a status of inferiority. He escaped from Kentucky and fled to Michigan via the Underground Railway, a mode of transportation mired in the blood of black men who had risked their lives in desperate attempts to attain freedom. Once safely in Michigan, he breathed deeply of the sweet, free air, found work, fell in love, married, and felt himself fortunate at last with a fireside and a sympathetic wife. When, in 1866, a son, Cassius, was born to this runaway slave, he must indeed have felt his cup of happiness almost overflowing; and he grimly determined that his son should have the things he had been denied, should be educated as he was not. But death struck heavily at the modest home, and the father was deprived of the companionship of a wife, the boy of the loving care of a mother.

Early in life, young Cassius showed evidences of the qualities essential to a brilliant and successful career, and the elder White made every possible sacrifice to keep the boy in Ann Arbor College, from which he graduated with high honors at the age of nineteen. Shortly afterward, he went to Indiana and accepted a teaching position. It was pleasant work, which he performed well and in which he made an enviable reputation; but destiny had touched this lad's brow and his restless spirit would not be content until he had found the work to which he felt he could contribute all of the energy in his make-up and of the flame of genius which burned brightly in his soul. The next few years found him seeking, but never satisfied. He went to St. Paul, Minnesota; from there to Spokane, Washington, where he became the proprietor of an elaborate and well-furnished cafe. He followed the elusive trail of prospecting to British Columbia and wrested considerable revenue from silver mining. A railroad magnate, J. J. Hill, had been considerably impressed with young White while he was in the cafe business in Spokane, and secured his services as a private car porter. This occupied him for several years; but, finally, one day while in San Francisco, sitting on the shore of the peaceful Pacific, looking out through the Golden Gate at the setting sun, he felt again the call to seek a field of greater usefulness and service to his people.

Back across the desert came Cassius M. White to the open spaces of Texas. He took a teachers' examination and made a First Grade certificate; applied for and secured a position in the City Schools and was made principal of a Grammar School in Austin, Texas. Always scholastically brilliant, he raised his First Grade Certificate to a Permanent Certificate in what was considered one of the most rigid examinations ever given in Austin.

While teaching in Austin, he joined a number of fraternal orders, among them the American Woodmen; and thus quietly did the door to a great opportunity open to him. In August 1904, he was elected clerk of Austin Camp No. 3, and he remained a member of this camp until the time of his death. In August 1910, he was called to Denver, Colorado, to assume the position and responsibilities of Supreme Commander of the American Woodmen—a title not sufficiently clothed in pomposity to conceal the naked need of the almost failing institution behind it.

When the new Supreme Commander of the American Woodmen assumed his duties, he found them to be a conglomerate mass of the duties of Supreme Commander, Supreme Clerk, Supreme Banker, Supreme Physician, Supreme Auditor and Supreme Prelate. In fact, for the first six months, the American Woodmen was C. M. White and C. M. White was the American Woodmen. The society had been in existence ten years, its operations extended over five states — Colorado, Texas, Georgia, Alabama, and Florida.

It had a membership of about 2,000 and assets of less than $8,000; a field force of one organizing deputy, one typewriter, one desk, one table, and the idea of a Fraternal Benefit Assocation.

But it now had C. M. White. Within a short time, with that unerring, almost uncanny judgment in the selection of men that was probably the keynote of his astounding success, the Supreme Commander had secured several competent men who shared with him the vision of a great fraternal institution to provide fraternal insurance for colored people on a sensible, practical modern plan, unburdened by excessive emphasis on aimless ritualisms and hollow ceremonials. White installed L. H. Lightner as supreme clerk, and to him committed the management of the home office. For himself he reserved the arduous task of traveling from city to city, from state to state, instilling new life into the hardening veins of old camps, sometimes just in time to forestall rigor mortis; setting up new ones and injecting into them the contagious enthusiasm for Woodcraft—speaking, pleading, working, worrying, with never a thought to the tremendous strain on his strength.

At the close of the first year of his administration, a very commendable gain in membership had been made. This growth continued during the life of Mr. White as is revealed in the history of the society.

While teaching in Austin, Texas, Mr. White met Mrs. Minnie F. Phillips, also a teacher; and her he married on December 27, 1896. To them were born three children, Grace, Frances, and John, two of whom — Frances and John — survive their illustrious father. There, too, he joined the Ebenezer Third Baptist Church and was baptized by the Reverend L.L. Campbell. For ten years, he was historical expositor of the Sunday school of that church; and he was a firm believer in the Baptist Church the remainder of his life.

Cassius M. White was respected and admired by all who came in contact with him. His advice and counsel were frequently sought in matters affecting the common interest of the group; and he never failed to meet any demand made upon his time and talent when he felt he could be of benefit to his people. He lived to see the institution which he had nurtured from a frail and feeble sapling develop into a mighty oak under whose spreading branches his people find security and happiness. His last words to his fellow-workers, to the comrades and friends who had worked with him, fought with him, and shared with him, were "Carry on."

The Supreme Commander of the American Woodmen died at 7:30 p.m., Wednesday, March 21, 1923, at St. Joseph Hospital, Denver, Colorado. The frame was gone; but the soul and spirit lived on in the good he had done, in the contribution he had made and in the memory of the thousands of woodmen he had led in Woodcraft.

LAWRENCE H. LIGHTNER, *Supreme Commander*

America has risen on the shoulders of self-made men. The record of her achievement, from the time when today's proud eminence was but a vision in the brains of her forefathers, is like a giant tapestry, woven in the bright colors of "rags to riches" epics. And glinting here and there are golden threads unwound from skeins held by dark hands.

Adolphus and Cora Jane Lightner were tenant farmers in Hearne, Texas, having exchanged the certain subjection of slavery for the uncertain poverty of tenant farming. There must have been times when Adolphus thought freedom's fire much hotter than slavery's frying pan, for fourteen children — ten boys and four girls — tumbled about the humble cabin, which meant fourteen ever-hungry mouths to fill and fourteen active bodies to keep clothed on the meager income which he could wrest from a fickle land and a vicious system.

Such was the crucible of poverty prepared for the molding of Lawrence H. Lightner, born September 6, 1884; and the habits of thrift and economy, branded on this child's mind, were to stand him in good stead in later years when the ability to spend wisely and save well was to mean the lifeblood of a great fraternal institution.

In the Lightner household, as in the many others on its economic level, there was one absorbing interest—one greedy master: the crops. During eight months of the year, it was a matter of all hands out in the fields. Bent backs and plucking fingers made obeisance to the cultivation of crops, the fruits of which would mean the difference between full pots and empty, between corn pone and batter cakes. Small hands, but recently grimed with mud pies, picked up hoes; and it was only when the work of cultivation had been done that any thought could be given to education. Four months out of a year, these children of toil could pursue a haphazard chase of the rudiments of reading, writing, and 'rithmetic in inadequately equipped, almost inaccessible school houses.

So for four months out of a year, for nine years, Lawrence attended school in Robertson and Falls Counties in the towns of Hearne and Marlin, Texas. But this boy was not satisfied with such scant preparation; and he found that his willing hands could sweep and clean enough floors to put him through high school. When that was done, his craving for education was still unsatisfied. Finding that his earnings would not be sufficient to sustain him while in college, he secured a student loan from the Board of Education of the Methodist Episcopal Church to pay part of his tuition at Samuel Houston College, supplementing his funds by doing janitor work and odd jobs about the campus. During the summer months, he worked as a porter and bus boy for hotels; but he could never save enough during the summer to finance the coming term in school; for, after purchasing necessary clothing, there were always the work-worn hands of his mother and father and the asking hands of his many brothers and sisters upturned to him for aid.

During the time young Lightner was at Samuel Houston College, he took part in all literary, athletic, and religious activities. He served as secretary of the literary society, president of the student Y.M.C.A., and taught a Sunday school class. He represented his school in an oratorical contest in which six state institutions participated, and received third honors. He served as student monitor of the Young Men's Building. On the baseball diamond, his lithe quickness made him top center fielder of more than six college baseball teams, and he served as captain of his school's baseball team for three years. A versatile student, he found keenest pleasure in mathematics and public speaking. There was also a natural love and taste for music; but most outstanding in his character was his unyeilding, scrupulous, exact sense of honesty.

Three years at Samuel Houston College gave this youth sufficient foundation on which to build the structure of success. He was, he thought, reasonably prepared; but his straitened finances did not permit much choice in his quest for employment. He had to accept the first offer, and it is the good fortune of the fraternal phase of Negro insurance that the first offer was to become connected with the American Woodmen, for it was not long after entering this field that the far-sighted lad saw the great possibilities for the building of a business that would give employment and render a positive service to the rank and file of the Negro group. The way was now clear — he had found his life's work.

In April 1911, young Lightner was brought to Denver on trial and placed in charge of the Woodmen office. After two years probation, he was elected to the office of supreme clerk. Expense funds were greatly limited; and the new clerk found good use for the practice of that strict economy he had learned in childhood. And even here he was still a janitor! For several years, the Supreme Clerk of the American Woodmen assisted the Supreme Commander in cleaning the office and doing general janitor's work. When he wasn't busy wielding a broom, he wielded a pen and directed the work of the home office and the correspondence with local camps and field agents.

In the fifteen years that followed, Lawrence H. Lightner became an integral part of the American Woodmen. He discharged the internal and technical operations of the organization. He shouldered the major responsibilities of investing the surplus funds of the society. He developed an individual office system for the business which is rated A-1 by actuaries and examiners; and trained and developed an office force of thirty clerks, stenographers, bookkeepers, and heads of departments. The home office of the American Woodmen is now widely known for its unquestioned efficiency and decorum.

Titles and offices do not make men. The qualities of real men assert themselves by bursting out of bounds of office technicalities to render necessary service. It was so in the case of the supreme clerk of the American Woodmen. Supreme Commander White died in 1923; but the consistent progress of the American Woodmen was not interrupted, due to the determined and progressive character of its supreme clerk, whose will predominated and whose policies obtained in a major way in the affairs of the concern.

Dr. E. W. D. Abner, Supreme Physician, succeeded the lamented C. M. White, serving the unexpired term, and was elected Supreme Commander in August 1925. But Abner was already an old man. The deputies, field agents, and many members of the American Woodmen foresaw that in the Supreme Quadrennium of 1933, to continue the progress of the institution, it would be necessary to place in the office of supreme commander a younger and firmer official.

It was a pill not at all relished by Supreme Clerk Lightner when leading spirits in the society informed him, in the weeks preceding the 1933 Quadrennium, that his services in the office of supreme commander were needed and that he probably would be drafted into the position. There was no personal profit for the supreme clerk in changing offices—the salaries for the two positions were the same; and, as supreme commander, he would have to give up the comforts of home and routine duties in a splendidly equipped office to subject himself to the uncertain conveniences and irregularities of travel. Moreover, being himself not particularly robust, he was by no means assured that the hardships of travel would not eventually undermine his health.

Reluctantly, however, he finally consented to be put forward for the office, at first with the hope that Dr. Abner could be persuaded to retire on some form of pension. It was finally thus arranged and Mr. Lightner was elected unanimously. Painstakingly accurate, precise, and conscientious, he controls the mighty machine under his direction with cool, unassuming demeanor, but with a very definite idea as to what he wants and how he wants it done.

He is an able presiding officer. His knowledge of parliamentary usage is almost infallible; and the smoothness with which he directs the legislation of any meeting over which he presides approaches perfection. The by-laws and constitution of the American Woodmen, exceptional in concise, orderly arrangement and also in the comprehensiveness with which they cover every phase of the work, are almost entirely the composition of L. H. Lightner.

Miss Geraldine Troutman was an employee of the American Woodmen; and young Lightner had opportunity to observe her charm and gracious poise. Both young people being more than ordinarily conservative, their friendship pursued an even tenor which culminated in a simple marriage, with no attempt at show or glamor. In the years since, he has been blessed with an understanding, sympathetic wife, whose steady faith and confidence have been a source of inspiration to him and whose calm presence has graced his home both as a hostess to his friends and a companion.

At the age of eighteen, this youth joined the Methodist Episcopal Church, Marlin, Texas, was immediately elected recording steward, and has served continuously in an official capacity in that church ever since. He is also a trustee of his local church, the Scott Methodist Episcopal Church, of Denver, Colorado; and is now serving the fourth continuous quadrennium as a member of the General Conference and World Service Commission of the Methodist Episcopal Church. For seventeen years, he has served as chairman of the Committee of Management of the Glenarm Branch Y. M. C. A., Denver, and, as chairman of that committee, played an important part in developing and executing the program for raising funds for the erection of the Glenarm Branch building. He represented the Western Region Y. M. C. A. in the World Conference held in Helsingfors, Finland, July 1926. He is regional director of the National Negro Business League; and has been a member of the board of directors of the N. A. A. C. P.

Texas claims many illustrious sons, but none has wrought more strongly nor woven the pattern of his life more clearly into a notable example for the youth of his nation and race than has Lawrence H. Lightner.

THE LATE DR. E. W. D. ABNER, *Former Supreme Commander*

Dr. E. W. D. Abner was born in Marshall, Texas, the son of the late famous David Abner who was a member of the Texas legislature and trustee of Bishop College of Marshall. The son, E. W. D. Abner, was educated at Bishop. He then taught public school in Texas, after which he completed a course in medicine.

Dr. Abner began the practice of medicine in Austin, Texas, and there built up a very lucrative practice. In Austin he was considered not only the leading physician, but the most outstanding colored citizen.

He became associated with the late C. M. White, former Supreme Commander of the American Woodmen, and was made Supreme Physician of the Society in 1911. He rendered the Order distinguished services in this capacity until 1923 when, on the death of the lamented C. M. White, he was elected Supreme Commander by the Supreme Council to serve the unexpired term of Mr. White. He was re-elected at the next Quadrennial Session in 1925 and, during the next four years, rendered brilliant and exceptionally energetic services in prosecuting the work of the society.

He was re-elected by acclamation at the Seventh Quadrennial meeting in 1929; and, at the Eighth Quadrennial in Denver in 1933, his health having become impaired in the meantime, he was retired from the office of Supreme Commander and elected to the honorary office of Past Supreme Commander for life, with an annual pension of $3,750.

Dr. Abner was married, but had no children. After moving to Denver, he erected a beautiful home, most lavishly furnished, on Downing Street. It was in this home on Sunday night, August 25, 1935, that, allegedly, some personal difference arose between Dr. Abner and a Miss Elnora Smith, a former clerk of Denver Camp No. 1, a local unit of the American Woodmen. It is reported that there was a struggle over a revolver. However this may be, the gun was discharged, fatally wounding former Supreme Commander Abner, who died as a result on August 27, 1935. The young woman testified at her trial that "there was a struggle over the gun and the gun went off." She was not convicted.

Dr. Abner had served the American Woodmen as Supreme Physician for a period of twelve years and eight months, as Supreme Commander ten years and five months, and as Past Supreme Commander for two years. He was buried at Denver, Colorado, August 31, 1935, with the ritualistic ceremonies and honors of the society he had served so well.

THE LATE G. W. NORMAN, *Supreme Banker*

It was with great confidence that C. M. White approached his friend and business associate, G. W. Norman, with a proposition that Norman join the American Woodmen. The two had just emerged from an interesting but unfortunately non-profitable venture in running a bus-line for colored passengers, following the passage of the separate streetcar law in Texas. So it required all of the sales talent with which the late Supreme Commander was so richly endowed to overcome the disinclination of his erstwhile business partner; for Norman was not a man to reach conclusions hurriedly. However, he was finally persuaded to become a member of the Order in which he was destined to play a prominent part.

Texas could claim G. W. Norman only as an adopted son. He was educated in Rutherford County, near Murfreesboro, Tennessee; and in Fisk University, Nashville, Tennessee. After spending three years at Fisk he taught in his native state and then moved to Weatherford, Texas. In the next few years, he taught at Stephensville, Granbury, Uvalde, and Manchaca; and in 1896 he was invited to move to Austin to become principal of the Wheatville City School, where he taught for three years. He was then elected principal of the Gregory School, serving in that capacity for twenty-three years. Then came a promotion to the Anderson High School, where he served as professor of Mathematics, resigning in 1928 after a creditable record of forty-six years in the schoolroom. In Austin and Travis County he was known as the "father of teachers," because so many of the teachers in that section had once been his pupils.

For a short period, from August 1910 to April 1911, Mr. Norman served as Supreme Clerk of the Supreme Camp; and was then elected Supreme Banker, filling this position with great credit for twenty-seven years.

No member of the American Woodmen loved more deeply the cause of Woodcraft than did this man who entered its ranks with such reluctance. No member was ever regarded with higher esteem. When the Quadrennium was held in Denver, in August 1937, the doctors had advised Norman not to attend. But perhaps the Supreme Banker was aware that this would be his last gathering with the friends and co-workers of a quarter of a century; and he would not be cheated of seeing and greeting them once again. Arriving in Denver, he found himself too weak to attend the meetings. It was a touching five minutes when he came into the morning session on the second day, supported by the willing arms of friends, to read his final report. When he bade the large delegation good-bye, nearly all realized that they were meeting the last time with the faithful veteran. He died on November 21 of the following year; and the expectation of his death did not lessen the widespread grief felt in Woodmen circles and by the many friends who knew and admired him.

BENJAMIN HARRISON GRAHAM, *Supreme Clerk*

Benjamin Harrison Graham was born and reared at Paris, Texas, the son of a merchant. He attended the Gibbons High School of that city. Following his graduation, he entered Atlanta University, from which he was graduated with a B. A. degree. Gifted with a pleasing voice, while in college he traveled as a member of the Atlanta University Quartet, and also saw service with the Atlanta Life under the supervision of the late Alonzo F. Herndon.

A few weeks after completing his college work, he had to return home because of his father's illness, and there assumed management of his father's grocery store. In the year 1915, he joined the American Woodmen. In 1916 he was appointed assistant principal of Gibbons High School in his home town, which position he held until 1922. He secured a year's leave of absence in 1918 to serve as secretary of the Y. M. C. A. at the Dupont Engineering Company, Penniman, Virginia, returning to his work at the high school when this work terminated with the ending of the World War. During this time, he served first as Commander of the local camp at Paris, Texas, then as clerk; and later as special deputy.

In 1922, the late Supreme Commander White, desiring to introduce Woodcraft into California, was impressed by young Graham, and selected him to do this important work. The choice was a splendid one.

His fine training, harnessed with his natural energy and ability, resulted in rapid expansion of the work in the state during his eleven years there as supervisor and district manager.

Nor did he neglect the importance of becoming identified with the religious, educational, civic, and political life of the city. He served as trustee, assistant superintendent of the Sunday School, and as a member of the choir of the Second Baptist Church; vice president of the N.A.A.C.P.; secretary of the board of directors of the Los Angeles Urban League; secretary of the local branch of the Negro Business League; assistant manager of the California Co-operative Improvement Association; member of the Y. M. C. A., and Kappa Alpha Psi Fraternity. In the primary election of May 1933, he was elected by popular vote to membership on the Republican County Central Committee of the Sixty-second Assembly district for the second time. He was subsequently elected Secretary, which position he still holds. He is a member of the Knights of Pythias and a Mason.

At the Eighth Quadrennial Convention of the American Woodmen held in Denver in August 1933, he was elected Supreme Clerk by unanimous vote. Filling the shoes of a predecessor who had made the office the heart of the institution was not an easy task; but Mr. Graham's record for the next four years was such that he was re-elected, again by acclamation, at the Ninth Quadrennial Convention in 1937. He is now serving the American Woodmen in this capacity.

In August 1921, while teaching in Gibbons High School, Paris, Texas, he married Miss Katheryn M. Campbell, an attractive young woman, also of Paris, and a teacher in the high school. Katheryn had been his childhood sweetheart; was a graduate of Fisk University; and in every way was suited to be an asset to her ambitious young husband. When he was called to Los Angeles in 1922, Mrs. Graham gave up her teaching position to go with her husband; and when the handsome couple took up residence in Los Angeles, the wife's graciousness was a major factor in their popularity. She is now a teacher in the Twentieth Street Public School, Los Angeles. They have one daughter—a girl, Benzell Harryetta.

DR. THOMAS THEODORE MCKINNEY, *Supreme Physician*

The degree of success of any life insurance company or fraternal organization, dealing with the uncertain quality of human health and life, must depend to a great extent upon the efficacy of those entrusted to supervise the selection of its risks. The American Woodmen is fortunate in that it is served by a man who not only has had a thorough grounding in the theory of medicine, but who has substantiated that foundation by a quarter of a century of active practice.

The hopes of Jane and Arch McKinney, of Van Alstyne, Texas, ran high when the stork left them a beautiful baby boy, Thomas Theodore, on August 16, 1869. The Emancipation Proclamation was on the lips of every colored man and woman. It was an idolized paper. Negroes felt that it laid the foundation of full liberty and unrestricted privileges. The McKinneys were farmers; but the brash promises of the new equality, spreading with fickle sweetness throughout the land, penetrated into their modest home, and they were stirred, as have been countless other dark parents in the history of the Negro, to hope that for their son there might be a brighter day, a fuller life. It was a vision of what their boy' might become under unrestricted opportunities that urged Arch McKinney and his faithful wife to toil ever harder on their farm, and to make greater sacrifices that he might receive the proper educational training.

At the tender age of seven, Thomas McKinney commenced to share with his father the exactions of farm labor, and for the next ten years he shouldered burdens more appropriate to maturer years; but even then, as ever in his life, whatever came his way to do, he did with the greatest ability of which he was capable. In 1887, although just eighteen years old, he was already locally distinguished for his scholarly attainments; and his services as a teacher were in demand. For the next nine years he taught school; but in the meantime, he had entered school at the Meharry Medical College, continuing to teach during summer vacations.

Completing his medical course in 1895, he followed the practice of medicine successfully in Texas for the next thirty years. In 1925 he was elected Supreme Physician of the Supreme Camp of the American Woodmen. This required that he move to Denver. Here his scholarly mind found the opportunity to apply itself in research and study of the health conditions of colored people. Upon his findings he laid the foundation of valuable reforms in the practices of risk selections for the great institution with which he is connected. The rigid carefulness of his methods naturally invited criticism from the more ambitious of the field men whose work it was to secure new members. Viewing the situation from a different angle, they thought he was unnecessarily technical. Notwithstanding that he found himself the target of vociferous complaints and stiff opposition from this influential element of the Order's membership at both the quadrennial meetings of 1929 and 1933, this farsighted medical director held steadfastly to his policy of rigid consideration of every application filed. It is due largely to the careful supervision of the risks accepted that this great fraternal organization has experienced such an exceptionally favorable mortality rate. The per cent of actual to expected mortality on gross amount of insurance at risk for 1938 was the lowest in the Order's history since 1922.

A man of versatile talents, throughout his life he has had many interests. While still in Texas he organized the Booker T. Washington Civic League; was at one time the organizer and leader of two brass bands; has served as medical director of the Odd Fellows, as president of the Denver branch of the N.A.A.C.P., and on the Committee of Management of the Y.M.C.A.

In the field of medicine Dr. McKinney is recognized as a leading authority. He is a member of the following: Medical Staff, Denver General Hospital; the National Medical, Dental and Pharmaceutical Association; the American Public Health Association; the First International Congress of Mental Hygiene; the Military Surgeons Association; the Medical Reserve Officers Association, U.S.A.; First Lieutenant, Medical Officers Reserve Corps, U. S. Army (retired); the Colorado Society of Vocational Guidance; and a Fellow of the American Geographical Society.

Dr. McKinney has also made outstanding contributions in the

field of journalism. He has written extensively for the columns of various newspapers and is the author of two widely read books, *Sparks from the Medical World,* and *All White America.*

This versatile physician believes firmly in the doctrine of separate Negro businesses. Among the difficulties to be overcome in building business units of the race he lists the following: the lack of sufficient capital; lack of trained personnel; lack of opportunity for practical experience in business organization and management; our inferiority complex; and the necessity of keeping business separate from politics.

Dr. McKinney and his wife, Mrs. Carrie L. McKinney, the latter formerly of St. Louis, Missouri, were united in marriage on November 26, 1896. Their forty-two years of hard work and happy companionship find, in their attractive home at 2401 Emerson Street, Denver, Colorado, deserved rewards in modern conveniences for rest, contentment, and comfort. They have four devoted children, Mrs. Ethel L. Young, and John, Archie, and Wendell McKinney. Archie finished Law at the University of Denver, June 7, 1939, receiving both the degrees of A.B. and LL.B. Young McKinney was the first Negro to receive his degree in law from this famous institution.

GOLDEN STATE MUTUAL LIFE INSURANCE CO., LOS ANGELES, CALIFORNIA

WILLIAM NICKERSON, JR., *President*

William Nickerson, Jr., was born January 26, 1879, near Cold Springs, San Jacinto County, Texas. The place of his birth, when William Nickerson was a boy, was a matter of a day's travel by horseback to the nearest railroad station. After he was ten years old, and until he entered the city school at Huntsville, he worked on the farm, cutting down trees, rolling logs and chasing cattle in that wild and wooded section of San Jacinto County, except during five months of the year, when he had to walk four miles over rough roads to the Wolf Creek School. William and Emma Nickerson, his parents, did not allow their limited income on the farm to defeat their ambitions to educate their son. Therefore, as soon as they could, they enrolled him in the Huntsville city school in the adjoining county of Walker, where in due time young Nickerson finished his high school course.

LIQUIDATIONS

Mississippi Life Insurance Company

THE LATE W. W. COX
Founder

THE LATE MRS. MINNIE M. COX
Secretary and Treasurer

THE LATE DR. W. A. ATTAWAY
Organizer and First President

HE LATE DR. WAYNE C. HOWARD
President

EDDIE THOMAS
First Policy Holder

LIQUIDATIONS

STANDARD LIFE INSURANCE COMPANY

THE LATE HEMAN E. PERRY
Founder

The scope of his vision now broadened; and, realizing the necessity for further educational preparation, he commenced to make plans to enter Bishop College at Marshall, Texas. He knew that his father and mother were not able to pay the required expenses; and so he proposed that if they could arrange to pay one-half of the required amount during the first year he would try to find work to pay the balance. William endured many sacrifices to work during his first year at Bishop. So well did he perform the tasks assigned to him that in his second year he had no trouble securing work sufficient to pay all of his expenses. Of his four years of college attendance, two and one-half years were spent at Bishop and one and one-half years at Prairie View.

On April 15, 1905, William Nickerson, on his way to breakfast, passed a well-lighted, inviting restaurant from which the aroma of appetizing food radiated. William could not enter that restaurant to eat. It was white. Some distance away, he sat down to eat in a poorly lighted, unsanitary, indifferently-serviced colored restaurant, lacking nothing to discourage relish. William wondered if there were anywhere any up-to-date colored business enterprises; and if not, why not. His thoughts were disturbed by the approach of a man who offered him an opportunity to become an insurance agent. "An insurance agent!" He had never thought of the business of life insurance before. He knew nothing about it but he accepted the job. Thus, accidentally, did the future president of Golden State Mutual Life Insurance Company enter the insurance business as an industrial agent for a white company. Soon, however, he realized that, as a colored agent for a white company, his ambition to rise could not be gratified, no matter what his merits.

In July 1908, therefore, with a number of associates at Houston, Texas, he became instrumental in the organization of the American Mutual Benefit Association, an assessment fraternal society. He was elected secretary, and by the year 1921 he was receiving a salary of $240 a month.

The brave services rendered by Negro soldiers overseas during the World War bred almost unanimous hope among colored people that there would follow a generally improved interracial feeling on the return of our soldiers. When the opposite condition seemed to prevail, the protest of some leading colored men in the South took concrete form. Houston, where lived William Nickerson with his

263

family, had its bitter and bloody experience in a riot that grew out of the presence of a Negro regiment of soldiers near that city.

Nickerson had a fine job in Houston with the American Mutual Benefit Association, then in its most prosperous days; but he also had a wife and eight children. It was impossible for him to view complacently the prospect of these children growing up in the conditions of restriction prevailing in that section of Texas; and so, on June 11, 1921, he, with his family, boarded a train for Los Angeles, California. He did not know whether or not he would find employment there; but he had an understanding with the trustees of the American Mutual Benefit Association that he would have charge of the affairs of that organization in Los Angeles if it could qualify for business under the laws of California. But he was to meet many difficulties before he was able to complete qualification, which he accomplished in the spring of 1922.

During the next three years in the city of Los Angeles he wrote a weekly debit of $1,300. In November 1924, the Houston authorities of the society decided not to renew their license in California for 1925. This decision confronted Mr. Nickerson with an embarrassing situation. He had made many friends out West; had cultivated patronizing confidence in the society he had represented. Now the decision of the Houston officers not to apply for license meant that all of the confidence built up by him would be destroyed. Nickerson realized that not only was his own reputation at stake, but the confidence of Negroes in their business leaders. This situation demanded that he do something definite, and in a short time, to save the business. He knew that it would be a well-nigh impossible task to cultivate sufficient confidence in a new venture to sell the capital stock required for a stock life insurance company.

But it was not a part of Nickerson's nature to cower in the presence of any challenge. However, this trait in his character was repeatedly put to the test in meeting a series of perplexing situations that arose to face him.

The Negro population of California was not much more than 39,000, somewhat scattered throughout the state. The laws of the state required a capital stock of not less than $250,000, fully paid, to establish a stock life insurance company. Before beginning to operate a mutual, the laws required a guarantee fund of $15,000 deposited with the Insurance Department and applications for insurance with premiums paid from not less than 500 applicants.

Applications for health and accident insurance, of which his $1,300 debit was largely composed, were not acceptable. The laws forbade stock subscriptions for a mutual company. How then was Nickerson to secure the $15,000 guarantee fund and 500 applicants for policies that he could not, as a certainty, promise to issue?

He consulted a lawyer to solve this puzzle. The lawyer said he knew the answer; but his fee would be $1,500. Nickerson thought that too much. Instead, he paid $27 for a set of law books; and resolved to find a way around the difficulty. But he had to hurry. For days and nights he shut himself up within the covers of his law books before he found a law sufficiently flexible to fit the situation.

In this situation, the resourceful Mr. Nickerson proposed to the Department of Insurance that he would issue to his subscribers "certificates of contribution," instead of certificates of stock subscription. That was something new under the laws of California. No law could be found against such a proposition, and none authorizing it; and, with the assistance of Mr. John H. Upton, an actuary, the Insurance Department of California was finally persuaded to approve Mr. Nickerson's "certificate of contribution" plan: with the provision that the Corporation Department of the state approve the forms also, which was done; that all of the "contributions" must be deposited in *escrow* in some bank; and that no part of the same should be used for sales commission or other expenses. This made it necessary for Nickerson to raise an additional surplus fund of $10,000 for the preliminary operating expenses. But here another difficulty arose. For a long time no bank in Los Angeles could be found willing to accept contributions to the fund in *escrow*.

This trouble, however, was finally overcome; and then it was found that no "contributions" to the guarantee fund or the surplus could be solicited until a charter had been secured, and a board of directors elected. Here again, resourcefulness was equal to the occasion. William Nickerson, Jr., Norman O. Houston, W. J. Benton, Edward T. Banks, Frank A. Gordon, James A. Evans, Henry H. Towles, Leroy A. Beavers, Edward R. Long, Otto A. Walker, S. B. W. May, W. T. Martin, George Williams, and Fitzhugh L. Banks, and George A. Beavers, Jr., were elected as a temporary board of directors, with the understanding that they would resign in favor of any others who would contribute the required $1,000 each to the guarantee fund.

On February 24, 1925, articles of incorporation having been filed for the Golden State Guarantee Fund Insurance Company of California, a charter was granted. Until this time, skepticism had dogged every step of the promoters in this venture; but, with the news that a charter had been granted, enthusiasm commenced to kindle, and things seemed more hopeful.

Just as promise seemed about to become a reality, another great obstacle placed itself, like a mountain of granite, squarely across the pathway of the ambitious William Nickerson and his associates. The California legislature was in session; and, if not actually to thwart the purposes of the promoters of the Golden State, certainly with the apparent intention of so doing, a bill was introduced in the legislature to raise the requirements for a mutual life insurance company from 500 applicants to 1,000, and the guarantee fund from $15,000 to $25,000. That bill was passed and made a law, to become effective at 12 o'clock midnight, July 23, 1925.

To some of those interested in the venture, the passage of this law seemed a definite defeat; but not to Nickerson. He was quick to perceive the silver lining, visible from behind the fringes of the dark cloud in which this newly enacted law seemed to take form. He turned the obstruction to quick advantage. He called public meetings of the colored people of Los Angeles; and told them that if this law seemed a deliberate attempt to obstruct the commercial progress of the race, they ought to rise to meet the challenge by making the necessary contributions before the law became effective. The dramatic words of Nickerson had an electrifying effect; colored people made many sacrifices and rushed to cooperate, with the result that on July 22, 1925, just one day before the law became effective, the last dollar was paid on new applications and on the guarantee fund.

Nickerson rushed to the office of the Insurance Commissioner with documentary evidences of guarantee fund deposits, and with all necessary papers. On July 23, 1925, the very day on which the new law became effective at midnight, the Golden State Guarantee Fund Insurance Company was qualified.

Deserved Recognition

In recognition of the achievement of William Nickerson, Jr., Bishop College of Marshall, Texas, where he had been a student thirty-five years before, conferred upon her worthy son the honorary degree of Doctor of Science in Business Administration on the occasion of the fifty-eighth anniversary convocation exercises of the college in May 1939. On this occasion the president of the college said to Mr. Nickerson: "You founded, and today are the chief executive officer of the largest business enterprise owned and controlled by Negroes in the State of California."

In 1906, William Nickerson, Jr., while still only a struggling insurance agent for a white company, married Miss Bertha B. Benton. There were born to them eight children, all of whom except one are living. They are Mesdames Willie B. Johnson, Quincella Kimbrough, and Jessie Mae Johnson; Messrs. Leslie A., Victor A., and Melvin B. Nickerson, and Miss Eloise Fay Nickerson. There are also five grandchildren to cheer and brighten the ripe and successful years of the Nickerson home.

LIEUTENANT NORMAN O. HOUSTON, *Secretary-Treasurer*

The Negroes' responsiveness and adaptability to the varying economic, social, and political conditions that obtain in the different sections have been sustaining factors in their progress and survival in America. One of the most vexing phases of race prejudice is the uncertainty of its extent—the variableness of its practices and applications in the numerous communities and sections of the country.

The courage, tact, and ready understanding of obtaining conditions which Lieutenant Norman O. Houston, secretary-treasurer of the Golden State Mutual Life Insurance Company, has always exercised in such a rare degree have enabled him to obtain recognition and work in capacities not usually open to members of the colored race. He was born in the far reaches of the West at San Jose, California, October 16, 1893, to Oliver and Lillian L. Houston. When still just a small boy his parents moved to Oakland, California, and Norman attended the graded schools. In due time he finished the Oakland Technical High School, and then completed courses in Business Administration at the University of California at Berkeley, the University of Southern California, and the International Accountants' Society.

The ambition to engage in business and to become an accomplished business man possessed Mr. Houston from childhood, and never was he diverted from the path that led to the realization of that ambition. Even while in college, he contributed to the payment of his expenses by finding work as a shipping clerk with the Oliver Typewriter Company, and he holds a five year service badge from that company. From 1917 to 1918 he was engaged in the rate and mailing department of the Board of Fire Underwriters of the Pacific, located in San Francisco.

In 1918, when, on account of the World War, the young man was called to the colors, his business training quickly received due recognition in his promotion to the rank of 2nd Lieutenant at the Third Officers Training Camp at Camp Funston, Kansas. When commissioned, he served as Regimental Personnel Adjutant in the 317th Ammunition Train, American Expeditionary Force. Even under rigid military restrictions, Mr. Houston's advancement was constant. Starting at $30 a month as a private, within a year he was receiving $166.

In a few months after his discharge from the army he was employed by E. E. Potter & Sons, General Insurance Agents of San Francisco, in which capacity he served until he saw an opportunity to become an agent for the National Life Insurance Company of the United States of America, and then a general insurance broker. Becoming friendly with some of the officers of the Pacific Mutual Life Insurance Company, he was encouraged to take a course in life insurance salesmanship, and graduated with distinction. While his services with these white insurance organizations were satisfactory and successful and the work congenial, yet, when in 1923 the American Mutual Benefit Association of Houston, Texas, qualified for business in California, the keen business mind of Mr. Houston quickly recognized the greater opportunities and broader field for him with the colored organizaiton. Starting as an agent, his effectiveness as a producer and his executive qualities soon brought him deserved recognition in his promotion to state superintendent.

In 1925, when the Golden State Mutual Life Insurance Company of Los Angeles was organized, Norman O. Houston became one of its co-organizers; and upon the company qualifying to do business, was elected secretary-treasurer. It is due largely to his thorough training in accounting systems and his long experience in various clerical capacities that the office work of the Golden State Mutual has from the beginning been systematized and coordinated according to the most efficient and approved methods of modern business.

Mr. Houston is a man of little leisure, for such time as he has away from his office of the Golden State he devotes to collateral civic activities. He is an active member of the A.M.E. Church; Past Commander of 92nd-93rd Division Officers Association; was Past Commander of Benj. J. Bowie Post No. 228 of the American Legion for several years; a member of the Department of California Americanism Commission; Judge Advocate of the 23rd District of the American Legion; chairman of Eastside Citizens Committee; chairman of Citizens Advisory Committee, East Area Health Program; member of Los Angeles County Commission of Fifteen on Rehabilitation; member of Board of Management and Senior Program Chairman, 28th Street Y.M.C.A.; member of City Wide Budget Committee, Y.M.C.A.; Life member, University of California Alumni Association; Past Polemarch of the Los Angeles Alumni of Kappa Alpha Psi Fraternity; and a member of the Los Angeles Chamber of Commerce County Flood Commission.

Mr. Houston is happily married to the former Miss Edythe A. Pryce, daughter of the late Dr. George S. Pryce of Lake Charles, Louisiana, and Los Angeles. They have four lovely children.

GEORGE A. BEAVERS, JR., *Vice President—Director of Agencies*

The Director of Agencies of the Golden State Mutual Life Insurance Company, George A. Beavers, was born October 30, 1891, in Georgia, the son of George and Annie Beavers, who, dissatisfied with the meager pay they had to accept doing janitorial and domestic service, left their native state near the shores of the Atlantic and moved entirely across the continent to the shores of the Pacific to settle down where their son could have better educational opportunities and a more liberal field in which to follow his life's work.

George Jr., having finished the public elementary and high schools, entered the Hoff Commercial School in the University of California; thus showing early evidences of his ambition to follow commercial work. Like many other colored boys, he had to find work to pay his expenses in college; and he did not disdain to do the work of a porter.

When young Beavers left college, equipped for a business career, he soon was forced to realize that even in the liberal state of California, most of the doors of business employment were kept closed to colored men, except in the few racial enterprises then in operation in the state. He, therefore, had to content himself with becoming a truckdriver in partnership with his father. In this he soothed his pride by styling the work "A Transportation Partnership."

When the American Mutual Benefit Association entered California, in 1922, Beavers immediately applied for work; and received an assignment as an agent. His success as an agent soon won him the position of superintendent of agents, the duties of which position he discharged with high credit until 1925. Then, in the organization of the Golden State, Beavers played a prominent part. He is a vice president and director of agencies of that company. Much of the company's rapid progress is due to the high type of ability which he exercises in this position.

At the meeting of the National Negro Insurance Association in Hot Springs, Arkansas, in 1931, Mr. Beavers represented his company and contributed in a very important way to the deliberations and legislation of the session.

Chapter VIII.

LIQUIDATIONS

THE liquidation of a life insurance company of a sizable volume of business is far more likely to be involved and difficult than other classes of corporations. No matter at what period in the company's history liquidation might be attempted, there would be thousands of immature policies outstanding, the face amounts of which could not be paid but of which some disposition must be made.

Prior to the 1929 depression, liquidations were usually completed without great difficulty, for then other companies more readily than now accepted the securities required to cover the reserves on the outstanding business of a liquidating concern.

Liquidations and receiverships of all kinds usually prove lush financial pastures for the lucky liquidators and their lawyers. In some cases the white receivers of Negro companies, untethered by any rigid legal restraints, have feasted for years *ad libitum* on the proceeds of the assets placed in their charge; and frequently with utter indifference to the interests of creditors. The following from the United States Department of Commerce's release in 1937 may be of value in explaining the causes of Negro Insurance Companies failures:

This report centers attention on the failures which the insurance business, as conducted among Negroes, has experienced. However, the contribution which Negro operated companies have made to the economic development of the Race should not be overlooked. During the past 20 years their services have caused them to be regarded as financial reservoirs from which funds may flow in times of stress. Today, after weathering the most serious depression in the nation's history, 30 odd Negro companies justify this confidence.

Cyclical Changes — The Negro workers are marginal workers whose wages are closely correlated with the rise and fall of the business cycle. Any diminution in their incomes is reflected almost immediately in the statements of companies

271

protecting Negro lives. — Widespread unemployment among Negroes drains the reserves of Negro insurance companies in the form of surrender values and policy loans.

The same Department sums up the specific causes of failures of Negro companies as follows:

1. Unwise, expensive and too rapid extension of agency territory;
2. Excessive expense of operation;
3. Failure to exercise competent and adequate supervision over claim payments;
4. Excessive payments;
5. Dividend payments on stock which apparently had not been earned;
6. Bad judgment exercised in reinsuring insolvent companies;
7. Manipulation of capital stock issues;
8. Lack of sound investment policy;
9. Lax or unwisely lenient supervision by superintendents of insurance.

Experiences Expensively Earned

Surely all races and nations blunder. It is a weakness inherent in the human race—not merely the Negro Race, as, strangely, even many Negroes appear to believe.

May the sensational details, hereinafter related of the rise and fall of notable Negro insurance companies, be read in the light of the fact that the leaders who sponsored these undertakings were the sons of a race not sixty years out of slavery, pioneering in a field in which the majority of similar institutions organized by white business leaders also proved unsuccessful.

THE CENTURY LIFE INSURANCE COMPANY OF LITTLE ROCK, ARKANSAS

EARLY in 1926 a number of wealthy, influential business and professional men of Little Rock, Arkansas, decided to organize a life insurance company. Prominent among these were A. E. Bush, who subscriped for approximately 45 per cent of the first issue of stock; the two Ish brothers, Dr. G. W. S. and J. G., subscribing for 22 per cent; Drs. L. L. Powell of Alabama and H. A. Powell of Little Rock, and B. G. Clanton of Chicago, B. G. Olive of Little Rock, and John L. Webb of Hot Springs subscribing for the balance.[1]

The formal organization of the company was accomplished November 2, 1926, and active operation begun January 1, 1927. A. E. Bush was elected president; J. G. Ish, first vice president and secretary; Dr. G. W. S. Ish, Medical Director; Reverend S. J. Elliot, vice president;[2] Dr. L. L. Powell, vice president;[3] B. G. Olive, vice president and agency director; Dr. H. A. Powell, treasurer; B. G. Clanton, general counsel,[4] and Mrs. Linnie Raines Bargyh, director.

It was at first the intention of these organizers to confine the operations of the company to Arkansas; and, therefore, the initial capitalization was only $50,000. The stock being sold at 25 per cent above par a subscriped surplus of $25,000 was created for operating expenses. All of the stock was bought and paid for, principally in cash, by the organizers; and this sound, clean organization probably would have been perpetuated had not the ambitions of its promoters triumphed over sound business principles.

Soon after organizing, the officers received information that the North Carolina Mutual Life Insurance Company was anxious to dispose of its business in Arkansas, Mississippi, and Oklahoma. This seemed to the directors a fine opportunity to secure a desirable volume of business as a foundation; therefore, the decision to reinsure the business of the North Carolina Mutual in these states.[5]

It was necessary to increase the company's capitalization to $100,000 so as to qualify in Mississippi and Oklahoma. In placing the additional required capital, steps were taken to interest other well-known Negro capitalists; and financial arrangements and credit extensions of a nature to produce future trouble were allowed. There was begun a series of complicated contracts involving all the stockholders, and out of these complications numerous lawsuits and lengthy litigation among the stockholders developed. The assist-

---

[1] Informant: J. G. Ish.
[2] Former National Grand Master, Mosaic Templars of America.
[3] Former State Grand Master of Alabama, Mosaic Templars.
[4] Former State Grand Master of Illinois, Mosaic Templars.
[5] The contract reinsuring this business was signed and became effective at midnight, December 31, 1926. The total business in force taken over, both industrial and ordinary, amounted to more than $8,000,000. This young company never actually recovered the shock of this sudden assumption of such a large volume of business.

ance of Jesse Binga of Chicago was sought; but, unfortunately, this was at a time when, although not known to the public, Binga's bank and his general financial affairs were in distress; and there is much to sustain the contention on the part of many that this Chicago capitalist's offer of financial assistance was inspired by his belief that in some way his own Chicago interests would be relieved by his connection with Century.

Then, as if to assure early dissolution, the ambitious directors began, even in their first year, to erect an office building at a cost of more than $100,000, which, to complete, they had to encumber with a debt of more than $47,000. Thus did inexperience and unbridled ambition cripple this fine organization from the very beginning.

Also, the aid of John L. Webb, Supreme Custodian of the Woodmen of Union Fraternal Order of Hot Springs was solicited. Then it was that this renowned financier became one of the principal stockholders. But here, too, at this very time, due partly to Webb's over-zealousness to furnish financial aid to distressed Negro property, a great portion of the assets of the fraternal order which he controlled had become frozen in farm loans and on other real estate. In short, the Woodmen of the Union itself was in the preliminary stages of financial difficulties. So, it appeared that a merger of the Century Life Insurance Company and this fraternal society might produce an organization sufficiently solvent to stand through the vexing times of the impending depression, now beginning to appear everywhere. It was unfortunate that this combination had to be attempted at such a time.

The combined organization, know as the Woodmen Union Life Insurance Company, operated about two years when the business was taken in charge by the Universal Life Insurance Company acting as liquidating trustees.

THE MISSISSIPPI LIFE

The Organization, Operation and Loss of the First Negro Old Line Legal Reserve Life Insurance Company

To understand properly conditions that inspired and made possible the organization of the first old line legal reserve life insurance company by and for Negroes it seems necessary to attempt to describe briefly the immediate territory surrounding the place of its birth; the economic conditions of the Negroes in that territory at the time of its organization and for many years prior thereto; and the interracial relations obtaining in that and the adjacent territory.

Moreover, so closely interwoven with the development of this section of Mississippi and the prevailing conditions thereof were the lives of two of the principal characters in the organization and operation of the Mississippi Life, it seems that the stories of their lives must form prominent features in any proper narrative of its history.

The Delta

There are two large areas in Mississippi known as deltas: the Yazoo Delta and the Mississippi Delta. These two areas adjoin and the character of the terrain and the conditions of life in them are so similar that they might well be mistaken for one. This combined area, a 250 mile strip of invariably flat and low land, the most fertile in the state, nowhere more than 60 miles wide, begins in the north at Lake View about twelve miles south of Memphis, Tennessee, and ends at the southern extremity near Vicksburg. The Mississippi River marks the western boundary, and a long, curving chain of hills bounds it on the east.

Low, marshy, undrained, subject always to the uncertainties of overflow, mosquito-infested and unhealthy, the few rough roads through the expanding forests impassable even by horse and buggy a great part of the year, comparatively few there were, prior to 1880, willing to brave the dangers and endure the hardships necessary to live on and improve this land. Its great agricultural and commercial possibilities were unforeseen except by a few of the far-sighted who had unshakable confidence in the future of the state, then yet largely in its undeveloped status.

Indianola

Indianola, the county seat of Sunflower County, lying in the heart of this wild and unsettled section, was just a small and struggling town in 1885. On account of the poor health conditions, there were not many white people in this county; and all but a few of them lived in the town. The Negroes were illiterate, poor, and for the most part, unambitious. All of the clearing of land and the farm work were done by them; but they owned little of the land, and were indifferent to possessing it, and were not in the least concerned about its future development until there came into their midst a young school teacher, willing to live the hard life required to stay there and teach school in a rough board church.

ECONOMIC DETOUR

Wayne W. Cox

This young man was Wayne W. Cox, born twenty-five years before in Holmes County, some sixty-five miles to the east, near Ebenezer, Mississippi, a village founded by a colored man, Perry Howard, the father of the lawyer by that name.

Cox, having finished the makeshift course provided by the county school, found his way to the new State College, the Alcorn A. &. M. College, near Port Gibson, which had been opened for Negroes by the state ten years prior. By his own labor on the college farm, he earned enough to maintain himself in school during the three years, when, lacking one year of graduation, he was forced to leave to seek work to support his aged and ailing mother. Returning first to the vicinity of Ebenezer, he had a minor clash with a white man, and, to avoid probable trouble, went to live at Indianola where he secured work as a teacher.

Almost immediately he visualized the great possible fortunes that lay in the development of this fertile farm land and was inspired with the ambition to own large tracts of it. By nature rigidly economical, he commenced, out of his meager salary as a teacher, to save some money which he invested in land, paying from 25c to 50c an acre for it.[6]

He not only bought all the land he could, but he persuaded other colored men to do likewise. Of the several who did, most of them later became associated with him in the financial enterprises which he led in organizing.

His Famous Wife

Soon after coming to Indianola the young teacher married Miss Minnie M. Geddings of Lexington, Mississippi, a woman who in later years was the central figure in an affair of such intense nature and of such magnitude as to bring national renown to both of them. She was also, after his death, to succeed him in the position of secretary-treasurer of the Mississippi Life Insurance Company.

W. W. Cox, in the rapidly developing county of Sunflower, soon became the leader among the colored people. He was a United States railway postal clerk on a line running through Indianola, the first colored man in that section of the state to hold such a position; and he became at once of such commanding prestige that the colored people generally confided their every interest in his hands. Such

[6] Some of this same land sold for $400 per acre after the World War.

was their confidence in him that in the fall, after they had their "settlements," they brought their money to him "to keep safe," and left it without security or written evidence of their deposits. He later said that at times he had of other people's money deposited in his name as much as $25,000.

This suggested the idea of the organization of a bank. However, he probably never would have organized the bank except for "the post-office affair." Through his influence, his wife had received appointment as postmistress of Indianola under President Harrison, in which office she served three years with great credit, but was not reappointed by President Cleveland. However, when President McKinley took office in 1897, Mrs. Cox was again made postmistress and served unmolested until the autumn of 1902, when trouble which culminated in her resignation was began.

Vitriolic Vardaman

By 1900, The Delta was rapidly taking form as a land of large plantations owned and operated by rich white planters and cultivated by large numbers of illiterate Negroes who constituted by far the greater part of the population. This was in contradistinction to the "hills section" of Mississippi where the majority of the population was composed of poor whites who, men and women, did their own field and other work. While these poor whites were not regarded as social aristocrats on a level with the rich white people of The Delta, they held the balance of political power, the Negroes being thoroughly disfranchised.

Greenwood, on account of its nearness to the "hills country", was the gateway to The Delta. About the beginning of the present century the hills-country white people in ever increasing numbers were coming to trade in Greenwood; and some of them to settle in and around that town. In the year 1901 the late James K. Vardaman came in from the near-by hills county of Montgomery. He had studied law, was politically ambitious; and began his life in Greenwood by founding the *Commonwealth*, a weekly newspaper of which he became editor. He was a master of spectacular appeal to prejudice and popular favor. Stately, nearly always meticulously attired in white, long locks of dark hair falling about his broad shoulders, he was a figure in his role as "White Chief," so picturesque as to attract marked attention and win popularity by his appearance alone.

But among the rich planters and merchants in and around

Greenwood only a substantial bank account could provide the necessary wherewithal for admittance to the best social circles. These rich whites looked upon the "White Chief," almost weekly borrowing to release his Commonwealth, with poorly concealed contempt; and Vardaman, countering with the verbose vitriol which made him famous began to thunder, on the platform and through his paper, his doctrine of social equality. This still further embittered the wealthy classes, who feared such preachments might cause race trouble and disturb their docile Negro labor. Perhaps their efforts might have been successful in confining the struggling editor to local oblivion, but for the Indianola Post Office Affair.

Minnie Cox, A National Figure

It was called to Vardaman's attention that in Indianola, twenty-five miles to the west, the white people had to have their mail "forked out to them from the black paws of a Negress." (The quotation is Vardaman's.) This was just the type of "visible evidence" the "White Chief" wanted to convince his increasing poor white following that there really existed an "impending crisis"—a threat of social equality and co-mingling of the races.

As a result of the agitation started by Vardaman, a number of white people of Indianola joined in a mass meeting in the autumn of 1902, and passed a resolution demanding the resignation of Mrs. Cox as postmistress, and fixing December 31st of that year as the final day of her tenure.

These were tense times for Cox and his wife. By "kitchen rumor" they knew, days before the mass meeting, that sentiment hostile to them was brewing; and, according to these rumors, brutalities and indignities far more dreadful than resigning the post office were being urged and contemplated. Mrs. Cox, out of consideration for her husband, wanted to relinquish the office at once; but neither the Post Office Department at Washington, nor her bondsmen, rich, brave white men of Indianola, would consent to this. Naturally, there were those who thought that Cox, himself an employee of the Government, would use his influence to keep the office in the hands of his wife.

The apparent danger that threatened the couple, as well as the nonchalance and inconsistency with which it was regarded by some of the sheltered white people, may be understood from the following, which appeared in the *Evening Scimitar* of Memphis, Tennessee, under date of January 7, 1903:

Minnie Cox is Safe

The life and property of Minnie Cox and her husband have never been jeopardized. Conservative citizens of Indianola scoff at the idea that they have been in danger of violence. . .

She left this town of her own volition, not for the reason that she feared intimidation or violence from anyone or party, but simply because her counsel laid down the old adage to her that where there is no fuel, no fire can be built.

Minnie is about thirty-five years old. Her husband is her senior by five years. Both are Mississippians, born at Lexington.

Minnie Cox is a small Negress, whose form and face bear all the leading characteristics of the black race. Her skin is as black as the proverbial ace of spades, her nose is flat and her ears small. Her husband is a mulatto of intelligent face and good bearing of person.

McKinley reappointed Minnie Cox to the office, and Roosevelt made no change when he assumed the Presidential duties.

The woman, therefore, has served eleven years as post-mistress. She gave eminent satisfaction. Always respectful to the white people, she was respected and commended by all who came in contact with her.

Witness, now, the chain of events that caused dissatisfaction among the whites over the fact that she held the office.

Last summer the match was struck that kindled the flame of popular sentiment toward the Negroes here.

It was early in June that a bricklayer of color, a skilled artisan and a man of some education and schemes, drifted into the prosperous little town of Indianola. He outbid white contractors and did his work just as well, if not better, than they. Not content with the good fortune he was enjoying, the Negro, who was of the new regime, endeavored to instill the idea of social equality with the whites into the dense craniums of his cocoa-nut-headed brethren and sisters.

Things rapidly reached a critical stage. It became almost impossible to endure the town Negroes. It was with difficulty

279

that washer-women could be secured to "do up" the soiled linen of their superiors.

Negro Disappeared

The Negro that was the prime factor in agitating this movement did not last long. He has not been heard of since the date of his abdication.

In the month of July another event occurred. M. Camp, a general merchandise man of Indianola, employed a Miss Bobbie Hendon to clerk for him. A Negro named Burnett was the errand boy. Burnett became industrious and was permitted to wait on the customers. He began to look upon himself as a regular clerk, and that Miss Hendon, being also a clerk, they were therefore social equals One day he made a remark to the young lady that was insulting. Miss Hendon burst into tears and ran into the street, calling for assistance

White citizens heard her story. They said little, but that night Burnett disappeared from off the face of the earth.* The fire was burning now. It needed no fueling.

Attention was turned at the same time toward Minnie Cox. Her face is also black. By common consent a mass meeting of citizens was held at the courthouse on October 17. A Committee of three, of which J. L. Davis, Mayor of Indianola, was Chairman, and G. P. Adair, Editor of the Pensee, Secretary, was appointed to draw up and circulate the following petition, addressed to the postmistress:

'We, the undersigned citizens, hereby request that you tender your resignation as postmistress of the Indianola post-office, to take effect November 1st.'

The undersigned numbered fifty-six of the most prominent citizens of the town.

Other excerpts will follow from which it will be seen that President Theodore Roosevelt closed the Indianola post office after some of the people there forced Mrs. Minnie M. Cox to resign. The office remained closed during the greater part of 1903, but Mrs. Cox drew her salary from the government until the expiration of her term of office.

In the meantime, the white citizens of Indianola organized their

---

* Note: And yet, according to the first paragraph of this excerpt "conservative citizens scoffed at the idea that Minnie Cox was in any danger."

own private post office, but they had to send all the way to Greenville, twenty-five miles distance, where their mail was delivered,
and have it brought by messenger to Indianola. When it is
remembered that there were no automobiles in Sunflower County
at that time, the full inconvenience of this situation will be appreciated. But Negroes in and around Indianola were not allowed to
receive any mail through this privately operated post office.

*What President Teddy Roosevelt, who Had the Courage of His
Convictions, Said About the Affair*

I cannot consent to take the position that the door of hope—
the door of opportunity—is to be shut upon any man, no-matter
how worthy, purely on the grounds of race and color. Such
an attitude would, according to my convictions, be fundamentally wrong. It seems to me that it is a good thing from
every standpoint to let the colored man know that if he shows
in marked degree, qualities of citizenship—qualities which in a
white man we feel entirely right to reward—then hè will not
be cut off from all hope of similar reward.

CINCINNATI INQUIRER, JAN. 3, 1903

TOWN
DENIED MAIL SERVICE
UNTIL CITIZENS ACCEPT A COLORED WOMAN
AS THE OFFICIAL DISPENSER OF POSTAL MATTER
FORCED TO RESIGN BY THE THREATS OF VIOLENCE

PRESIDENT AND CABINET CONSIDERED THE CASE
AND ROOSEVELT CONSULTED GENERAL PAYNE

STATEMENT ISSUED FROM EXECUTIVE OFFICE
GIVING A HISTORY OF THE TROUBLE AND
DETAILING THE ACTION THAT HAS BEEN TAKEN

Washington, January 2.—The troubles of a colored woman
today occupied the chief attention of President Roosevelt and
the members of his Cabinet. The woman is Mrs. Minnie Cox,
Postmistress at Indianola, Mississippi.

The Indianola affair has been under consideration for some
time,

SHE HAD TO RESIGN

It was made so unpleasant for this colored woman that she was forced to resign, her life threatened if she continued to act.

President Roosevelt was aroused and ordered that the resignation be not accepted. At the Cabinet meeting today it was decided to notify the citizens of Indianola that the office would remain closed, and the town be shut off from all postal connections until the people are willing to accept the woman as their postmistress. The reports of Postoffice Inspectors show that she is at all times courteous and honest in the discharge of her duties. Her moral standing in the community is of the highest. Few offices of this grade in any state are conducted better.

Life in Danger

The Mayor of the town and the Sheriff of the County both told the Postoffice Inspector that if she refused to resign they could not be answerable for her safety.

Memphis Commercial Appeal — Jan. 8, 1903

The End Not Yet In Sight

ROOSEVELT WILL NOT OPEN INDIANOLA OFFICE

FEELS HE WAS JUSTIFIED

HINTS OF STARTLING PRIVATE INFORMATION ARE HEARD

Washington, Jan. 7. — (Staff Special) — From reliable sources the Commercial Appeal learns that the administration takes the view that there was sufficient justification for closing the office. Hints are made that officials have some sort of startling private information that is being held up the sleeve. What this is no one on the outside knows.

Sunflower Tocsin, Jan. 6, 1903

NEGROES IN OFFICE

Minnie Cox, postmistress, or ex-postmistress, of Indianola, Mississippi, knows that she is not wanted as postmistress any longer. Her husband also has plenty of horse sense.

Now, why should the President be unwilling to let her out of office when she desires to get out?

LIQUIDATIONS

Memphis Commercial Appeal, Jan. 7, 1903

NEGROES NOT WANTED

Several colored professional men were attempting to locate in Indianola. This was resented by the whites engaged in similar vocations, and was another inspiration to the postoffice trouble.

"They told me if I didn't leave, my home would be on the long bridge some night," explained Dr. Fulton. The long bridge crosses the Indian bayou in the center of the town. Fulton lived on the opposite side from the courthouse.

From a Local Paper:

Let Teddy take "coons" to the White House. I should not care if the walls of that ancient edifice should become so saturated with the effluvia from their rancid carcasses that a "chinch bug" would have to crawl upon the dome to avoid asphyxiation.

The Organization of a Bank

The spirit of venture and of courage which so greatly actuated the conduct of W. W. Cox was imparted to a large number of his substantial colored friends in the county.

The reader should get no impression that the Negroes in Sunflower County were frightened by the terrible conditions that for a time hung like a threatening cloud over the community.

The storm aroused by Vardaman's propaganda had scarcely blown away before Cox set about to establish on the scene an enterprise of far more importance to Negroes than the position of postmistress.

He quietly called together a number of his substantial friends, some of whom he had persuaded to buy delta land eighteen years before. He told them of his plan to organize a bank. A bank! A Negro bank in Indianola? Many of the white people, when they heard about it, laughed at the idea. But some of Cox's white friends remarked, "You don't know Wayne Cox."

Even while the rumor was being treated as a joke, W. W. Cox, Reverends William Coates, Walter Stephens, Peter Miles, William Peyton, P. W. Capshaw, H. C. Bell, Dan McKinney, Albert Johnson, M. B. Burnett, and others had already subscribed and paid in the capital, $25,000; and before the end of 1903 they had a charter for

283

the Delta Penny Savings Bank. It was a prosperous institution from the beginning.

Just about the time that Vardaman made his debut in Greenwood, a young colored physician, Dr. W. A. Attaway, also settled there. He was a brilliant conversationalist, and had just enough stammer in his manner of speech to throw into every conversation an atmosphere of cordial amusement. This shadow of a defect was in fact an advantage. People liked to hear him talk and to talk to him.

Almost over night he was becoming a leader of the colored people in Greenwood, but he became too openly vocal in his replies to Vardaman's tirades against the postmistress in Indianola. He was not permitted to remain long thereafter in Leflore County.

He opened offices at Moorehead, Mississippi, ten miles east of Indianola. In 1906, W. W. Cox requested the popular physician to become president of the Delta Penny Savings Bank.

Soon after becoming president of the bank, Dr. Attaway suggested the organization of an even bigger financial venture—an Old Line Legal Reserve Life Insurance Company—to be owned and operated by Negroes.

This suggestion became a concrete reality on September 1, 1908, when the initial capital of $25,000 was all subscribed and the Charter of Incorporation signed by the incorporators.

On the call of W. W. Cox, acting clerk, the stockholders again met in the Delta Penny Savings Bank on September 28, 1908. The charter of incorporation was read and approved.

An election was held and the following were elected directors to serve for two years or "until their successors are elected according to law": W. W. Cox, W. P. Kyle, N. Baines, W. A. Attaway, C. C. Johnson, T. S. Crawford, H. W. Nichols, J. E. Walker and A. B. Grimes.

After the election of the directors, the board met and proceeded to elect the following officers: W. A. Attaway, president and manager; H. W. Nichols, first vice president; J. E. Walker, second vice president; T. S. Crawford, third vice president; W. W : Cox, secretary-treasurer.

Charter Secured

On January 9, 1909, the State of Mississippi granted the charter. Under this charter, authorization was granted for the sale of stock not to exceed $25,000, and for making application for license to do an industrial insurance business when the sale of stock had been completed. It did not take long to dispose of the stock, for Cox, once convinced of the wisdom of the course, subscribed and paid for most of it himself. Before the end of the year the company was operating and had organized several districts in the state.

First Old Line Legal Reserve Negro Life Insurance Company Organized

Its capitalization being only $25,000, the Company was not permitted under the laws of the state to write policies for death benefit in excess of $500. This necessarily limited the field to industrial business. Dr. Attaway wanted a company that could write all forms of life insurance and in which the policies would not be limited in the amount of individual risks. Therefore, at the annual meeting of the stockholders of the Mississippi Beneficial Insurance Company in November 1910, it was voted to amend the charter, increasing the capital to $100,000. This having been done and $25,000 of the increased authorization sold, the Mississippi Beneficial Insurance Company in that year was granted license to do Old Line Legal Reserve Life Insurance business, and thus became the first such company in the world to be organized among Negroes.

Eddie Thomas, the First Policyholder

Among the stockholders and admirers of Dr. W. A. Attaway was a well-to-do young farmer of Louise, Mississippi. He was the first person ever to apply for and to receive an Old Line Legal Reserve Life Insurance Policy in a Negro Company. It was a ten-year endowment policy for $1,000.[7] Thomas kept the policy in force until its maturity in 1920, when he became the first Negro to be paid $1,000, matured endowment, by a company owned and operated by Negroes.

Early Difficulties

The officers of the Mississippi Beneficial Life had to find and "make out" with such makeshift agency material at first as were cast off by the white companies. This was a class of poorly trained colored men. Hence, the company sustained many losses from poor selections, extravagance, and dishonesty in the years from 1909 until 1914.

[7] Dr. Attaway solicited this application, medically examined Thomas, and then, as president, signed the policy.

The white agents of white companies catering to Negro patronage criticized and fought the Mississippi Beneficial Life in every way. In some communities, as agents of the colored company weekly delivered their policies to the homes of their people, white agents would trail them, take away the policies and destroy them.

The office of Insurance Commissioner in the State of Mississippi was and is elective. The commissioner, at the time the Mississippi Beneficial was licensed, was discouragingly frank in stating that it could continue to operate only as long as it did not get into trouble with the white agents and the white companies.

The white agents knew his attitude; hence, they lost no time in filing charges against the company, charging it with "switching business." The commissioner promptly threatened to cancel its license; and it required the assistance and influence of important white friends to persuade him not to take this step.

During 1913, friction developed between the president and the secretary and became acute before the end of the year. The former wanted the home office moved to Greenville, where he resided. Cox, holding controlling interests, insisted that the office remain in Indianola.

At a meeting of the stockholders in January 1914, Professor A. J. Howard, brother of Perry W. Howard and wealthy merchant, planter, and former president of Alcorn College, was elected president of the company, and M. S. Stuart, former cashier of the American Trust and Savings Bank of Jackson, Mississippi, was elected general manager.

A. J. Howard, although he accepted the office, never did visualize the possibilities for service and financial expansion at his finger tips. He invested nothing in the company, notwithstanding his pledges before his election so to do. Residing at Ebenezer, sixty-five miles away, he gave no more of his time to the interests of the company than was necessary for attending monthly executive meetings at Indianola, when he insisted always that the meetings be adjourned in time for him to obtain his salary check and catch the next train to Ebenezer. Of the official personnel, therefore, Stuart alone had to undertake the operation of the Mississippi Beneficial Life at the beginning of 1914, and he was of limited experience in this field.

It was a gloomy prospect, with discouraged and absconding agents, claims long past due and unpaid all over the state, pending judgments and threats of cancelling the license from the Department of Insurance. The "book capital" stock was at this time $50,000; but there was an impairment of $13,000 and threats of application for a receivership from disgruntled stockholders.

The industrial debit was less than $1,400, scattered over the state, under twenty-seven district offices, most of which were operating at a weekly loss. Objections from powerful influences in the company embarrassed the management's program for combining field offices to reduce expenses.

However, with a saving of more than $11,000 in the district overhead effected in 1914, most of the overdue claims were satisfied. Several educated young men were induced to accept agencies; clerical systems were installed, and regular weekly reports were required. Notwithstanding the economic disturbances caused by the war in Europe and stagnation in the cotton market, things seemed brighter for the company at the beginning of 1915. During that year the debit increased more than $400.

Another Major Misfortune

It was during 1915 that the causes of another major misfortune began to appear. Then it was that Mississippi began enforcing its recently enacted guaranty banking law. It was no secret that the State Banking Department did not intend to qualify any of he five or six colored banks. The white banks objected to being taxed to guarantee deposits in Negro banks.

Had the doors of the Delta Penny Savings Bank been closed, that would have paralyzed the Mississippi Beneficial Life. Cox and his friends became greatly alarmed. They knew that his bank could meet the financial requirements, but how could they overcome the hostile sentiment of the white banks?

Bank examiner Love said: "Cox, I do not think that I will qualify your bank under any circumstances; and certainly, I am going to make the requirements doubly as rigid as for any other bank in the state." Twice Cox met the requirements laid down by the examiner, only to have them made more difficult. At last he was informed that he would have to secure the endorsements of the two white banks in Indianola. To the credit of these white competitors and to the surprise of the examiner, they readily gave their endorsement; and the bank was qualified, being the last bank, and the only Negro bank, admitted into the guaranty league.

287

But W. W. Cox never recovered from the weeks of mental strain of this ordeal. Throughout 1915, he was physically a weak man, though not fifty-five years old.

When it became known late in 1915 that he was gravely ill, all the colored people and the leading white people of the town became alarmed. White leaders said, "Indianola needs Wayne Cox and we must save him." They insisted that the authorities at the exclusively white resort at Stafford's Springs, Mississippi, build a cottage especially for Cox's accommodation. It was done, but he remained there only two weeks. He wanted to go to the hospital at Tuskegee; and here he died in April 1916—a martyr to the cause of Negro business.

Scores of white people attended his funeral; and, over the body of a man who, just thirteen years before, had to slip into the town under cover of darkness to meet and steal away his persecuted wife, tears flowed as freely down white as down colored cheeks.

A. J. Howard resigned the office of presidency and Dr. Joseph Edison Walker, who was serving as vice president, was elected president.

The improvement and growth of the company started with reforms effected in 1914, continued with accelerated pace.

By the end of 1916, the company's annual premium income was more than $125,000. December 31, 1917, the premium income was $194,074, and the total income, $201,168. In 1917, the company qualified for business in the State of Arkansas; and, during 1919, in Alabama and Tennessee. By the end of 1919, the premium income had passed the half million dollar mark, being $544,189.

Moved to Memphis

During 1918, it began to appear to the officers of the company that, in a few years, the Mississippi Life[8] would tower too spectacularly over all other business enterprises at Indianola and all other insurance companies domiciled in Mississippi for comfort and security.

There were indications that many white people in Mississippi were already viewing with amazement and puzzled concern the progress of this institution under the management of colored people. While these suspicions may have been without any basis at all, yet, seeking a base of operation with greater facilities, it was decided,

[8] The name was changed to the Mississippi Life at a prior meeting of the stockholders.

in 1919, that the home office of the company be moved to Memphis, Tennessee. But here the directors ran into difficulty. The Insurance Commissioner was unwilling that the securities of $100,000 on deposit with the treasurer of Mississippi be transferred to Tennessee. His consent to move was gained only on condition that the company remain legally and theoretically domiciled in Mississippi. However, in the summer of 1920, the affairs and effects of the home office of the Mississippi Life Insurance Company were moved to Memphis, and offices were opened at 234 Hernando Street. The theoretical domicile of the company was Kosciusko, Mississippi, and a seal was left there in charge of W. W. Phillips, one of the directors.

At the end of the year 1920, the company's total income amounted to $905,117; but, at the end of 1921, the total income amounted to only $884,958, a decrease of slightly more than $200,,000. Out of this fact came subsequent important and sensational developments.

Actuarial Trouble

After the close of the year 1920, the Mississippi examiner came, and, with him, an actuary. The result of their examination made it appear that the company was impaired in the sum of some $20,000. They contended that all of the loss had been sustained in the Ordinary Department which had been supervised by an Ordinary manager or agency director.

Contribution to Surplus

In this emergency, Dr. J. E. Walker, president, and Mrs. Minnie M. Cox, secretary-treasurer, came to the company's rescue, and contributed to the surplus of the company $20,000 in securities to which they had to relinquish all title in favor of the company.

At a meeting of the stockholders at Clarksdale, Mississippi,[9] in February 1921, the services of the Ordinary supervisor were dispensed with, nothwithstanding that he contended that these losses were not real; but due to errors in lapsing forfeited policies.

However that may have been, allegedly through the resourcefulness and activity of this supervisor, Mrs. Cox, who continued a boarder in his home, purchased sufficient additional of the capital stock of the company from various stockholders to increase her holdings to a majority. She then demanded that her son-in-law,

[9] Theoretically domiciled in Mississippi it was thought legally compulsory that the stockholder's meetings be held in that state.

Dr. Wayne Cox Howard of Bessemer, Alabama, be elected president of the company.

Dr. J. E. Walker had in this year (1922) already been elected for a two-year term; and he refused to resign until his large block of stock had been purchased and an adjustment made of his compensation for the unexpired term. His resignation was made effective as of February 22, 1923.

Dr. Howard was elected president at the meeting of the stockholders immediately following the resignation of Dr. Walker; but he stated repeatedly that he had no relish for the office. He was wealthy in his own right; and he never did move to Memphis to assume the duties of president. Apparently he was even more blind to the great financial possibilities within his grasp than his brother had been in the infant days of the company at Indianola; for now he was treating with indifference the direction of an enterprise already collecting a million dollars yearly.

The Mysterious Visit of an Actuary

In this situation, the responsibilities of operating the company in 1923 fell upon the shoulders of Marshall B. Burnett, active vice president, and M. S. Stuart, general manager. President Howard came to Memphis so infrequently as to cause delay in making important decisions affecting the proper prosecution of the business.

But, if the young president did not appreciate the luscious business plum dangling before him, there were others, old in the game, eying this prize with eager craving and design; and they were already laying plans to capture it.

This was at a time when the juggling of corporate units, stock manipulations, quick deals and glaring financial combinations had become the sensational order of the day in American business. Rogers Caldwell, Luke Lea, Samuel Insul, and other smart dealers held the spotlight among white people. Among colored people Heman Perry dominated the center of the stage. It was, therefore, a crass tempting of fate for Dr. Howard, garbed in the hood of inexperience, to be caught out in the financial jungles with such a tempting morsel in his unprotected basket. He was not destined to go far with it.

Unexpectedly, early in 1923, a prominent actuary dropped into the offices of the Mississippi Life in Memphis. He asked to be allowed to "look over your last annual statement," after which he inquired how it was that with "such an income and such low overhead you don't have a large surplus and pay heavy stock dividends." Told that the Mississippi commissioner opposed stock dividends, he replied: "That's because you don't have your own Actuary"; and he further stated that if the company would engage him he would "develop" the large surplus which he said the company already had; and then, if the Mississippi commissioner did not approve it, he would submit his findings to a "Committee of Actuaries of national standing" and force his hand.

The active officers of the company employed this actuary to make an examination of the company's affairs. They knew that he was the actuary for Standard Life of Atlanta; but they did not know that Heman Perry of that company was scheming to get possession of the majority stock of Mississippe Life and its large surplus of cash to aid him in overcoming impending bankruptcy of Standard, nor that information gained by the examination would be used by Perry in formulating his plans to capture the Memphis company.

Later developments revealed that the scheme was first to deprive the company of the services of either one or both of the active officers. That alone, it later was disclosed, was the motive that inspired the letter from Perry to Stuart reproduced herein.

The actuary left Memphis without completing the examination and revealing the "large surplus" he had promised. He later returned; but then his chief purpose seemed to have been to secure the services of the general manager to manage the "great Industrial Department" which he said Standard was going to operate. He said that Stuart would soon receive a "flattering offer" from Perry; and that offer was received on September 26, 1923. (See facsimile on page 292.)

M. S. Stuart, knowing nothing about the financial straits into which Standard Life had fallen, and sharing the high confidence which the Negro public everywhere had in its solvency and pledges, resigned his office as general manager of the Mississippi Life; and, in response to telephoned request, went to Atlanta expecting to begin the formulation of plans for organizing "the great industrial department" which he believed Standard was about to organize.

Puzzled that he could not get Perry nor any of his representatives to manifest that degree of interest in projecting the industrial department which he knew such an important venture

JNO. A. COPELAND
Consulting Actuary
JAS. R. COTHRAN
Associate Actuary
HURT BUILDING
ATLANTA GEORGIA

September 25th, 1923.

Mr. M. S. Stuart,

Memphis, Tenn.

Dear Sir:-

The Standard Life contemplates entering the
Industrial field and considerable additional -territory
and will require a Manager for the proposed expansion.

We would be glad to have you form a connection with the Standard Life and offer you a salary of
$6,000.00   a year.

We expect to commence operations in accordance
with our plans at an early date and would like to have
your connection with us completed as of November first.
Should you see fit to accept our offer herein contained,
kindly advise us at the earliest possible moment.

Yours very truly,

STANDARD LIFE INSURANCE CO.

President.

292

should command, he, after almost two idle days in Atlanta, protested the indifference and loss of time. Soon after that, Perry, affecting an air of one who has news of great moment to impart, said to Stuart: "It begins to look like we are going to be able to place in your hands all of your old Mississippi Life organization as a nucleus with which to begin your department." To Stuart's demurrer that he would have no part in any attempt to disaffect the agents of his former employers, Perry said that, that would not be necessary, since he had information which caused him to believe that the Insurance Commissioner of Mississippi intended to cancel the license of the Mississippi Life because its officers had employed an actuary without his consent. He further stated that such a step would probably make the stock of that company almost worthless; but that he preferred to "save the situation" by buying all of the stock and reinsuring the business. He wanted Stuart to attempt to persuade Dr. Howard and Mrs. Cox to sell him their stock. This he declined to do; but agreed to go to Jackson, Mississippi, to ascertain from the Insurance Commissioner there if he meant to cancel the license of the company; and, if so, to go on to Washington, D. C., to lay the entire matter before the Honorable Perry.W. Howard, General Counsel of the Mississippi Life and legal adviser of his brother, Dr. Wayne Howard.

Heman Perry, the Liberal Pauper

The Mississippi Insurance Commissioner said that on account of constant "confusion and disobedience to my orders"[1] he intended to cancel the license of the Mississippi Life as of December 31, 1923.

On October 2, 1923, Stuart arrived in Washington and lost no time in reporting all of the circumstances surrounding the company to Perry Howard, Assistant United States Attorney General and Mississippi representative on the National Executive Committee of the Republican party.

This eminent jurist expressed himself as not disturbed about the intention of the Insurance Commissioner to cancel the company's license. "That", he said, "isn't worth talking about. I can fix it in fifteen minutes. What concerns me most is your leaving the company."

After taking the matter under consideration until the next day

---

[1] Once before when the company in Indianola had engaged the services of Andrew Sigtenhorst, a popular actuary, he had ordered that this particular actuary never be employed again; but had not mentioned any other actuaries.

and talking to his brother at Bessemer, Alabama, by telephone that night, he said that he would advise the sale of the stock held by his brother and Mrs. Cox on the following conditions: (a) That the entire amount be paid in cash;[2] (b) that the price be $125 per share;[3] (c) that his fee be borne entirely by Heman Perry or Standard Life.

A message was immediately dispatched to Perry at Atlanta suggesting that he probably should come on to Washington to complete negotiations. In reply, two telegrams were received. See facsimiles, page 295.)

Perry,[1] on his arrival in Washington, was informed very explicitly that $125 per share was the price *proposed by Mr. Howard*. Yet in less than twenty minutes he agreed to pay $150 per share, Howard's fee and the $20,000 contribution to surplus which Mrs. Cox had made in 1921. Was this unnecessary liberality due to a desire to curry favor as a foundation for indulgence of pledges that he knew were soon to be broken? That seems the only plausible explanation.

Pressed by Lawyer Howard as to his ability to pay in cash, Perry, with a casual gesture of indifference, said: "Why, Mr. Howard, Standard Life and its affiliated Service Companies turn deals like this every day or two."

But this pretense that a deal of $106,000 was a matter of trivial routine was soon to be exposed, along with the pauperism of Perry. When Dr. Wayne Cox Howard, his wife, Mrs. Ethyl Cox Howard, Mrs. Minnie M. Cox, Heman Perry and Perry W. Howard met in Bessemer, Alabama, the first week in November 1923 to conclude the deal, it was found that Perry did not have the cash to pay for the stock. Saying that he had been too busy to transfer the required funds to "my open account," he offered Dr. Howard four personal checks of $5,000 each to cover the initial payment and three promissory notes of $20,000 each, due respectively as follows: November 15, 1923; December 1, 1923; December 15, 1923; and one note for $26,000 due December 31, 1923. He also, at this time, gave Perry Howard his check for $4,500 to cover his fee. All of these checks were drawn on the Citizens Trust Company of Atlanta, one of the affiliates of Standard Life. None of the checks was honored when presented at the bank. The failure to pay the checks

---

[2] Mr. Howard stated emphatically and repeatedly that he would advise the sale only for cash.

[3] The total cost at this rate would amount to about $90,000.

322AGHB 508FM 21

Q ATLANTA GA OCT 3 346

W H STUART

     WHITELAW HOTEL 13TH ST WASHINGTON DC

FERRY OUT OF TOWN UNTIL FIVE PM WILL WIRE ON HIS

ARRIVAL WHO IS COMING AND WHEN STAY ON THE JOB

         JNO A COPELAND

XA449 16

                                                   1923 OCT 3 PM 5 44

      ATLANTA GA 5 45P

B S STUART   1580
       WHITELAW HOTEL 13 AND TEE STS WASHINGTON DC

FERRY LEAVES TONIGHT MIDNIGHT SOUTHERN ARRIVING WASHINGTON ABOUT

TEN THURSDAY NIGHT WILL MEET YOU WHITELAW HOTEL

     JOHN A COPELAND.

and Perry's flimsy ruse in trying to cover up the financial stress of his tottering corporations and his own bankruptcy, by claiming that he had discovered that the Mississippi Life was impaired, aroused the ire of Perry Howard as will be seen from correspondence herein reproduced.[4] (See pages 297-8.)

Many informed persons in both white and Negro business circles now knew that Perry, Standard Life, and all of its affiliates were in the most desperate of financial difficulties.[5] Evidently, some one did make an effort to induce the Insurance Commissioner of Mississippi to turn the business over to Standard without Perry having to pay for the stock, as intimated in the letter of P. W. Howard. Actually, this state official did threaten to take such action; and he was persuaded not to do so only after Perry W. Howard in a letter had declared he would file stiff legal resistance; and after G. W. Lee and M. S. Stuart in a personal interview had stated they would lead a movement to disorganize all of the debits and dissipate the business if Perry attempted to take charge without paying for the stock.

Faced with the necessity of complying with his contract, Perry began a wandering search for funds. He went to all of the financial centers where Negroes were supposed to have money or extensive credit; but without success.

A Devious and Doubtful Detour of Finance

In desperation the daring president of Standard now urged a procedure of doubtful rectitude. He tried to induce Dr. Howard and Mrs. Cox, the two principal officers of the Mississippi Life, to deposit all of the company's cash surplus[6] in his bank, the Citizens Trust of Atlanta, allegedly intending to borrow it from his bank to pay these officers for their personal stock.

The superficies of such a transaction would, of course, expose no symptoms of irregularity; but in the light of their knowledge that this bank had not honored its president's checks, and that he was vainly trying to borrow money to pay for their stock, the president and secretary-treasurer of the Mississippi Life woud have been venturing dangerously close to the fringes of integrity in making the

---

[4] Informants: Dr. W. C. Howard, P. W. Howard, H. E. Perry.

[5] In less than sixty days afterward, Eric D. Walrond, sponsored by Perry, was in Atlanta preparing an article for *Forbes Magazine,* picturing Perry as a millionaire.

[6] Probably about $80,000, certainly not less than $60,000.

IN REPLY REFER TO
INITIALS AND NUMBER

Department of Justice,
Washington.

November 16, 1923.

Prof. M. S. Stuart,
679 Mississippi Avenue,
Memphis, Tennessee.

Dear Stuart:

I shall be in Memphis Monday morning.

I am sending you copy of letter written to Perry. It may be a little rash, but from the information in his letter, I would not like to express myself full of him. If he gets by with this deal, I shall expose him to the whole nation.

There were no representations made at all by Mrs. Cox and my brother in the conference at Bessemer. It was very brief on account of the illness of Mrs. Cox. He and his actuaries said they had more information than we, and they acted on that information.

I do not believe that there is a d-- bit of impairment, and the whole thing is a scheme to get this boy's stock for nothing and I shall dedicate my whole life to getting even on such a scheme as this, and you know that I am vindictive. They are going to pay him every dime or the whole scheme is going to be exposed and it will stink to hell.

Pardon my expressions, but my very soul revolts at such d-- rottenness.

I sincerely appreciate your stand for right in the matter.

Your friend,

Perry W Howard

PWH/LRL.

297

C O P Y

November 16, 1923

Mr. Heman E. Perry, President,
Standard Life Insurance Company
Atlanta, Georgia.

Dear Mr. Perry:

I read your letter very carefully and I want to say that
I was never more surprised or deceived in a human being than I am
in the deception your letter purports to set up.

You know the representations you make are absolutely in
error. In your insistence to get this business, you stated that
if there was any impairment you had a way to take care of it. You
said that there was no way for us to know just how the situation
was, but, on the other hand, the insurance examiner and your actuaries were getting this information as nearly as it could be got.
When we were in Bessemer, you stated that you had Mr. Copeland to
go to Jackson and Mr. Cothran to Memphis to make cursory examinations, which seemingly satisfied you. You bought after your representatives and actuaries and the representatives of the Insurance Department had made an examination. Not only that, but this
matter was O. K.d, approved and urged by Mr. S. P. Henry, representative of the Insurance Department of Mississippi.

I shall see and talk with you in Memphis. In the meantime, let me assure you that I trust that I am mistaken in the
opinion formed from your letter that you are planning a coupe to
defeat payment of your just debts. You and I will lock horns on
this proposition, and the best man will win. If you win, you are
welcome. But saddest of all is my disappointment in you writing
such a letter.

Respectfully yours,

(Signed) PERRY W. HOWARD

PWH/LRL.

P. S. Mrs. Cox and Dr. Howard did not make any such
statement to you as to the assets of the company, and you know
it quite well and knew it when you said this; for all investigations as to the resources, etc., of this company, were made by
your representatives and the representatives of the Insurance
Department of Mississippi. --PWH.

LIQUIDATIONS

money of the corporation, in which all other stockholders and policyholders held interest, available to a man who, they knew, probably
intended to borrow it to pay them. They declined to transfer the
entire amount but they did deposit $20,000 in the Citizens Trust
and soon thereafter Perry's four checks for $5,000 each, totaling the
first payment on the stock, were honored.[7]

Even after that first installment and P. W. Howard's fee had
been paid, there was great doubt as to Perry's ability to go through
with the deal. None of the promissory notes, except the last, was
paid when due.

After about six weeks of suspense, during which Perry tried
every art of persuasion to get additional funds of Mississippi Life
transferred to his bank in Atlanta, he succeeded in effect in doing
that which he probably intended doing in the first place, namely:
*Use the Mississippi Life's own funds to buy the majority of the
capital stock of that company and then sell the industrial business
to get money to pay on Standard's great debts.*

The benefits of this jugglery were destined to be short-lived.

On December 26, 1923, Heman Perry, president; William H.
King, vice president; and James A. Robinson, secretary, of Standard
Life; T. M. Henry, Insurance Commissioner of Mississippi; and
Silas Davis, a white officer of the Southeastern Trust Company of
Atlanta, Georgia, came to Memphis for the purpose of consum-
mating the transfer of the stock and the business of the Mississippi
Life to Heman Perry or Standard Life.[8] Davis had in his hands
a cashier's check for $86,000[9], the balance due on the stock. He re-
fused to pay it over to Dr. Howard and Mrs. Cox until the stock had
been transferred and Perry elected president, Robinson, secretary,
and King, vice president of the Mississippi Life. Then these new
officers immediately drew checks, transferring all of the Mississippi
Life's money to Atlanta to repay, it was alleged, the money Perry
had borrowed from the Southeastern Trust through Silas Davis.

Although on its way, the first Old Line Legal Reserve Life
Insurance Company of the Negro race had not yet passed out of

[7] Refuting any charge that this deposit had been made with the understanding
that it was to be used to pay them, they immediately commenced to draw company
checks against it in payment of death claims. The bank, however, after about
$6,000 had been withdrawn, refused further payments until a representative of the
company presented a demand check for the balance.

[8] Technically it was transferred to the Service Holding Company.

[9] The total amount of the stock and the contribution to surplus was $106,000.

the hands of Negroes. There was still hope; for the promised merger with Standard Life, the preliminary ruse Perry had employed as an inducement to get consideration for his proposal to buy the stock[10], was still promised with as fine an imitation of sincerity as Perry and his satellites could stomach for such a feat of duplicity. On December 27, 1923, the Mississippi Life's new president dictated, signed, and released a letter to the field forces of the company. (See facsimile page 301.).

James A. Robinson, the Executioner

That letter, pregnant with promise, probably was meant only as an opiate to quiet the unrest, caused by many wild rumors, among the field forces. Meanwhile the conduct of these new officers of the company seemed to the observant to confound the hopes raised by those glittering promises. Their conduct on their visits to Memphis was enshrouded in an air of mystery. They made no move to transfer the office to Atlanta. It was not hard to see that their pretended interest in the affairs of the company, which the more aggressive employees pressed on their attentions, was not sincere.

At last, without having evinced any interest in the annual statement, they called a meeting of the stockholders at Holly Springs, Mississippi, Saturday February 16, 1924. This proved to be the day of interment of the race's first Old Line Legal Reserve Life Insurance Company.

Strangely, neither Perry nor any of his henchmen appeared at the time set for the meeting. After more than an hour, James A. Robinson, the double-barreled secretary of Standard and Mississippi Life, came; and calling the meeting to order, requested M. B. Burnett to preside. All present were dumbfounded when he arose and offered a resolution empowering the president and secretary to sell and reinsure all of the business of the company in any company or corporation that might to them seem best.[11] He explained that this blanket resolution was merely a necessary legal formality for merging the business with Standard Life. No one present believed that explanation.

The procedure now became so ridiculous that Robinson himself

[10] Mr. Perry's first promise was to purchase all of the stock, minority as well as majority.

[11] Privately, Robinson admitted that the business was already being sold to a white company, and expressed his distaste for the part he was compelled to play in this sad, commercial tragedy.

MEMPHIS, TENNESSEE,
December 27, 1923.

To The Field Forces,
Mississippi Life Insurance Company.

GENTLEMEN:

You will be interested and elated, we are sure, to know
that the Service Company of Atlanta, has acquired a controlling
interest in the Mississippi Life Insurance Company.

This change in the capital stock of this Company means a
great deal in the way of progress. It means that the Mississippi
Life Insurance Company with assets of over $500,000--with more than
$20,000,000 of Business in Force--with Policy Reserves of more than
$400,000, together with its excellent field organization, will be
merged with or joined to the great STANDARD LIFE INSURANCE COMPANY,
an orgainzation whose assets are more than $3,000,000 and whose
Business in Force after the merger will be more than $50,000,000.

Standard Life has not heretofore written any class of
Industrial Insurance Business, but now it will also enter this field.
Therefore, as soon as the details of this union are completed, we will
be ready to commence the Industrial Business in eight additional states.
You will readily realize the large number of splendid openings for promotion for you. Competent men will be much in demand, and you will
have a chance if you are prepared.

We have already made arrangements to retain the services of the
present management of the Mississippi Life Insurance Company to direct
its field forces, and the same contractal basis will continue to be
maintained as has heretofore obtained with the agents and field forces
of the Mississippi Life. The services of all competent insurance
men are desired, and no employee of the Mississippi Life need have
any fear of being disturbed in his present employment. If any
changes be made at all in the working conditions of the employees,
they will be for the better and not for the worse.

Therefore, let us all join hands and work enthusiastically, for
the BIGGEST and STRONGEST Negro Insurance Company in the world afor ated

Mr. H. E. Perry, Mr. Wm. H. King and Mr. Jas. A. Robinson have
already been elected President, Vice-President and Secretary respect-
ively of the Mississippi Life Insurance Company instead of Dr. W. C.
Howard, Mr. M. B. Burnett and Mrs. M. M. Cox who resigned.

Yours very truly,

Heman E. Perry

PRESIDENT.

had to join in the laughter[12] when he had to both move and second the adoption of his resolution. He held the majority of the stock, and, of course, forced through this death warrant of the Mississippi Life.

The decision to sell the business of the Mississippi Life to the Southern Life of Nashville, Tenn., had been made months before, probably even before Perry had finished paying for the stock. The instrument of reinsurance bears date of February 16, 1924, the same day the stockholders met. Of course, no proper notice of intention to sell could have been given.

Thus passed this enterprise, the pride of hundreds of thousands of aspiring Negroes, not because it was not in the robust vigor of solvency, but because its financial life-blood was desired for trans-fusion into the veins of the prostrate and gasping form of Standard Life.

Perry Driven Out of Memphis

Whether or not W. W. Cox intended that the institutions of business that he established should stand as monuments of protests to the injustices inflicted upon him and his wife, the very circum-stances in which they were conceived remained until the end a source of especial pride and inspiration to those who carried them on after his death. The insurance company was organized and all of its business secured around the idea of race pride. It was ever kept before the agents on the field that they were having a part in the building of an enterprise that might stand through the ages as a credit to the ability of Negroes to construct and operate financial units comparable to the average among white people. Familiar enough were these men and women with the every day discourtesies they had to tolerate in commercial transactions with whites. They, and their prospects, therefore, had responded with ready enthusiasm and faithfulness to the vision of an insurance company of their own, in the patronage of which, in the sanctity of their homes, they would not have to submit to the humiliation of collectors who collected their money with offensive airs of arrogance and imagined superiority.

Since the time the Mississippi Life began to secure an important and noticeable volume of business, a haunting fear that some of its

[12] It was laughter fraught with bitter irony, scorn, and sorrow.

capital stock might fall into the hands of white capitalists or traders had, like a shadow, followed the moving spirits of the company.

When, therefore, it became known that Heman Perry was the "human instrument" through whose manipulations they had become victims of that which they had so long dreaded, bitter and threatening hostility to him became vocal among the employees of the company in Memphis. While the plan to move the home office to Atlanta had been deeply deplored by the leading colored people of Memphis, it had been quietly accepted in the belief that the business would be merged with Standard to make a greater Negro enterprise. But when the plot was exposed in its true light, Perry became the object of a raging tide of indignation and denunciation.

A few days after the last meeting of the stockholders at Holly Springs, Perry came to Memphis to confer with his white attorneys. When he visited the company's offices at 234 Hernando Street, several of the young women hurled bottles and other missiles at him, while others spat on him from the windows of the second floor as he hastily ran out of the building.

A number of agents from the office of District Manager G. W. Lee, led by H. P. Johnson, believing that Perry might return to the Hernando Street office after the young women had quit work for the day, waited there, vowing bodily harm to him if he should return; but the perplexed president of Standard Life had taken refuge in the offices of his attorney "up town" where he remained until he could hire a taxi to drive him to a station outside of the city limits, where he boarded the train for Atlanta, never again to set foot in Memphis, Tennessee.

THE STUART-ANDERSON AGENCY

ALTHOUGH the Southern had, in legal theory, "bought the field business—"[13] the right to collect the premiums—it was able through its white agents to take charge of only a negligible portion of the

[13] Under the contract of reinsurance the Southern was due to take over only so much of the assets of the Mississippi Life as was required to cover the reserves on the reinsured business. The total assets were in round figures $500,000. To this, $204,000, the amount the Southern paid for the business, should be added. From this sum ($704,000) the amount of the reserves was due to be deducted. Actuary Sigtenhorst figured $288,127 to be sufficient for reserves. Standard's Actuary said $435,900 should be deducted. If Sigtenhorst was right the Southern got $147,773 more than was due it. Yet, out of the balance, minority stockholders of Mississippi Life received dividends of 185% of the par value of their stock. How could the Mississippi Life have been insolvent?

collections. In Alabama and Tennessee, where it had white agency organizations, most of the policyholders refused to pay premiums to these white agents, but instead applied for insurance with other Negro companies.

In Arkansas, Mississippi, and Texas where the Southern had no agency organization, all of the more than 300 Negro agents who had served the Mississippi Life refused to accept service with the Southern until assured that they would not be used for only a short time until the company could organize a white agency force.

It was out of this situation that the Stuart-Anderson Agency was born. This was an insurance entity unlike anything ever operated before or subsequent to its existence.

The following were among the terms and powers of the contract which created this Agency.

1. While operated technically in the name and under the charter of the Southern Life Insurance Company, it was for all practical purposes (except the investment of funds and the issuance of ordinary policies) a separate company.

2. It had the exclusive right to write business, both ordinary and industrial, for the Southern in the States of Arkansas, Mississippi, and Texas.

3. It had charge of the collection of the premiums on all the business in force which the Southern had purchased from the Mississippi Life. (This was about 80 per cent of the total collections of the former Mississippi Life, about 96 per cent of all of the business of the Mississippi Life Division of the Southern, and amounted in 1925, the last full year of operation, to $836,999.30.)

4. It was for a period of ten years, with the optional right to repurchase the business and convert it into an independent company at any time before the expiration of the ten year period.

5. The terms of purchase (ten times the industrial debit and $7 per thousand for the ordinary) were provided in advance.

6. That white agents could not write insurance on, collect premiums from, or otherwise transact insurance business with colored people for the Southern in this territory during the life of the contract.

7. It had the use of the former home office building of the Mississippi Life at 234 Hernando Street, with all of its equipment.

8. Here it received all reports, issued all industrial policies and directed the services of 33 home office clerks, 19 field clerks and 360 agents and district managers.

9. It authorized salaries of $5,000 per year each for the three general agents (M. S. Stuart, M. E. Anderson and V. L. Reuben[14]) and in addition, 50 per cent of the net profits from the agency operation.

10. It authorized the agency to employ its own actuary,[15] as a result of whose advice and calculations the general agents were paid earned profits amounting to $25,500 for the years 1924-5.

This agency operated successfully for a period of two years and five months, (from April 7, 1924, to September 6, 1926) earning a gross profit of more than $51,000 for the Southern.

Be it said to the credit of the officers of the Southern Life Insurance Company—Will Harris, Sr., Oury Harris, and Will Harris, Jr.—that in every way they faithfully complied with every pledge they made as long as possible. They proved to be men as fine, fair, and agreeable to work with as any men of any race could have been.

However, in the Spring of 1926, the financial trouble of the Southern became acute; and, the Insurance Commissioner of Tennessee took charge of the affairs of that Company. It then was clear that the Southern was headed for liquidation or reinsurance by some other company.

The distressed condition of the Southern was a matter of great concern to the Stuart-Anderson Agency. Its operators were not yet ready to repossess the business. They had not had time to assemble sufficient capital for a new company.

There had been a tentative understanding with J. M. Avery that the North Carolina Mutual would reinsure the business at any time the owners of the option were ready. But at the very time when the general agents had to exercise their option or lose it, the North Carolina Mutual was preparing to withdraw from Arkansas and Mississippi, two of the agency states of operation. Therefore, the

[14] Died Sept. 1924.
[15] Andrew Sigtenhorst of Waco, Texas.

general agents transferred their option and their rights under it to Universal Life Insurance Company. By virtue of the terms of that option Universal saved more than $150,000 over the rate which Southern received for similar business sold to another company.

But of more importance than all else: the field forces of the Mississippi Life had prevented the debits they had built from passing out of the control of Negro men and women; for now, even technically, they were again a major part of a Negro life insurance company.

STANDARD LIFE INSURANCE COMPANY OF GEORGIA

IN 1908 Heman E. Perry, a young Texas-born Negro, who had served as an agent for two white companies, startled Negroes of Atlanta and of Georgia generally by announcing that he was going to organize an old-line legal reserve life insurance company with a capital stock of $100,000. "Impossible! Just a dream!" said popular opinion. "Why even Alonzo Herndon couldn't raise that much money," said one old Atlantan.

Be it remembered that this was just three years after most of the benevolent mutuals had been compelled to disband because of the $5,000 deposit law passed by the Georgia legislature; and yet Perry was undertaking to raise $100,000 where even Herndon had been able to raise only $5,000.

Perry did not succeed. He sold stock amounting to $70,000, but, under the Georgia law the entire authorization of $100,000 had to be sold within two years; otherwise all money received had to be returned to the subscribers with interest. Perry was legally compelled to return all of this money; and yet, shrewd salesman that he was, he took full advantage of the prevailing skepticism that the subscribers would get their money back. Through his prompting, this situation was made a publicity egg, out of which, amid much crowing and cackling, Perry hatched out as a heroic chanticleer dominating the entire commercial barnyard of the race.

He was adroitly laying the foundation for the appearance of an encore, and right well did it succeed. His second campaign to sell $100,000 of stock made its *debut* dressed up in the colors of a response to a demand on the part of the public. This time he perfected better plans, for actually he had a majority of the authorization already pledged before he again applied for state permission to sell. That meant that, for the most part, he had only to complete transactions already arranged. And yet Perry did not actually sell the entire $100,000 issue this time. However, the cash he lacked was secured on a note endorsed by T. H. Hayes of Memphis, A. L. Lewis of Jacksonville, and Alonzo F. Herndon of Atlanta. So that Standard Life actually came into existence already burdened with a secret stock obligation which had to be paid out of its first earnings.

On March 22, 1913, Standard Life Insurance Company of Atlanta, Georgia, began business, being the first Negro legal reserve company organized to write only ordinary business, and the third to qualify as a legal reserve, the Mississippi Life being the first, the North Carolina Mutual the second.

Standard Life grew rapidly. Perry surrounded himself with the most intelligent and efficient talent to be found in the colored race; and, although he was always a dominating figure, his magnetic personality attached men to him with great admiration. At the end of 1913, the company's business in force was $381,500; its premium income, $10,293; assets $116,702. Within ten years Standard's insurance in force had increased to $22,881,575; its premium income, $1,178,022; assets, $2,042,439. At this time the company was operating in Alabama, Arkansas, Georgia, Kentucky, Louisiana, Missouri, North Carolina, Oklahoma, Tennessee, Texas, Virginia, and the District of Columbia.

However, Perry soon gave almost his entire time and thought to the creation and organization of various affiliated financial schemes. In some way connected with or heading up in Standard, he organized the following affiliates:

> Service Engineering & Construction Company
> Service Farm Bureau
> Service Foundation, Inc.
> Service Fuel Corporation
> Service Holding Company
> Service Laundry
> Service Pharmacy
> Service Printing Company
> Service Realty Company

The Citizens Discount Corporation
The Citizens Trust Company [16]
Penny Savings Bank (Augusta, Georgia)
Sunset Hills Development Company

There were many to say that much of Standard's money was invested in these subsidiary enterprises, and that the cause of Standard's failure lay in this diversion of its funds. No doubt this condition was a contributory factor, but it was not entirely responsible. The early failure of this, the most spectacular and widely advertised Negro institution, was probably due to a combination of some or all of the following causes:

1. Standard commenced business burdened with an obligation which it had incurred in completing its sale of stock.
2. It encountered those natural difficulties inevitable in trying to operate an exclusively ordinary company on the support of patrons largely industrial.
3. Perry's visionariness.
4. The lack of sufficient capital surplus to sustain such rapid growth.
5. The extremely high rate of reserves required by the type of ordinary with which Standard began business.
6. The enormous amount of premium notes accepted in the payment of insurance assumed.
7. The inevitable entanglements and complications resulting from interlocking interests of the same directors in several corporations.

· Standard's first financial troubles came to the surface when it was subjected to an examination by state examiners in 1919. According to their findings, Standard was then impaired in excess of $60,000. Due to Harry Pace's resourcefulness, this was overcome by substituting and delivering to policyholders policies[17] requiring lower reserves than those originally issued.

The exact time that Perry secured a loan of $300,000 from

[16] This bank, despite all the turmoil and the great crash of Standard and most of its affiliated institutions, has survived, even through the years of depression. Reputedly, it now enjoys prosperous operation.

[17] This was a financial sacrifice made out of pride of race, willingly and understandingly, by Standard's policyholders, which was reluctantly accepted by the white examiners.

308

Will Harris, president of Southern Insurance Company of Nashville, Tennessee, in the name of Service Holding Company, cannot be ascertained; but it is now known that Perry was heavily obligated to Harris or to the Southern's interest[18] in 1923 prior to the beginning of negotiations to secure possession of Mississippi Life. An additional loan of some $200,000[18] had already been or was later secured from New York financiers. Harris was induced to assume also this obligation and to advance approximately $50,000 more, so that the total indebtedness to Will Harris in 1924 amounted to $550,000[18]. At this time 1251 of the 2500 shares of Standard were held by the Service Holding Company which Perry dominated. He had pledged this majority block of stock to Harris. Harris also held as additional security a mortgage covering all of the assets of Service Company. The final date of grace on all of these obligations was December 15, 1924. At that time Harris could elect either to foreclose on the mortgage or to have the majority block of stock in Standard Life recorded in his name. Of course, he preferred the latter course because control of Standard meant also control of all of its affiliates.

When the stockholders of Standard met on January 15, 1925, Will Harris, the reluctant holder of the majority stock, proposed to merge Standard with Southern. He also magnanimously proposed to give the minority stockholders[19] stock in Southern[20] in exchange for stock they held in Standard. He offered, moreover, not to take possession of Standard if the minority stockholders or any other group of financiers would make him a substantial cash payment and pledge satisfactory security for the remainder of the debt. It was by the vote of the stockholders present, not by Will Harris' insistence, that the merger proposition was accepted, by which Standard Life passed from the control of Negroes.

News of the loss of this company cast a pall of gloom over colored Atlanta. Women wept and men who had invested their all on their confidence in Perry now swore vengeance on him.

The Ghost of the Klan

That the losses of Standard and of Mississippi Life were the result of plans deeply laid by the Ku Klux Klan, is alleged by "Dame

---

[18] Informant: the late T. J. Ferguson, former treasurer of Standard, February 13, 1939.

[19] All colored.

[20] A white company.

Rumor" and in George Lee's "Beale Street." However, the story that Harris and Perry were willing tools in such a scheme is not sustained by careful investigations. There is every indication that Harris became involved only because of the prospects of legitimate profits on loans. He sustained tremendous losses from his connection with Standard.

The Southern operated Standard for not quite a year as a separate entity, with its home office in Atlanta. In this time the officers of Southern were forced to realize that in Standard they had assumed obligations that would soon sink both Standard and Southern. In a desperate effort to save themselves, Southern officials inspired the organization of Standard Life of Eureka Springs, Arkansas, a sort of corporate wet-nurse, to take troublesome Standard Life of Georgia out of Southern's lap, and to keep it until it could find an opportunity to drop it on some other corporation's doorstep. It soon found this opportunity in National Benefit Life Insurance Cmpany of Washington, D. C.; and thus did Standard Life come back home to Negroes only to die in the arms of another expiring Negro company when the National Benefit ceased operation in 1931.

THE LATE HEMAN E. PERRY, *President*

Heman E. Perry was born in Houston, Texas, March 5, 1873. He completed the sixth grade of the grammar school in that city, and so far as is known that was the extent of his technical education.[10]

Since details of his life's work were so closely connected with the development, operation and disposition of Standard Life that they must be disclosed in its history, their repetition is here unnecessary. Therefore, these observations are confined to his personal traits.

Heman Perry was by nature a genius. Like all such, he was visionary, a slave to caprice and novelty, impatient of routine, prone to shun the drudgery of details, fickle, unstable; and entirely unfitted for any role in business, save, perhaps, that of promotion and salesmanship. His mind was prolific in the conception of plans and schemes that on the surface appeared feasible and profitable. Some of them, perhaps, if the thread of theory had been followed with diligent persistence as Perry conceived them, might have worked out successfully. But, most often, when the novelty of organization and the preliminary stages had worn off, Perry tired of his projects and was ready to turn them over to others.

[10] Perry, after leaving school, started life as a cotton sampler.

LIQUIDATIONS

Heman Perry was not dishonest for any selfish purposes, if at all. None of his schemes and manipulations were entered into with motives of profit for himself. There is much to indicate that he cared little for personal pleasure or luxuries. He devoted nearly all the salary of $800 per month, which he received from Standard, to the financing of other schemes. He never owned an automobile, did not gamble or drink, and, although he never married, there is no evidence that he was given in the least to dissipation or social extravagances. He had to be persuaded by those close to him to buy presentable wearing apparel. About a year before the collapse of his enterprises, he completed a fine new home, contemplating marriage, some said. Others said it was only to induce other people to buy and build homes in his real estate project. He lived only a few lonely months in that fine home.[11]

After the loss of Standard he went to St. Louis, Missouri, and there made a feeble attempt to rehabilitate and revive the Mid-West Life Insurance Company. He met discouragement on every hand. He went to Kansas City in 1928 trying there to interest investors in Mid-West; but was not there long before he was found dead in the bathroom of the home in which he was stopping. Was it suicide or heart failure? That question has never been answered. Heman Perry lived and died a martyr to his wild zeal to build a combination of Negro financial enterprises of favorable comparison with any in America. His body was taken to Houston and there, surrounded by relatives and only a few loyal friends, was laid to rest.

Let it not be thought that no substantial improvement for Negroes resulted from Perry's dreams and manipulations. The entire West-side of Atlanta, where many intelligent colored families now live, some of whom own their homes or are buying them, was acquired and developed by him through Service Realty Company. True, with the collapse of Standard and its affiliates, the title or controlling interest in it passed from his hands. Nevertheless, the section through him became a Negro residential area and probably will indefinitely remain so.

It is reported that in the developed portion of this area there are about 200 blocks with twenty-four residences to the block, with an average value of $4,500[12] per residence, or a total value of $21,-600,000. The project is said to cover an area two miles square;

[11] Informant: Mrs. Ludella Dawkins, former secretary.
[12] Informant: T. J. Ferguson, former treasurer of Standard Life.

311

and the value of the land still undeveloped is placed at $357,350. It is interesting to note that Perry's first venture in this section was highly profitable. He purchased twenty acres, and in a short time sold ten of them to the city for a Negro High School at a profit of $20,000. Then Service Engineering Company was the successful contractor for the erection of the school. This deal is said to have been the inspiration that lured him into attempting the subsequent project on such an enormous and visionary scale.

With certain omissions, there is here reproduced an article about Standard Life and Heman Perry by Eric D. Walrond in *Forbes Magazine* of New York, in its issue of February 2, 1924. It undoubtedly, was a "managed" production. Very probably it was arranged by some of Perry's smart advisers that Walrond be guided into contact only with those sources interested in making Perry appear fabulously wealthy so as to create an "eastern atmosphere" in which he could secure further large loans. The article follows with clarifying authoritative footnotes:

THE LARGEST NEGRO COMMERCIAL ENTERPRISE IN THE WORLD

AMAZING STORY OF HEMAN E. PERRY, COMMERCIAL BOOKER
WASHINGTON, FOUNDER OF $30,000,000 STANDARD LIFE
INSURANCE COMPANY

By Eric D. Walrond

Recently it was my privilege to go down to Atlanta, Georgia, for 'Forbes Magazine,' to look in on what is by all odds the largest Negro commercial enterprise in the world—the Standard Life Insurance Company, the oldest,[13] old-line legal reserve company operated by Negroes. . .

When I entered the $152,000 office building of the Standard Life I felt like one in a trance. I could not imagine Negroes owning or operating anything like it (the office equipment alone cost close to $100,000.) I saw dozens and dozens of colored men and women, of the very finest type, employed as clerks, stenographers, bookkeepers, statisticians, accountants, actuaries[14] and executives. In the words of one of the leading white corpo-

[13] This is in error. The Mississippi Beneficial Life was authorized as an Old-Line Legal Reserve Company in 1910—Standard in 1913.

[14] Except Miss Sadie T. Mossell of the North Carolina Mutual Life Insurance Company, there were no Negroes even considered actuaries at that time.

ration lawyers of Atlanta, "These people are no longer serfs—fit to be cooks and butlers. Educated, they must be helped; the South must go out of its way to help them realize their ambitions." Fresh from the North, I concurred; for I knew there was not anything like it anywhere up there. Altogether this Company and its affiliates have 2,500 people, all colored, on its payroll.

In addition to the Citizens Trust Company, whose total deposits up to December 5, 1923, amount to $846,998.79, an increase of $550,422.83[15] over the previous year's, it operates the Service Company which, in its turn, operates twelve other corporations with combined assets of $8,498,217.37

The Service Company was organized in 1917 with an authorized capital of $100,000; this was increased in 1920 to $500,000, and in 1923 to $1,000,000. Later it grew, in its varied and ramified way, until today it owns $2,000,000 worth of real estate; 300 acres of land within the city limits of Atlanta; seven four-ton trucks; eight box-car loads of building material; 1,000,000 feet of lumber; 1,000 acres of agricultural land in Calhoun County; $50,000 worth of hoisting apparatus, concrete mixers, tools and office equipment; the Verdery Estate, a $138,-350 piece of property situated in the business district of Augusta; and a $50,000 printing plant.[16]

Also, the Construction Company is in possession of contracts to the extent of $448,576.00, exclusive of a $212,000 contract recently awarded it by the municipality of Atlanta for the construction of a public school house.

Singularly, the man who founded Standard Life and who is responsible for its gigantic success, while the busiest, brainiest Negro in the South, is modest, brisk-moving, unassuming. He is Heman E. Perry, whose forbears, according to legendary history, were owned by Judge Heman Perry, of Waynesboro, Georgia.[17]

Wherever I went, whether to banker or college president, lawyer or minister, laborer or politician, farmer or millionaire,

---

[15] It was alleged that almost all of this $500,000 increase in deposit was created by discounting Standard's premium notes, only a negligible percentage of which was ever paid.

[16] This plant was purchased by the Scott News Syndicate, from which it now publishes the *Atlanta Daily World,* the only Negro daily newspaper.

[17] Perry was unquestionably of mixed blood.

313

white or black, I heard in glowing terms of the financial genius of Heman Perry.

For, let it be remembered, Heman Perry is the directing genius of a $30,000,000 enterprise, earns $75,000 annually, is insured for $1,000,000 and is said to be worth $8,000,000: (These figures, let me assure you, I did not get from Mr. Perry himself or from any one in his organization, but from disinterested white men in Atlanta whose business it is to know these things.)

It was toward the end of the second week in Atlanta that I had an opportunity to interview Mr. Perry.[18] Said Mr. Perry, "I went to New York with the idea of getting rich. I decided to go to Georgia and start all over again in cotton. I went to a pawn shop and disposed of my cuff buttons for $5. I went down to a river boat and gave the purser the $5 to work my way to Savannah. Before the boat got out in the water I made 65 cents in tips."

With a capital of 65 cents the indomitable Perry, managed to keep alive for a week, eating ten-cent meals at two-day intervals, until finally he got a job with a cotton broker. . .

How Insurance Company was Formed

"Trying to get an insurance agency," Perry said, "I wrote a letter to about every life insurance company in the United States. Out of twenty answers I received there were about three that used colored agents and they confined their agents to endowment policies."

This brought to a head a matter Mr. Perry had been thinking over for a number of years—the organization of an Old Line Legal Reserve company for colored people.

"I called together about twenty men in the old Y.M.C.A. Building. I made each man pay $20 as a sort of entrance fee. I then put the proposition up to them. Few of them felt that an Old Line Legal Reserve company could be floated."

In spite of which Mr. Perry went ahead. Mr. Perry, minus a salary, agreed to defray all the expenses of organization with the exception of $125, which was the incorporation fee.

[18] There is much to sustain a prevalent rumor that it was a part of Perry's game to keep important out-of-town visitors waiting a week or ten days for an interview to impress them with his importance.

Refunds Subscriptions

"After two years of hard labor, spending largely one day in a town and traveling at night in the 'Jim Crow' cars, we had $85,000 cash.

"Reluctantly, we voted to return the money to the people, for it was the only thing to do. The $85,000 with the 4 percent interest was refunded to the subscribers without any strings tied to it. I sent a letter along with each remittance saying that I had paid the total expenses which amounted to $4,740.[19]

"I remember the evening well," Mr. Perry continued reminiscently. "It was cold and windy, the fire had gone out, and it was fast growing dark. One of the men remarked, 'It's getting dark, boys. Let's light the gas.' And another said, 'No, don't light the gas; don't put Mr. Perry to any more expense.' And they filed out, one by one, and left me there alone at the fireless stove thinking things over."

THE NATIONAL BENEFIT LIFE INSURANCE CO.

IN 1898, S. W. Rutherford, who had been a sewing machine agent and then a deputy for the True Reformers, conceived the idea of founding a mutual aid society in Washington. At the beginning he had very little capital, but he managed to secure a table and two chairs and rented an office. He organized an assessment association and named it the National Benefit.[20]

A little later Rutherford assembled $2,000 as capital, but still restricted the operation of the association to writing combination sick benefit and small life policies. Until 1903, he was the president, manager, collector, office clerk, and office boy all in one. In 1903, the capital was increased to $5,000 and the association began to offer small endowment insurance policies, but not on a legal reserve basis.

The company grew rapidly and in a few years changed its name to National Benefit Life Insurance Company. Until 1918, the concern was owned almost exclusively by the Rutherford family. At this time additional capital stock was sold and the entire issue of $100,000 was paid. Even then for the next five years, the operating

[19] According to Walrond, Perry had worked at a job with a cotton broker and in a warehouse only a short time, since he arrived in Savanah, penniless, before he commenced to sell stock for Standard. From whence then came the $4740 used to cover expenses?

[20] W. J. Trent, Jr., *Development of Negro Life Insurance Enterprises*, 1932.

officers seemed to have retained undisturbed control; and the Company moved on without major trouble.

But, in 1923, this great company entered upon evil days. It was then that its officers sponsored an authorization to increase the capital stock to $250,000 so that nine or ten new states might simultaneously be entered and developed, and numerous, lavish sub-offices equipped. Except great white companies, heavily capitalized and just starting business, and Victory Life, there is no record of any company ever qualifying for business in so many states at once. From this burden the National Benefit never recovered. To sell this large issue of stock, loans were made which were ridiculously under-secured. Prospective stock buyers were granted loans far in excess of the value of their real estate holdings and some without security at all, to induce them to buy stock. For example, the following is from the report of the state insurance examiners as of December 31, 1927:

> On August 11, 1923, an increase in the amount of Capital Stock to $250,000 was authorized at a special meeting of the stockholders.
>
> On December 31, 1926, the Company increased its Capital Stock account the sum of $14,550 and its Surplus Account the sum of $135,450 through money borrowed from the Delta Penny Savings Bank, Indianola, Mississippi, and the Solvent Savings Bank, of Memphis, Tennessee.
>
> No. 1: This report further shows that this money was used to purchase stock in the name of certain individuals closely connected with the Company; that they gave no security for the loans and that in May 1927 the Company sent $90,000 to the Solvent Savings Bank to pay on the loan.

Further excerpts from the report of these examiners follow:

> This insolvent condition of the Company, on December 31, 1926, was caused principally by their writing entirely too much business for their surplus. In the Company's annual statement for the year 1926 to the Insurance Department, the market value of real estate owned was increased arbitrarily and various liabilities not included.
>
> On December 31, 1927, the Company sold 9,000 shares of its Capital Stock to R. H. Rutherford, President, S. W. Ruther-

ford, Secretary, and M. F. Smith, Assistant Secretary, for the sum of $382,500. This amount was borrowed by Rutherford, Smith and Rutherford from the National Park Bank, New York City, and placed to the credit of the Company, and certificates issued to the Company for a like amount and held by the National Park Bank as security for the loan.

The above excerpts from the report of the joint examination in 1928, while explaining at great length the irregularities of the colored officers and employees involved, said not a word about the conduct of a white actuary of New York City, who committed suicide as a result, it was alleged, of his grave involvement in the financial complications of National Benefit.

In June 1931, Negro newspapers in glaring print stated that the National Benefit was insolvent to the extent of more than one million dollars, and that application would be made for the appointment of a receiver.

About three months prior to this time the board of directors of the company, in meeting in Washington, D. C., had been informed about the financial troubles of the company and the involvement of some of its operating officers. John T. Risher, who at the time was engaged in the real estate business, had become conversant with the affairs of the company by way of negotiating large loans from it for the building of the Masonic Temple in that city. Following the disclosures, Risher, a former pharmacist of Mississippi, who had received signal recognition as a clerk in the United States Navy Department in Washington, was elected president of the company. Without practical experience in the business of life insurance, he was, from the start on this account, seriously handicapped in coping with the abnormal and difficult situation.

The affairs of the company were vexingly entangled; and it was realized that any steps towards rehabilitation would be all the more difficult because of the inexperience of the newly elected president.

On July 22, 1931, the president of the National Negro Insurance Association, seeking to minimize the harm that might result to all Negro companies from the failure of the National Benefit, addressed a communication to the officials of a number of the larger Negro companies suggesting that a conference be held to consider what should be done in the emergency. All the officials except one wanted the conference; but it was not called until after it had been ascertained that it was desired by the newly elected president of the National Benefit.

On July 28, 1931, the invitation was sent out to all of the larger Negro companies. It was not an official call nor meeting of the National Negro Insurance Association, but a voluntary gathering. Present at this conference were C. C. Spaulding, Harry H. Pace, A. L. Lewis, W. S. Hornsby, Dr. J. E. Walker, M. S. Stuart, B. L. Jordan, John L. Webb, Dr. L. T. Burbridge, James T. Carter, C. B. Gilpin, S. Jackson; and, of course, John T. Risher.

The conference met at 12 o'clock noon Tuesday, August 18, 1931. Notwithstanding the fact that Risher had informed the president of the National Association that there were some serious and urgent developments which he wished to lay before the conference, the conferees were astounded when he arose and stated that he had no plan to propose by which other Negro companies could be of assistance to the National Benefit nor did he desire any assistance from them, nor any of their officials.[21]

In the situation created by this queer conduct of Risher, the conference could only appoint a committee to draft a statement to release to the public, setting out that the officials of other Negro companies had tendered their good offices in behalf of National Benefit.

Early in March 1932 white receivers were appointed by the courts of the District of Columbia.

The president of the National Association, acting on the suggestion of George W. Cox, treasurer, on March 10, 1932, addressed a letter to these receivers proposing the cooperation of Negro companies in any way that seemed feasible to protect the interests of the thousands of Negro policyholders of National Benefit. An insulting reply was received from one of the receivers, from which the following is quoted: "Any attempt by the colored companies to disturb the business of the National Benefit would reflect on the business acumen of the said companies." There had been no attempt at, nor suggestion of, disturbance of the National Benefit's business by any Negro company.

John Risher continued to entertain ambitions to administer the assets and affairs of the company; and in 1933, he filed a suit

---

[21] Later this erstwhile president of the company sought to be appointed receiver for it.

asking dismissal of Frank Bryan and Gilbert A. Clark, the white receivers. This resulted in prolonged litigation that is still pending; for, notwithstanding the dismissal of these receivers in March, 1939,[22] they appealed from the decision of the court dismissing them, and seek to be reinstated, according to the following from the *Memphis World:*

VICTORY ENDS SIX-YEAR FIGHT

President of Company named New Receiver

WASHINGTON—March 17, 1939.—A six-year fight to end the extravagant spending of the white receivers for the National Benefit Life Insurance Company came to an abrupt halt Saturday when Justice Peyton Gordon of the U. S. district court of the District of Columbia dismissed Frank Bryan and Gilbert A. Clark, receivers since April, 1932, and appointed John T. Risher, President of the insurance company, to succeed them.

The suit, which was filed in 1933 by Risher, pointed out that when receivers were appointed for the company, there were assets of $3,700,000. It is alleged that the receivers had collected an additional $1,500,000 and had disposed of all of the company's assets, including the money collected by the receivers, with the exception of $353,000. None of this money, Risher pointed out to the court, had been paid out to policyholders. All of the money spent went to administrative expenses and fees for the receivers and their lawyers.

Property owned in Georgia and valued at $1,225,000 was sold for $700,000, the court was informed. The Odd Fellows building in Atlanta, which was owned by the Company at a value of $225,000, was sold for $50,000. The record further showed that one of the receiver's attorneys in Atlanta received a fee of more than $30,000.

Among the causes given for the troubles of the National Benefit Life was that of reinsuring the business and taking over the assets of the Standard Life. This was accomplished early in 1927.

There is no doubt that the obligations of the Standard's business and the inflated figures of its assets assumed by the National Benefit contributed to some extent to the difficulties that finally proved the

---

[22] It is alleged that the salaries of these two white men were $500 per month each during their seven years of "liquidation."

undoing of the Washington company; but there is also evidence to show that the National Benefit was already in trouble when it took over Standard Life.

The real estate owned by the Standard Life Division of National Benefit, December 31, 1927, was listed at $1,865, 530 and first mortgages at $328,892. The appraisers at the instance of the state insurance examiners as of December 31, 1927, fixed the value of this real estate at less than $900,000, a depreciation of more than a million dollars under the book value. Any degree of diligence should have disclosed to National Benefit officials the inflated valuations at which they accepted this real estate. It is alleged that an old frame hotel in the country town of Eureka Springs, Arkansas (market value about $50,000), was listed and assumed by the National Benefit at $500,000, notwithstanding no valid deed attesting its conveyance could be found.

THE UNION GUARANTY, JACKSON, MISSISSIPPI

Soon after the beginning of the present century there was a home or other Grand Lodge office of some kind of a fraternal order in nearly every important city in Mississippi.

These fraternal orders collected hundreds of thousands of dollars every year; and, dependent upon them or in some way connected with them, a dozen Negro banks sprang up in the state and flourished for a time. Not until Dr. W. A. Attaway and Wayne W. Cox organized the Mississippi Beneficial Life in 1909 did it dawn upon some of the fraternal leaders that their benefit societies were not organized upon enduring principles.

In 1912, the Honorable Louis Kossuth Atwood, lawyer, former member of the Mississippi State Legislature, president of the Southern Bank of Jackson, and head of the Independent Order of Sons and Daughters of Jacob, suggested plans for the organization of a Negro life insurance company in Jackson. He associated with him in its organization: Professor E. H. McKissack, of Holly Springs; the Reverend Edward P. Jones, the Honorable W. E. Mollison, brilliant attorney, president of the Colored Woodmen and the Lincoln Savings Bank, of Vicksburg; the Honorable William J. Latham, prominent civil attorney of Jackson; Professor William Singleton of Kosciusko, and other substantial business men and farmers of the state.

The capital stock of $50,000 was soon paid in and the company secured its charter and license to do business in the summer of 1912. T. A. Dixon became the director of field activities.

Soon after its organization, the company reinsured all of the Mississippi business of the Union Mutual Aid Society of Mobile, Alabama; and, with this nucleus, began rapidly to acquire a promising volume of industrial health and accident business. The company moved with satisfactory progress until 1915. It was in this year that Latham, one of the attorneys of the company, became dissatisfied with the manner in which the election of officers had been conducted. He was a brilliant lawyer in civil matters, and when he appealed to the courts of Hinds County for settlement and satisfaction of his grievances it was known by all concerned that the company was facing major trouble. This litigation resulted in the appointment of a white receiver for the assets of the company. The policyholders were protected by reinsurance in the Mississippi Beneficial Life. The fine debits written by the agents of the Union Mutual Aid along the Mississippi Gulf Coast were taken in charge by the Mississippi Beneficial Life and remained a profitable part of its business until 1923, passing by reinsurance over to Standard, thence to the Southern, thence to Universal Life in 1926.

UNDERWRITERS MUTUAL LIFE INSURANCE CO.

To succeed, insurance enterprises must have the opportunity to contact sufficiently large number of persons to whom policies may be sold. In this respect, two reasons may be advanced to account for Negro insurance enterprises not flourishing in the North, as in the South, prior to 1918.

First, in most northern states the Negro population was small and widely scattered. Second, the northern Negro was not then as race conscious as the southern Negro, due to a more subtle type of race prejudice in the North.

This picture underwent a radical change as the result of labor conditions created in the North by the World War. A most acute labor shortage occurred in the large manufacturing centers north of the Ohio River. The northern manufacturer then realized that his opportunity to secure labor lay in bringing it from the South where the Negro was growing increasingly dissatisfied under adverse economic, political, and social conditions.

Northern labor and the Negro population in the larger cities of the North increased almost unbelievably within a few weeks.

Not only skilled and semi-skilled laborers but professional and business men also came North. One of these was the late William J. Latham, a prominent attorney from Jackson, Mississippi. Latham located in Chicago. Immediately, he began to express his ideas of organizing an insurance company to the acquaintances whom he had made. Out of conversations had with them and others, plans were made for organizing the first insurance company by Negroes in the North—the Underwriters Insurance Company.

The company was authorized to do business in November 1918. It began in a modest way as a Mutual Health and Accident Company, operating under the Illinois Mutual Act of 1915. A few agents who had received agency training in the South were secured and the writing of applications was begun. The policies provided weekly sick and accident benefits from $1 to $10 and a funeral benefit of $100. The officers were William J. Latham, president; Claborn Shelby, vice president and secretary; and William J. Wright, treasurer. These, together with William H. King of theatrical fame, and John Seymore, constituted the first board of directors. During the last week in November 1918, its first policy was issued and by the close of the year the weekly debit was $125.

J. E. Mitchem, who, with Frank Gillespie of Liberty Life fame, and others, got his initial experience with the Royal Life Insurance Company in 1915, was elected secretary of this company in June 1919, and continued in that position until June 1933, when he became secretary of Victory Mutual.

The Underwriters Life made rapid progress and, in 1924, its charter was changed to make it a mutual assessment life company and its named changed to Underwriters Mutual. Under the new charter it wrote industrial and ordinary life as well as health and accident. In this same year the company purchased its home office, and the employees now required for the business numbered nearly 100. At the close of business December 31, 1931, its total income was $175,546, assets, $67,292, liabilities, $50,830, surplus, $16462, and life insurance outstanding, including health and accident, $5,621,000.[23]

The company was built on the lives of the industrial class who came North to work during the War, and when they lost their work when the depression of 1929 struck the country, its business gradually dwindled, and in 1934 its assets were liquidated by the Illinois Insurance Department.

[23] Informant: J. E. Mitchem.

Chapter IX.

THE NATIONAL NEGRO INSURANCE ASSOCIATION

LIEUTENANT GEORGE W. LEE, vice president of Mississippi Life Insurance Company, was requested to deliver an address on Negro life insurance in the 1920 session of the National Negro Business League. The life insurance section of the League was then presided over by Mr. John L. Webb, of Hot Springs, Arkansas; and fraternal insurance held the spotlight in the meetings.

The business of the several important life insurance companies was receiving scant attention. When Lee returned to Memphis he voiced his protests to other officials of the Mississippi Life Insurance Company. This Company sent M. S. Stuart to represent it in the next session of the League, which convened in Atlanta in 1921.

There were a number of companies, Atlanta Life, Mississippi Life, North Carolina Mutual, Standard Life, Afro-American and others, growing larger every year and encountering many new problems; hence, it was suggested that there ought to be an association composed only of the men engaged in the business of life insurance. At this meeting of the Business League, an assembly of gentlemen representing nine Negro insurance companies, met in Bethel A. M. E. Church on Auburn Avenue in Atlanta, on August 19, 1921, for the purpose of organizing a national association of Negro insurance men. The meeting was organized by the election of C. C. Spaulding of the North Carolina Mutual as temporary chairman and M. S. Stuart of the Mississippi Life as the temporary secretary. The idea of creating a separate organization was approved by all present. On motion of T. K. Gibson, a committee on permanent organization was appointed. It was decided that the temporary organization should be known as the National Association of Negro Insurance Underwriters. The following committee on permanent organization was appointed: M. S. Stuart, chairman; Charles A. Shaw, secretary; and T. K. Gibson, J. H. Goode, J. L. Wheeler, R. W. Chamblee, J. J. Allen, and C. C. Spaulding, ex-officio.

323

It was decided that a call should be issued to all colored insurance companies to send representatives to meet in Durham, North Carolina, on October 27, 1921, for the purpose of organizing a permanent association of colored insurance men. Pursuant to this decision the call was duly prepared and signed by the Committee on Organization, and issued to thirty-six colored companies.

At ten o'clock on October 27, 1921, sixty representatives from thirteen of the leading colored insurance companies assembled in the new home office of the North Carolina Mutual Life Insurance Company in Durham. C. C. Spaulding of the North Carolina Mutual acted as temporary chairman, and M. S. Stuart of the Mississippi Life Insurance Company served as temporary secretary.

The purpose of the meeting was explained by the chairman. The minutes of the preliminary meeting held in Atlanta on August 19 and the official call for the first meeting of the Association were read by M. S. Stuart.

Of thirty-six colored insurance companies to which the call had been sent, the following thirteen were represented by the delegates named:

Atlanta Mutual Life Insurance Company, Atlanta, Georgia; Cyrus Campfield, N. B. Herndon.

Afro-American Life Insurance Company, Jacksonville, Florida; L. D. Ervin.

Georgia Mutual Life Insurance Company, Augusta, Georgia; H. T. Singleton.

Mutual Relief and Benevolent Association, Columbia, S. C.; J. H. Goode.

Mississippi Life Insurance Company, Memphis, Tennessee; V. L. Ruben, M. E. Anderson, Jackson, Mississippi; A. J. Topps, Greenwood, Mississippi; R. A. Ross, Montgomery, Alabama; M. S. Stuart and G. W. Lee, Memphis, Tennessee.

North Carolina Mutual Life Insurance Company, Durham, North Carolina; J. L. Wheeler, Atlanta, Georgia; Dr. L. H. Stinson, Augusta, Georgia; J. H. Thorpe, Kittrell, N. C.; G. W. Cox, R. J. Garrett, Jackson, Mississippi; B. G. Olive, Little Rock, Arkansas; M. L. Johnson, Decatur, Alabama; W. H. Harvey, Columbia, S. C.; D. C. Deans, Richmond, Virginia; H. C. Bell, Clarksdale, Mississippi; A. E. Spears, Charlotte, N. C.;

J. S. Thompson, Weldon, N. C.; C. C. Spaulding, W. J. Kennedy, J. M. Avery, T. A. Riveria, Durham, N. C.

Pilgrim Health and Life Insurance Company, Augusta, Georgia; W. S. Hornsby, A. B. Singfield.

Richmond Beneficial Life Insurance Company, Richmond, Virginia; C. B. Gilpin, J. E. Harris, W. H. Thompson.

Bankers' Fire Insurance Company, Durham, North Carolina; W. Gomez.

Standard Life Insurance Company, Atlanta, Georgia; L. E. Graves, Raleigh, N. C., J. E. Wallace, Greensboro, N. C.

Winston Mutual Life Insurance Company, Winston, North Carolina; J. A. Blume.

International Mutual Life Insurance Company, Reidsville, North Carolina; E. D. Miller and E. M. Townes.

In addition to the thirteen named above, the names of twenty-nine unrepresented companies were recorded. It appears then that the total number of Negro insurance organizations, exclusive of fraternal orders, societies and benevolent associations, in operation in October 1921, was forty-two.

M. S. Stuart read the report of the Committee on Organization, consisting of ten articles and sub-sections and submitted tentative resolutions and by-laws for consideration.

Lengthy discussions were provoked by Article I, dealing with the name of the organization. The name, *National Negro Insurance Association,* suggested by G. W. Cox, was unanimously accepted.

Section 3 of Article IV, dealing with the composition of, and representation in, the Association provoked further lengthy discussion. This section provided that each representative of any member company present should have the right to cast one vote, and that each company should have the right to cast five votes. This meant that as long as this section remained in effect officers, district managers, agents, office clerks, or any other type of employee whom member companies saw fit to send as representatives would compose the Association. It remained in force, unattacked until the fourth annual session of the Association which convened in Chicago, August 18, 1924, when W. A. Jordan of the Southern Aid Society raised the question of representation. When the fifth session was held in Louisville, August 6, 1925, it was provided that "insurance companies owned, controlled and operated by men and women of African descent" should comprise the membership.

The committee on the revision of the constitution made the following recommendation, which was adopted:

> The National Negro Insurance Association shall be an Association composed of accredited delegates of insurance companies. Each insurance company shall be allowed as many representatives in the Association as it shall care to send, but each company shall be entitled to only two votes in the Convention.
>
> The vote of each accredited delegate in the Convention shall be such proportion as the number of delegates from his company bears to two. The fee shall be $25 for each member company and $2 for each accredited member.

The adoption of this provision was regarded by the field men of Negro insurance companies as making of the Association an organization composed almost entirely of executives of the companies. Even among the executives there were those who held to the opinion that agents and other field representatives should be entitled to full participation in all meetings of the Association. Out of this division of opinion there developed a long drawn-out contention, springing up at each one of the subsequent meetings until the twelfth annual session, held in Jacksonville, Florida, April 20, 21, and 23, 1932, at which time George W. Cox sponsored a proposal to admit local associations, composed of agents and other field men on the same basis as companies. This to some extent again opened the doors to the field men and women.

MAMIE C. HICKERSON, *Statistician*

Miss Hickerson is a graduate of Northwestern University School of Commerce, having completed a four year course in accounting. She has been employed by the Supreme Liberty Life Insurance Company, Chicago, for eighteen years, in various capacities. In September 1937, she was made a junior officer of the company, and statistician; and in 1938 was elected statistician of the Association. Ambitious and eager to keep abreast of every development in her chosen field, Miss Hickerson has kept up her studies and has completed courses in insurance (principles— economics and life insurance law and taxation—statistics) and is

CHARLES C. SPAULDING
First President

THE LATE JOHN A. BLUME
President, Winston Mutual Life Insurance
Company, Treasurer, N. N. I. A.

MISS MAMIE C. HICKERSON
Statistician

Field Workers

J. H. COATES
Assistant Agency Director,
Universal Life

CAPT. CHARLES H. FEARING
District Manager, North Carolina
Mutual

J. R. BEAVERS
Winner First Prize, Industrial, 1936-1937
North Carolina Mutual

R. A. CHEEK
Agent, North Carolina Mutual

NATIONAL NEGRO INSURANCE ASSOCIATION

Field Workers

T. R. NEAL
District Manager, Atlanta Life,
Orlando, Florida

C. J. ADAMS
Winner First Prize, Ordinary, 1938
North Carolina Mutual

GRADY SIMS
Winner First Prize, Industrial, 1938
North Carolina Mutual

MISS HERTICINE TURNER
Edwards, Mississippi
Winner First Prize, National Essay Contest,
1939

now studying advanced statistics and advanced organization and management. She graduated from Supervisors' School conducted by International Business Machines Corporation. This young business woman is a credit to her race, her profession, her sex, and her company.

SCHEDULE OF THE ANNUAL MEETINGS

Session Number	Where Convened	Date	Number Companies Represented	President Secretary Treasurer, Elected	Important enactments and decisions
1ST	Durham, N. C.	Oct. 21 1921	13	C. C. Spaulding M. S. Stuart Thad Tate	To publish an insurance journal. Course of study recommended. Adopted name. Fixed annual fees and dues.
2ND	Atlanta, Ga.	Sept. 14-15 1922	19	C. C. Spaulding M. S. Stuart H. E. Perry	Approved fund of $3,000 to establish chairs of insurance in colleges.
3RD	Jacksonville, Fla.	Sept. 5-7 1923	21 (by 500 delegates)	C. C. Spaulding M. S. Stuart H. E. Perry	Group sections arranged for executives, district managers, local agents
4TH	Chicago, Ill.	Aug. 18-19 1924	17	F. L. Gillespie C. A. Shaw & C. W. Greene J. M. Avery	Agree not to employ agents dismissed by any member Co., "for improper conduct." Technical discussions.
5TH	Louisville, Ky.	Aug. 6-8 1925	16	A. L. Lewis W. E. Stewart H. E. Hall	Rejected recommendation to hold joint session with Nat'l. Bus. League. Technical discussions.
6TH	N. O. La.	Aug. 4-6 1926	19	Dr. J. E. Walker W. E. Stewart H. E. Hall	Annual individual membership fee discontinued. Valuable papers and discussions.
7TH	Memphis, Tenn.	April 20-22 1927	27	Dr. J. E. Walker W. E. Stewart H. E. Hall	Addressed by State Ins. Commissioner, A. S. Caldwell. Vote $300 for Nat'l. Negro Press Association. Vote to secure national charter of incorporation.
8TH	Columbus, Ohio	April 25-27 1928	22	H. H. Pace W. E. Stewart E. M. Martin	Addressed by J. A. Jackson of U. S. Dept. of Commerce. Agree to exchange impairment lists and vote uniform Med. Ex. Fees, establish Bureau Health.
9TH	Little Rock Ark.	April 24-26 1929	24	A. Overton W. E. Stewart W. H. Lee	Annual company dues levied according to assets. Technical papers on various subjects of the business
10TH	Atlanta, Ga.	April 23-25 1930	28	L. T. Burbridge W. E. Stewart J. H. Lewis	Addressed by Mrs. Mary McLeod Bethune. Technical papers on subjects related to the business.

SCHEDULE OF THE ANNUAL MEETINGS

Session Number	Where Convened	Date	Number Companies Represented	President Secretary Treasurer, Elected	Important enactments and decisions
11TH	Hot Springs, Ark.	April 22-24 1931	24	M. S. Stuart W. E. Stewart G. W. Cox	Annual Company dues increased as follows: assets an. dues $250,000 $50.00 to $1,000,000 $75.00 over $1,000,000 $100 Technical papers.
12TH	Jacksonville, Fla.	April 20-22 1932	18	W. H, Lee W. E. Stewart J. A. Blume	Recommend c r e a t e "Old Age" Pension Bureau for employees. Agency associations admitted to membership. Technical papers and discussions.
13TH	Chicago, Ill.	June 21-23 1933	15 and (2 agency associations)	E. M Martin W. E. Stewart J. A. Blume	Receivership "racket" condemned. Cooperative advertising through Negro press approved. High lapsation discussed. Other papers read.
14TH	Richmond, Va.	July 25-27 1934	17 and (3 associations)	G. W. Cox W. E. Stewart J. A. Blume	Uniform agency contract recommended. National Negro Insurance W e e k approved. President Roosevelt memorialized about unfairness to Negro labor and in dispensing relief. Technical discussion.
15TH	Durham, N. C.	May 22-24 1935	17 and (6 associations)	C. B. Gilpin W. E. Stewart J. A. Blume	Office National Historian created. Advisory Council of former Presidents created. Voted $500 for Health Week. Voted $1,000 for. Ins. Week. An. company dues increased to $50, $100 and $150 according to assets. Agency Institute adopted.
16TH	Detroit, Mich.	July 8-10 1936	17 and (6 associations)	W. S. Hornsby W. E. Stewart B. L. Jordan	First report of Nat'l. Negro Insurance Week. Address by Walter White of N.A.A.C.P. Actuary's report. Technical papers and discussions.
17TH	Augusta, Ga.	May 26-28 1937	21 and (7 associations)	G D. Rogers C. L. Townes C. H. Fearing	B u r i a l Associations admitted to membership. Baby Clinic recommended. Created Office of Nat'l. Medical Director. Decided to observe Nat'l. Collection Month.
18TH	Cleveland, 'Ohio.	June 15-17 1938	32 and (7 associations)	L. C. Blount C. L. Townes H. L Street	N e g r o Newspapers and Nat'l. Negro Bus. League commended and approved. First Report Committee on Social S. Taxes. Additional Technical sections approved, to wit: Actuarial, Auditors, Statistical. Technical papers approved.
19TH	Los Angeles, Calif.	July 12-14 1939	31 and (7 associations)	Dr. P. P. Creuzot C. L. Townes H. L Street	American Woodmen represented and membership approved. SSA C o m m i t t e e Report showed compensation of agents of eight Companies exempt from Tax. MS of History approved.

NATIONAL NEGRO INSURANCE WEEK

Prize Winning Agents		Company Represented	Ind. Prem. Written	Ordinary Insurance Written
1936				
J. R. Beavers	1st	N. C. Mut'l.	$19.13	
C. H. Bragg	2nd	Atlanta Life	17.05	
Albert Stone	3rd	Afro.-Amer.	16.10	
W. C. Ross	1st	Sup. Lib. L.		$10,000
J. V. King	2nd	Universal L.		9,500
L. M. Argrett	3rd	Afro.-Amer. L.		8,000
1937				
J. R. Beavers	1st	N. C. Mut'l. L.	$75.55	
J. R. Gregg	2nd	N. C. Mut'l. L.	57.49	
J. B. Flood	3rd	Rich. Benf. L.	53.15	
R. A. Cheek	1st	N. C. Mut'l. L.		$77,000
C. J. Adams	2nd	N. C. Mut'l. L.		43,500
G. W. Nickens	3rd	Vic. Mut'l. L.		40,100
1938				
G. W. Sims	1st	N. C. Mut'l. L.	$51.39	
C. V. Cruse	2nd	Mammoth L.	30.39	
C. J. Adams	1st	N. C. Mut'l. L.		$52,000
G. B. Darby	2nd	Vic. Mut'l. L.		21,000
1939				
A. Pace	1st	Sup. Liberty	$55.48	
H. Strong	2nd	Sup. Liberty	54.18	
A. Pearson	3rd	Sup. Liberty	38.00	
W. C. Ross	1st	Sup. Liberty		$27,000
Ezra Brown	2nd	Sup. Liberty		26,250
C. J. Adams	3rd	N. C. Mut'l.		23,000

PRODUCTION OF LEADING COMPANIES, NATIONAL NEGRO INSURANCE WEEK

		Industrial	Ordinary
1936			
N. C. Mut'l. L.	1st	$921.81	$58,500 2nd
Atlanta Life	2nd	893.04	55,000 3rd
Sup. Liberty L.	3rd	618.52	84,500 1st
1937			
N. C. Mut'l.	1st	$1870.55	$561,000 1st
Atlanta Life	2nd	1737.47	
Sup. Liberty L.	3rd	1360.36	321,000 3rd
Victory Mut'l.			355,000 2nd
1938			
N. C. Mut'l	1st	$2110.27	$420,025 1st
Sup. Liberty	2nd	1746.04	218,500 3rd
Atlanta Life	3rd	1239.35	
Gold State Mut'l.			275,350 2nd
1939			
N. C. Mut'l.	1st	$2436.29	$607,250 1st
Sup. Liberty	2nd	2406.76	304,000 3rd
Atlanta Life	3rd	1910.00	244,000
Gold. State			310,500 2nd
Total production 1939		$17,623.47	$19,154,686

The National Association conducted its first National Essay Contest in 1939. The prize winners with the cash prizes won follow:

Miss Herticine Turner, Southern Christian Inst. Edwards, Miss. $100 1st.
Miss Lorraine Crenshaw, Central High School, Cleveland. Ohio   50 2nd.
Miss Majorie E. McKinney, San Diego High School, San Diego, Calif.   50 2nd.

Chapter X.

AT THE DETOUR'S END — WHAT?

It seems appropriate that these pages should close by attempting to direct some thought to the future economic status in which Negroes will live in this country. So that the pressing necessity of this should be fully appreciated it seems necessary to keep before us the uncertain status under which the group has groped about during the past seventy-five years. This unfixed status has obtained because the attempt to give liberty to, and to make citizens of, the Negro slaves of the United States was badly bungled. It was a job left incomplete. No definite program in the interests of the freedmen and the national welfare was adopted and followed. Four million human beings, untrained in the responsibility of earning a livelihood, were turned loose, and without guidance left to project themselves into the economic channels of the nation. Injury and confusion inevitably resulted from the shock and the incredible lack of vision on the part of statesmen.

Because this happened in an undeveloped land of plenty, where even the weak could extract a tolerable existence out of the crumbs of prosperity spurned by the more shrewd and powerful, the full effects of this great national mistake have been strung out, and the clash between whites and Negroes in the struggle to live was deferred until it was made inevitable by the depression of 1929. Prior to that time there were "white men's jobs" and Negro jobs." There were many types of work in which white men disdained to engage, especially in the South.[1] The depression forced the issue. Its results now force white men to seek and to take any kind of work. Even southern white women, once pampered idols in idleness and cloistered luxury, now compete with Negroes to serve as waitresses, elevator operators, and in other classes of work once considered the exclusive field of "Negro menials."

The competition that is always a product of class distinction is now keen between Negroes and white people for the American standard of living. It is idle to censure the ordinary white man for taking such advantage as he can; for despite the interest of lofty

[1] Forty years ago most white men disdained to be letter carriers in the South.

331

white leaders in the Negro's welfare, the poor white man will not —cannot—have much relish for generosity and fair play when the wolf is howling at his own door, and, perhaps, his furniture piled on a city street. The Negro's security cannot safely be left dependent upon voluntary justice or magnanimity from such a source; or upon only the theories of laws, the practical application of which is left in the local hands of authorities whose friends and relatives need and contend for the profit derived from inequitable enforcement. Moreover, the Negro cannot well afford to lose the good will of white neighbors, which he must often forfeit if he tries to get a fair share of the community economic opportunities and benefits. In this plight Negroes are rapidly descending to a level of general dependency upon public relief. A change to something more definite and secure is sorely needed. The remarkable economic agility by which colored people have clung to precarious situations in the past is now meeting tests too severe to be mastered. The Negro population has now increased to the point at which tips, chance jobs, nondescript opportunities, fringe occupations, ledge holds, second tables, leavings and "somehow" existence will no longer suffice. This detour is running out to a dead end of disappointment and poverty.

Thirty-six per cent of employed Negroes in 1930 worked in agricultural pursuits, yet approximately 25 per cent of the whole race were tenant farmers with an annual average cash income of $105, for a family of five—about $1.75 each a month.

Twenty-eight per cent of the employed were engaged in domestic service with a weekly cash income of not quite $5 for a work week of ninety-four hours. But even so, there is frequently heard an insistent demand that this work be given to white males and females.

Labor unions that do not definitely deny membership to Negroes flagrantly discriminate in the assignment of available work. Thus it is that the Negro is gradually losing his place in industry.

Prior to 1929 there was promise in the professions. Now each graduating class in medicine and dentistry is smaller than the one before. The number of Negroes able now to finance completion of these and other costly courses of special preparation grows constantly smaller. Without some improvement in the situation Negro doctors and dentists will pass from the scene.

"In some of the towns and cities of Mississippi, many Negroes, due to under nourishment, are starving and do not know it. They are not getting work enough from government projects or private enterprise to provide adequate food for themselves."[2]

Social Equality

This subject is brought in here with no thought of bitterness and resentment. It is not among the purposes of this work to take issue with those intangible, proclaimed objectives of its doctrines. It is the economic by-products of this dogma that are so deadly to the Negro—its bread and butter effects. If SOCIAL EQUALITY would stay dressed up in only its social clothes, well might the Negro shed no tears over the loss of those parlor privileges which, it is pretended, it was invented to protect. In its every day attire its very expensiveness to the Negro makes of it a symbol of hostility. Its annual cost to him in employment denied in the private enterprises, which his patronage helps to maintain, and in municipal, state and federal governmental jobs, amounts to more than $220,000,000.

Social Equality. It is a discouraging, ambition-chilling, road-closed detour sign that aspiring Negroes—aspiring only for material welfare—meet on every main highway of life. The material efficiency of this dogma forces the question: Is destitution, actual starvation or criminality the price the Negro must pay so that the sentimental fears of society may be sustained?

Social Equality. Did its authors intend that it should have credit for thousands of undernourished, weak, disease-ridden Negro children? Was its real purpose to be an instrument of destruction and extinction? If so, let its sponsors fear not. It is an ingenious weapon—an effective blockade athwart the Negro's lifeline. It is working. Its stranglehold grows ever tighter around the colored man's neck. The Negro cannot cope with the adroit subtleties of its pretenses. The social armor under which it is cloaked is invulnerable in our democracy.

Social Equality. It is getting results. Thirty-three per cent of the victims on relief are Negroes. The Negro death rate is 82 per cent higher than the white, and Negro criminality, is, of course,

[2] The Honorable S. D. Redmond, Jackson, Mississippi, in the *Pittsburg Courier,* January 13, 1940.

higher. If this group becomes "a race on relief," let it be charged to the triumph of social equality.

Social Equality. It is getting results—not in the South alone. The statistics of just one nation-wide, Northern-domiciled, large, white life insurance company that refuses to employ Negroes shows its total assets for 1938 to be $4,942,900,416.98. Being a mutual, all that great amount belongs to the policyholders. One-eleventh of its industrial policyholders are Negroes. It is estimated that one-twentieth of that company's assets belong to Negro policyholders. This means that the officers of this company alone hold away from the fields of Negro employment $247,145,020. Mind you, these are officers of a mutual company, a cooperative, servants of the policyholders. Administrators in trust, honor-bound to see that all the benefits derived from the premiums they collect become equitably available to all the policyholders. Employment, though incidental and somewhat indirect, is yet a very important benefit resulting from premiums collected in large amounts. This company, moreover, is investing these funds in the financing of slum-clearance and many other units of construction in which the employment of Negro workmen is negligible. Are not these officers contributing to the idleness, the delinquency, the criminality, the starvation of Negro youth? Are not their hands stained with the contributory prostitution of young Negro women, who educated for business careers, find only idleness and disappointment? But they are no worse than the officers of many other life insurance companies—no worse than the owners and operators of thousands of other types of corporations that accept Negro patronage but refuse to employ Negroes.

The total, in this way held away from Negro employment, runs into the billions of dollars—dollars *paralysed* in their power to employ those by whose spending they are amassed.

The colored race is neither superhuman nor marvelous. This spending away from itself; spending "across the river"; this constant economic drain will surely, and soon, place on the doorsteps of this nation a ragged, relief-dependent, disease-spreading, demoralizing, humiliating unit of its population in a plight that will mar the whole picture of democracy.

No more than any other group can the Negro survive in decency, deprived of the reactive benefit in employment from his buying power.

AT THE DETOUR'S END—WHAT?

About Solutions

No definite solution can be found in the dimness of the obtaining twilight status. The Negro must be either an American citizen with all the rights and opportunities that others enjoy; or he must be separate, definitely separate, with all of the opportunities and advantages that will arise from the combined power of his numbers. The role of an economic chameleon, first separate and then unseparate, to suit the convenience of exploitation, brings the race ever nearer to exhaustion of its economic resources.

Three solutions, all admittedly fraught with complicated difficulties, appear, nevertheless, to be feasible. They are:

1. Sufficient governmental supervision and power over private enterprises to compel the employment of Negroes by those industries that accept patronage from Negroes.

2. Give back to Negro business the accumulated assets that Negro patronage has produced in white businesses. This might be done, at first, in the form of subsidiaries. Certainly the Negro assets in the big life insurance companies that have insured Negroes can, in most companies, be identified and turned over to Negro branches under Negro personnel and white auspices.

3. Legal authority by which the Federal Government could subsidize Negro business and give to it proper financial support for adequate expansion and development.

It was Mrs. Eleanor Roosevelt who said: "Lincoln's plea for equality of citizenship and for freedom has never been quite accepted in our Nation." She said this about the fight of Washington Negroes for the privilege of attending a white theatre. It would be far more important to the race as a whole if she would turn her powerful influence to bring about equality of economic opportunity for a group that, even on the rising tides of prosperity, can only get a taste when the cup of plenty splashes over, and that then may lap up only the stray drops that the more powerful may spurn.

APPENDIX

A. Bibliography

ANDREWS, R. MCCANTS. *John Merrick, A Biographical Sketch.* The The Seeman Printery, Durham, North Carolina, 1920.
Annual Compilation of Industrial Insurance. The Industrial Salesman, Cincinnati, 1938.

BRACKET, J. R. *The Negro in Maryland.* John Murphy & Company, Baltimore, 1889.

BROWN, W. H. *Education and Economic Development of Negroes in Virginia.* University of Virginia Publications, Phelps-Stokes Papers, vol. 6.
By-Laws of the Free African Society.
Cyclopedia of Insurance in the United States. The Index Publishing Company, New York, 1932.
Dunne's International Insurance Report, James E. Dunne, Editor, New York, 1938.
Forbes Magazine, New York, February 1924.
General Laws of Grand United Order of Odd Fellows in America and Jurisdiction. Odd Fellows Journal, Washington, 1925.

DABNEY, WENDELL P., *Maggie L. Walker, Her Life And Deeds.*

HOUCHINS, JOSEPH R. "Causes of Negro Insurance Company Failures," *U. S. Department of Commerce, Bureau of Foreign and Domestic Commerce Bulletin* 15, Washington, 1937.
Industrial Life Insurance. Metropolitan Life Insurance Company. New York, 1938.
Minutes of the Supreme Camp of the American Woodmen, Denver.
Negroes in the United States, (1920-32). U. S. Department of Commerce, Bureau of the Census. Washington, 1933.
Proceedings of Annual Meetings of the National Negro Insurance Association, 1921-39.

CAMPFIELD, CYRUS. *Annual Reports of the Statistician to the National Negro Insurance Association.* 1930-36.

HICKERSON, MAMIE C. *Annual Report of the Statistician to the National Negro Insurance Association.* 1937-8

SPAULDING, ASA T. *Reports of the Actuary to the National Negro Insurance Association.*

STEVENSON, JOHN A., *The Penn Mutual Life Insurance Company, Address,* 32nd Annual Convention, Life Insurance Presidents.

TIBBS, ESTHER O. *Reports of the Actuary to the National Negro Insurance Association.*

Selling Accident and Health Insurance. The Health and Accident Underwriters Conference. Chicago, 1938.

TRENT, JR., W. J. *Development of Negro Life Insurance Enterprises.* University of Pennsylvania. Thesis. Philadelphia, 1932.

Vision, The, Atlanta Life Insurance Company Publication, Atlanta, July 1928.

Whetstone, The, North Carolina Mutual Life Insurance Company Publication, 40th Anniversary Number, 1938.

NEWSPAPER ARTICLES

Cincinnati Inquirer, Cincinnati, Ohio. January 3, 1903.

Commercial Appeal, Memphis, Tennessee. January 7-8, 1903.

Commercial Appeal, Memphis, Tennessee. January 1, 1940.

Evening Scimitar, Memphis, Tennessee. January 7, 1903.

Sunflower Tocsin, Indianola, Mississippi, January 6, 1903.

Pittsburg Courier, Pittsburg, Pa. January 13, 1940.

PERSONAL INTERVIEWS

Davis, B. J., Former District Grand Secretary, Georgia Grand Lodge of Odd Fellows.

Dawkins, Ludella, Stenographer.

Ferguson, T. J., Former Treasurer, Standard Life Insurance Company.

Mitchem, J. E., Former Secretary.

Numerous other personal interviews and questionnaires.

B. NEGRO LIFE INSURANCE ORGANIZATIONS IN THE UNITED STATES OF AMERICA

Afro-American Life Insurance Company, Jacksonville, Florida
American Woodmen, Denver, Colorado
Atlanta Life Insurance Company, Atlanta, Georgia
Central Life Insurance Company, Tampa, Florida
Douglas Industrial Life Insurance Company, New Orleans, Louisiana
The Domestic Life and Accident Insurance Company, Louisville, Kentucky
The Dunbar Mutual Insurance Society, Cleveland, Ohio
Excelsior Life Insurance Company, Dallas, Texas
The Federal Life Insurance Company, Washington, D. C.
Fireside Mutual Insurance Company, Columbus, Ohio
Golden State Mutual Life Insurance Company, Los Angeles, California
Good Citizen Mutual Benefit Association, New Orleans, Louisiana
The Great Lakes Mutual Life Insurance Company, Detroit, Michigan
Guaranty Life Insurance Company, Savannah, Georgia
The Independent Order of St. Luke, Richmond, Va.

338

Keystone Aid Society, Philadelphia, Pa.
Liberty Industrial Life Insurance Company, New Orleans, Louisiana
Louisiana Industrial Life Insurance Company, New Orleans, Louisiana
Mammoth Life and Accident Insurance Company, Louisville, Kentucky
North Carolina Mutual Life Insurance Company, Durham, North Carolina
Pilgrim Health and Life Insurance Company, Augusta, Georgia
Peoples Industrial Life Insurance Company, New Orleans, Louisiana
Protective Mutual Life Insurance Company, Chicago, Illinois
The Richmond Beneficial Life Insurance Company, Richmond, Virginia
Provident Home Beneficial Society, Philadelphia, Pennsylvania.
Safety Industrial Life Insurance Company, New Orleans, Louisiana
Southern Aid Society of Virginia, Inc., Richmond, Virginia
  Southern Life Insurance Company, Baltimore, Md.
Standard Industrial Life Insurance Company, New Orleans, Louisiana
Superior Life Insurance Society
Supreme Liberty Life Insurance Company, Chicago, Illinois
Mutual Benefit Society of Maryland
Southern Life Insurance Company, Baltimore, Maryland
Union Protective Assurance Company, Memphis, Tennessee
United Mutual Benefit Association, New York, New York
Universal Life Insurance Company, Memphis, Tennessee
Unity Industrial Life Insurance Company, New Orleans, Louisiana
Unity Mutual Life Insurance Company, Chicago, Illinois
The Victory Industrial Life Insurance Company, New Orleans, Louisiana
Victory Mutual Life Insurance Company, Chicago, Illinois
Virginia Mutual Benefit Life Insurance Company, Richmond, Virginia
Winston Mutual Life Insurance Company, Winston-Salem, N. C.
Western Mutual Life Insurance Company, Dallas, Texas
Western Union Mutual Life Insurance Company, Detroit, Michigan
Booker T. Washington Burial Insurance Company, Fairfield, Alabama
Commonwealth Burial Association, Chicago, Illinois

INDEX

ERRATA

The following errata occur in the Index:

References to Standard Industrial Life refer to Standard Life, and not to Standard Industrial Life, except on pages 59 and 339. Standard Life of Georgia has been liquidated, but Standard Industrial Life of Louisiana is experiencing successful operation.

References to Liberty Industrial Life refer to Liberty Life, and not to Liberty Industrial Life, except on pages 59 and 339.

The entry under T. H. Fairchild refers to T. M. Fairchild.

The entry under T. T. Spaulding refers to A. T. Spaulding.

The entry under J. Z. Bargy should read Bargyh.

Black Swan Photograph Company should read Black Swan Phonograph Company.

On page 174 Dr. J. Z. Barghy should read Bargyh.

INDEX — (continued)

INDEX — (continued)

INDEX — (continued)

INDEX — (continued)

Harmon Medal, 1930, 86.
Harris, J. E., 230, 325.
Harris, Mrs. M. E., 110.
Harris, Oury, 305.
Harris, W., 305, 309, 310.
Harrison, President, 277.
Harvey, W. H., 324.
Hatfield, H. D., 227.
Hawkins, John, 207.
Hayes, C. M., 152.
Hayes, T. H. & Sons, 2.
Hayes, T. H., Jr., 2, 307.
Hayes, Thomas H., Sr., 76.
Haynes, M. M., 247.
Haywood, J. W., 247, 248.
Haywood, L. H., 124, 125.
Heath, Rev. J. J., 110.
Hendon, Miss Bobbie, 280.
Henry, Edward W., 31.
Henry, S. P., 298.
Henry, T. M., 299.
Herndon, A. F., 75, 117-124, 131, 196, 258, 307.
Herndon, Mrs. A. F., 124, 125.
Herndon, A. F., II, 125.
Herndon, N. B., 124, 125-6, 324.
Hickerson, Miss M. C., 326-7.
Hill, W. D., 57, 219-220.
Hill, J. J., 250.
Holcomb, Henry, 66, 67.
Holder, Julian, 67.
Holloman, John, 96, 97, 108, 152.
Holmes Gold Medal, 100.
Holsey, Bishop L. H., 75.
Home Security Life Ins. Co., 222.
Hooks, Julia, 102.
Hopkins, J. A., 117.
Hornsby, T. J., 156, 157, 158.
Hornsby, W. S., 93, 156, 160-1.
Hornsby, W. S. Jr., 164-5, 318, 325, 328.
Houston, William L., 26, 27, 28.
Houston, N. O., 265, 267-9.
Howard, A. J., 171, 286, 288.
Howard, B. F., 30.
Howard, Mrs. Ethyl Cox, ix, 294.
Howard, J. A., 97.
Howard, Perry, 27, 28, 31, 276, 293-4, 296-9.
Howard, W. C., 290, 293, 294, 296, 298, 299, 301.
Howell, L. A., 132, 135.
Hubbard, J. E., 97.
Hueston, William C., 31.
Hughson, J. S., 229.
Hughes, G. P., 137, 138.
Hunter, Frank H., 30.

I

Improved Benevolent Protective Order of Elks, 30, 80, 234.
Independent Order of Good Samaritans, 163.
Independent Order of Odd Fellows, see Odd Fellows.
Independent Order of St. Luke, 20, 33, 34, 233.
Independent Order of Sons and Daughters of Jacob, 19, 320.
Independent Order of Temple Builders, 160.
Index Publishing Co., ix.
Indianola Post Office Affair, 278-82.
Ingram, Birl S., 25.
Insurance, Industrial, 36-62.
Insurance in force, 41-44.
Insurance lapsation, 44-5.
International Mutual Life Ins. Co., 325.
Interstate Life Ins. Co., 168.
Ish, G. W. S., 272, 273.
Ish, Jefferson Gatherford, Jr., 89-93, 272, 273.

J

Jackson, H. T., 30.
Jackson, N. J., 237.
Jackson, S. Jr., 230, 318.
James, Mrs. L. E., 93.
James, S. T., 201.
Johns, H. A. M., 239, 240-1, 242.
Johns Hopkins University, ix.
Johnson, A., 283.
Johnson, C. C., 284.
Johnson, Charles Jr., 232.
Johnson, E. F., 230.
Johnson, Frank, 30.
Johnson, H. P., 303.
Johnson, Henry Lincoln, 24.
Johnson, M. L., 324.
Johnson, S. J., 110.
Johnson, W. E., 152, 155.
Jones, Absalon, 4.
Jones, Mrs. Charles Etta, 140.
Jones, Edward P., 26, 27, 30, 180.
Jones, George P. Institute, 181.
Jones, J. L., 246, 247.
Jones, J. McHenry, 26, 27, 28.
Jones, M. B., 237.
Jones, Sarah G., Memorial Hospital, 237.
Jordan, B. L., 234, 242, 318, 328.
Jordan, W. A., 235-6, 237, 325.
Joseph, I. J., 97.
Josey, T. Walter, 162.
Judge, A. H. Y., 31.

INDEX — (continued)

K

Kelley, James E., 31.
Kelso, William J., viii, 29, 188-9.
Kennedy, J. C., 245.
Kennedy, W. J. Jr., 216-18, 325.
Kenney, R. J. Jr., 248.
Keystone Life Ins. Co., 59, 133.
Kilgo, J. C., 202.
King, J. V., 329.
King, W. H., 299, 301, 322.
Kinney, Albert E., 66, 67.
Kirk, Edward R., 2.
Kittrell College, 227.
Knights and Daughters of Tabor, 20, 33.
Knights of Pythias, 19, 68, 114, 146, 149, 160, 165, 233, 235.
Ku Klux Klan, 131, 309.
Kyle, W. P., 284.

L

Lake, E. F., 245.
Lampkins, Hazel, 93.
Lampton, Bishop E. W., 33.
Lanier, M. B., 138.
Latham, W. J., 320, 322.
Latson, E. W., 109.
Lee, G. W., 30, 122, 125, 129-32, 296, 303, 310, 323, 324.
Lee, Wm., 246.
Lee, W. H., 110, 113-114, 327, 328.
Leeward Islands Government Scholarship, 107.
Lewis, A. L., 109, 110-113, 307, 318, 327.
Lewis, J. H., 109, 110, 327.
Lewis, J. Leonard, 57, 110.
Lewis, Z. D., 232, 233.
Liberty Industrial Life, 36, 59, 73, 74, 79, 82, 322.
Licenses, 56.
Life and Casualty Ins. Co., 176-8.
Lightner, L. H., viii, 246, 248, 251, 252-6.
Lincoln Hospital, 200.
Lincoln Institute, 91.
Liquidations, causes of, 271-2.
Littlejohn, T. S., Sr., 33.
Long, E. R., 265.
Long, Theodore L., 110.
Louis, Joe, 67, 71.
Louisiana Industrial Life Ins. Co., 59, 141-150.
Love, Bank Examiner, 287.
Lowrie, Dr. T. L., 110.

M

Mack, O. P., 138.
Mahoney, Barney, 67.
Mahoney, Charles H., 66, 67-70.
Mammouth Life and Accident Ins. Co., 58, 59, 97, 150-6.
Manufacturers Life Ins. Co. of Canada, 108.
Martin, E. M., Jr., 125-8, 327, 328.
Martin, J. B., 170, 179.
Martin, N. H., 133.
Martin, W. T., 265.
Mason, D. B., 192.
Masonic Order, 32-34, 91, 112, 160, 165.
May, S. B. W., 265.
McAllister, H. P., 248.
McDonald, Bill, 32.
McDougald, R. L., 219.
McDowell, Mrs. J. E., 152, 154, 155.
McGill, S. D., 110.
McGaughey, M. M., 192.
McKinley, President, 277, 279.
McKinney, D., 283.
McKinney, Majorie E., 329.
McKinney, T. T., 247, 248, 260-2.
McKissack, Ephriam H., 26, 27, 28, 320.
McKissack, M. M., 170.
McLane, J. S., 110.
McMechen, George W. F., 31.
Mechanics and Farmers Bank, 200.
Memphis Commercial Appeal, 282 283. 283.
Memphis Evening Scimitar, 279.
Merchant, W. T., 152, 153, 154.
Merrick, E. R., 213-16.
Merrick, John, 195, 196-203, 206, 210.
Merrick-Moore Memorial Scholarship, 196.
Metropolitan Life Insurance Co., 25, 43.
Metropolitan Mutual, 120.
Middleton, G. S., 132, 133.
Mid-West Life Ins. Co., 149, 310.
Miles, P., 283.
Miller, E. D., 325.
Mills, James E., Dr., 31.
Mississippi Beneficial Ins. Co. See Mississippi Life.
Mississippi Life Ins. Co., 36, 168, 169, 171, 172, 174, 178-181, 184, 185, 224, 225, 274-303, 304, 305, 306, 307, 309, 312n, 320, 321, 323, 324.
Mitchem, J. E., 97, 102-106, 322.
Moon, The, 75, 76, 77, 103.

INDEX — (continued)

INDEX — (continued)

INDEX — (continued)